The

VIRGINIA

DYNASTY

The

VIRGINIA

DYNASTY

∞

Four Presidents and the
Creation of the American Nation

LYNNE CHENEY

VIKING

VIKING

An imprint of Penguin Random House LLC
penguinrandomhouse.com

LIBRARY OF CONGRESS CONTROL NUMBER: 2020940885

ISBN 9781101980040 (hardcover)
ISBN 9781101980064 (ebook)

Printed in the United States of America
1   3   5   7   9   10   8   6   4   2

Set in Stempel Garamond LT Pro
Designed by Cassandra Garruzzo

For Dick, for always

CONTENTS

Prologue

Put the spike of a drawing compass into a map of Virginia at Ferry Farm, George Washington's boyhood home. Extend the other leg of the compass so that it reaches out sixty miles and draw a circle. Within it, not only Washington, but also Thomas Jefferson, James Madison, and James Monroe were born, grew to manhood, and made their homes. From this small expanse of land on the North American continent came four of the nation's first five presidents—a dynasty whose members led in securing independence, creating the Constitution, and building the Republic. One of them doubled the size of the United States. Another extended its border to the Pacific Ocean. Sometimes they worked as a band of brothers, but not always. They quibbled, they quarreled, and they fought. Were political parties a bane or a boon? What were the limits of dissent? How should a republic prepare for war?

George Washington, the most charismatic of the dynasty, was lionized in his lifetime and worked to become a legend in praiseworthy ways, such as embodying good character and staying above politics—or at least politics as he understood it. Tall and power-fully built, he heightened his presence with elegant dress, even wearing fashionable yellow gloves on special occasions. He was a man of few words, which enhanced his natural dignity and helped conceal his explosive temper. He had countless admirers but few friends.

Jefferson, tall, long-limbed, and with reddish hair, was known for receiving visitors in well-worn waistcoats and run-down slip-pers, his way of demonstrating that for all his ties to Virginia's aristocracy, he was a man of the people. Gifted with a soaring imagination, he was a master of language, able to set forth ideas that would inspire generations. He delighted in everything from high art to scientific discovery to gadget building. His often-shifting views made him a hard man to know.

Madison, the most profound thinker of the group, usually dressed in black. To strangers he could seem stern, but with friends after dinner he was a charming conversationalist. A small, compact man, he could disappear in a crowd, particularly when accompanied by his glamorous wife, Dolley, but when he entered debate, as at the Constitutional Convention, his powerful mind made him impossible to ignore. A well-grounded man, he was the least likely of the dynasty to disparage others, but he was expert at digging in his heels in defense of ideas.

Monroe, the last of the Virginia dynasty, was also the last pres-ident to wear knee breeches. Old-fashioned and awkward, he let his ambition show, but kept his temper under wraps by writing blistering letters to those who offended him—and not mailing them. Because he lacked the intellectual prowess of a Jefferson or Madison, he can seem a symbol of the dynasty's winding down, but through a remarkable career in Congress, the diplomatic corps, and the cabinet, he learned one of the secrets to being a good president: Listen to smart people.

How to account for this gathering of talent, aspiration, and achievement? Part of the answer—and all explanations of human beings are partial—is the transformative time in which these men lived. As children of the Enlightenment, they imagined a society in which reason replaced dogma and individual rights were honored. Other nations had been founded "in the gloomy age of ignorance and superstition," as George Washington put it, but the United States had its beginnings in "an epoch when the rights of mankind were better understood and more clearly defined than at any former period." Establishing a nation built on what Washington called "the researches of the human mind after social happiness" was an irresistible calling, one that animated the four Virginians and drew them together.[1]

Washington taught himself about the exceptional age into which he had been born. Jefferson, Madison, and Monroe attended schools and colleges steeped in the new learning of the Enlightenment. They studied Latin and Greek, as was expected of young gentlemen, but they also had teachers from Scotland's esteemed universities who placed great value on natural philosophy, as science was called, and moral philosophy, which concerned ethics and politics. William Small (Jefferson's beloved tutor at William and Mary), Archibald Campbell (founder of the academy where Monroe studied), and Donald Robertson (whose school

Madison attended) had all breathed the air of the Scottish Enlightenment and understood well its distinctive practical side. Science and the study of man were more than ends in themselves; they could be used to better the world.

Madison attended Princeton, which was presided over by the Reverend John Witherspoon, a formidable man and the preeminent student of the Scottish Enlightenment in the colonies. In Nassau Hall, he lectured about the natural rights of life and liberty and justified the overthrow of tyrannical governments, ideas of clear application in revolutionary times. Madison was the only one of Witherspoon's students to become president, but among the others were a vice president, thirty-nine members of the House of Representatives, and twenty-one senators. Witherspoon himself was a member of the Continental Congress and a signer of the Declaration of Independence.[2]

How, one wonders, would the men of the Virginia dynasty have fared in another time? A generation earlier, revolution was not on the table, and viewed from America the Enlightenment was a mere glow on the horizon. The era in which these men lived determined their destiny—as did their place on the planet.

Virginia was on the periphery of civilization, where the dictates of tradition had less force. It was easier to question assumptions about monarchy than it would have been at the imperial center. It was easier to imagine a new society in which citizens could worship as they pleased rather than bow to a long-established church.[3]

Being far from England had this practical benefit: As subjects of a distant monarch, Americans became adept at governing themselves. Operating under a royal governor, Virginians (or, to be accurate, some white male property owners in Virginia) elected the legislature, which in turn passed bills and levied taxes. Talented young men of the gentry class were expected to participate. Washington and Jefferson entered the House of Burgesses at ages twenty-seven and twenty-six, respectively. Madison became a member of the House of Delegates at twenty-five, and Monroe at twenty-four.

Virginia, ironically, was the most English of the colonies. Royalists who left England after Oliver Cromwell's ascent to power gravitated there and set its culture, and one of the first royal governors of Virginia, Sir William Berkeley, perpetuated it by recruiting younger sons from prestigious English families to immigrate.[4] They and their descendants built homes in the English style, even scoring wood siding and applying sand to it (as at Mount Vernon) so that it looked like the stone facing of a British manor. They hired instructors to teach their children the formal steps of the minuet and collected books and pamphlets from Europe.

At the same time, the British took pleasure in pointing out how far American efforts at sophistication fell short. Their cultural achievements were scant to nonexistent, according to Sydney Smith, an English cleric known for his scathing critiques. "Who reads an American book?" he asked. "[Who] goes to an American play? Or looks at an American picture or statue?" Smith failed to mention New England painters such as Gilbert Stuart and passed over poets Anne Bradstreet and Phillis Wheatley, both of whom had been published in London. But Smith's assessment and others like it hit close to home in the Upper South, and Virginians did not lodge a defense. Instead they emphasized what set America—and Virginia—apart: land that stretched on forever, full of beauty and possibility, a "goodly field" Washington called it, which promised "a fruitful harvest." Jefferson described "the passage of the Potomac through the Blue Ridge [as] perhaps one of the most stupendous scenes in nature" and the Natural Bridge as "the most sublime of nature's works.⁵

Virginia was the largest of the colonies. The land grant of 1609 to the Virginia Company of London had an eastern border that extended along the East Coast from Cape Fear to Barnegat Bay. The grant included the territory northwest of the Ohio River, an area larger than any European country except Russia. Even after ceding its western lands and the Northwest Territory to the federal government, Virginia dominated in size, and Virginia's leaders understood the influence that resulted. One politician, holding up a snuffbox so small that he could barely fit a thumb and forefinger into it, declared the actions of Delaware, Georgia, Massachusetts, and South Carolina of little consequence. "When compared to Virginia they are no more than this snuff box is to the size of a man." Outsiders observed Virginia's influence and disapproved. A Marylander complained that at the First Continental Congress, Virginians had "juggled the whole conclave of the delegates."⁶

By 1790, the free population of Virginia was 516,230, the largest of the thirteen states. Adding to its power was an enslaved population of 305,057. At the Constitutional Convention in 1787, delegates had debated whether the enslaved should be counted in determining how many representatives a state could send to Congress. The South would gain a political advantage if every person in slavery were counted and the North if none were. Knowing that without a compromise the convention would fail, delegates settled on counting three of every five of those enslaved ("all other persons" was the language), and Virginians increased their sway in both the House of Representatives and the Electoral College—though not as consequentially as some have supposed.[7]

The Virginians, unshakable advocates of liberty and equality, held people in bondage, which they knew was wrong. Jefferson called slavery a sin against God, a "fatal stain" on Virginia. The men of the dynasty were aware of the contradiction in which they lived but unable to resolve it, unable to find a way to the total emancipation that justice demanded. They determined nonetheless to pass down concepts of freedom and equality, principles that became mighty weapons, perhaps the mightiest, for ending slavery. Abraham Lincoln honored Jefferson for enshrining the idea of equality in the Declaration of Independence, where it would forever be "a rebuke and a stumbling block to the very harbingers of re-appearing tyranny and oppression." Frederick Douglass observed that there was nothing in the Constitution that justified one human being owning another. Were the country to live up to the words in the preamble, such as "liberty" and "justice," Douglass said, "slavery would go reeling to its grave." Both the Declaration and the Constitution remind us today of the miles left to go before we live up to our national ideals.[8]

The time in which they lived and the place do not fully account for the Virginia dynasty. "The talent must exist," as a contemporary of the four men noted. Gifts of commanding and uplifting, of being wise, diligent, and persevering, are not called forth by time and place unless, at least in some nascent form, they are already there.[9]

The effect these men had on one another drove their achievements. They lifted one another up, as in Chapter One, "The Warriors," when General Washington's resolve strengthens Monroe on the long retreat through the Jerseys, or in Chapter Two, "River Crossing," when Jefferson takes Monroe under his wing after the younger man, a hero at Trenton, has his hopes for the future blasted. Disagreements among dynasty members changed opinions, as in Chapter Three, "The Intellectuals," when Jefferson tries to undermine Madison's plan for ratifying the Constitution, and Madison "rectifies" Jefferson's thinking. Disagreements also changed relationships, as in Chapter Four, "Untrodden Ground," and Chapter Five, "Schism," when Madison and Jefferson, dismayed by the direction of the Washington administration, organize an opposition party and break with the president forever. In later chapters, Virginia presidents clear the way for the next Virginian in line. One strategy was to put in place old vice presidents who were unlikely to threaten Virginia succession.[10]

The men of the Virginia dynasty were politicians, although they didn't like to admit it. They were also patriots and philosophers, as well as leaders who could bring the country through war. Living in the time they did, they also saw themselves as scientists who had devised a unique experiment, a nation where reason and justice would prevail.

But as years passed and the ideas of liberty and equality made slavery ever more intolerable, it seemed that the experiment would fail and the country be torn apart. Madison, the longest lived of the dynasty, may have had the most acute sense of what lay ahead, and he wrote a note to his fellow Americans to be published only after his death when "it may be considered as issuing from the tomb, where truth alone can be respected and the happiness of man alone consulted." The note was both counsel and plea: "The advice nearest to my heart and deepest in my convictions is that the Union of the States be cherished and perpetuated."[11]

ONE

The Warriors

From Triumph to Catastrophe

On July 2, 1775, a rainy Sunday, George Washington, the newly appointed commander in chief of the American army, arrived in Cambridge, Massachusetts. The next day the weather lifted, and skies were sunny as he inspected troops to the sound of trilling fifes and beating drums. He wore a blue coat faced in a buff-colored wool that matched his vest and breeches. Decorated with shining gold buttons and gilt epaulets, the uniform was part of "the pride and pomp of war" that Washington knew inspired men at arms. It added to the calm, assured demeanor that was key to his leadership, and the men he inspected on that July day were cheered. "It seemed as if the spirit of conquest breathed through the whole army," one of his generals wrote.[1]

Washington was an expert at conveying confidence to others,

even when he had grave doubts, as he did when he inspected the American troops that Congress had appointed him to command. His army was a motley collection of farmers, mechanics, students, and shopkeepers. They had no uniforms, no standard weapons, and were woefully lacking in military discipline and organization. At Cambridge, Washington began to attend to the multitude of details that would form them into a real army, issuing orders that dealt with everything from keeping track of the number of troops to forbidding gambling.[2]

On February 16, 1776, he convened his war council in a Georgian mansion on Brattle Street that served as his headquarters. He was ready to undertake the task for which he had come to Massachusetts: driving the British out of Boston. For more than a year they had occupied the city, and for many months American forces had been keeping them under siege. Congress had instructed Washington to seek approval from generals in his war council before major action, and he proposed an assault on Boston, which the council immediately rejected as too dangerous. Washington, thoroughly disgruntled, agreed to a plan to fortify Dorchester Heights, an elevation overlooking Boston and its harbor, with guns that a tall, brawny twenty-five-year-old named Henry Knox had recently hauled from Fort Ticonderoga.[3] A sustained bombardment from the heights, everyone agreed, had a good chance of bringing the redcoats out.

Because troops ascending Dorchester Heights would be vulnerable to enemy fire, Washington used diversions. He placed heavy ordnance at Lamb's Dam, Cobble Hill, and Lechmere Point, all distant from the heights, and ordered bombardments on the nights of March second and third. On the night of March 4, while the boom and flash of cannon captured British attention, three hundred oxcarts weighed down with preassembled barricades moved up the hills, wheels muffled by straw. Teamsters whispered. Three thousand soldiers followed, concealed from British eyes by a fog over Boston Harbor. By the time the troops reached the top, they had broken through the haze into moonlight so clear that they made quick work of constructing fortifications. By dawn, they had built several imposing structures and emplaced ordnance that Henry Knox had dragged from northern New York on the Dorchester hills.[4]

The next morning, General William Howe, in command of the British army, saw full-blown fortifications threatening his men and ships. "The rebels have done more in one night than my whole army would have done in months," he was heard to say, and by 8:00 p.m. he and his war council had decided to evacuate the city.[5] On March 17, British ships lifted sail and dropped down the harbor. On March 27 they stood out to sea.

Washington confessed to a friend that he could "scarce forbear lamenting" the British withdrawal. His men had been ready for a battle. But the bloodless victory more than pleased his fellow Americans. The Massachusetts Assembly rushed to laud him and Congress resolved to strike a gold medal in his honor. John Hancock, president of the Continental Congress, took rhetorical flight, telling Washington, "The Annals of America will record your title to a conspicuous place in the temple of fame."[6]

Washington was the hero, the man of the hour, and he looked the part. More than six feet tall, he was muscular yet moved with grace, particularly on horseback. Thomas Jefferson called him "the best horseman of his age." He was also a superb dancer and "very gallant," according to Judge Francis T. Brooke, who noted that Washington always paid particular attention to "the most beautiful and attractive ladies at the balls."[7]

Washington's combination of powerful physique and gentlemanly manner was most impressive. When Abigail Adams met him, she scolded her husband, John, for not preparing her adequately. "I thought the one half was not told me."[8]

In addition, Washington was wealthy. As the son of a second marriage, he'd had few prospects as a youngster, but after his father died when Washington was eleven and his beloved half brother Lawrence and Lawrence's daughter and widow died when he was in his twenties, he inherited the Mount Vernon estate. He also married wealth in the person of Martha Custis, the five-foot-tall, kind, and capable widow whom he wed in 1759.

Years later, John Adams, a more cynical soul than his wife, made a list of what he called Washington's "talents." First was "a handsome face," second, "a tall stature," third, "an elegant form," fourth, "graceful attitudes and movements," and fifth, "a large, imposing fortune."[9] Adams's point that much of what propelled Washington ahead in the world was not earned but given is a fair one, but it should be observed that many a tall, fine-looking rich man has rested on his gifts rather than using them to advance the cause of freedom.

In Washington's mind, his gifts and achievements did not make up for what he called his "defective education." In the years before he came into his fortune, his family did not have the means for him to acquire classical knowledge, as his older half brothers had.[10] He grew adept at geometry, a skill crucial for his work as a surveyor, and although he did not study Latin, he became familiar, likely through popular translations, with Rome's history and heroes.

Washington learned the ways of the gentleman not only by observing men such as his brother Lawrence, but also by studying etiquette. He copied *The Rules of Civility and Decent Behaviour in Company and Conversation,* maxims that provided guidelines for a young man striving to be part of Virginia's ruling class: Be respectful of others; be in command of facial expressions, hand gestures, and posture; be in control of emotions.[11] The last was a particular challenge for Washington, who from youth onward was given to notable outbursts of temper.

The 110th rule of *Civility and Decent Behaviour* may have impressed Washington most. "Labor to keep alive in your breast that little spark of celestial fire called conscience," it read. Throughout Washington's life, people commented on his ongoing effort to do what was right, to strip himself of bias and partiality and act with "disinterestedness." Even critics who came to believe that Washington was ruining the Republic had to acknowledge that he tried to act from honest motives, or as Washington himself put it, with a "consciousness of upright intentions."[12]

The praise and admiration that came Washington's way after Boston, pleasing though they were, did nothing to solve the deep problems that plagued his army. But whatever progress he made would not last. Army enlistments, which were for one year, expired at the end of 1776. A short-term army was exactly what Congress and most of the country wanted. A permanent arrangement was deemed a threat to liberty, an "armed monster," as one orator put it. But for Washington, short enlistments meant disbanding one army and recruiting another in the middle of war, creating chaos and inhibiting the development of an effective force. "The reflection upon my situation and that of this army produces many an uneasy hour when all around me are wrapped in sleep," Washington wrote while in Boston.[13] In April, as he marched his men to New York, he had to know there were many sleepless nights ahead.

By mid-August, so many British ships had gathered off Staten Island that it looked as though a forest had sprung up in the Lower Bay. The masts of more than a hundred ships were an awesome and discouraging sight. The British armada had arrived, bringing an army of more than thirty thousand, including nearly nine thousand German mercenaries, to put down the American rebellion. The American army numbered around twenty thousand men, but among them, according to Washington biographer Douglas Southall Freeman, were "no more than ten thousand effectives."[14]

Washington was sure that the British would try to seize New York City, on the southern tip of Manhattan Island, but he could not be certain that was where the first attack would come. He dispersed his forces to cover other points, including Long Island, where the critical location was Brooklyn Heights, a palisade overlooking the East River. Washington dispatched about a third of his men to the heights and set them to digging ditches and strengthening fortifications.

Starting the morning of August 22, the British put twenty

thousand troops ashore at Long Island's Gravesend Bay. By the twenty-third they were within three miles of American lines on Brooklyn Heights, and on the twenty-seventh they dealt the patriots a mighty blow. Washington had ordered three thousand of the army's best men positioned outside the fortifications. While fire from Hessian mercenaries provided a distraction, General Henry Clinton, Howe's second-in-command, took ten thousand men through a lightly guarded pass, turned the left flank of the Americans positioned forward, and attacked from behind while Hessians charged from the front. Terrified Americans scrambled to escape. Some made it to safety within the fortifications, but many were captured and many killed by bayonets. Philip Fithian, a chaplain watching from behind the ramparts, described the dreadful scene: "O doleful! doleful! doleful!—Blood! Carnage! Fire! . . . Many, many we fear are lost. . . . Such a dreadful din my ears never before heard!—And the distressed wounded came crying into the lines."[15]

Washington organized a masterful night retreat from Brooklyn Heights across the East River to Manhattan that saved 9,500 patriot troops, but as many as a thousand more, Washington reported to Congress, had been killed or taken prisoner. The rest were disheartened, their minds filled "with apprehension and despair." Large numbers of militia "have gone off," he wrote from New York City, deserting "in some instances almost by whole regiments."[16]

John Adams, chairman of the congressional Board of War, offered a cold-eyed assessment. "In general, our generals were outgeneraled," he wrote to Abigail.[17]

⚭

The Battle of Brooklyn Heights changed Washington for a time. He had come into the war eager for bold and open fighting. Now, in a war council with his generals, he indicated that he wanted no more of putting "young troops . . . against their superiors both in numbers and discipline," and the council discussed a "war of posts," which meant defending strong positions and not engaging the enemy unless there was clear advantage. It was an approach that Washington may have first known as a Fabian strategy, after the Roman general Fabius Maximus, who had used it effectively against Hannibal, although he had to endure the "contempt and calumny" of the public and Roman officials for supposed timidity, which was hardly the reputation that a warrior would wish. It had, however, preserved Fabius's army, which was no small accomplishment as Washington viewed matters through the lens of September 1776.[18]

But what did a defensive strategy mean for New York City? Should he defend it or abandon it? he asked Congress in a letter. He offered opinions on both sides until by the end his letter was so clotted with contradiction that historians have offered dramatically different interpretations of what Washington meant.[19]

The war council's decision was as muddled as Washington's letter: nine thousand men stationed at the north end of the island, where a rocky plateau known as Harlem Heights would provide a strong post; five thousand men to be left in the city; and several thousand others at various points.[20] If, as Washington had said in his letter to Congress, his entire army would be hard put to defend the city, five thousand men—a third of the army—were surely doomed to fail.

Fortunately the generals of the war council had second thoughts. Major General Nathanael Greene, sure that the army should evacuate, was a force behind the collective change of mind, and a congressional resolution declaring that the decision whether to stay or go was entirely up to Washington eased the way. On September 14, Washington wrote to the Congress that his war council had "not only determined a removal of the army prudent but absolutely necessary."[21]

The battered army began withdrawing to the north just as Lieutenant James Monroe arrived from the south. Together with his roommate at William and Mary, John Francis Mercer, he had left college to enlist in the 3rd Virginia Infantry, and after "rapid marches" of four hundred miles, he arrived with his regiment on the heights near the Harlem River. Wearing fringed hunting shirts, Monroe and other officers of the 3rd Virginia were warmly welcomed, as were the more than six hundred men they led. Their high spirits were infectious, and their obvious training a source of confidence.[22]

But they were far from the fighting when the attack came. Instead of landing near Harlem Heights, as Washington had expected, the British came ashore some five miles to the south. On September 15, a clear, bright Sunday, Connecticut militia guarding Kip's Bay saw dozens upon dozens of flatboats packed with

British troops heading toward them. The red-uniformed regulars on the transports "appeared like a large clover field in full bloom," a fifteen-year-old private named Joseph Plumb Martin observed. Then came a blistering cannonade from British warships in the East River, and Martin thought his head would "go with the sound." He and the rest of his unit abandoned their shallow trenches and ran, allowing British troops and blue-clad Hessians to splash ashore and form up unopposed.[23]

Washington and his aides galloped up as Massachusetts militia and Connecticut Continentals arrived. He shouted directions: "Take the walls! Take the cornfield!" But when sixty British grenadiers appeared, the patriot reinforcements panicked and were soon "flying in every direction and in the greatest confusion," as Washington described it. In a fury, he rode among them, even striking officers to try to preserve order, but all to no effect. "Are these the men with which I am to defend America?" he roared, throwing his hat to the ground.[24]

Washington usually succeeded in keeping his temper under control, but the panic at Kip's Bay brought it out—and a dark mood with it. After the flight of the troops, only Washington and a few aides were left on the field. It was time to withdraw, but as the British approached ever closer, Washington remained in place. Finally, an aide seized the reins of his horse and moved the commander in chief to safety. As Major General Nathanael Greene, who was very close to Washington, analyzed it, Washington had been courting destruction, putting himself in harm's way in order to be harmed. He was "so vexed at the infamous conduct of his troops," wrote Greene, "that he sought death rather than life."[25]

Washington had been thinking about martial glory since his

youth. When he was just fifteen, he had purchased a small book from his cousin Bailey about the military achievements of the Duke of Schonberg, whose heroics "replenished the world with astonishment and made him if not superior at least equal to . . . the Caesars of our age."[26] Washington had tasted what such renown was like after Boston and hungered for a full measure of it, but what possibility was there now? He was going up against one of the greatest military powers in the world with militiamen who ran before firing a single shot. Even Continentals, as he had just seen, could not always be counted on.

Perhaps for a moment he was also struck by his own failures. He had seen the troop positioning on Long Island the day before the battle and not objected.[27] Now, misjudging where the British would land on Manhattan Island, he had stationed some of his greenest troops at Kip's Bay and thus provided the enemy easy entry. For a man who had spent his life seeking a reputation that would lift him high, the realization that the losses were on his shoulders would have been dreadful.

The moment passed, but the months ahead would be full of gloom and self-doubt. Washington had entered a slough of despond and did not know when—or if—he would emerge.

An encounter the next day briefly lifted spirits—and gave James Monroe his first taste of battle. On the morning of September 16, a probing party of Knowlton's Rangers was sent out from Harlem Heights and soon came upon a detachment of British Black Watch infantry. After a skirmish, the Americans drew back toward the heights, and as the British pursued, their buglers sounded a tallyho—as though the Americans were fleeing before them like a fox before hounds. The taunt struck Washington's adjutant, Colonel Joseph Reed, to the core. "I never felt such a sensation before," he wrote. "It seemed to crown our disgrace."[28]

Washington was quick to respond. The British advance party was far in front of its lines, and he had some of his best fighters at hand. He ordered three companies of Virginia riflemen to cut off the advance force, and thus it was that Lieutenant James Monroe, until recently a college student, headed into the fray.[29]

The tall, rawboned Monroe was a fighter at heart. Even while enrolled at William and Mary, he had participated in a raid on the royal governor's palace to seize muskets and swords for the Williamsburg militia. Monroe was fired by the cause for which he fought and aware that distinction in battle could bring him the notice that he needed to move up in the world. He had been born into Virginia's gentry class, but at the modest end of it. His father owned 500 acres when Monroe was born. The Washingtons owned 6,000.[30]

There were a multitude of other differences between Washington and Monroe, starting with one being a general and the other a lieutenant, but there were also similarities in their personal stories and in their personas. Both lost their fathers before they reached adulthood and took on early responsibility. Monroe lost his mother as well. Both men were reserved and received praise for honesty and judgment rather than quick wit. Both were deeply ambitious—no fault in a warrior. "To take a soldier without ambition," Francis Bacon wrote, "is to pull off his spurs." But Washington knew how to conceal his ambition, as a gentleman was expected to do. Monroe did not. Even his political mentor Thomas Jefferson, who regarded him with affection, recognized how jealously and obviously Monroe attended "to his own honor and grade."[31]

Wanting to rise in the world and even achieve glory did not mean that either Washington or Monroe undervalued the cause of liberty. Indeed, it was a source of inspiration. "Let us . . . rely upon the goodness of the cause," Washington wrote early in the war, "to animate and encourage us to great and noble actions."[32]

Both men, when their ambitions were thwarted, became deeply discontented, and the Revolutionary War had times of frustration for both. As the end of fighting neared, however, Washington was the hero of the nation and the world, while Monroe, despite bravery and effort, felt like an outcast. The Revolution, so thrilling in the beginning, left him distrustful near the end—and among those he distrusted was the great Washington. It was a small fissure that foreshadowed a great schism.

At Harlem Heights, the Virginia companies joined in a resolute attack upon the British and, strengthened with reinforcements, "charged the enemy with great intrepidity," as Washington described it, driving them from "the wood into the plain." They "were pushing them from thence," Washington wrote, when he decided to order a withdrawal rather than risk an overwhelming British reinforcement. The troops were not enthusiastic about returning to camp. As Joseph Reed described it, "The pursuit of a flying enemy was so new a scene that it was with difficulty our men could be brought to retreat." Their reluctance soon gave way to exhilaration at the blow they had delivered. Wrote Washington, "This affair I am in hopes will be attended with many salutary consequences, as it seems to have greatly inspirited the whole of our troops."[33]

But in case inspiration was not enough, Washington issued orders that any officer or soldier who fled in the face of the enemy "be instantly shot down." He also ordered reliable officers to be placed to the rear of battalions so they would be well positioned to do the shooting.[34]

A few nights later, flames leapt skyward from New York City, and some thought Washington was behind the burning. Congress had forbidden harm to the city, and there is no evidence that he overrode their wishes. For someone else to have taken the initiative, however, was perfectly fine with him. Describing the fire to his cousin Lund Washington, he wrote, "Providence—or some good honest fellow—has done more for us than we were disposed to do for ourselves."[35]

The Battle of Harlem Heights did not change the army's perilous situation. In three and a half months, Continental enlistments would expire. The regular army would be gone, and a new one would have to be raised. Meanwhile, militiamen wandered into camp, used up scarce ammunition and stores, and went home when they pleased. Washington had daily reminders that he did not have the army he needed to prevail.[36]

He kept his composure for the most part. Kip's Bay had been an exception. But he needed an outlet for his frustrations, someone he could talk to who would not betray his inmost thoughts. One he trusted was thirty-five-year-old Joseph Reed. Reed was a pleasant-looking man with a narrow face that widened agreeably at the jawline. A London-educated lawyer, he had been in the party that accompanied the new commander in chief to Boston, and along the way Washington recruited him to become his aide-de-camp. Several months later, after Reed left to rejoin his family and resume his Philadelphia law practice, Washington pleaded with him to return. He missed Reed's "ready pen," which had lifted from his shoulders some of the burden of correspondence with the Congress, letters to his generals, orders to his army. Moreover, he told Reed, he needed someone with whom he could "live in unbounded confidence."[37] When Washington persuaded Congress to promote Reed to adjutant general with the rank of colonel, the Philadelphian agreed to return. Washington had, or so he thought, someone from whom he did not have to hide his irritations and concerns.

To Reed Washington felt free to express his disgust with the economically ambitious New Englanders who surrounded him. "Such a dearth of public spirit and want of virtue," he wrote, "such stock jobbing and fertility in all the low arts to obtain advantages . . . Such a dirty, mercenary spirit pervades the whole." New Englanders had their prejudices, too. They considered the Virginians haughty and imperious. But Washington was the commander in chief, and when Reed told him that word was beginning to circulate in Philadelphia about his opinions, Washington stopped speaking ill of New Englanders.[38]

But he continued to despair about his army, and on September 30, 1776, he sat down at his headquarters on Harlem Heights and penned a long lament to his cousin Lund. For a year, he wrote, he had been pointing out to Congress "the evil consequences of short enlistments, the expenses of militia, and the little dependence that was placed in them." Congress's failure to respond had left him torn in a way he had never before experienced:

> I see the impossibility of serving with reputation or doing any essential service to the cause by continuing in command, and yet I am told that if I quit the command, inevitable ruin will follow from the distraction that will ensue. In confidence I tell you that I never was in such an unhappy, divided state since I was born.

He was, he told his cousin, "bereft of every peaceful moment."[39]

As Washington's spirits began to sink, forty-four-year-old General Charles Lee, effectively second-in-command of the Continental army, was on his way to Harlem Heights. For the next two years, the presence of this brilliant but eccentric former British officer would reveal much about both Washington and Monroe.

Lee, now resident in Virginia, had attended fine schools in England and Switzerland and was the master of many languages. He had years of military experience and deep admiration for the American cause. Washington had strongly urged his appointment, and John Adams had worked for it as well, calling Lee "the best qualified for the service." After Mercy Warren, one of the most accomplished women of the age, met Lee, she seconded

Adams's assessment: "No man was better qualified at this early stage of the war to penetrate the designs, or to face in the field an experienced British veteran, than General Lee." He had the attributes of a fine warrior, she wrote, being "fearless of danger, and fond of glory," as well as possessing "a bold genius and an unconquerable spirit." Having seen much of the world, he could also be good company, "frequently agreeable in narration and judicious and entertaining in observation." Warren did not gloss over his appearance. Lee was painfully thin with a nose so large that it overwhelmed his face. He was "plain in his person even to ugliness," she wrote. He could also be a boor, "careless in his manners to a degree of rudeness."[40]

Recently in charge of the Southern Department of the Continental army, Lee had been celebrated for his role in turning back a British attempt on Charleston. But even gracious South Carolinians could not overlook his eccentricities. "We must put up with ten thousand oddities in him on account of his abilities and his attachment to the rights of humanity," General Charles Cotesworth Pinckney observed. Lee's dress was slovenly, his manner caustic, and he traveled with a pack of dogs, taking his favorite, Spado, into even the politest company. At a reception in Boston, he had maneuvered none other than Abigail Adams into a handshake with the large black Pomeranian.[41]

Lee's opinion of his fellow man fell far short of his opinion of dogs, and he was often unable to keep his feelings to himself. During the French and Indian War, the Seneca had named him Boiling Water because of his scathing outbursts.[42] They were often directed at those in authority, usually when they had somehow thwarted him, but sometimes even when they had not.

Despite Washington's losses at Brooklyn Heights and Kip's Bay, there was continued admiration of his integrity. Colonel John Haslet, commander of the 1st Delaware Regiment, wrote that Washington's "character for disinterestedness, patience, and fortitude will be had in everlasting remembrances." But Haslet also noted that his indecisiveness had the army concerned: "We have alarm upon alarm, orders now issue[d] and the next moment reversed." The army was yearning for steady leadership: "Would to heaven General Lee was here is the language of officers and men."[43]

The troops were thrilled when Lee rode into camp. Tench Tilghman, one of Washington's aides, reported that his presence helped "our people feel bold." Lee had arrived shortly after Washington had learned of the British landing a large force at Throg's Point, from which they had to advance just nine miles to block the bridge that was the escape route from Manhattan. Being cut off was the nightmare that Washington had worried about for weeks, but his report to Congress seemed confident. Throg's Point at high tide was actually an island, he explained, and the grounds from the point were "strong and defensible, being full of stone fences both along the road and across the adjacent fields."[44]

Washington knew that Congress viewed Manhattan as critical to guarding the Hudson River, "the nexus of the northern and southern colonies," as John Adams called it, and "a kind of key to the whole continent." This view had recently been reinforced by Congress resolving "that General Washington be desired if it be practicable by every art and whatever expense" to block British use of the Hudson. Thus Washington made preparations for a battle to defend his position. On October 13, he ordered that the mess "be kept cooking" and "the butchers constantly killing." He exhorted his men to "act with bravery and spirit becoming the cause in which they are engaged."[45]

Lee was appalled to learn that with a formidable enemy at work to outflank him, Washington intended to defend his foothold on Manhattan Island. Lee blamed the Congress in part, declaring that its members were "unhinging the army by their absurd interference." But Washington was also at fault. He ought to threaten to resign, Lee wrote, unless the Congress stopped meddling.[46]

Lee was not the sort to hide his opinion, and by October 15, Washington agreed that it was no longer "practicable," to use Congress's word, to stay on Manhattan. The British had committed so many men and resources to the flanking movement that if they failed at Throg's Point they were certain to try somewhere else. At a council of war, which met at Lee's quarters, Washington read aloud "sundry accounts of deserters shewing the enemy's intentions to surround us." The council voted to evacuate Manhattan except for the garrison at Fort Washington, an enormous earthwork atop a rocky mound on the highest point on the island. With guns trained on the river, Fort Washington and its twin, Fort Constitution in New Jersey, provided security for the Hudson, or at least that was the idea. Just a week before, the British had sailed the *Roebuck*, the *Phoenix*, and the *Tartar*, together with supporting vessels, past the forts. But the emphasis of Congress on preventing British ships from navigating the Hudson helped clear doubts away.[47]

Any resentment that Washington felt at Lee's swooping in and redirecting patriot efforts he kept to himself. Two days after the council of war, as patriot troops were rolling their tents to depart, he thanked Lee by renaming Fort Constitution. Henceforward it would be known as Fort Lee.

The withdrawal across King's Bridge to White Plains, New York, was long and miserable. Draft animals were in short supply, leaving soldiers to strain and pull to move heavy artillery. Food was short, according to Private Martin, who abandoned a cast-iron kettle he had been carrying. Since there was nothing to cook in it, he decided, there was no sense hauling it a step farther.[48]

The encampment at White Plains, as Joseph Reed observed, offered "every advantage of ground," but on October 28 the British army appeared, bayonets glittering in the sun, and quickly put an end to the idea that the patriot position was too daunting for them. During a fierce cannonade, "brisk on both sides," an observer noted, the British advanced on Chatterton's Hill, the high point of the battleground, and all too soon the militiamen stationed on the hill gave way.[49]

Washington retreated for the third time in two months, this time to the heights around North Castle. He waited for another attack, but in the early morning hours of November 3, the rumbling of cannon carriages alerted patriot sentries to enemy troop movement. The British marched off in a southwesterly direction, leading optimists in the American camp to believe they were headed into winter quarters in New York City. Washington suspected that General Howe intended to invade New Jersey—and attack Fort Washington.[50]

In a letter to the Continental Congress, Washington vowed to send a force across the Hudson into New Jersey and even lead it himself in order to prevent the British from moving southward and attacking Philadelphia, where the Congress was meeting. But because there were imperatives east of the Hudson as well, he decided to take just two thousand men into New Jersey with him. He would leave four thousand under General William Heath at Hudson Highlands thirty miles north and another seven thousand with General Lee at North Castle to guard the approach to New England.[51] Meanwhile, the garrisons at Forts Washington and Lee were to remain.

Washington was counting on the main body of the army, under General Lee, augmenting, if necessary, the small force that he was taking across the Hudson, but he communicated his plan in a remarkably diffident way: "If the enemy should remove the whole or the greatest part of their force to the west side of Hudson's River," he wrote to Lee, "I have no doubt of your following with all possible dispatch." Washington could be a forceful commander, ordering men shot, lashed, and hanged to enforce discipline, but his note to Lee was more respectful request than firm command, as though he had lost his self-confidence during the bruising months since Boston.[52]

He may also have been constrained by the rules of gentlemanly behavior. On some level, he might have regarded a firm order to a top general as a breach of civility. One of the entries he had copied from *Rules of Civility*, the book that did so much to instill in him a sense of decorum, warned against being "excessive in commanding."[53] Whatever the reasons for his diffidence, it did not always serve him well.

About the same time that Washington was making suggestions to General Lee, he sent a letter to Major General Greene, now in command of Fort Washington and Fort Lee. Three more British ships had sailed past Fort Washington, leading the commander in chief to ask, "What valuable purpose can it answer to attempt to hold a post from which the expected benefit cannot be had?" The answer was obvious. There was no valuable purpose. But Washington did not tell Greene what to do. "As you are on the spot," he wrote, "[I] leave it to you to give such orders as to evacuating [Fort] Washington as you judge best."[54]

Washington was fond of the thirty-four-year-old Rhode Islander, a strong, stocky man who walked with a pronounced limp. His gait had held him back in the early days of his military career, when he had not been made an officer in a local militia company because of it. In the Continental army, he quickly became a brigadier general, then a major general and one of Washington's most trusted officers. The commander in chief, largely self-educated, may have favored Greene because he, too, had schooled himself, reading Euclid, Horace, and Seneca as a young man, as well as moderns, such as Locke and Hume. To the chagrin of his Quaker family, he had studied historic battles, read the memoirs of renowned general Maurice de Saxe, and immersed himself in the writings of Marshal Turenne, whose campaigns Napoleon would recommend for instruction. Although Greene had no battlefield experience, he had gained a reputation as "a first-rate military genius," in the words of Tench Tilghman. He was "one in whose opinions [the commander in chief] places the utmost confidence."[55]

Washington moved the men directly under his command north to Peekskill, across the Hudson, and down to Fort Lee, where he met with Greene, who was confident that Fort Washington could be successfully defended. Washington vacillated between

Greene's reassurances and his own growing doubts—"warfare in my mind," he called it—until finally it was too late to make a decision. On November 16, General Howe brought the full force of the British army against the fort. Washington, standing on a high bank near Fort Lee, watching smoke rise and listening to cannon fire, sent a brave officer across the river to tell the commander of the fort, Colonel Robert Magaw, that if he could hold out until nightfall, he and his men would be evacuated to New Jersey. The messenger returned with dreadful news: Magaw was negotiating a surrender. He had little choice. His men were jammed into the earthen fort that the British had encircled with murderous artillery.[56]

The fall of the fort was a catastrophe. Washington calculated that two thousand men had been lost, as many as he had led across the Hudson into New Jersey. In fact, the toll was worse—nearly three thousand lost, and this at a time when army enlistments were expiring. Bleak as the situation had been before, nothing matched this calamity.

Certain the British would soon cross the Hudson, Washington ordered an immediate evacuation of Fort Lee. Stores of food, hundreds of tents, and thousands of weapons were left behind. Washington consolidated his army at Hackensack, and it was there that he received a letter from Charles Lee. "Oh General," Lee wrote, "why would you be overpersuaded by men of inferior judgment to your own?"[57]

In a single sentence Lee questioned Washington's judgment and faintly praised it, while raising doubts about Greene. He was not the only one to lament Greene's advice and Washington's indecision, which had effectively implemented the Rhode Islander's strategy. But Greene was forthright, loyal, and smart, and the advice he offered was usually good. He had urged evacuation of New York City—and burning it on the way out. His latest recommendation was that Washington station "provisions and provinder" at key points along the route through New Jersey that the army was likely to take.[58] As fall weather turned to freezing winter, the men would be cold, miserable, and hungry, but at least there would be some food for them and their horses.

As the retreat began, Washington wrote to Lee, "I am of the opinion and the gentlemen about me concur in it that the public interest requires your coming over to this side with the Continental troops." It was not quite an order. Lee would call it a "recommendation."[59]

During the next few weeks, Washington repeatedly urged and even entreated Lee to join him, but he did not issue a command. Lee explained that he hesitated to leave New England unguarded and that his men were ill-equipped for a long march. When Washington pressed him to hurry and help defend Philadelphia, Lee answered that he did not think Philadelphia was the British target (which it turned out not to be) and that he had information that the British intended to move toward New England (which a large part of their army did). When Lee finally crossed the Hudson, he proposed that rather than join Washington he harass the British from the rear, thus distracting and weakening them.[60] Lee had a military rationale for every demurral, but since the fall of Fort Washington, he had become utterly disenchanted with George

Washington—which no doubt inclined him to find reasons not to join the commander in chief.

Lee's failure to heed Washington's recommendations added to the burdens that the commander in chief was already shouldering—as perhaps did his own failure to issue Lee a definitive order. He had an army of Continentals whose terms would be up at the end of the month and several brigades of militia that were already departing, a Congress that issued poor military guidance and failed to supply even basic necessities to the troops, and a record of military defeat that was causing many to doubt his leadership. On top of all this came betrayal from someone with whom he thought he could "live in unbounded confidence."[61]

At Burlington, Washington was handed a letter addressed to Colonel Reed during a time when Reed was absent from camp. Thinking the letter to be an official communication, Washington opened it to read a note to Reed from General Lee:

> I received your most obliging, flattering letter [and] lament with you that fatal indecision of mind which in war is a much greater disqualification than stupidity or even want of personal courage. Accident may put a decisive blunderer in the right, but eternal defeat and miscarriage must attend the man of the best parts if cursed with indecision.

It was evident that after the debacle at Fort Washington, Reed had gone behind Washington's back and criticized him to Lee. Washington forwarded the letter to Reed along with a note:

The enclosed was put into my hands by an express from . . .
White Plains. Having no idea of its being a private letter, much
less suspecting the tendency of the correspondence, I opened
it, as I had done all other letters to you from the same place and
Peekskill, upon the business of your office.[62]

In its dispassion, the note was fully aligned with the gentleman's
code, though one can hardly miss the anger underneath. Washington's lack of emotion, at least on the surface, was essential at this
point. He needed Reed in the days directly ahead, as well as Lee and
the troops he commanded. It was not the time for an open break.

Washington hid well the cares weighing on him. Young Lieutenant James Monroe watched him pass by as the Continental
army retreated from Newark, New Jersey, southwest toward
Brunswick. Lieutenant General Henry Cornwallis and his troops
were not far behind. As Monroe remembered it:

> I saw him in my earliest youth in the retreat through Jersey at
> the head of a small band, or rather in its rear, for he was always
> near the enemy, and his countenance and manner made an im-
> pression on me which time can never efface. . . . A deportment
> so firm, so dignified, so exalted, but yet so modest and com-
> posed, I have never seen in any other person.[63]

Monroe wrote this description long after he and Washington
had become estranged, but he nonetheless captured an essential

element of his greatness. Washington was not a brilliant general, although there were moments of brilliance, one of which lay directly ahead. But he was determined and honorable, someone who towered above other men not only in stature but also in character.

TWO

River Crossing

∾

Victory Hard Won

Washington and his army arrived at Trenton on December 2, and over the next five days and nights retreated from New Jersey across the Delaware River into Pennsylvania. Charles Willson Peale, an artist who had come with the Philadelphia Associators to reinforce Washington's army, described a night scene he came upon as the "most hellish" he had ever beheld: "The shores . . . lighted up with large fires; the boats continually passing and repassing, full of men, horses, artillery, and camp equipage; the hallooing of hundreds of men in their difficulties of getting horses and artillery out of the boats." As Peale was watching, one of the men who had crossed over the river "staggered out of line and came toward me. He had lost all his clothes. He was in an old dirty blanket jacket, his beard long and his face so full of sores." Only when the man drew very close and spoke did Peale realize it was his brother James.[1]

James Peale was hardly the only man in distress, and Washington, as he had before, wrote to the Congress asking for simple necessities. "The clothing of the troops is a matter of infinite importance," he wrote, "and if it could be accomplished would have a happy effect . . . many of them being entirely naked and most so thinly clad as to be unfit for service."[2]

Washington was relieved when reinforcements began to arrive. Two thousand men assigned to Charles Lee's command appeared on December 20—but the general was not with them. After bringing his men to New Jersey, Lee had decided that he needed a comfortable bed and, perhaps, some female companionship. He had spent the night with a few aides at Widow White's lodgings, several miles from his lines. He had just finished a letter about Washington's shortcomings ("*Entre nous,* a certain great man is most damnably deficient") when a British detachment that had been alerted to his location moved in and carried him off.[3]

Lee's capture was widely regretted. Jonathan Trumbull Jr., an army paymaster, wrote to his father, the governor of Connecticut, "This is a misfortune that cannot be remedied as we have no officer in the army of equal experience and merit." Colonel John Cadwalader noted that Lee's capture "had dampened the spirit of the army very much." Washington wrote to his cousin Lund, "Our cause has . . . received a severe blow in the captivity of General Lee."[4]

At the same time he was regretting Lee's loss, Washington suddenly found himself free from congressional interference. On December 12, 1776, Congress, worried about the British capturing

Philadelphia, decided to find another meeting place, and before leaving town gave Washington "full power to order and direct all things relative to the department and to the operations of war." Wasting no time in taking advantage of his new stature, Washington wrote a forceful letter to the Congress. Members had by now authorized an 88-battalion army, but Washington made clear this was insufficient. He needed 110 battalions, and if members thought he was pushing too hard, he wrote, they should understand that "desperate diseases require desperate remedies."[5]

The British army, in eighteenth-century fashion, went into winter quarters but left three posts along the Delaware at Bordentown, Burlington, and Trenton. Joseph Reed, now directing a network of spies in New Jersey, reported enemy activity to Washington and kept him informed about the spirited attacks that American militia were carrying out on enemy posts.[6]

Trenton, where Colonel Johann Rall commanded three regiments of Hessians, had been under extreme pressure from patriot militia, and it was there, suggested Reed, that Washington ought to attack. "Some enterprise must be undertaken in our present circumstances," Reed wrote, "or we must give up the cause." Reed was certainly not the only one to arrive at this conclusion. Everything pointed to it, from the expiration of enlistments in little more than a week to New Jersey citizens who were losing enthusiasm for the American cause. But Reed offered specific recommendations: take advantage of the collected American troops and "the scattered, divided state of the enemy" and try to "possess ourselves again of New Jersey or any considerable part of it." The effects of such a move, he advised, "would be greater than if we had never left [New Jersey]."[7]

A shattering blow to the enemy—or a "brilliant stroke," as Washington called it—would overshadow the retreats and defeats of the past year, and the pieces were in place.[8] In addition to the advantages Reed set forth, Washington had commandeered all the boats along the Delaware and had skilled mariners to man them. Colonel John Glover and his Marbleheaders, a Massachusetts regiment that counted free black men among its numbers, had proved their worth in the evacuation from Brooklyn Heights, across the East River to Manhattan. They were brave and disciplined, and when the red-haired Glover assured Washington and his war council that he and his men could handle a Delaware crossing, they had confidence in his judgment. Washington knew he could depend on the inventive Henry Knox, and he put him in charge of the logistics of the crossing. Nathanael Greene was also at Washington's side and would lead a column into Trenton.

As they readied to cross the Delaware, Washington's men had almost nothing by way of warm clothes, but they did have the inspirational words of Thomas Paine, a radical Englishman who had marched as a volunteer on the long retreat. An essay he had written circulated in the camps along the river. "These are the times that try men's souls," it began. "The summer soldier and the sunshine patriot will, in this crisis shrink from the service of his country; but he that stands it NOW deserves the love and thanks of man and woman."[9]

The time set for the attack on Trenton was "Christmas Day at night," Washington wrote to Joseph Reed on December 23, admonishing him to tell no one. The next evening a visitor noticed Washington writing on bits of paper. When one dropped to the floor, the visitor read the words "Victory or Death," the phrase that would be the password for the attack.[10]

By now the 3rd Virginia had lost two-thirds of its men to illness. Only five officers remained, one of them Lieutenant James Monroe, still eager to fight after the grueling march through the Jerseys. When Monroe learned that Washington had chosen Captain William Washington to lead an advance party across the Delaware, he immediately volunteered to serve under him. At dusk on Christmas Day, the advance party crossed the river at Coryell's Ferry, north of where Washington would cross. After landing, the officers and fifty men moved to a point three miles outside Trenton, where they had been ordered to set up a roadblock and "make prisoners of all going in or coming out of town."[11]

Although the men proceeded stealthily, they nonetheless alerted a dog, whose owner investigated the ruckus and discovered the advance party. Thinking they were British, he ordered them away, his curses loud in the night, but when he found out they were Americans, he introduced himself as Dr. John Riker and offered to accompany them in case his services were needed.[12]

The advance party made prisoners of many traveling to and from Trenton that night and at dawn spied a column of the Continental army approaching. General Greene was in command, with General Washington accompanying. The men in the advance party became the vanguard of the column for the march to Trenton. It was full daylight when the town came into sight, and Washington was concerned. To achieve surprise, he had hoped to strike before dawn; nevertheless, when the Americans surged into Trenton, the Hessians were totally unprepared.

William Washington and James Monroe were among the first into the town. They came in at the north end of King Street just as Hessians dragged two cannon into position at the south end. "The Hessians were just ready to open fire," an eyewitness wrote, "when Captain Washington and Lieutenant Monroe with their men rushed forward and captured them." Both men were wounded, Washington in the hand and Monroe, as he described it, "through his breast and shoulder." Monroe bled profusely and later said he would have died had Dr. Riker, the man with the barking dog, not been near and "promptly taken up an artery."[13]

Because of Captain Washington and Lieutenant Monroe, the Hessians were unable to stop the American advance. They had no time "to form and reflect," as a participant in the battle put it. Had they been able to do so, he continued, they might well have retreated over a bridge to their rear, thus putting a barrier between themselves and the Americans, who in a "half-naked, half-frozen condition," would have found it difficult to prevail.[14]

The next day, as triumphant Americans recrossed the Delaware into Pennsylvania with nearly one thousand Hessian prisoners, Monroe was carried to a ferryman's house, where he spent ten days. The faithful Dr. Riker dressed his wound and perhaps told him of the American victory at Princeton. Crossing into New Jersey once more, Washington and his army had dealt the British a second stunning blow. When American troops had momentarily faded, Washington, astride a light gray, half-Arabian horse, had rallied them and led them forward until the British line broke and the redcoats began to flee.[15]

Washington moved his army into winter camp at Morristown, New Jersey, and not long after wrote to physician William Shippen Jr. that he had determined to inoculate American troops against smallpox. Washington had been trying to protect the army against the disease since Boston by using quarantine and isolation, but had decided that inoculation, or variolation, as it was called, was essential. The procedure involved inserting fluid from a pustule of an infected person into a cut in the skin of the person being immunized, thus causing a mild form of the disease. But the inoculated could pass it on until they had fully recovered, and city fathers almost everywhere did not want the procedure happening in their town, no matter how carefully it was regulated. Washington instructed Shippen to keep the project secret, but made clear that inoculation was as important as any military battle.

> This expedient may be attended with some inconveniences and some disadvantages, but yet I trust in its consequences will have the most happy effects. Necessity not only authorizes but seems to require the measure, for should the disorder infect the army in the natural way and rage with its usual virulence, we should have more to dread from it than from the sword of the enemy.

Threats to victory, he knew, came in many forms.[16]

Monroe was moved to a home in Bucks County, Pennsylvania, where he recuperated for nine weeks. He had been promoted to captain for his bravery at Trenton, but the regiment in which he was to serve had to be raised. As soon as he was able, he traveled to Virginia to recruit, but the task was nearly impossible. Enlisting men for three years, which the Congress had recently authorized, was much more difficult than recruiting for one, and the competition was stiff. The Virginia hills were filled with recruiters not only from Virginia, but from Georgia and South Carolina as well. Some recruiters addressed the disparity of supply and demand by enlisting those who were unfit, too young, or totally drunk at the time they signed up, but Monroe shied away. "I am thoroughly convinced we shall not get another man without using those arts which I would avoid and which no man of honor should use," he wrote. Monroe's uncle, Joseph Jones, a well-connected Fredericksburg lawyer who had watched over Monroe and his siblings after they were orphaned, wrote a letter to George Washington emphasizing Monroe's hard work: "He has been diligent in endeavoring to raise men, but such is the present disposition of the people of Virginia, neither Captain Monroe, nor any other officer preserving the character a gentleman ought to support, can recruit men."[17]

Monroe returned to Washington's camp and became a volunteer aide to one of Washington's brigadiers, William Alexander, whom everyone called Lord Stirling. In his autobiography, Monroe made this assignment sound matter of course, but giving up one's rank to serve as a volunteer was no small matter. When John Lacey, a captain from Pennsylvania, was asked to serve as a "volunteer without command," he wrote that it was like "a thunderbolt." He "felt such a load of degradation, [and] of injured innocence" at receiving what was a "deadly blow to all my future hopes of comfort or preferment." For Monroe to lose his rank, particularly after he had just been promoted for bravery, was difficult. He was now simply James Monroe, Esquire.[18]

Lord Stirling was not really a lord. His claim to a Scottish earldom had been rejected by the British House of Lords, but he insisted on being addressed as "Lord," and perhaps because he carried himself in noble fashion and had a fine estate in Basking Ridge, New Jersey, everyone went along. A jovial fellow, Stirling was famous for the amount he drank, no mean achievement in the eighteenth century, when enormous amounts of alcohol were consumed. There were many jokes about Stirling's drinking—but none about his bravery. He had stood with Smallwood's Marylanders at the Battle of Brooklyn Heights, holding off the British and Hessians until the main body of his soldiers had a chance to escape. Officers at that battle called him "as brave a man as ever lived."[19]

In August 1777, the British landed thirteen thousand men at Turkey Point in Maryland and by early September were marching toward Philadelphia. Trying to prevent its capture, Washington met the enemy at Brandywine Creek, which the British had to cross to reach Philadelphia. As had happened at Brooklyn Heights, the British knew more about the battlefield than Washington did. Generals Howe and Cornwallis took eight thousand men across unguarded fords to flank Washington's army. Stirling turned his division to meet the flanking British and took the brunt of the enemy attack. In the end the Americans were forced to withdraw, but Lord Stirling's corps, said a division commander, had "remarkably distinguished themselves."[20]

The British occupied Philadelphia with three thousand troops and stationed another nine thousand at Germantown, some five miles away. In what James Monroe characterized as an act of defiance, Washington decided to go on the attack. The Fabian strategy had brought him grief just as it had to the Roman general after whom it was named. John Adams called it "this execrable defensive plan." New England troops despised it, Adams said. It left them "dispirited."[21]

On the night of October 3, 1777, patriot columns marched toward Germantown. The leading brigades achieved surprise, overran a British light infantry battalion, and drove back other units. A Hessian officer observed that the Americans achieved "something I had never seen before, namely the English in full flight." But when a heavy fog blanketed the battlefield, Washington's army fell into confusion. In less than three hours, the Americans were withdrawing, exhausted but, according to Thomas Paine, not discouraged. "They appeared to me to be only sensible of a disappointment, not a defeat," he wrote. Lord Stirling offered what may have been an ironic assessment. The British had learned from the encounter, he said, "that we can drive them before us several miles together and that we know how to retreat in good [order] and defy them to follow us."[22]

Washington moved his army into winter camp at Valley Forge, a wooded region on the Schuylkill River some twenty miles from Philadelphia. Lord Stirling's division served as rear guard, and thus Monroe was among the last to enter camp. He was officially Stirling's aide, now with the rank of major, a change for which he would have been grateful, but he had no regimental or brigade authority. He wanted to command men in battle but instead found himself a message carrier, bearing "the orders of his general to the troops under him . . . or on the march . . . taking those of the commander-in-chief daily from the adjutant general of the army to report them to his own general." Many years later, Monroe cast his experience as an aide in a positive light. It had given him an intimate view of "the most interesting occurrences of our revolutionary conflict," he wrote. He met the commanders of Washington's army and got to know other young aides at Valley Forge, including Alexander Hamilton and John Laurens, both in their early twenties.[23]

Hamilton, whose birth in Nevis in the West Indies was illegitimate, had managed to educate himself at King's College in New York, and by his skill, bravery, and sparkling intellect had attracted Washington's attention. Hamilton also had a flair for paperwork. Washington continued to try to impose efficiency on his army through a myriad of detailed instructions: to keep track of the number of men who were sick, to calculate the cost of a single ration in a uniform manner, to provide soap to the troops "without delay."[24] Hamilton was proficient at translating Washington's wishes into formal orders and able, with just a few hints, to compose graceful letters to important persons. Washington considered him indispensable.

Laurens, an elegant young man of high ideals and reckless courage, also worked as one of Washington's secretaries. The son of the president of the Continental Congress, Henry Laurens,

John had joined the army over his father's objections. He and Hamilton had a close bond that, at least on Hamilton's part, seems to have grown beyond friendship into an unusually strong emotional attachment.[25]

Another of the bright young men in Washington's military family was the twenty-year-old Marquis de Lafayette. A fervent believer in the American cause and wealthy as well, he had purchased his own ship to sail from France to America. Congress had made him a major general, but his warmth and charm made it difficult for his peers to envy him. Particularly when taken all together, Hamilton, Laurens, and Lafayette radiated dash and glamour. Hamilton's grandson would write, "There was something about them rather suggestive of the three famous heroes of Dumas."[26]

Washington attached a log structure to the two-story stone house in which he and his aides lived and worked, and they typically took an afternoon meal there. Washington must have welcomed the energy and enthusiasm of Hamilton, Laurens, and Lafayette at a time when he was weighed down by an assault on his reputation that he believed was aimed at replacing him as commander in chief. His losses were being unfavorably compared to the spectacular October victory at Saratoga in New York, where General Horatio Gates had defeated British general John Burgoyne and captured his army of five thousand. A Virginia neighbor of Washington's, Dr. James Craik, warned him that a "strong faction" was "holding up General Gates to the people and making them believe . . . that Philadelphia was given up by your mismanagement and that you have missed many opportunities of defeating the enemy."[27]

But Washington's main concern was his army. The men had

shelter of a sort, crude wooden huts that they had built themselves, many without floors, which meant they were sleeping on
the cold ground, probably without blankets, since they were in
short supply. Soldiers pieced together uniforms, but usually not
complete ones. This soldier would lack a coat, another a shirt, and
some even breeches. Many had no shoes. One of the most affecting images of Valley Forge is of bloody footprints in the snow.[28]

Provisions were an even greater problem. Not long after he
entered Valley Forge, Washington had written to Congress that it
was impossible to field an army that had nothing to eat. Without
food, there were three options, he wrote: "starve—dissolve—or
disperse." But Congress, with no authority to raise revenue by
taxing the states and having already printed so much continental
currency that it was nearly worthless, was hard pressed to provide
money for provisions. Months later, Washington wrote to New
York governor George Clinton that part of the army had been
without meat for a week.[29]

In February 1778, perhaps the worst month at Valley Forge, he
began to fear that his freezing, starving army would mutiny or
simply leave. February was also the month when Martha Washington arrived. She had been traveling to troop encampments
since Cambridge, and upon her arrival at Valley Forge she began
attending to the sick, wounded, and dying. She urged officers'
wives to knit socks and make shirts for the troops with her. She
loved her tall, distinguished husband "madly," Lafayette wrote,
and when she wasn't there, Washington longed for her comforting
presence. The perceptive Mercy Warren described her this way:
"Her affability, candor, and gentleness qualify her to soften the
hours of private life . . . and smooth the rugged scenes of war."[30]

Trying to distract Washington from his cares, Martha arranged evening get-togethers, simple affairs at which the drink was tea or coffee, and the entertainment, conversation—or sometimes one of the guests would sing. Washington's general officers and their wives attended, including Lord and Lady Stirling, along with their daughter Kitty and Kitty's companion, Nancy Brown, "a distinguished belle," according to one of Monroe's friends. Nineteen-year-old James Monroe probably accompanied the Stirlings, but it is impossible to imagine him taking to the floor to sing. Six feet tall with a dimple in his chin, he was reserved and awkward. His usual demeanor was so serious, according to one young woman, that it was a subject for joking and teasing.[31]

Monroe's circle of friends included John Francis Mercer. He was someone in whom Monroe confided about everything from rivals to women to plans for the future. Pierre Du Ponceau, who arrived with Baron von Steuben in February 1778, also became Monroe's good friend. Von Steuben, who would earn deserved fame for training the army at Valley Forge, spoke little English. While he quickly impressed the American troops with his ability to swear in both French and German, he needed a translator for most interactions, and thus Du Ponceau had come with him to America. The eighteen-year-old was a language prodigy, who would become a fabled linguist and a champion of American literature. At Valley Forge, however, Monroe lent him British books, which Du Ponceau claimed to like, long and lugubrious though they might be.[32]

When spring came to Valley Forge, the army was largely intact. Most of the men, inspired by Washington's "prudence and wisdom," had stayed, and they drew deserved praise. Wrote Nathanael

Greene, "Such patience and moderation as they manifested under their sufferings does the highest honor to the magnanimity of the American soldiers."[33]

Washington set May 6, 1778, aside "for gratefully acknowledging the divine Goodness and celebrating the important event which we owe to his benign interposition." France had agreed to a military alliance with the United States, and to mark the occasion, brigades formed up at their parade grounds, and after wheeling right marched to their posts, displaying skills they had learned from von Steuben. As Washington reviewed the troops, they saluted him smartly, and when the review was finished, cannon sounded, the signal for a *feu de joie*. The brigades fired their guns in succession, the sound traveling around the army once, then twice, then three times, each round followed by huzzahs, the last "to the American States." John Laurens declared that the celebration "gave sensible pleasure to everyone present."[34]

Five days later, despite a congressional ban on theater, young officers performed Joseph Addison's play *Cato*, in which Cato the Younger sacrifices himself rather than live under Julius Caesar's tyranny. General and Mrs. Washington were in "the numerous and splendid audience," as were Lord and Lady Stirling and probably Monroe. Washington, a frequent theatergoer before the war, had seen *Cato* many times and found its affirmation of liberty inspiring. He used lines from the play to model behavior for himself and others, as when he congratulated a young officer by paraphrasing Addison: "It is not in the power of any man to command success, but you have done more—you have deserved it."[35]

Fortune now seemed to be smiling on the Americans—and on Washington in particular. The support from France would translate into weapons, men, and ships. At the same time, opposition to him from inside the United States had failed and fallen away. At the end of May, he dismissed those who had wanted to replace him as commander in chief as "men who wanted to aggrandize themselves," but now had "slunk back."[36]

The other happy news was that General Charles Lee had been released. An American raid in Rhode Island had captured a British officer of equal rank, Major General Richard Prescott, who, like Lee, had imprudently chosen to spend a night several miles from his army and had been captured. Washington had pushed hard for an exchange, telling Colonel Elias Boudinot, who was in charge of such matters, that Lee "was never more wanted . . . than at the present moment." Finally Lee's release had been secured, and as he approached Valley Forge, Washington rode out to meet him, greeting him, Boudinot recorded, "as if he had been his brother." The two men entered camp to the martial music of fifes and drums.[37]

Lee, once again second-in-command of the American army, had aides assigned to him, one of whom was John Francis Mercer. It was probably through Mercer that Lee came to know Monroe well and to bolster the young Virginian's sense of himself. Lee's confidence that Monroe had a bright future would have come like a spring rain to Monroe's parched ego. He would remain Lee's friend even when others had abandoned him.[38]

Knowing that they were now going to have to fight the French, the British evacuated Philadelphia and headed toward New York. Washington wanted to attack, but in a war council the majority of his generals, with Lee taking the lead, voted not to, arguing that since the French alliance would eventually bring American victory, it made no sense to risk the army at present. Indeed, said Lee, the Americans ought to build the British army "a bridge of gold" to hasten them on their way.[39]

But after von Steuben's training, the American army was now better than it had ever been, and with Hamilton, Lafayette, and Greene urging him on, Washington overrode his council and ordered an attack on the British once they moved out of camp at Monmouth Court House in New Jersey.[40] An advance party of several thousand was to make the attack while the rest of the army remained close by to provide reinforcement if necessary.

Lee irritated everyone at the outset by changing his mind about whether he would lead the advance party. Finally he decided he wanted the command, and Washington obliged. On June 28, 1778, with orders to attack the British rear, "if possible," Lee advanced with four to five thousand men. They moved eastward into rough and un-reconnoitered territory that was crossed by ravines, but despite the difficult terrain, Lee felt that he could prevail, particularly after he learned that the British rear guard was only two thousand strong.[41]

Positioning his men for an attack, Lee put General Charles Scott in command of the extreme left of the American line and sent Lafayette to the right. Trouble began when Lafayette, concerned that he and one of his regiments were too exposed, drew back. He had no orders from Lee to do so, but would later say that someone whose name he could not remember had told him that Lee wished the pullback. General Scott, believing Lafayette was retreating, also drew back—without orders—and kept withdrawing. Lafayette, meanwhile, ordered a battery on the right flank to draw back. When the battery commander refused on the grounds that he had orders from General Lee to hold his position, Lafayette told him that General Lee had ordered a withdrawal—although the general had not.[42]

At the same time that the line was collapsing, Lee realized that he was fighting more than an ordinary rear guard. British general Henry Clinton, who had replaced General Howe as commander of British forces, had stationed his second-in-command, General Cornwallis, and a division of the elite of the British army behind his rear guard. He had turned them to attack the American advance and was bringing up reinforcements. Lee, although not aware of these details at the time, observed enough to conclude that the odds were now heavily against him. He decided to make as orderly a withdrawal as possible to a strong defensive position.[43]

Lee withdrew to the west toward an "eminence" that he believed his troops could hold. The day was blisteringly hot, like "the mouth of a heated oven," as Private Joseph Plumb Martin described it. Men and horses were collapsing and dying of the heat, and Lee's withdrawal, while controlled, became somewhat disorganized. One brigade sent to occupy the eminence did not stop marching when the soldiers reached it, but kept moving to the rear.[44]

Washington had last been told that Lee was cutting off the British rear guard, but now he heard that the Continentals were in retreat. As he rode forward in disbelief, Lee, who was helping his men cross the ravine to the hill they were to occupy, learned that the commander in chief was nearby and rode to meet him. Upon seeing Lee, Washington furiously demanded to know what the retreat was about. What was all the confusion? "Sir, sir?" Lee responded, perhaps not hearing, but more likely not comprehending. As he saw it, he had done a fine job of getting his detachment out of a dangerous situation—one that had not been of his making. There was no confusion, he told Washington, "but what had arisen from his orders not being properly obeyed."[45]

There are different versions of what else was said, but Washington apparently castigated Lee for retreating without sufficient cause and suggested he had done so because he had not approved of the attack in the first place. A Major Morton, who witnessed the confrontation, said that it was not Washington's words that were extraordinary, but his manner: He was "violently excited," his face "like a *thunder* cloud before a lightning flash." Lee later called Washington's accusations "thundering charges."[46]

Washington rode off, Lee following, but after his temper cooled, Washington placed Lee in command of the force covering the retreating troops. He was to check the enemy while Washington formed up the rest of the army—which the commander in chief did in a way that demonstrated his finest characteristics. "I never saw the general to so much advantage," Alexander Hamilton wrote. "His coolness and firmness were admirable." Lafayette agreed, writing that Washington's "presence of mind, valor, and decision of character were never displayed to greater advantage."[47]

As the main body of the army moved up and joined the battle, Lord Stirling's division took the left flank, locating on the eminence that Lee had chosen. After a long exchange of cannon fire, the British struck on the left with light infantry and grenadiers. Sometime in the early hours of fighting, Stirling's adjutant,

Lieutenant Colonel Francis Barber, was wounded, and Monroe took his place. For the first time since Trenton, he found himself in action. After the British fell back, he led a scouting party of seventy to see where they would next attack. In a note to Washington, he advised it would be on the American right, which it was. The British were no more successful at breaking the line there than they had been on the left, and at the end of that blazingly hot day, General Clinton withdrew his troops to a camp outside American artillery range. Washington, hoping to make a counterstrike the next day, kept his men in the field. He spent the night lying on a cloak under a tree talking with Lafayette about Lee.[48]

The British campfires flickered through the night, but they turned out to be a ruse. When morning came, the Americans found the British had departed and were once more on their way to New York. The battle was essentially a draw, but Washington advertised it as a victory, writing to his brother John that it had been "a glorious and happy day."[49]

Meanwhile, Lee, seething over the public upbraiding he had received from Washington, imprudently decided to take up the matter with the commander in chief. He had a letter delivered in which he blamed Washington's "singular expressions" to him in the field on "misinformation of some very stupid, or misrepresentation of some very wicked person." The injury Washington had done him must be the work of "those dirty earwigs who will forever insinuate themselves near persons in high office," he continued, for he knew that Washington himself would never be guilty of such "an act of cruel injustice."[50]

By this time, Washington may well have been ready to let the matter drop. He had, after all, left Lee in a command position after their encounter on the field. But Lee's letter goaded Washington into repeating charges he had made in that angry moment. As far as he was concerned, he wrote, Lee had disobeyed orders and conducted an unnecessary and "shameful" retreat.[51]

Lee responded with an insult. "I trust that temporary power of office and the tinsel dignity attending it will not be able by all the mists they can raise to [obfuscate] the bright rays of truth," he wrote. He then decided to raise the stakes, writing another letter to Washington to request a court-martial in which he could make his case. Washington complied, Lee was arrested, and the trial was announced in the General Orders of the next day. The charges were "disobedience of orders in not attacking the enemy," "an unnecessary, disorderly, and shameful retreat," and "disrespect to the commander in chief."[52]

Lee was clearly guilty of the third charge, but not the first two. Washington had ordered Lee to attack "if possible." He had reported that to the Congress. Moreover, it would have been absurd to order an attack no matter what, a point that Alexander Hamilton, testifying against Lee in the court-martial, had to admit. The charge that Lee had made a "shameful," i.e., unjustified, retreat was likewise without foundation. Washington himself had seen how hard it was to repel the British with his entire army. Lee's advance party would have been no match for what it had encountered. John Laurens tried to make the case that the retreat was disorderly by saying Lee had given no orders for how it was to occur, but under questioning from Lee, who acted as his own counsel, Laurens had to admit that orders might well have been given out of his hearing. In his final statement, Lee made the point that he had managed a retreat of two miles over difficult ground "without the loss of a single piece of artillery, a single battalion, or even a single company."[53]

On August 12, 1778, Lee was found guilty on all three counts, although the court did omit the word "shameful" in describing his retreat. Lee was suspended from any command in the army for a year, a sentence so light for the offenses of which he had been convicted that many concluded that the court was not convinced of his guilt. They had handed down the verdict they did because it was unthinkable to rebuke Washington, which an innocent verdict would have done. Dr. William Shippen Jr., chief of the medical division of the Continental army, reported that "many very good officers in camp" approved of Lee's conduct at Monmouth and were dismayed at the verdict. Aaron Burr, who had fought at Monmouth, defended Lee, as did John Francis Mercer, who had testified on his behalf at the court-martial, and James Monroe, who would continue to respect and reach out to Lee even as the general became a pariah.[54]

No one had the perspective on Lee that Washington did: the long march through the Jerseys, during which Lee had repeatedly avoided reinforcing him; the correspondence between Reed and Lee, questioning his fitness for leadership. Through it all, Washington had treated Lee with courtesy, but at Monmouth he exploded, and Lee's behavior afterward probably convinced him that Lee's insubordination had gone so far that it was damaging his command. Little wonder that Washington had been willing to pile on the court-martial counts.

Monroe began to think seriously about studying in France, which caused difficulty with a young woman, Nancy Brown, the "distinguished belle" who had attracted notice at Valley Forge.

She believed that she and Monroe had a commitment to one another, and she objected to his leaving. Monroe's response suggests just how unserious a suitor he was. He turned for advice to the witty and beautiful Theodosia Prevost, whom he met while the army rested near her home after the Battle of Monmouth. The Hermitage, as her home was known, was a place where young officers "talked and walked and laughed—and frolicked and gallanted," and Monroe seems to have been one of their number. He was smitten with his hostess, as were others, including twenty-two-year-old Lieutenant Colonel Aaron Burr. Monroe's letter to Mrs. Prevost about Nancy Brown was less an appeal for counsel than a display of what he apparently judged to be clever flirtation. In truth it was an example of his social awkwardness.[55]

He should not have taken Miss Brown's objection lightly. She was not only the companion of Lord Stirling's daughter, but also the orphaned niece of Susannah Livingston, wife of the governor of New Jersey and a woman unaccustomed to letting offenses pass. Lord Stirling, who was Mrs. Livingston's brother-in-law, had tangled with her before, and fortunately for Monroe he stepped into the social roil on his behalf. In a letter to Joseph Jones, Stirling offered assurances that Monroe had behaved honorably.[56]

Congress was required to ratify Lee's court-martial verdict, and at the end of October, Gouverneur Morris, a Pennsylvanian whose lively company Washington enjoyed, thought it was uncertain which way the vote would go. "Lee's affair hangs by the eyelids," he wrote. Physician Benjamin Rush, not a friend of

Washington, was pessimistic about the outcome. As he saw it, members of Congress were reluctant to appear to oppose the commander in chief. "I blush for my country," Rush wrote to John Adams, "when I tell you that several members of Congress leave the House when the affair is brought on the carpet."[57]

On December 5, 1778, Congress voted to uphold the court-martial verdict. Two weeks later James Monroe resigned from the Continental army. John Francis Mercer also decided to resign.[58]

The Lee verdict brought a very different reaction from Washington aide John Laurens, who challenged the convicted general for his insinuations about the commander in chief. Lee, caustic as ever, observed that although one person did not usually defend another's honor, he would accept the challenge on the assumption that Laurens was invoking an ancient custom that allowed a third person to take up the cause of "monks, old women, and widows." The two men met in a wood near Philadelphia on December 23 at half past three, Alexander Hamilton accompanying Laurens as his second and a Major Evan Edwards accompanying Lee. The first shot left Laurens unscathed, but Lee was hit in the side. He pronounced the wound inconsiderable and proposed another shot, which Laurens agreed to, but the seconds, with Major Edwards leading the way, talked them out of it.[59]

When Lee realized that he would not get the vindication he wanted, he decided on revenge. Before he left Philadelphia to take up residence on his farm in Virginia, he published a series of questions, "whacking queries," he called them, "which are to spoil Gargantua's digestion." One question harked back to the letter that Joseph Reed had written to Lee about Washington's indecision—the one that elicited the response from Lee that fell into Washington's hands. Since that incident Reed had been all praise and compliment as far as Washington was concerned, and Lee asked whether "this gentleman . . . does really think his Excellency a great man, or whether evidences could not be produced of his sentiments being quite the reverse?" It is not known if Lee still had the letter, but the hint that he did and might produce it forced Reed to make a painful public confession that he had indeed been a critic of the commander in chief.[60]

Another of Lee's queries asked whether it was consistent with the "spirit of liberty and republicanism to inculcate and encourage in the people an idea that their welfare, safety, and glory depend on one man." He was not the only one concerned about the adulation of Washington. John Adams worried about "the superstitious veneration which is paid to General Washington." William Tudor, a well-regarded Massachusetts lawyer, delivered an oration in Boston warning of the emergence of a new Cromwell or a new Caesar.[61]

But Lee's words brought out a mob. Thirty men broke into Goddard's, the print shop in Baltimore that published the queries, and destroyed the type. Another mob confronted William Goddard, owner of the press, and convinced him to offer a public apology for "a piece so replete with the nonsense and malevolence of a disappointed man." As Lee summed it up after departing for Virginia: "No attack, it seems, can be made on General Washington, but it must recoil on the assailant."[62]

A corollary to Lee's view was that having Washington's approval lifted one's reputation. Monroe visited Washington's camp and received a letter from the commander in chief that called him "brave, active, and sensible." It was a recommendation that would be useful to his plans, which he described to Lee as going to Europe "in the character of an officer."[63]

But the Virginia assembly had no interest in the kind of diplomatic appointment Monroe sought, and he planned, he told Lee, to spend a year in Fredericksburg, Virginia, with his uncle Joseph Jones, now "the chief justice of this state." Perhaps aware that Lee was living in a primitive one-room structure, Monroe wrote that he wished that the general could come live with him, but the house in Fredericksburg was not his. "I only live in expectation of it," he wrote.[64]

It was as though he were tempting fate. The fifty-two-year-old Jones, heretofore childless, became the father of a son, who would inherit all Jones's property. When Monroe realized that he would not be an heir, he went into a downward spiral. He wrote to a friend that he did not often leave his lodgings, "nor join society, nor do I feel a disposition for it." Instead of spending the year with his uncle, he obtained an appointment from the Virginia legislature to command a regiment—but again it had to be raised, and again that proved impossible. As a result, he was "thrown out of the service," as he described it. He did not let Jones know of his disappointment, but instead sought his advice. He had decided to go to Williamsburg and study law, and he asked Jones, should he attend George Wythe's lectures or accompany Thomas Jefferson to Richmond to study law there? In a friendly letter Jones advised that he choose Jefferson, and Jefferson, fortunately, chose Monroe. He had noticed him and, having formed a good opinion of him, invited him to join several young men, including John Francis Mercer, who were reading law under his tutelage. If Monroe was not exceedingly clever, neither was he worrisomely cunning, and Jefferson appreciated his military experience. In May 1780, after the British delivered a mighty blow to the American garrison at Charleston, South Carolina, Jefferson sent Monroe to scout the preparations being made to oppose a full-scale British invasion. At Jefferson's instructions, Monroe also set up a system of express riders so that news could move quickly from North Carolina to Virginia.[65]

As Jefferson's protégé, Monroe began to thrive in a way he had not while in Washington's army. In Berkeley, Virginia, General Lee heard how well the young man he had befriended at Valley Forge was doing and wrote to tell Monroe of the pleasure the news gave him. "It not only assures me of the certainty you have of well establishing yourself in fame and fortune (if from the whimsical circumstances of country there can be any such thing established as fame and fortune) but of the good figure you make." The general was especially pleased that Monroe was now putting himself forward. "I rejoice in it with all my soul, as I really love and esteem you most sincerely and affectionately."[66]

In one of the most personal of his letters that survives, Monroe expressed his gratitude to Jefferson for having rescued him from despondency:

A variety of disappointments with respect to the prospects of my private fortune previous to my acquaintance with your Excellency, upon which I had built as on a ground which could not deceive me and which failed in a manner which could not have been expected, perplexed my plan of life and exposed me to inconveniences which had nearly destroyed me. In this situation, had I not formed a connection with you, I should most certainly have retired from society with a resolution never to have entered on the stage again.

Monroe had been so bitter, he told Jefferson, that he had even thought of breaking off connection with his uncle, who had been the father figure in his life since he was fifteen, but then Jefferson had reached out: "You became acquainted with me and undertook the direction of my studies, and believe me I feel that whatever I am at present in the opinion of others or whatever I may be in future has greatly arose from your friendship."[67]

Late summer 1780 brought awful news from the southern theater. About the time that Monroe was writing to Jefferson, the British under Cornwallis dealt the patriots a mighty blow at Camden, South Carolina, killing nearly a thousand Americans and taking another thousand prisoner. Congress relieved the southern commander, Horatio Gates, and Washington nominated Nathanael Greene in his stead. Greene repaid the trust of the commander in chief by imposing a dramatic number of casualties on Cornwallis's army in a battle at Guilford Courthouse in North Carolina. Twenty-five percent of Cornwallis's men were killed or wounded. His force reduced, Cornwallis decided to move north and unite with British troops in Virginia. It was a march that would take him to Yorktown.

Washington and the Comte de Rochambeau, who was in command of French land forces in the United States, agreed to confer in Wethersfield, Connecticut, on May 21, 1781. There, in the parlor of a gambrel-roofed house belonging to merchant Joseph Webb, Rochambeau, fifty-six, short, and portly, hinted that a French fleet in the West Indies might sail north in the summer to aid the American cause. Washington replied that should that happen, the allied forces would have command of the water, be able to transport ground forces readily, and thus have options for where they might attack. In the meantime an operation against New York, some thirty miles from where Washington's army was encamped, had the highest importance.[68]

Rochambeau agreed to make New York the priority, even though he preferred to have the fleet sail into the Chesapeake Bay. Within a week of signing an agreement with Washington, Rochambeau wrote to the Comte de Grasse, commander of the French fleet, recommending the Chesapeake as the place to go on the offensive against the British.[69]

Rochambeau was saying one thing and doing another, but was he the only one? Three days after he wrote to de Grasse, Washington sent a message to Lafayette and described the agreement at Wethersfield: "An attempt upon New York . . . was deemed preferable to a southern operation as we had not command of the water." The letter was intercepted by John Moody, who, in the pay of the British, so regularly stole Washington's mail—and so regularly escaped—that one has to consider whether Washington used him to pass disinformation to the British. In this case

Moody's haul convinced General Henry Clinton, headquartered in New York, that he now had "the most perfect knowledge of the designs of the enemy." Sure in his belief that New York was Washington's target, he ordered Cornwallis to send six regiments, some two thousand men, to defend the British enclave. Later commenting on this decision, a British writer praised Washington's cleverness in alarming Clinton so much that he failed to send appropriate aid to Cornwallis.[70]

Later Washington was accused of having been so fixated on New York that he changed plans with reluctance. Washington strongly objected, writing that the intention of the allied forces was always *to strike the enemy in the most vulnerable quarter.* He underlined for emphasis. That might have meant New York, or Virginia, or even Charleston. He had made New York seem the definitive object, hoping to get assistance from eastern and middle states as well as "for the interesting purpose of rendering the enemy less prepared elsewhere."[71]

Washington's claim that he was trying to set the enemy on the wrong path is bolstered by his having used disinformation from near the beginning of the war to near the end. During the siege of Boston, he had discovered that American forces had so little gunpowder that each man had fewer than nine rounds, but no spy peering into the powder house outside Cambridge could have guessed that. There were an impressive number of barrels on display—all "filled with sand," according to an American officer. In 1780, Washington had concocted a scheme with Lafayette to issue a proclamation in French indicating that a combined American and French force would attack Canada and inviting French Canadians to join in. Among those deceived was Benedict

Arnold, whose treachery was not yet known. He passed what he thought was genuine intelligence about an assault on Canada along to General Clinton.[72]

Assuming that Washington's repeatedly pointing to New York as the target was a deception, it was a massive one, including not just the enemy but also his own army and highest officers. The idea of keeping vital information in extremely close hold was not a departure from habit, but his preferred way of proceeding. He had once written Patrick Henry, "There are some secrets, on the keeping of which so depends, oftentimes, the salvation of an army: secrets which cannot, at least ought not to, be entrusted to paper; nay, which none but the commander in chief at the time should be acquainted with."[73]

Still, many historians have agreed with Washington biographer James Thomas Flexner, who wrote that Rochambeau "forced [Washington] to undertake the Yorktown campaign against his better judgment." He was "fixated" on New York, writes one. He had "nearly an obsession" about winning New York back from the British, writes another. He had "botch[ed] this major strategic call," according to a third historian.[74]

There is support for this point of view, including the inflexibility that Washington's contemporaries noted about him. Once he had made a determination, it was hard to move him from it. But even harder to ignore is how consistently he indicated that he would attack where victory seemed likely. It was a theme running through his writing from Wethersfield on, as was his concern about attacking in Virginia without command of the sea. Washington was not fixated on New York; he was fixed on victory.[75]

Before he left New York, Washington had thirty boats mounted on carriages, counting on the British to think they were for crossing to Staten Island. Ovens were built, some near Sandy Hook, a curving barrier spit at the entrance to Lower New York Bay. The purpose was to convince the British that Sandy Hook was where the American and French armies would join with de Grasse's fleet prior to an attack on New York. So convincing were these maneuvers, wrote Jonathan Trumbull Jr., now one of Washington's aides, that "our own army no less than the enemy are completely deceived."[76]

Deceptions in place, Washington set out with the French army and most of the American army for Virginia. He was headed toward a glory greater than even he had imagined.

Monroe, meanwhile, tried again to enter the fight, visiting Lafayette's headquarters in Williamsburg and volunteering his services. Once again, he found there was no need for officers, no part for him to play. As the country celebrated the great victory at Yorktown, Monroe determined on a future far removed from the military. He would study in France and become a diplomat, thus removing himself from Washington's orbit. He would burnish a different set of skills from those of the first great man he had known.

THREE

The Intellectuals

Poetry and Prose

Both Jefferson and Madison were lifelong students, and love of learning helped bind them in one of the most significant friendships in American history. But the two also differed in many ways, as the tone and tenor of the documents most famously associated with them illustrate. The Declaration of Independence, which Jefferson wrote in 1776 in a second-story rented room in Philadelphia, begins with prose that soars and uplifts:

When in the course of human events it becomes necessary for one people to dissolve the political bands which have connected them with another and to assume among the powers of the earth the separate and equal station to which the laws of nature and of nature's god entitle them, a decent respect to the opinions of mankind requires that they should declare the causes which impel them to the separation.

In a single sentence—a long one, to be sure—Jefferson linked American independence with the long span of the ages ("the course of human events") and even the timeless ("the laws of nature and of nature's god"). Then he set out the enduring principles on which the new nation was to be built:

> We hold these truths to be self-evident; that all men are created equal; that they are endowed by their Creator with inherent and inalienable rights; that among these are life, liberty, and the pursuit of happiness.

The power of these lines is remarkable—and even more so when one compares them to a source, the draft of the Virginia Declaration of Rights:

> That men are born equally free and independent and have certain inherent natural rights, of which they cannot, by any compact, deprive or divest their posterity; among which are the enjoyment of life and liberty, with the means of acquiring and possessing property, and pursuing and obtaining happiness and safety.

Writing on his portable desk, Jefferson expressed the same ideas, but took out the prosaic and negative and added a spiritual dimension. Men are not merely born, they are created, and their rights, coming from their Creator, are not merely self-evident, they are immortal. He did not use the word "property," as the Virginia Declaration did, but the more elevated and poetic "pursuit of happiness."[1]

Jefferson paid attention to cadence, as in the phrase "pursuit of happiness," which lilts along on iambic feet (unaccented syllables followed by accented ones). Later in his life, Jefferson would write an essay on English prosody pointing out the importance of pauses to poetic language, a subject he was already thinking about at the time of the declaration. He marked the rough draft to indicate where someone reading the document aloud should break.[2]

Jefferson once explained that his purpose in writing the declaration was "not to find out new principles or new arguments never before thought of, not merely to say things which had never been said before." Instead, the document "was intended to be an expression of the American mind and to give to that expression the proper tone and spirit called for by the occasion."[3]

James Madison had a different task with the Constitution: to draw up plans for a new government. In a boardinghouse at 19 Maiden Lane in New York City, he laid out his ideas in workmanlike prose and sent them first to Jefferson, who in 1787 was the U.S. envoy to France. The foundation of the new system, he wrote, was "ratification by the people themselves," thereby making it "paramount" law. A few weeks later, in letters to Edmund Randolph, the governor of Virginia, and to George Washington, who, having resigned as commander in chief, was tending to his beloved Mount Vernon, Madison laid out a three-part structure for the new government, including a "legislative department [that] might be divided into two branches." He wrote that "a national executive will also be necessary," and that "national supremacy ought also to be extended as I conceive to the judiciary department."[4]

Madison was not striving for ringing words; he was laying out ideas. As the time of the Constitutional Convention neared, he incorporated his thoughts into what became known as the Virginia Plan, the convention's agenda that he drew up with colleagues from the Old Dominion. Again, the language was stripped down and to the point. "Resolved that a national executive be instituted," read article 7. "Resolved, that a national judiciary be established," stated article 9.[5]

The Constitution signed in Philadelphia at summer's end in 1787 benefited from delegates to the Constitutional Convention giving elevated names to the departments of government. The "national executive" became "the president of the United States." The "national judiciary" became "the Supreme Court." And it benefited even more from the elegant preamble of Gouverneur Morris, who knew how words ought to go together. But Morris's noble opening aside, the Constitution was the natural successor to the plainly worded letters and drafts in which Madison had earlier set forth its key features. For all its practicality, however, the Constitution created something wholly new—a republic of vast extent and, as time would show, of long duration.[6]

John Quincy Adams observed that the effect Jefferson and Madison had on one another was decided but hard to pinpoint. "The mutual influence of these two mighty minds upon each other is a phenomenon, like the invisible and mysterious movements of the magnet in the physical world, and in which the sagacity of the future historian may discover the solution of much of our national history," he said.[7] Looking over the course of their lives, one sees that they improved one another. Jefferson's lofty and wide-ranging intellect was inspiration for Madison, whose more precise and practical way kept Jefferson tethered to earth. They combined to make a mighty force when they fought for freedom of expression, which both saw as essential to a free nation.

Establishing intellectual freedom was far from the only effort that Jefferson and Madison undertook in the nation's early years, but it is woven like a ribbon through much of their work. A darker theme is as well: their gradual estrangement from George Washington, whom both Jefferson and Madison came to see as a threat to the Republic.

In June 1779, in Williamsburg, Virginia, Jefferson and Madison first worked closely together. Madison, twenty-eight, had been defeated in a bid for the Virginia Assembly when he had refused to treat voters to bumbo (otherwise known as rum). Despite the loss, he was regarded as a promising young man. The legislature elected him to Virginia's executive council, where he was serving when Thomas Jefferson became governor. Eight years Madison's senior, Jefferson was a person of distinction whose service to Virginia had begun a decade before. But disparities in status did not stand in the way of friendship. During the three or four months that Jefferson's first term as governor coincided with Madison's time on the council, "an intimacy took place," as Madison described it.[8]

The years directly ahead were not kind to Governor Jefferson. Worried that the British would invade, he moved the capital from Williamsburg to Richmond, which was farther inland, but not even that was safe. Benedict Arnold, the notorious turncoat who had tried to deliver West Point to the British, advanced on Richmond with loyalists, hired Hessians, and British troops, forcing Jefferson to flee. Arnold and his men spent twenty-four hours burning and pillaging.

During a subsequent invasion, General Cornwallis sent a detachment of white-coated dragoons to Charlottesville, where the Virginia Assembly was meeting. A young soldier named Jack Jouett, known for his scarlet cloak and plumed hat, spotted the raiders as they rode past the Cuckoo Tavern, and he galloped ahead to sound the alarm. When he reached Monticello, Jefferson greeted him graciously and invited him in for some early-morning Madeira. The governor then arranged a leisurely breakfast for Virginia Assembly delegates who had been staying with him and saw them off. He made arrangements for his family and, after watching them depart, collected up papers to take with him. It was as though he knew that one more precipitous flight before the enemy would damage his reputation irreparably, but he cut it very close, riding off on Caractacus, his fastest horse, just before the raiders arrived.[9]

His unhurried departure did not protect him from criticism. A few weeks after his narrow escape, a motion was introduced in the House of Delegates to inquire into his conduct during the

British invasions. The investigation came to nothing. Indeed, the assembly ended up passing a resolution praising Jefferson as governor. Nevertheless, when he was subsequently elected to the House of Delegates, he declined to serve.

Madison, now in the Confederation Congress, was dismayed by Jefferson's refusal. When called to serve the country, as Virginians called their state, it was understood that one accepted. Madison wrote to Governor Edmund Randolph, "Great as my partiality is to Mr. Jefferson, the mode in which he seems determined to revenge the wrong received from his country does not appear to me to be dictated either by philosophy or patriotism." James Monroe, a new member of the House of Delegates, joined in encouraging Jefferson to reenter the world, writing him that disapproval of his refusing to serve was widespread. Jefferson responded by calling the investigation that the House of Delegates had proposed "a wound on my spirit which will only be cured by the all-healing grave."[10] Few politicians have been more sensitive to criticism than Jefferson, which meant that public life, wherein no one escapes reproach, was unusually miserable for him.

Jefferson also told Monroe that his wife was "very dangerously ill." Martha Wayles Skelton Jefferson, a small woman not yet thirty-four, had borne six children in ten years, and the birth of the last child, a daughter, had left her feverish and bedridden. In the following months, Jefferson helped nurse and comfort her, staying constantly in her calling. Shortly before she died in September, as Jefferson's oldest daughter, Martha (called Patsy as a child), recalled, "He was led from the room almost in a state of insensibility" and fell into a "long fainting fit." After Martha's death, he stayed in his room for three weeks and then began to ride incessantly.[11]

Rumors circulated about Jefferson's "swooning away," but Madison found them hard to believe, given what he called his friend's "philosophical temper."[12] Determined to end Jefferson's self-imposed isolation, Madison moved in Congress to appoint him a commissioner to peace negotiations with the British. Drawing friends who wanted to retire from public life back into the political arena was a skill that Madison would find useful in the years ahead. Jefferson left Monticello intending to sail for France, but news that a peace treaty was close caused him to wait several weeks for final instructions. He joined Madison at a comfortable boardinghouse owned by a Mrs. House and run by her daughter, the insightful and empathetic Eliza Trist.

The two men had time to talk about books, for which they both had a passion. Each was drawing up a list, Madison of books that members of Congress would find useful and Jefferson of his library at Monticello, as well as of books he hoped to buy in Paris. There were marked differences, partly because of their different missions, but personality also entered in. Jefferson had an extensive section on fine arts, while Madison had no poetry, no plays, no musical scores. Madison knew the enchantment of "poetry, wit, and criticism," but thought study of the real world "more substantial, more durable, more profitable."[13]

The lists also revealed important meetings of the mind. The first publication on Madison's list, *Encyclopédie Méthodique*, was a product of Enlightenment thought, an ongoing effort to summarize and systematize subjects ranging from grammar to pharmacy to military art. Jefferson was already buying the *Encyclopédie* and would eventually have 136 volumes in his library. Both men were fascinated by the sixteenth- and seventeenth-century voyages that had spurred the Enlightenment and listed works by and about explorers such as Martin Forbisher, who had tried to find a Northwest Passage, and William Dampier, whose adventures circumnavigating the globe inspired Jonathan Swift's *Gulliver's Travels*. Another explorer on both lists was Richard Chancellor, who in the sixteenth century found the opening to the White Sea, landed at Archangel, and visited Moscow.[14]

Jefferson's and Madison's interests ranged around the world, but they also kept Virginia very much in mind. Jefferson was doing research to expand *Notes on the State of Virginia*, the only book he ever wrote. In it he described everything from the rivers and mountains of the commonwealth to its roads and laws. He laid out a plan "to diffuse knowledge more generally through the mass of the people" by establishing free three-year schools to teach reading, writing, and arithmetic. He also took up the topic of race and argued that black men and women were inferior to those who were white, a view not uncommon in the eighteenth century, but shocking to read today. In *Notes*, he also condemned slavery, calling it a sin for which there would be a day of reckoning. "I tremble for my country," he wrote, "when I reflect that God is just; that his justice cannot sleep forever."[15]

It is a measure of the time in which he lived that Jefferson feared condemnation not for what he said about race, but for denouncing slavery. He gave a friend permission to publish extracts from the *Notes* in France, but put "the strictures on slavery" off-limits. He was concerned, he wrote, that they might push his fellow Virginians into even more fervid opposition to emancipation.[16]

Jefferson also wrote about religious freedom in *Notes*, declaring, "It does me no injury for my neighbor to say there are twenty gods or no god. It neither picks my pocket nor breaks my leg." His enemies would pounce on this passage, citing it as proof that Jefferson was an atheist. Wrote one, "Let my neighbor once persuade himself that there is no God, and he will soon pick my pocket and break not only my leg but my neck."[17]

Madison had been committed to religious freedom since prerevolutionary days, when he had been enraged by the persecution of Baptists, and he had already moved Virginia beyond the Enlightenment standard for religious freedom. Philosopher John Locke had argued for "toleration," but as Madison saw it, the concept of civil authorities' tolerating beliefs wrongly implied that the state had authority in spiritual matters, when in truth they were within the individual's purview. In 1776, at the convention to create a Virginia constitution, Madison had managed to change Virginia's Declaration of Rights from "all men should enjoy the fullest toleration in the exercise of religion" to "all men are equally entitled to enjoy the free exercise of religion." He was only twenty-five at the time, but the religious article in the Virginia declaration, as he modified it, was a turning point in the history of religious freedom.[18]

In the brick boardinghouse at Market and Fifth Streets, Jefferson and Madison would have discussed Jefferson's work to revise Virginia's legal code, including a statute he had drafted that would put religious freedom into legal effect. Jefferson had been unable to get this revision passed, and it would not become law until he was in France and Madison had returned to the Virginia House of Delegates. In a makeshift capitol in Richmond, where delegates were then meeting, Madison fanned the fires of a controversy over tax support for Christian churches and asked this key question: "Who does not see that the same authority which can establish Christianity, in exclusion of all other religions, may establish with the same ease any particular sect of Christians, in exclusion of all other sects?" Madison reintroduced Jefferson's proposal, and it passed both houses, becoming law in January 1786. In a letter to Jefferson, he exulted that the legislation had "extinguished forever the ambitious hope of making laws for the human mind."[19]

Given Jefferson's and Madison's aspirations, it is easy to overlook that they were men, after all, and that their concerns were not always intellectual. Both had chronic ailments. Jefferson suffered from migraines that laid him low for days and even weeks. Madison experienced what he called "sudden attacks," which he described as "somewhat resembling epilepsy and suspending the intellectual functions," a description that suggests he suffered from what are today known as complex partial seizures. Afflicted persons remain conscious, but with their ability to understand and speak impaired. Stress was a trigger for both men, and both sought relief from infusions of Peruvian bark, which came from the cinchona tree and contained quinine. Eighteenth-century men often talked about their health, and Jefferson and Madison surely took up the topic during their time at Mrs. House's.[20]

Jefferson observed his young friend falling in love with the daughter of New York congressman William Floyd, who was staying with his family at Mrs. House's. Kitty Floyd was pretty, round-faced, and fifteen years old, an age deemed quite marriageable in the eighteenth century. Jefferson took it upon himself to move the courtship along. He made Madison's case to Kitty and reported back, "She possessed every sentiment in your favor which you could wish." But Jefferson, characteristically, was too optimistic. Several months later, Miss Floyd broke off the romance, leaving the typically imperturbable Madison in distress. Jefferson advised "firmness of mind and unintermitting occupations." He also observed how surprised he was at the breakup. "Of all machines," he observed philosophically, "ours is the most complicated and inexplicable."[21]

Three months after arriving in Philadelphia, Jefferson learned that his mission had been canceled. Agreement on a peace treaty was so close that he was no longer needed as a negotiator.[22] He accepted appointment by the Virginia Assembly to serve in the Confederation Congress and traveled with Madison to Annapolis, where the Congress was meeting. Madison, term-limited out of Congress after three years, rode on to Virginia, and Jefferson set up housekeeping in rented quarters with James Monroe, who had secured a seat in Congress. Jefferson brought books with him—and a French chef, Monsieur Partout.

Jefferson found the Confederation Congress frustrating. "Our body was little numerous, but very contentious," he wrote in his autobiography, but his creativity was nonetheless on display. One of his proposals was to use the decimal system as the basis for the value of U.S. coins, an idea so appealing in its simplicity that the Confederation Congress adopted its basic principles. This "landmark in monetary history" as Jefferson biographer Merrill Peterson called it, effected a change that we continue to benefit from today.[23]

Jefferson also proposed the Ordinance of 1784 to create states out of the vast stretch of wilderness between the Mississippi River and lands claimed by the British and Spanish. The new states, ten or more that Jefferson placed in a grid, were not to be colonies of the country that already existed, as had been the pattern for most of recorded time. They were to enter the Union as equals. After 1800 they were to be free of slavery. The Confederation Congress eliminated the slavery clause by a single vote, and within a few years the entire act would be superseded by the Northwest Ordinance, in which important Jeffersonian ideas remained. The Northwest Ordinance forbade slavery, as Jefferson had earlier proposed, and also mandated a grid to divide up the land. Flying across the United States on a clear day, it is possible to look down and see the lingering effects of Jefferson's orderly mind.[24]

The most moving event of the session occurred on December 23, 1783, when George Washington resigned from command of the Continental army. "Having now finished the work assigned me," he said, "I retire from the great theater of action, and bidding an affectionate farewell to this august body under whose orders I have so long acted, I here offer my commission and take my leave of all the employments of public life." As he handed his commission to the president of the Congress, onlookers wept. Of all Washington's deeds, none would surpass his surrender of power. Years after, George III would weigh in, telling artist Benjamin West that Washington's renouncing power "placed him in a light the most distinguished of any man living and that he thought him the greatest character of the age."[25]

On May 7, 1784, Congress appointed Jefferson to serve with Benjamin Franklin and John Adams to negotiate commercial alliances with European powers, a post he quickly accepted. He sold his books to Monroe, left Monsieur Partout with him, and agreed to do him a favor. Monroe had been struck by James Madison's rise in the world, which he attributed to perseverance, and wanted to begin a correspondence with him. Jefferson liked bringing people together and arranged for it, writing to Madison that "the scrupulousness of [Monroe's] honor will make you safe in the most confidential communications. A better man cannot be."[26]

In August, Jefferson arrived in Paris, accompanied by his eleven-year-old daughter, Patsy. The younger children, six-year-old Maria (sometimes called Polly) and two-year-old Lucy, the last child of Martha and Thomas Jefferson, had stayed in Virginia with relatives. Another member of the party was an enslaved man in whom Jefferson placed much trust, James Hemings.

Jefferson fell ill for at least six weeks in Paris, as new arrivals frequently did. He managed to joke with Abigail Adams that stomach problems were not his only issue. Another affliction was getting his hair powdered and dressed every day. Given the time required by this nod to etiquette, he fully expected to lose a year of his life in the hairdresser's chair.[27] But soon there was news of tragic dimensions. His little girl Lucy had died in Virginia of whooping cough. Jefferson wanted her older sister, Maria, to be with him and Patsy and began working on ways to bring her to Paris. It would be two years before she arrived, accompanied by James Hemings's enslaved sister, fourteen-year-old Sally Hemings.

In May 1785, Jefferson replaced Benjamin Franklin as United States minister to the Court of Versailles and continued trying to negotiate trade agreements. By this time he had many friends in high places, among them the Duc de La Rochefoucauld and the Marquis de Condorcet. He became close to the Marquis de Lafayette, now in his late twenties, who mentored him on the ins and outs of French politics. The Marquis de Chastellux burnished Jefferson's reputation with his book *Travels in North America*. He had visited Monticello and described Jefferson as tall, "with a mild and pleasing countenance." He noted his intellectual achievements, ranging from music to natural philosophy to statesmanship, and concluded, "It seemed as if from his youth he had placed his mind, as he has done his house, on an elevated situation."[28]

The most sophisticated and intelligent women invited Jefferson to their homes. He spent pleasant hours at Château de Chaville, the country home of Madame de Tessé, often in the company of Lafayette, who was her nephew. Conversations ranged from horticulture (Chaville had extraordinary gardens) to architecture to politics. At Chaville and at her Paris home, Madame de Tessé frequently turned the discussion to establishing a constitutional monarchy in France. From her and the people invited to her small, elegant salon, Jefferson learned of the radical ideas (or so they seemed at the time) being advanced in polite society.[29]

Paris offered many pleasures. Jefferson loved music, the "passion of my soul," he described it. He heard the Te Deum sung in Notre Dame and listened to Handel and Haydn in the Palais des Tuileries. He attended the opera and the theater—and he shopped energetically. By the time he returned to Virginia, he would have so many paintings, books, and busts that he required some forty crates to ship them home.[30]

He admired Parisian architecture, and during a visit to the Halle aux Blés, a newly completed Paris grain market that had an ingenious, skylit dome, he met twenty-six-year-old Maria Cosway, an English expatriate's daughter, who had been born and educated in Italy. She was visiting Paris with her wealthy husband, a portrait painter famous for his miniatures, who seemed undisturbed by Jefferson's quick interest in his wife. Hardly had Jefferson and the Cosways exchanged greetings when Jefferson began canceling other plans so that he could spend the rest of the day and evening in Mrs. Cosway's company. A beauty with golden curls and violet eyes, Maria Cosway was neither bookish nor political. She was an accomplished painter and a musician with a "softness of disposition," as Jefferson described her. One excursion they shared took them over the Pont de Neuilly and along the Seine to the royal retreat at Marly, which Jefferson declared "the most beautifully situated and the most pleasant" château in all France. They went on to other lovely places: the château and gardens at St. Germain, the Château de Madrid, and the Bagatelle château. "Every moment was filled with something agreeable," Jefferson wrote.[31]

Jefferson knew that Maria and her husband would be in Paris for only a matter of weeks, but he still seemed unprepared for their departure. He bid her farewell, handed her into her carriage, and walked away, "more dead than alive," as he described it.[32]

In a long missive, probably written over a period of days, Jefferson penned one of history's most famous love letters, a dialogue between heart and head. The heart described Cosway's beauty and the loneliness Jefferson felt without her, but the head declared that he had been foolish to fall in love with her. He had known there was no future for the two of them and created pain for himself by ignoring that simple fact. Answered the heart: The pleasure of her company was well worth the pain.[33]

The heart ended the dialogue, but Jefferson nevertheless stepped back from Mrs. Cosway. Perhaps to distract himself, he sent a note to Sophie de Tott, an exotic young woman whom Madame de Tessé had taken under her wing. Even in the freewheeling days of prerevolutionary France, de Tott stood out. She had once had her portrait done as a bacchante, with grape leaves entwined in her hair, an open-mouthed smile (forbidden by artistic convention), and one breast bared (forbidden by the Académie Royale).[34]

Madame de Tott responded to Jefferson's note immediately. She saw herself as Jefferson's acolyte, and he encouraged the notion, sending her a fine edition of Homer and tutoring her in Greek prosody. There were more superlatives than imagination in the notes she wrote to him, and his to her, while flirtatious, had a perfunctory air—except for a revealing observation about himself in a letter he sent to her from Marseilles. He explained that he searched always to find something positive in even the most miserable situations. "The plan of my journey," he wrote, "as well as of my life [is] to take things by the smooth handle," a metaphor that explained his habit of avoiding conflict and unpleasantness. He regarded this approach to living as so important that thirty years later he would offer it as a rule of conduct to ten-year-old Paul Clay, the son of a neighbor.[35]

Jefferson was in Marseilles as part of a three-month journey through southern France and northern Italy, a trip that marked the end of his flirtation with Madame de Tott. While he wrote her no more letters, he did write Madame de Tessé from Nîmes, when he became enthralled by a Roman temple. "Here I am, Madame, gazing whole hours at the Maison Carrée, like a lover at his mistress." The temple would be his inspiration for Virginia's capitol in Richmond.[36]

Jefferson saw Maria Cosway again in 1787, and after that they corresponded, although years often passed between letters. She established a convent school in Italy, but one of her last letters to Jefferson, written in 1819, was from London, where she was caring for her sick husband. She described herself as "happy in self-gratification of doing my duty," but remembered his long-ago love letter. "In your dialogue," she wrote, "your head would tell me, *'that is enough.'* Perhaps your heart will understand I might wish *for more.*"[37]

During Jefferson's time in Paris, Monroe married Elizabeth Kortright, a petite and beautiful seventeen-year-old from a well-regarded New York family. Monroe, twenty-seven, had met her while the peripatetic Confederation Congress was meeting in New York. After their marriage, they moved to Virginia, where Monroe planned to work as a lawyer in Richmond and pay some of his debts. Joseph Jones, seemingly unaware of the psychological turmoil that had engulfed Monroe after the birth of Joseph Jones Jr., convinced him that Fredericksburg would be a better place to practice than Richmond and offered him use of a house on Caroline Street. Monroe accepted and soon became a member of the Virginia legislature.[38]

Madison and Monroe kept Jefferson up to date on happenings in Virginia, and Jefferson opined upon them. His flair for words, their correspondence shows, made him not only an inspiring writer, but also a master of cutting commentary. When Madison told him that Patrick Henry had blocked revision of the Virginia constitution, Jefferson responded, "What we have to do I think is devoutly to pray for his death."[39]

Jefferson convinced Madison to look up from his books and help him challenge French naturalist Comte de Buffon, who had a theory that the animals of the new world were smaller than those of the old. Madison enthusiastically began to dissect quadrupeds found around his Montpelier home, including a weasel. He kept careful notes to show that it was larger than the belette, or weasel, that Buffon had described. Its tongue, for example, was an entire line (or one-tenth of an inch) longer.[40]

Madison sent pecan nuts and sugar tree seeds to Jefferson and in turn received delightful inventions: phosphorescent matches, a pedometer, and a cane with a telescope cleverly tucked inside. But Madison's greatest pleasure came when Jefferson filled his request for books. He had expressed particular interest in volumes that would throw light on the constitutional arrangements "of the several confederacies which have existed," and when he received a "literary cargo" from Jefferson, he found it "perfectly to my mind." It became his habit to retire to his room right after breakfast and immerse himself in books. A visitor to Montpelier noted that he came out of his room only "a little before dinner."[41]

The constitutional arrangements of the United States, known as the Articles of Confederation, were a conspicuous failure. The Congress of the Confederation was unable to levy taxes for national needs. States, strapped for revenue, were printing money willy-nilly and imposing onerous taxes on one another. As Madison used the books Jefferson had sent to consider a more effective form of government, the situation grew even more critical. A series of protests that would become known as Shays's Rebellion erupted. Farmers took up arms to protest tax collections and land foreclosures. In Massachusetts, they shut down county courts and marched on the Springfield armory. In Madison's view and in George Washington's, with whom he was corresponding, the lawlessness portended calamity. A national government was needed if liberty were to be secure.

That was not how Jefferson saw it from Paris. "The late troubles in the eastern states so far as I have yet seen . . . do not appear to threaten serious consequences," he wrote, a reasonable enough observation, but he went on: "I hold it that a little rebellion now and then is a good thing, and as necessary in the political world as storms in the physical."[42] Madison, aware as he was of Jefferson's abstract turn of mind, must still have been surprised. While he was scrambling to create a central government that could secure the nation, Jefferson, dwelling on theoretical heights, was arguing that armed civil unrest was a welcome turn of events. Madison had little time to consider what Jefferson's lofty view might portend. In fact, it would soon strain their friendship.

In September 1786, Madison attended a meeting at Mann's Tavern in Annapolis that was intended to discuss trade, but evolved, no doubt with help from Madison, to a more comprehensive consideration of how to strengthen the young nation. With only five states represented in Annapolis, the delegates unanimously resolved that another and larger meeting be convened in Philadelphia in May 1787. Although Madison had doubts about whether the convention proposed could create a more workable nation, he threw himself into trying to organize it. He arranged to be elected to the Confederation Congress and rode through a January blizzard to New York to make sure that body would pose no obstacle. He worked to persuade a reluctant George Washington to attend the convention. The general had told his fellow citizens in 1783 that his retirement from the army was final, that he was determined not to have "any share in public business" thereafter. The gesture had established him as a new Cincinnatus—the famed Roman who gave up power to return to his plow. What effect would it have on his reputation for all future time if he participated now in what was clearly public business?[43]

Madison, fast becoming the persuader in chief of the Virginia dynasty, stressed the importance of the convention, its "preeminence over every other public object." Washington's attendance would guarantee that other "most select characters" would attend. When Washington still turned him down, Madison sent him the names of distinguished citizens who had already agreed to be delegates. Knowing that he would be with such worthies as John Rutledge of South Carolina and Elbridge Gerry of Massachusetts might, Madison thought, help assuage any fears Washington had of becoming involved with a failed effort.[44] Six and a half weeks before the convention was scheduled to begin, Washington finally agreed to be there.

By the time Madison arrived in Philadelphia, he was already a man of reputation. "Mr. Madison is a character who has long been in public life," Georgia delegate William Pierce observed, "and what is very remarkable, every person seems to acknowledge his greatness." He lacked physical presence, but his political acumen and intellectual abilities were readily apparent. "He blends together the profound politician with the scholar," Pierce wrote.[45]

Before the convention's formal opening, Madison met with fellow delegates from the commonwealth to work out the Virginia Plan. It set forth ideas that he had been contemplating for months, including proportional representation. For each state, large and small, to have a single vote, as was the case under the Articles of Confederation, was incompatible with the national union he had in mind.

Madison left the introduction of the Virginia Plan to Governor

Edmund Randolph, a well-liked fellow, perhaps because he had little talent for political machination. On May 30, after Washington called the delegates to order, Randolph read the first proposition, a bland statement about revising the Articles of Confederation. Gouverneur Morris, a worldly man of many mistresses, observed that the proposition did not match the more radical ones that followed and wanted it changed. Randolph acceded and the first resolve became "that a national government ought to be established consisting of a supreme legislature, judiciary, and executive." Delegates protested that the resolve violated their congressional mandate—which it did—but passed it and began an exploration of uncharted territory."[46]

Madison addressed the convention on every important matter. His contribution to a May debate about popular election suggests a touch of poetry in his soul. "The great fabric to be raised," he said, "would be more stable and durable if it should rest on the solid foundation of the people themselves." Madison also took part at key moments to accomplish crucial alterations, as when he and Elbridge Gerry moved to change Congress's having the power to "make" war to authorizing it to "declare" war, thus providing for executive leadership of armed conflicts. All the while Madison was taking notes that remain our most important record of the convention.[47]

Madison's achievement in organizing and orchestrating the convention in Philadelphia was one of the most consequential in American history, but as the gathering concluded its work, he was disheartened. In order to give the central government sufficient strength to control the wayward states, he believed that a national veto over state actions was necessary, but delegates had sent that proposal down to defeat. Thus he found himself unsure that the government provided for would "effectually answer its national object."[48]

It took him weeks to reconcile himself, but by the end of October he wrote to a friend that it was an error to compare the Constitution to an ideal concept. The comparison should be to what it replaced, and when one considered the instability that prevailed under the Articles of Confederation, the Constitution promised to be a firm anchor. He also began to consider how difficult a job the delegates in Philadelphia had taken on. On October 24, he wrote to Jefferson that the drafting of the document had been "a task more difficult than can be well conceived by those who were not concerned in the execution of it. Adding to these considerations the natural diversity of human opinions on all new and complicated subjects," he continued, "it is impossible to consider the degree of concord which ultimately prevailed as less than a miracle."[49]

Alexander Hamilton had also been dissatisfied with the final document, seeing the government it created as much too weak. In a speech at the convention, he had proclaimed that the United States needed an arrangement more like Britain's, with an executive and senate serving for life. This would bring "the rich and well-born" into government, from whence they could control the "turbulent and changing" masses, in which Hamilton placed little trust.[50] At the end of the convention, however, Hamilton, like Madison, faced up to practicalities and signed the document. Between the Articles of Confederation and the Constitution there was no choice.

In an alignment that would be short-lived, the two men joined with John Jay to rally public opinion, writing a series of essays for New York papers that would be compiled as *The Federalist*. Writing under the pen name Publius and working at breakneck speed, they explained the Constitution and the importance of its ratification. Madison's most famous essay is the first he wrote, *Federalist* 10, in which he took up the inevitability of "factions" developing in civil society, perhaps because of interest in a cause or allegiance to a charismatic leader. An advantage to a large republic such as the Constitution set forth was that it would have "a greater variety of parties and interests," he wrote, which lessened the possibility of any one of them becoming monarchical.[51]

In 1788, in a burst of creative energy, Madison wrote twenty-two essays in just forty days, among them *Federalist* 51, in which he explained the necessity of partitioning power in the government. "If men were angels, no government would be necessary. If angels were to govern men, neither external nor internal controls on government would be necessary." In the absence of angelic leaders, separating power meant that each part could check and balance the others. "Ambition must be made to counteract ambition," he wrote.[52]

It was likely during this intense time that Madison heard back from Jefferson, who was entirely undaunted by Madison's suggestion that people who had not been in Philadelphia might fail to appreciate the difficulty of the constitutional task. Jefferson was perturbed that there were no term limits for the president. For one person to be in office many years could lead to an elective monarchy, he believed. He was also shocked that there was no bill of rights. Without knowing the details of what had gone on in Philadelphia, he wrote to Madison as if speaking *ex cathedra*, "A bill of rights is what the people are entitled to against every government on earth."[53]

Madison did not oppose a bill of rights in principle. In 1776, he had happily participated in George Mason's project to create the Virginia Declaration of Rights. But he did not think it necessary to include a bill of rights in the Constitution, because the powers granted by that document to the central government did not include the authority to infringe upon rights. The overwhelming majority of delegates to the Philadelphia convention were apparently in agreement. When George Mason and Elbridge Gerry proposed a bill of rights in the last week of the gathering, every state save for Massachusetts, which abstained, voted the measure down.

Madison, used to Jefferson's habit of expressing himself "strong and round," did not confront his friend about his pronouncement. Instead, he described a very specific situation to him: In Virginia, certain opponents of the Constitution were likely to seek a bill of rights in order to prevent ratification. Should the Constitution as accepted by Virginia be amended so that it was different from the document ratified by other states, there would be need for a second convention. The result would be chaos and discord—and the end of hopes for the Union.[54]

But damage had already been done. From his home at the Hôtel de Langeac on the Champs-Élysées, Jefferson had broadcast his dissatisfaction with the Constitution far and wide. He wrote to John Adams that the president set forth in the document "seems a bad edition of a Polish king." To Adams's son-in-law,

William Stephens Smith, he suggested that the document was an overreaction to the armed mobs of farmers. The United States had not had many rebellions, after all, and a few lives lost here and there were of no great import. "The tree of liberty must be refreshed from time to time with the blood of patriots and tyrants," he wrote. "It is its natural manure."[55]

Jefferson targeted ratification in Maryland, where the convention was to be held in April 1788. He sent Marylander William Carmichael a list of objections to the Constitution. He predicted ratification would fail in Virginia and noted the advantage should the document be defeated nationally: "Another convention shall be assembled to adopt the improvements generally acceptable and omit those found disagreeable."[56] In his pronouncement, he neatly avoided having to explain exactly how a second convention would come together.

To another prominent Marylander, Uriah Forrest, Jefferson sent an excerpt from the letter he had written to Madison detailing his objections to the Constitution. He authorized Forrest to "make what use you please of the contents of the paper but without quoting its author." Forrest arranged to have it passed around the Maryland convention, where Jefferson was quickly pegged as the author. Marylander Daniel Carroll wrote to Madison that he could scarcely believe that Jefferson had done something so "inconsistent with his character for understanding and discretion... [and] that delicacy of friendship I thought he possessed."[57] Madison, who no doubt agreed, kept his frustration to himself. For him and Jefferson to be on opposing sides of an issue would prove to be as rare an occurrence as Madison's alliance with Hamilton.

By the time Maryland ratified the Constitution, Madison had already begun deploying his formidable political skills in Virginia, and in nothing was he more artful than in turning Edmund Randolph into a proponent of ratification. The Virginia governor had refused to sign the Constitution in Philadelphia. He found parts of it objectionable, such as the absence of term limits for the president, and wanted Virginia to add amendments to meet his complaints before ratification. Like Jefferson he thought that the different amendments of different states could be harmonized at a second convention.[58]

Madison had known Randolph well since the days leading up to independence, and he kept in touch with him after the convention, sending him issues of *The Federalist* and confiding that he had written essays for the anonymous project. In another letter he flattered Randolph for the influence he had in Virginia affairs—and warned that opponents to the Constitution were using his good name in efforts to dissolve the Union. Little by little Randolph began to think of Madison's ideas as his own. In April 1788, he wrote to Madison that he had always been concerned that under the cover of amendments previous to ratification "a higher game might be played."[59]

The convention in Richmond drew crowds so large that delegates moved from a temporary capitol building to more spacious quarters, a wooden building on Shockoe Hill, recently built to house a French academy. On the first day of debate, Governor Randolph took to the floor and declared that if Virginia adopted amendments prior to ratifying, it would lead to "inevitable ruin to the Union." He raised his arm and declared, "I will assent to the lopping of this limb before I assent to the dissolution of the Union."[60]

Madison used less dramatic language to convey the good news of Randolph's about-face. That night, in his room at the Swan, he wrote to Washington: "The governor has declared the day of previous amendments past, and thrown himself fully into the federal scale."[61]

There were still formidable foes, the chief of whom was fifty-two-year-old Patrick Henry. For more than a dozen years, Madison had been watching the gaunt, bewigged Henry win over audiences with his passionate, if not always well-reasoned rhetoric, and he watched again now in the packed building on Shockoe Hill. Henry launched a broadside at the Constitution, claiming that it would "oppress and ruin the people." He attacked on more than a dozen points, taking up some several times. The Constitution "squints toward monarchy," he declared. It would lead to federal excise men joining state tax collectors in "sucking [the] blood" of Virginians.[62]

Madison politely but mercilessly challenged Henry to provide evidence for his claims. He pointed out Henry's numerous inconsistencies and demonstrated where his line of thought led. In the absence of federal taxing power, "how is it possible a war could be supported," he asked. Bushrod Washington wrote to his uncle George Washington that Madison performed "with such force of reasoning and a display of such irresistible truths that opposition seemed to have quitted the field."[63]

But the next day, Saturday, Madison was less sure-footed, perhaps because he heard delegates buzzing that Jefferson had weighed in. The American minister to France had written to Alexander Donald, a Richmond tobacco broker, describing his plan for nine states to ratify the Constitution but four "refuse to accede" until a declaration of rights was added. Word of Jefferson's letter circulated in the capital in early June—as did reports that New Hampshire would soon become the ninth state to accept the Constitution. In that case, were the delegates in Richmond to grant Jefferson's wish, Virginia would refuse to ratify.[64]

Madison made a half-hearted attempt to counter the effect of Jefferson's letter, but then stopped abruptly. "I shall no longer fatigue the committee at this time," he said, "but will resume the subject as early as I can." He left for his room at the Swan, afflicted, he said later, by "a fit of illness," a description that suggests he had suffered a sudden attack.[65]

The following week, Henry took advantage of Jefferson's sentiments. With such an "illustrious citizen" urging that nine states adopt and four reject the Constitution, what choice did Virginia have? Madison, who had returned to the convention, snapped back with a blunt query. Jefferson was an "ornament" to the state, he observed, but how could the convention be led by someone who was not there?

> Is it come to this then that we are not to follow our own reason? Is it proper to introduce the opinions of respectable men not within these walls? . . . Are we who . . . are not to be governed by an *erring world* now to submit to the opinion of a citizen beyond the Atlantic?

Besides, Madison declared, "I believe that were that gentleman now on the floor, he would be for the adoption of this Constitution." He immediately began to qualify, saying that he was only making a surmise, which, indeed, he was—and one that was unjustified. In the last letter that Madison had from Jefferson about the Constitution, his friend had favored the exact plan upon which Henry was expounding. Whether Madison's assertion was a slip or a tactic, it apparently had a positive effect. Delegate Archibald Stuart wrote to a friend, "Madison came boldly forward and supported the Constitution with the soundest reason and most manly eloquence I ever heard. He understands his subject well and his whole soul is engaged in its success and it appeared to me he would have flashed conviction into every mind."[66]

The vote was closer than it had been in most ratifying conventions, 89 to 79, but the Constitution was approved with no amendments attached. Recommendations for changes would be forwarded to the Congress.

Madison took nearly a month to write Jefferson with the news. When he finally did, he was respectful—but he made no effort to soften the fact that opponents of the Constitution had used Jefferson's letters to try to prevent ratification. Jefferson did not apologize, but he was effusive in his compliments to *The Federalist*, which Madison, after long delay, had sent to him. Suggesting that Hamilton's and Jay's portions must have been minimal, Jefferson called it "the best commentary on the principles of government which ever was written," and he confessed graciously, "It has rectified me in several points."[67]

One of the votes against the ratification of the Constitution in Virginia was cast by James Monroe, now serving in the House of Delegates. In his speeches he emphasized the dangers of the presidency created by the Constitution. Might not foreign governments corrupt the president? Might not the Senate collude with him? Might not the Congress interfere with the electoral system to ensure the election of someone whom members approved?

Monroe's complaints may have been related to his not having been appointed as a delegate to the Constitutional Convention. A likely reason was that he was out of politics when delegates were chosen, off practicing law in Fredericksburg. He nonetheless blamed two supporters of the Constitution, Governor Randolph and James Madison. He wrote Jefferson:

> The governor I have reason to believe is unfriendly to me and hath shewn (if I am well informed) a disposition to thwart me; Madison, upon whose friendship I have calculated, whose views I have favored, and with whom I have held the most confidential correspondence since you left the continent, is in strict league with him and hath, I have reason to believe, concurred in arrangements unfavorable to me.[68]

If Monroe's hostility was not the primary cause of his negative vote, it might well have made it easier for him to see the document's faults.

Monroe's ill will toward Randolph and Madison was a minor matter compared to his hostility toward George Washington. In a long essay that he wrote around the time of the ratifying convention, Monroe undertook to show how Washington—or the Statesman, as he called him—had orchestrated his grand career. What better way "to add a brilliancy to his character and secure his success" than to give up command of the army in a ceremony of great solemnity? As he thought back on that occasion—which he had witnessed—he imagined the calculations Washington had made leading up to it:

> His resignation should be received by the sovereign power of the country that employed him, with the highest acknowledgements for his services. Its benedictions should be poured upon his head, and he should take his leave with solemn declarations never to engage in public life again.

The idea that Washington deliberately tried to create a heroic image of himself has been a theme of modern scholarship, but note is usually taken that he also believed resigning was the right thing to do.[69]

Washington's life in retirement was similarly staged, as Monroe described it. The plan was for the Statesman to be "affable and communicative, yet preserve such a degree of gravity and dignity in his deportment that whilst he gained the esteem, he might secure the respect of society."[70]

Monroe took a deeply cynical view. By exaggerating "a trifling tumult," such as Shays's Rebellion, he wrote, the Statesman encouraged "men of reputation [to] urge a general reform in the system," and after much persuasion and showing great reluctance, he left his much-vaunted retirement to chair the convention that resulted. There, with "aged men," he worked to create a form of government as close to monarchy as could be achieved "without creating a public alarm."[71] And it was the Statesman, of course, who would become the monarch.

Monroe had just begun to connect his description of Washington's self-invention with reasons to fear the Constitution when he broke off the essay. He had no compelling reason to finish. He could not have intended such a diatribe for publication. Monroe, like Washington, seems to have had an explosive temper that he found ways of controlling—such as a private rant.[72]

Even after those who favored the Constitution won the day at Virginia's ratifying convention, opponents continued their resistance. Patrick Henry used his sway with the legislature to have Madison passed over for the U.S. Senate and tried to keep him out of the House of Representatives by seeing to it that his district lines were redrawn to include pockets of anticonstitutional sentiment. Henry probably also had a hand in fielding Madison's opponent—none other than James Monroe.

Monroe wrote hundreds of letters portraying himself as the candidate who favored rights of conscience. The proof was that he had supported amendments to the Constitution guaranteeing such rights, while James Madison had not. But Madison, who had a long history of defending Baptists against persecution, began his own letter-writing campaign. In a neat turn from his opposition to amendments at the Virginia convention, he explained that circumstances had now changed. As he wrote a Baptist friend in Orange County,

The Constitution is established on the ratifications of eleven states and a very great majority of the people of America; and amendments, if pursued with a proper moderation and in a proper mode, will be not only safe, but may serve the double purpose of satisfying the minds of well-meaning opponents, and of providing additional guards in favor of liberty.

Amendments, he went on, ought to be proposed by the first Congress under the Constitution.[73]

Although it was the middle of winter, Madison and Monroe went on the stump, even making some joint appearances. After a Lutheran service, they listened to the lively music of "two fiddles" and debated one another on the church steps. "We addressed these people," as Madison described it, "and kept them standing in the snow listening to the discussion of constitutional subjects. They stood it out very patiently—seemed to consider it a sort of fight of which they were required to be spectators." Riding twelve miles home after the event, Madison learned that winter campaigning has its risks. His nose was frostbitten, and the resulting mark remained the rest of his life.[74]

Madison won the election handily. Afterward he assured Jefferson in a letter that both he and Monroe had managed to keep the campaign civil. "Between ourselves," he wrote, "I have no reason to doubt that the distinction was duly kept in mind between political and personal views, and that it has saved our friendship from the smallest diminution." He added, "On one side I am sure it is the case," a comment that was a wink at Jefferson. They both knew that Monroe was likely to hold a grudge, though he would hide it. Later Jefferson would describe Monroe this way: "Everything from him breathed the purest patriotism, involving, however, a close attention to his honor and grade."[75]

Madison understood Jefferson's affection for Monroe, who took every word and suggestion of Jefferson's straight to heart. When Jefferson recommended from Paris that Monroe, Madison, and William Short, a Virginian acting as Jefferson's private secretary in France, settle in the vicinity of Monticello so that the four of them could form an "agreeable society," Monroe began to look for land.[76]

FOUR

Untrodden Ground

❧

A Nation Wholly New

Even before he was officially elected president, Washington was concerned about his inaugural address. He had a seventy-three-page draft that he was doubtful about, and he asked Madison to stop at Mount Vernon on his way to New York, where the inaugural was to be held. At the end of Madison's weeklong stay, Washington had a much shorter speech. It was moving and modest, and if the sentence structure was somewhat convoluted, as Madison's sometimes was, it contained a lovely image of "the sacred fire of liberty" that had been entrusted to the American people.[1]

On April 30, 1789, Washington officially became the president of the United States. Dressed in a dark brown suit made of American broadcloth and wearing silver shoe buckles, he took the oath of office on the second-floor balcony of New York City's Federal

Hall, the temporary Capitol of the United States. When he finished, he kissed the Bible on which he had placed his hand during the swearing in, and with bells ringing and the crowd below cheering, he reentered the hall and delivered his address to the Congress. The president's mannerisms were unusual; Senator William Maclay wrote that he was "agitated" and "trembled." Maclay thought he was self-conscious, but just as likely his emotions had broken through. Even the most stoical of men could have been overwhelmed by the mighty course he had run and what lay ahead.[2] Everything that he and those around him did would be without precedent.

Madison composed the response of the House of Representatives to the president's address. At Washington's request, he also authored the response of the president to the House's response, and if that were not enough, he also wrote the president's response to the Senate. It was as though Madison's voice were echoing off every wall and column of Federal Hall.

Madison was not the Speaker of the House. That task fell to Frederick Muhlenberg of Pennsylvania. But Madison was recognized as the leader of the House, "our first man," as Congressman Fisher Ames of Massachusetts put it. Ames, a passionate and colorful speaker, did not think Madison's leadership was the result of commanding presence or oratorical skills. "He speaks low, his person is little and ordinary," Ames wrote. But he was trusted as a man of "sense, reading, address, and integrity."[3]

He was also master of every element of the legislation he introduced. Nowhere was this clearer than in the way he managed what we today call the Bill of Rights. He reviewed the more than two hundred amendments that had been proposed in state ratifying conventions and then neatly set aside all of those that would weaken the central government. Amendments having to do with individual rights remained, and he incorporated them into proposals for the Congress.

At the Virginia ratifying convention, Madison had warned that listing rights would be dangerous. If the list did not set forth every right that individuals possessed, it could imply that the state had power over rights not included. To avoid this trap Madison constructed his propositions to emphasize that fundamental rights were inherent in individuals, not government: "The people shall not be deprived or abridged of their right to speak, to write, or to publish their sentiments"; "The right of the people to keep and bear arms shall not be infringed." Lest anyone still think that rights not mentioned were fair game, Madison proposed an amendment specifically taking up the topic: "Exceptions here or elsewhere in the Constitution made in favor of particular rights shall not be so construed as to diminish the just importance of other rights retained by the people."[4] In edited form this proposition became the Ninth Amendment.

The heated battle to get the amendments through the Congress went on for months. Wrote Madison, "The difficulty of uniting the minds of men accustomed to think and act differently can only be conceived by those who have witnessed it."[5] Madison kept at it, and at the end of September 1789, Congress approved amendments to send to the states for ratification. Madison was not only deeply knowledgeable and politically creative, he also had persistence—a characteristic that James Monroe found worthy of emulation.

In Paris, Jefferson was witnessing what he called a "great national reformation," and he viewed it optimistically, seeing it as a sign that the people of France had awakened to their oppression and with "quietness [and] steadiness" would gain their rights. He had hope for a happy outcome even after angry mobs stormed the Bastille on July 14, 1789, and afterward carried the bloody heads of prison officials on pikes through the streets. In a letter to Maria Cosway, he joked, "The cutting off heads is become so much à la mode that one is apt to feel of a morning whether their own is on their shoulders."[6]

Jefferson had applied for permission to travel to Virginia months before the violence began. He wanted a leave of absence, he explained to President Washington, "to carry my children back to their own country and to settle various matters of a private nature." Waiting in Paris for the document that would permit him to sail, he had the satisfaction of learning that the National Assembly had issued the Declaration of the Rights of Man and of the Citizen, a document asserting "natural, unalienable, and sacred rights." Jefferson had advised his friend Lafayette as he drafted the declaration.[7]

He also heard from Madison, who was helping George Washington fill out his administration. Would Jefferson be willing, Madison asked, to accept an appointment in the new government? It was not what Jefferson wanted to do. His plan was to return to

Paris after six months. If he were to leave his diplomatic post, he told Madison, his wish was to retire to Monticello.[8]

Before he left Paris, Jefferson wrote another letter to Madison, this one developing a concept that he said had grown out of his time in Paris. "The earth belongs in usufruct to the living," he wrote. "The dead have neither powers nor rights over it." The concept had natural appeal for someone witnessing a revolution against a regime that had perpetuated injustice for centuries, but a reason personal to Jefferson may also have played a part. He had acquired an enormous debt from the death of his father-in-law, John Wayles. In the time since Wayles had died in 1773, creditors had been pressuring Jefferson, and he had been putting them off, but matters had reached a point requiring face-to-face negotiations. The "matters of a private nature" that he had mentioned to Washington was debt from the past that burdened him.[9]

Pondering what he had written about the earth belonging to the living, Jefferson did not send the letter to Madison for months. When Madison finally received it, he responded in a decidedly practical way. Were not some debts incurred for purposes "which interest the unborn, as well as the living"? Warding off conquest was an example. And would not the frequent changing of laws and constitutions lead to instability? Jefferson had calculated that nineteen years was the length of time that a generation was at its height and set that as the limit for debts or constitutions to continue, but, Madison pointed out, generations did not either come of age or leave the stage all at once. It was a constant process that made a time limit unworkable. It would give him great pleasure, he wrote, if the concept that the earth belonged to the living would be "always kept in view as a salutary curb on the living generation from imposing unjust or unnecessary burdens on their successors." But he also wrote how unlikely that was: "Our hemisphere must be still more enlightened before many of the sublime truths which are seen through the medium of philosophy become visible to the naked eye of the ordinary politician."[10]

Once again Jefferson was the speculative master of grand ideas, and Madison was rooted in the realities of human nature and political life. But the exchange also captured an essential similarity, what the editor of the Madison Papers called the "admiration and respect for the qualities of mind which each found in the other."[11]

Jefferson arrived in Virginia to learn that even as he had sailed from France, President Washington had nominated him to be secretary of state, and the Senate had confirmed him. A few days after Christmas, Madison arrived at Monticello to try to persuade his friend to accept. The two men had not seen one another in more than five years, but their happy reunion did not change Jefferson's mind. A week or so after Madison had departed Monticello, Jefferson wrote to say that he hoped the president would not urge him to accept the nomination, although if he did, he planned not to object.[12]

Madison, once more in his persuasive mode, kept up the pressure on his friend. Jefferson finally succumbed, agreeing to become secretary of state even though his personal inclinations were otherwise. "I . . . shall endeavor to subdue the reluctance I have to that office," he wrote to Madison, even though his aversion to it had "increased so as to oppress me extremely."[13]

When Jefferson arrived in New York on March 21, 1790, he found that Madison had just lost a battle with Treasury Secretary Alexander Hamilton over how government securities should be redeemed. Madison had thought Hamilton's proposal to have the Treasury buy them at par value was unjust. Speculators, who had purchased many securities at a deep discount from the military men who had originally owned them, stood to make handsome profits. In Madison's view, the men who had fought in the Revolution deserved to receive a portion of any benefit. As Hamilton saw it, the government had a contractual obligation to the present owners, and his was the argument that prevailed.

Madison was soon opposing Hamilton's proposal for the federal government to assume state debts, and he had the votes to defeat it. Hamilton decided to take his case to Jefferson and on a spring day waylaid the new secretary as he was going into a townhouse that the president had rented on Broadway. Looking "somber, haggard, and dejected beyond description," as Jefferson reported, Hamilton grabbed his arm and walked him back and forth before the president's door, all the while painting an alarming picture of contention in the Congress. Eastern states were even threatening to secede should assumption be rejected.[14]

The result of the encounter was the most famous and consequential dinner party ever held in New York. Jefferson invited both Hamilton and Madison to his rented quarters on Maiden Lane, where Hamilton dominated the conversation. One imagines him striding across the drawing room, his posture erect, his hair back from his face, throwing out numbers and expounding on the importance of assumption. Madison would have asked a clarifying question now and then—and worked to move the numbers a little to gain advantage for Virginia. Jefferson probably listened gravely, intent on absorbing a subject far removed from those that had engaged him in Paris.

By the end of the evening, as Jefferson told it, Madison had agreed that while he would not vote for assumption, neither would he continue strenuously to oppose it. Meanwhile, to soften the blow to southern states, where hostility to assumption ran high, the permanent seat of government would be in the South. By the end of July, assumption had passed, and the permanent national capital was slated for a wild, beautiful, and mosquito-infested swamp on the banks of the Potomac River.[15] Until the new capital was built, the U.S. government would meet in Philadelphia.

When assumption later proved deeply unpopular in Virginia, Jefferson changed his account to portray himself as having been thoroughly duped by Hamilton. For the moment, however, there was the pleasing image of political leaders compromising on a matter of great import—and it lasted until Hamilton made his next move, which was proposing a national bank.

The bank proposal established once and for all Hamilton's belief that the authority of the federal government reached far beyond the specific powers granted to it in the Constitution. Madison argued forcefully on the floor of the House that such an expansive view was in error. Appeals to certain clauses in the Constitution, such as those that gave Congress authority to "provide for the general welfare" or "pass all laws necessary and proper to execute the specified powers" did not give Congress "unlimited discretion."[16]

In *Federalist* 44, Madison had described the "necessary and proper" clause in a commonsensical way. It gave the Congress limited authority to accomplish constitutionally sanctioned ends, but a bank was not that, he argued on the floor of the House, and to pretend it was would deny the concept of limited government.[17]

Madison was unsuccessful in convincing a majority of his colleagues to vote against the bill, but he hoped to be more successful with the president. Jefferson and Attorney General Edmund Randolph advised President Washington that the bank plan was unconstitutional, and the president had gone so far as to ask Madison to draw up a memo justifying a veto. But he gave Hamilton the final word, letting him review the advice that Randolph and Jefferson provided. On February 25, 1791, Washington put his signature to the bank bill. To Madison and Jefferson this was proof positive of Hamilton's sway over the president.

After the First Congress adjourned, President Washington set out on a southern tour. He had visited New England early in his presidency and now planned an excursion through Virginia, the Carolinas, and Georgia. Jefferson and Madison decided to take a tour of their own, one which would begin in New York City, where they could visit Philip Freneau, Madison's classmate at

Princeton. They wanted to talk to him about starting a newspaper in Philadelphia that would be aligned with Republican views.[18]

Madison and Jefferson met with Freneau, making clear that the newspaper would not be his only source of income. He would also receive $250 a year from the State Department, an arrangement that would not pass ethical muster today but bore similarities to Hamilton's agreement with reliably Federalist publisher James Fenno, for whose newspaper Hamilton raised money. Jefferson and Madison left Freneau to consider their proposal and set out on the part of their excursion that had as its object, according to Madison, "health, recreation, and curiosity." A journey into largely unsettled parts would be a welcome diversion from the pressure of politics.[19]

From Poughkeepsie, they traveled through the spectacular landscape that would later inspire the painters of the Hudson River School. They marveled over plant specimens then unknown in Virginia, including a shrub with large, fragrant pink blossoms, probably a rhododendron. They sailed on the crystal-clear waters of Lake George and fished for trout, salmon, and bass.[20] They toured revolutionary battle sites—Bennington, Fort Ticonderoga, Saratoga. And, of course, they talked politics. While they left no record of their conversations, it was inevitable that some were about Hamilton and the power he exercised over the president.

The story of the relationship between Washington and Hamilton was more complicated than they could have known. There had been a time during the war when Washington had hoped to find in Hamilton a person in whom he could confide and trust. He wanted the kind of connection he had sought—and so spectacularly not found—with Joseph Reed, but Hamilton wanted his independence. In 1781, he had seized on an opportunity to leave Washington's service, telling his father-in-law, Philip Schuyler, that he had felt no friendship for Washington since the time of Valley Forge. "Indeed, when advances of this kind have been made to me on his part," Hamilton wrote, "they were received in a manner that showed at least I had no inclination to court them and that I wished to stand rather upon a footing of military confidence than of private attachment."[21] Now, ten years later, their relationship seemed to be professional, but a present-day historian, even with access to personal letters, cannot be sure how much the past lingered.

At the end of their botanical excursion, both Jefferson and Madison felt better than they had for some time. Jefferson wrote to Washington that the trip may have rid him of his debilitating headaches, and he noted that Madison's health was "visibly mended." But the sense of well-being with which they emerged from the wilderness would be short-lived. Thanks to Hamilton's bank bill, the country had been caught up in a speculative frenzy, a "public plunder," Madison called it.[22] A scene more perfectly calculated to fix their conviction that Hamilton would destroy the Republic is hard to imagine.

In the opening months of the Second Congress, Hamilton presented yet another plan, this one for the government to subsidize manufacturing. Madison sent the proposal to a friend, observing that it interpreted the Constitution so loosely that it rendered the document meaningless. "The parchment had better be thrown into the fire at once," he wrote.[23] Madison's efforts to defeat the bill were aided by the bursting of the speculative bubble. With people on all rungs of the economic ladder losing everything they had, further government involvement in the economy lost its appeal, and Hamilton's plan for manufacturing was shelved.

Determined to end Hamilton's influence over the government, Jefferson repeatedly criticized the Treasury secretary in meetings with the president. Madison took his complaints public, spelling out on the floor of the House the horrors of a loose interpretation of the Constitution: Government could take control of religion and education; Congress could regulate activities great and small. Madison also wrote a number of anonymous essays for the newspaper Philip Freneau had founded in Philadelphia, the *National Gazette*. Madison returned to the idea of factions or parties that he had addressed at the Constitutional Convention. Parties had been a factor since the Revolution, he wrote, and they were so now. One party was promoting the interests of the influential and the moneyed. Its members believed mankind "incapable of governing themselves." The other party, the "Republican party," Madison called it, rejected distinctions of wealth and class and was firmly for the people.[24]

As he had for the Constitution, Madison was laying a theoretical groundwork, this time for an organized opposition. He knew that parties were widely disdained. Jefferson had once said that if he "could not go to heaven but with a party," he "would not go there at all." But Madison presented parties as inevitable and argued that they served a useful purpose by providing checks on one another.[25] His argument undercut the idea that the government currently in place was above party. By arguing for equal standing between those in power and the opposition, Madison initiated a transformation of the American political landscape.

The political battle that ensued was as hard fought as any in American history. Both Federalists, who favored administration policies, and Republicans, who opposed them, believed the future of the nation was at stake. Hamilton, the chief Federalist spokesman, believed in using government power to move the United States as rapidly as possible into the modern commercial world. The Virginians were repelled by the idea of government hastening the many into the miseries and dependency of factory life, while encouraging scandalous opulence for the few.

The Virginians were relentless. They move "in a solid column," wrote one observer, "and the discipline of the party is as severe as the Prussian. Deserters are not spared."[26] But one notable Virginian was not in the phalanx. Indeed, Washington perceived himself an object of its attack, which was one reason he did not want to stand for a second term.

In a meeting he requested with Madison, the president explained that he thought that someone else could do the job better than he. As Madison later recorded his words:

> He had from the beginning found himself deficient in many of the essential qualifications, owing to his inexperience in the forms of public business, his unfitness to judge of legal questions, and questions arising out of the Constitution; . . . that he found himself also in the decline of life, his health becoming sensibly more infirm and perhaps his faculties also; that the fatigues and disagreeableness of his situation were in fact scarcely tolerable to him.

The president also said that his presence in office seemed to animate the spirit of party, which was causing so much harm by dividing the government and the people. If he stepped down, it would be consistent with the public interest.[27]

Madison assured him that no one could have served the country better. Another four years of Washington's "temperate and wise administration," he said, could give the government "a tone and firmness" that would allow a successor to administer it safely. As for parties, he told the president, they "did not appear to be so formidable to the government as some had represented." Washington, seeming unconvinced, turned the discussion to different subjects.[28]

As Madison left Washington's office, he must have felt at least a little abashed, knowing that he was in large part responsible for the party turmoil that Washington cited as a reason to retire. It would be many months before another of Madison's essays appeared in Freneau's paper.

When the first session of the Second Congress was over, Madison traveled home to Virginia with the Monroes. The two men had been adversaries at the Virginia ratifying convention and opponents for a seat in the First Congress, but now Monroe was in the U.S. Senate, appointed to fill a vacancy. The two had become allies, united with Jefferson against Hamilton and the direction he favored for the country.

As the party rode south, they probably discussed what Monroe had recently learned about the Treasury secretary. Reports had come to Congress that Hamilton was covering up personal speculation by conducting it through a certain James Reynolds. A delegation of three, one of whom was Senator Monroe, had visited Hamilton and, with Oliver Wolcott Jr. as a witness, shown him letters indicating payments to Reynolds and asked for an explanation. The one they received was jaw dropping. Hamilton had been transferring money to Reynolds, he said, but not for speculation. He was paying blackmail because he had been sleeping with Reynolds's wife. The three members of Congress agreed, as gentlemen did, that such a private matter should be kept confidential, and it was—for nearly five years.

Through the summer of 1792, the hostilities in Washington's cabinet continued. The president grew increasingly irritated with Jefferson's constant carping and told his secretary of state that he simply did not believe that there were plans afoot to establish a monarchy in the United States, as Jefferson kept saying, and that the attacks on Hamilton had gone too far. The latter conclusion would have been easy to reach since Hamilton had not yet entered the fray. Soon, however, he was in the middle of it. Writing under a variety of pseudonyms, he publicly raised Freneau's connections to Madison and Jefferson, surfaced the story of Jefferson's not having been entirely pleased with the Constitution, and hinted at scandal in Jefferson's personal life.

Monroe joined Madison in defending Jefferson in the newspapers, thus further roiling the waters. The president pleaded with his cabinet members to end the bitter fighting. To Jefferson he wrote:

> My earnest wish and my fondest hope . . . is that instead of wounding suspicions and irritable charges, there may be liberal allowances—mutual forbearances and temporizing yieldings on all sides. Under the exercise of these, matters will go on smoothly and, if possible, more prosperously. Without them everything must rub, the wheels of government will clog—our enemies will triumph—and by throwing their weight into the disaffected scale, may accomplish the ruin of the goodly fabric we have been erecting.

He sent a similar message to Hamilton—and both men rejected his pleas. Jefferson replied that he had to fight back when Hamilton's system "was calculated to undermine and demolish the republic." On an unpleasant personal note, he added that he would not allow his reputation "to be clouded by the slanders of a man whose history, from the moment at which history can stoop to notice him, is a tissue of machinations against the liberty of the country." Hamilton, although more polite, stubbornly refused to break off the battle. He could not quit, he wrote, when he was being attacked personally and a party had been formed "deliberately bent upon the subversion of measures, which in its consequence would subvert the government."[29]

Jefferson and Hamilton might have refused a direct order from Washington, just as they refused his pleas. Still it is a wonder that the president did not forcefully tell them to stop feuding. Instead, perhaps seeking the gentlemanly way, he gave hints and made requests, as he had sometimes done with officers under him in the Revolution. At one point, he hinted to Jefferson that he ought to fire Freneau—but the hint was not so strong that Jefferson felt obliged to respond. In personal notes, Jefferson indicated that if an answer became necessary, he would be definitive. "I will not do it," he wrote. Perhaps Washington had expected refusal and deliberately avoided a confrontation. He did not want Jefferson to leave office, or Hamilton either. How would he find someone as knowledgeable about foreign affairs as Jefferson or as versed in matters of finance as Hamilton? Thus, the contention in cabinet meetings continued. As Jefferson described it, "Hamilton and myself were daily pitted in the cabinet like two cocks."[30]

Washington began to wonder if the very spirit of party that made him want to retire was a reason he could not. Perhaps the split in government was too threatening for a change in the presidency. When Jefferson visited Mount Vernon on October 1, 1792, the president told him he was still uncertain, but "if his aid was thought necessary to save the cause to which he had devoted his life principally, he would make the sacrifice of a longer continuance."[31]

In November, a long letter from a friend, Elizabeth Powel, may have ultimately persuaded him. George and Martha Washington had known Eliza and her immensely wealthy husband, Philadelphia merchant Samuel Powel, since the days of the Continental Congress. During the Constitutional Convention, while Martha stayed at Mount Vernon, Washington and Mrs. Powel had seen one another frequently, sometimes for large dinners at the handsome Powel house on Third Street, sometimes for tea or the theater. They went out in the company of others, but there was a flirtatious edge to their relationship. When Washington had to decline an invitation to see Richard Sheridan's play *The School for Scandal*, he wrote to her, "The general can but regret that matters have turned out so unluckily, after waiting so long to receive a lesson in the school for scandal."[32]

Eliza was more than charming and witty. She was a person of surpassing intelligence who was trustworthy, someone in whom Washington could confide. In telling her of his plans to retire, he apparently questioned his capacities, as he had to Madison, causing her to warn him against "a false diffidence of abilities which those that best know you so justly appreciate." She laid out what she saw as his great strengths:

> Your very figure is calculated to inspire respect and confidence in the people, whose simple good sense associates the noblest qualities of mind with the heroic form when it is embellished by such remarkable tenets of mildness and calm benevolence— and such I believe was the first intention of nature.

"You are," she told him, "the only man in America that dares to do right on all public occasions."[33] Washington remained silent about his candidacy for a second term until finally his silence was interpreted as assent.

As had happened in the election of 1788, the electoral vote for Washington was unanimous. The approval of his fellow countrymen was satisfying, he admitted, but "to say I feel pleasure from the prospect of commencing another tour of duty would be a departure from truth."[34]

Toward the end of February 1793, Washington must have particularly regretted his decision to serve a second term. First Freneau's *Gazette* attacked the grand way in which his birthday had recently been celebrated. The city militia had marched and there had been a banquet where important personages offered toasts. It was a high-toned affair that smacked of monarchy, claimed the *Gazette*. At about the same time, the House of Representatives took up a series of resolutions aimed at removing the secretary of the Treasury from office on the grounds that he had played fast and loose with appropriations, using them for purposes for which they had not been intended. Hamilton further inflamed his critics by saying he had to have spending discretion. It would be "pusillanimity" for him to strictly adhere to appropriations.[35]

The attack on Hamilton was led by William Branch Giles, a stocky Virginia congressman said to drink "wine or cherry bounce from twelve o'clock to night every day."[36] Giles was immediately suspected of acting on behalf of Jefferson, who had indeed provided him a draft of resolutions for Congress to use condemning Hamilton. It was typical Jefferson, wanting to make a point, but not wanting to make it himself. Madison also seems to have acted in a customary way. The resolutions presented by Giles were much softer than Jefferson's draft. Madison was accustomed to toning down his friend's rhetoric.

In the end, the resolutions failed. Jefferson blamed speculators in Congress and claimed that even though the resolutions had been voted down, they had accomplished some good by "showing the public the desperate and abandoned dispositions with which their affairs were conducted."[37] They may have made Washington momentarily more cautious about Hamilton. When the Treasury secretary asked him for a letter to Congress stating that he had approved the uses to which Hamilton had put appropriated monies, the president responded with a missive so lukewarm that Hamilton's adversaries cheered.

On a partly cloudy day, Washington rode alone to Congress Hall and after being sworn in delivered an inaugural speech of just 135 words.[38] Had Madison assisted him, as in 1789, the speech would not have been so brief, but Washington had not asked for the younger man's help, perhaps because he now knew that the bright fellow from Orange had turned his intellectual firepower on the Washington administration. Since the time that Hamilton had revealed the connection between Madison, Jefferson, and Freneau, Washington had not written to Madison to seek his advice on any matter.

The revolution in France, on which so many had placed so much hope, grew increasingly violent. In August 1792, Jacobins and sansculottes stormed the Tuileries, forcing the royal family to seek refuge with the Legislative Assembly. An orgy of killing followed in September; mobs killed hundreds of priests, prisoners, and aristocrats, among them the Duc de La Rochefoucauld, one of Jefferson's intellectual companions in Paris. He had been stoned to death while his young wife, Rosalie, and his mother watched.[39]

The bloody turn led many to condemn the Jacobin leaders of

the Revolution, but Jefferson wanted to hear none of it. He regretted the loss of life, he told his protégé William Short, who was on a diplomatic mission in Europe, but added:

> The liberty of the whole earth was depending on the issue of the contest, and was ever such a prize won with so little innocent blood? My own affections have been deeply wounded by some of the martyrs to this cause, but rather than it should have failed, I would have seen half the earth desolated. Were there but an Adam and an Eve left in every country and left free, it would be better than it is now.

Short must have been appalled. He was deeply in love with Rosalie de La Rochefoucauld and had been desperately trying to comfort her since the murder of her husband.[40]

In January 1793, King Louis XVI was taken to the Place de la Révolution and guillotined. The executioner held up his bloody head for the multitudes to see. Jefferson received reports of the king's death with sangfroid, writing to a friend, "Should the present ferment in Europe not produce republics everywhere, it will at least soften the monarchical governments by rendering monarchs amenable to punishment."[41]

As Jefferson saw it, the United States and France were part of an ongoing effort to bring liberty to the world, and if violence resulted, so be it. "We are not to expect to be translated from despotism to liberty, in a feather-bed," he had once written.[42] Federalists, on the other hand, were horrified by the slaughter in France and admired British stability. When France declared war on Britain, they could not imagine joining cause with the French.

On April 22, 1793, Washington, with advice from Hamilton, issued a proclamation of neutrality—an action that Madison saw as "an assumption of prerogatives not clearly found in the Constitution." Jefferson became nearly frantic when Hamilton, writing under the pseudonym Pacificus, defended the proclamation in the *Gazette of the United States*—and attacked those who opposed it as enemies of the president. "For God's sake, my dear sir," Jefferson wrote to Madison, "take up your pen, select the most striking heresies, and cut him to pieces in the face of the public."[43] It was not the last time he would make such a request.

Madison, at Montpelier, was reluctant to take on the task. He did not have the right books with him, and being away from Philadelphia, he was not sure he understood the political situation. Did the president intend the proclamation to invalidate treaties the United States had signed with France during the American Revolution? Despite his qualms, Madison began work on the assignment, using the pen name Helvidius to write a series of essays. His main argument was that the president had no constitutional authority to make a proclamation declaring the stance of the nation with regard to war. Such a matter belonged to the legislative branch.

Both Madison and Jefferson believed that Washington's proclamation demonstrated how little he understood the American people's attachment to France and its struggle for liberty. The Virginians' view had been reinforced by the reception accorded the envoy of the new French Republic to the United States. Jubilant crowds had greeted Edmond-Charles Genêt (otherwise known as Citizen Genêt) when he landed in Charleston in April. He was the center of festivity after festivity as he traveled north, all leading to a grand dinner in his honor in Philadelphia. Lovers of France sang "La Marseillaise" and took turns donning a bonnet rouge, the red cap worn by French revolutionaries.[44]

The red-haired, florid-faced Genêt took his enthusiastic welcome as encouragement to fit out privateers for the French to sail against Britain and to recruit Americans to move against Spain in the New World. When the United States government objected, thousands of his supporters paraded through the streets of Philadelphia, shouting their support for France and threatening to drag President Washington out of his house. "Terrorism," John Adams called the demonstrations.[45]

Jefferson, who had been quite taken with Genêt at first, agreed with other members of Washington's cabinet that the United States should request Genêt's government to recall him. "I adhered to him as long as I could," Jefferson wrote to Madison. "Finding at length that the man was absolutely incorrigible, I saw the necessity of quitting a wreck which could not but sink all who should cling to it." The visit that he had counted on to increase support for France had harmed the cause, and as a result, the best thing for Republicans, Jefferson wrote to Madison, was to support neutrality and "avoid little cavils" about whether it had been constitutional for the president to declare it.[46]

Madison had told Jefferson at least three times that he did not want to write the Helvidius essays, but he had undertaken the task. Indeed, he had nearly finished it when Jefferson let him know that the constitutional approach he had taken would not do. The patient Madison responded by tactfully reminding Jefferson that he had encouraged him to edit previous numbers of Helvid-ius and did again in the last two essays he enclosed. As Madison no doubt suspected would happen, his careful arguments about legislative and executive power remained at the center when the essays appeared in the *Gazette of the United States.*[47]

Madison never confronted Jefferson about whether it was nit-picking to question the president's constitutional power, but he did join with Monroe to write resolutions that could be taken up by supporters of France in Virginia. First on the list was that "the Constitution of the United States ought to be firmly and vigi-lantly supported against all direct or indirect attempts that may be made to subvert or violate the same." Also resolved: The United States ought to maintain goodwill for France, which had embraced "the cause of liberty and republican government." Madison sent Jefferson a copy of the memo.[48]

The furor over Citizen Genêt brought ever more vitriolic at-tacks on Washington and ever greater frustration for him. Since the Revolution, he had been the object of adulation. Now he was being compared to Louis XVI. Henry Knox, surprisingly un-aware of the president's sensitivities, passed around a broadside that described Washington being taken to the guillotine. Wash-ington erupted, Jefferson reported, "into one of those passions when he cannot command himself":

> The president . . . ran on much on the personal abuse which had been bestowed on him; defied any man on earth to pro-duce one single act of his since he had been in the government which was not done on the purest motives; . . . that by God he had rather be in his grave than in his present situation; that he

had rather be on his farm than to be made Emperor of the World; and yet that they were charging him with wanting to be a king.

When the rant ended, an awkward silence set in. One cabinet member tried to get the meeting back on track, then another. The president decided to reconvene the next day.[49]

A virus halted the political warfare—at least temporarily. Yellow fever, a disease of blinding headache, black vomit, and severe jaundice, struck Philadelphia in the fall of 1793. Because Congress was in adjournment, Madison and Monroe were in Virginia. Washington departed the city on September 10, leaving Jefferson to provide this description: "Deaths are now about thirty a day. It is in every square of the city. All flying who can."[50]

A diarist reported that tar was being burned in the streets. The doors of the infected were being marked, and the dead buried quickly and unceremoniously. Jefferson left on September 17, but not before he once more allowed Hamilton to bring out the worst in him. Upon hearing that the secretary of the Treasury was stricken and might die, he suggested that Hamilton was being overdramatic, that he was "as timid in sickness" as he was on the battlefield.[51] It was a claim for which Jefferson had no basis since he had never been in battle, let alone with Hamilton.

President Washington broke a long silence with Madison, but only to ask if the Constitution provided him the power to change the meeting place of Congress. Madison replied that it did not. Only the Congress had such power. Fortunately, by December, when the Congress gathered, frost had killed mosquitoes carrying the disease. No one at the time understood why the fever had occurred or why it ended, but Philadelphia was once more habitable.

On the last day of 1793, Jefferson submitted his resignation and the president accepted it. The secretary of state had long wanted to retire, but Washington, despite his annoyance with him, had dissuaded him. One revealing argument that the president offered was that he needed "the check of [Jefferson's] opinions in the administration." The president recognized the need for a counterweight to Hamilton.[52]

Washington's first choice to replace Jefferson was James Madison. Although the relationship between the president and congressman was frosty, Washington wanted Madison's brainpower—and the Republican balance he would provide. But Madison, having long listened to Jefferson's complaints about being a lone voice in the cabinet, wanted no part of the executive branch.

Monroe, meanwhile, tried to keep up the attack on Hamilton. Hearing rumors that the New Yorker would soon receive a diplomatic appointment to Britain, he wrote to the president to object and offered to explain his reasons in person. An irritated Washington wrote back that if Monroe had objections he should put them in writing and reminded Monroe, "I alone am responsible for a proper nomination." Monroe should have stopped at that point, but wrote a letter laying out his case: Hamilton was a monarchist, known to favor England, and his appointment would hurt American ties with France—and that was the way "the community at large" understood it. Washington, averse to being lectured about his ignorance of public opinion, did not respond.[53]

Despite what seemed unending political strife, James Madison had an excellent spring. He was strolling the streets of Philadelphia when the gorgeous Dolley Payne Todd passed by. A tall, shapely brunette, she had fair skin that she had learned as a child to protect from the sun, blue eyes, and black curls. She wore the bosom-baring necklines then in fashion, displaying what the French called *une belle poitrine*. The forty-three-year-old Madison was not at all put off that she was at least two inches taller than he, and though he had a reputation for being reserved, he immediately looked for a way to meet the twenty-six-year-old Widow Todd. She had lost her husband, John, to yellow fever and was now the single mother of a two-year-old boy.

Madison arranged for Aaron Burr, who had been a student with him at Princeton, to make the introduction. Dolley, wearing mulberry satin and yellow glass beads, received "the great little Madison," as she called him, in her parlor, and soon he was letting her know through her friend Catharine Coles how he felt about her. "He told me . . . he thinks so much of you in the day that he has lost his tongue," Catharine wrote. "At night he dreams of you and starts in his sleep a calling on you to relieve his flame, for he burns to such an excess that he will be shortly consumed."[54] Coles's letter is remarkable not only for its intimate expressions, but also because Dolley saved it. Had Martha Washington,

Martha Jefferson, or Elizabeth Monroe had such a missive in hand, she would have destroyed it rather than leave it for posterity to read. But Dolley was different, a woman who did not feel obliged to conceal personal details from history. In fact, as the decades ahead would show, she was intent on making her mark.

The couple married at Harewood, the estate of George Steptoe Washington, the president's nephew. Washington and his wife, Lucy, who was Dolley's sister, lived in an imposing stone house, and it was there, on a sunny September day, that James Madison and Dolley Payne Todd took their vows.[55]

As the newlyweds were traveling in Northern Virginia, President Washington ordered thirteen thousand militia from four states to march into western Pennsylvania. Long-simmering resentment among farmers over an excise tax on whiskey and the federal agents who tried to collect it had erupted into violence. The rebels tarred and feathered tax collectors and burned down the estate of John Neville, a tax inspector. Six thousand farmers gathered in a field to show their power and their anger. Washington, urged on by Hamilton, was determined to put the insurrection down. On September 30, with Hamilton at his side, he set out in a carriage for Carlisle, Pennsylvania. As he approached points of rendezvous for gathering troops, he changed to a horse, knowing full well that was how the men would expect to see him. At one stop, an eyewitness reported, "He pulled off his hat and in the most respectful manner, bowed to the officers and men, and in this manner passed the line." The men were greatly affected, the onlooker wrote, as if they had encountered "an honored parent."[56]

When Washington was satisfied that his plans for subduing the rebellion were in place, he rode back to Philadelphia in his carriage, leaving Hamilton in charge. The younger man performed in a way that showed why Washington was comfortable leaving him in command. He directed the impressive army into the heart of the insurgency, and the mobs melted away.

Madison was one of many who suspected that Hamilton would use what became known as the Whiskey Rebellion for some purpose of his own, perhaps, he wrote to Jefferson, to show the need "for a standing army to enforce the laws." When Madison arrived in Philadelphia for the second session of the Third Congress, that was all the talk. Madison was not much bothered, since he did not think such a measure would succeed. Jefferson, busy at Monticello pulling down parts of his house in order to build the grand home we know today, joked that given the large force Washington had assembled, he expected to hear any day that the Americans had attacked Detroit, where a significant British troop buildup was under way. He was also curious, he told Madison, about how the administration was going to justify bringing "such an armament against people at their ploughs."[57]

The judgment that it was excessive to call out thirteen thousand militia to deal with half that many malcontents was perhaps justified, but it was also easy to mock the federal government's response when one was not in charge of it. And in the end the show of massive force worked.

FIVE

Schism

~

Breaking the Bonds of Attachment

Tall windows lent an air of grandeur to the sparsely decorated House chamber of Philadelphia's Congress Hall.
Daylight poured through the windows, though not much
warmth, and it was left to stoves fitted into fireplaces at opposite
ends of the room to take the chill off the November air.[1]

As President George Washington delivered his sixth annual
address to Congress from in front of the dais on the chamber's
west side, Congressman James Madison listened from one of the
black leather armchairs arranged on risers facing the commander
in chief. Madison had a mahogany desk in front of him that was
fitted out for pen, ink, and paper, and perhaps he recalled for a
moment his note-taking at the Constitutional Convention seven
years before. Delegates had met in the Pennsylvania State House
next door.[2]

If Madison's mind wandered briefly, he focused soon enough on the president's words. Washington was condemning "certain self-created societies" for fostering bitterness and discontent over the excise tax. Their lies, said the president, had encouraged suspicion of public officials, undercut people's faith in their duly elected government, and brought about the Pennsylvania insurrection.[3]

Madison knew that Washington had little use for "democratic societies," as their members called them. Formed around the time that enthusiasm for Citizen Genêt was running strong, the societies, some three dozen of them across the country, were decidedly pro-French. As the democratic society in Pennsylvania put it, its members were attached to France "by sentiments of the liveliest gratitude for the great and generous service she has rendered us while we were struggling for our liberties and by that strong connection which arises from a similarity of government and of political principles." The societies passed antitax resolutions, including condemnations of the much-despised excise tax, and published essays usually critical of administration policies. They also repeatedly affirmed faith in the Constitution and in the people as the backbone of government.[4]

Even though he knew Washington's opinion, Madison had not thought that he would go so far. For the highest official in the land to blame the societies for fomenting rebellion was, in his view, a violation of "the most sacred principle of our Constitution," the right of citizens to speak freely—even when their subject was the failings of their government.[5]

Whether citizens of a republic should feel free to criticize duly elected officials was a question that would split the Virginia dynasty.

Members of the democratic societies used newspapers to broadcast their views. Philip Freneau, who had encouraged the founding of the societies, opened the pages of the *National Gazette* to them. The *Philadelphia Gazette* published members' letters, including one from David Reddick of the Democratic Society of Washington County, Pennsylvania. How was it, Reddick inquired, that his society was being blamed for the insurrection when protests over the whiskey tax predated the society's founding? Circular letters were another way that societies made their viewpoints known. The largest society, the Democratic Society of Pennsylvania, sent one to other societies asking, "If it be deemed a heresy to question the infallibility of the rulers of our land, in the name of God to what purpose did we struggle through and maintain a seven years war against a corrupt court?" Whether democratic societies in the western counties of Pennsylvania actually took part in the rebellion has been disputed, but so far as is known, no society in any part of the country voiced approval of it. There were, on the other hand, many condemnations. "This society are opposed to every outrage of this nature," declared a group in Massachusetts.[6]

The rank and file of the democratic societies were working class, but membership rolls also listed some prestigious figures. David Rittenhouse, astronomer and inventor, was one; linguist Pierre Du Ponceau, Monroe's friend from Valley Forge, another. Jefferson and Madison were not members, but they defended the right of those who were to speak out without being accused of sedition. In a letter to Madison from Monticello, Jefferson declared that the president's denunciation of the societies was "an attack on the freedom of discussion, the freedom of writing, printing, and publishing." In a letter to Monroe, who had left his seat in the Senate to become minister to France, Madison asserted that the president had made "perhaps the greatest error of his political life." His speech provided a precedent for the government to "stifle all censures whatever on its misdoings, for if it be itself the judge, it will never allow any censures to be just, and if it can suppress censures flowing from one lawful source, it may those flowing from any other—from the press and from individuals as well as from societies."[7]

Madison also described to Monroe the political game being played. The Federalists wanted to connect the insurrection, which everyone condemned, to the democratic societies, and at the same time link the societies to the Republicans. Guilt by association was not the only advantage of this strategy. Presidential attacks on the societies would become attacks on Republicans and position Washington with the Federalists, which would add luster to their cause. This multistage scenario flowed easily from Madison's complicated mind, as did what he saw—mistakenly, it would turn out—as the final outcome. "The result," he wrote, "cannot fail to wound the president's popularity more than anything that has yet happened."[8] The president's reputation with the people would turn out to be remarkably resilient.

The administration had many supporters in the House, and Madison was hard pressed to keep the representatives' response to the president's address from heaping further condemnation on the democratic societies. On the floor of the House chamber, he noted that it was not the business of the House to censure viewpoints that members of the societies expressed. "Opinions are not the objects of legislation," he declared, and he warned fellow members of the slippery slope. "How far will this go?" he asked. "It may extend to the liberty of speech and of the press." He managed to water down criticism of the democratic societies, and the next day at noon, he and two others walked to the handsome brick house that the president rented on Market Street and presented the House response.[9]

The president was polite but firm in reply: Forces that fomented unrest should be universally condemned. As he had written to his cousin Burgess Ball, the societies had no business criticizing "acts of Congress, which have undergone the most deliberate and solemn discussion by the representatives of the people." They dared to declare, "*This act* is unconstitutional—and *that act* is pregnant of mischief." Doing so worked "to destroy all confidence in the administration." Washington believed, as did most Federalists, that the responsibility of citizens was to vote and leave those whom they elected to govern in peace. Madison thought that this attitude came from a presumption "that mankind are incapable of governing themselves."[10]

Jefferson blamed Washington's advanced years for the errors of his second term. "His memory was already sensibly impaired by age, the firm tone of mind for which he had been remarkable was beginning to relax, its energy was abated, a listlessness of labor, a desire for tranquility had crept on him and a willingness to let others act and even think for him." Washington had confessed many of these failings to Jefferson, and the Lansdowne portrait done from life by Gilbert Stuart in 1796 seems to confirm them. Washington is sixty-four, about the age that the other members of the Virginia dynasty would be in their second terms, but he looks older. He projects no energy, and his eyes are locked in a blank stare. His lips are pressed together, and the area around them oddly swollen. Stuart pointed out that Washington had recently received a new set of dentures and said that he "wanted him as he looked at the time."[11]

New, ill-fitting dentures were one more burden for the president. He had lost his last tooth, which had anchored his old dentures, and the new set, probably made of ivory, was uncomfortable, unstable, and caused his face to bulge.[12] Washington's various sets of dentures were state of the art in his time, but seeing the only surviving example at Mount Vernon today—a rude contraption— one wonders how he managed to speak while wearing them.

Jefferson believed that Washington's declining health made him increasingly susceptible to the Federalists in his cabinet. Certainly Hamilton had a hand in shaping the view of the democratic societies that Washington laid out for Congress in November 1794. There were American precedents for the societies, such as the Sons of Liberty, but Hamilton encouraged Washington to see their resemblance to the Jacobin Club in Paris, a national organization with branches across France whose radical elements had propelled the French nation into the Reign of Terror.[13]

Washington saw the democratic societies and those who championed them as a threat to the Union. They gave "artificial and extraordinary force" to parties, he said, and parties could become "potent engines, by which cunning, ambitious, and unprincipled men will be enabled to subvert the power of the people and to usurp for themselves the reins of government." Washington saw himself as "disinterested," a word that did not mean "unconcerned" as we might think today, but rather "objective" or "unbiased." He saw himself as making decisions according to what was just and right, not from self-interest or party interest. Thus attacks on his administration by democratic societies were not challenges by one organized viewpoint to another; they were assaults by a biased group with no official standing on the duly elected government and the fair-minded president at the head of it.[14]

Washington's conviction that criticism of the government undermined the Republic set him apart from the younger members of the Virginia dynasty. They believed that there could be legitimate opposition—and Madison, in particular, was hard at work organizing it.

The dispute over the democratic societies was inflamed by a widening war in Europe. In the early months of 1794, word had reached Philadelphia that the British were seizing American ships sailing to or from the French West Indies with French produce on board. They confiscated the cargo and declared the ships prizes of war. They stripped crews of their clothes and belongings, and threw the men into rusting prison hulks. Congress responded with proposals to build warships and raise an army.

Washington had long favored strengthening the military, but the last thing he wanted was war with Great Britain. He believed that the United States was not yet strong enough to fight and win. Someday, it would likely be. "Twenty years peace," he wrote, "with such an increase of population and resources as we have a right to expect, added to our remote situation from the jarring powers, will in all probability enable us in a just cause to bid defiance to any power on earth."[15] But in 1794, as he saw it, war was out of the question.

A breach with Great Britain was also the last thing that Alexander Hamilton wanted. It would destroy his economic program, he told Washington, by interfering "with the payment of the duties which have heretofore accrued and bring the Treasury to an absolute stoppage of payment—an event which would cut up credit by the roots." Hamilton knew that Washington intended to nominate an envoy to Great Britain to try to improve relations between that country and the United States. Indeed, Hamilton had been suggested, but he was aware of the controversy that the president's naming him would provoke. He took himself out of the running and recommended the chief justice of the Supreme Court, John Jay, a tall, slender New Yorker, who despite his exceedingly grave mien, revealed more than a touch of vanity in the apparel he chose for a sitting with Gilbert Stuart—a showy garment decorated with great swathes of salmon-colored silk that he had received from Harvard four years before.[16]

The democratic societies immediately weighed in against Jay for his well-known Federalist tilt toward Great Britain. They also took up the cause of Kentuckians and others living on the frontier. These southerners and "westerners," as they were called, had not forgiven Jay for the agreement he reached with Spain while serving as foreign secretary to the Confederation Congress. He and Diego de Gardoqui, the Spanish minister, had agreed that the United States should forgo its navigation rights on the Mississippi

River for thirty years in exchange for a commercial treaty with Spain. Such an agreement would have meant disaster for those who depended on the Mississippi for trade and transport, and Congress rejected it.

Despite substantial opposition, Jay won Senate confirmation and by July 1794 had arrived in London, set up housekeeping in the Royal Hotel in London's West End, and was being lavishly entertained by Lord Grenville, Great Britain's shrewd secretary of state for foreign affairs. Grenville had learned from one of Jay's associates that the chief justice might be "attached by good treatment," a perception no doubt underscored by the affair of the Spanish horse. The king of Spain had presented Jay with an Andalusian stallion during negotiations between Spain and the United States. Jay, aware that the emoluments clause of the Articles of Confederation forbade gifts from "any king, prince, or foreign state," suggested that Congress approve the gift of the horse and consider it in tandem with a miniature portrait of Louis XVI set in diamonds given to Benjamin Franklin by the French king. Associating his gift with the eighty-year-old Franklin's cast a pleasant glow upon it, and on March 3, 1786, Congress permitted both men to keep their presents.[17]

Jay's instructions for negotiating with Great Britain in 1794 were delivered to him by Edmund Randolph, whom Washington had moved from being attorney general to secretary of state after Jefferson's retirement. The instructions had been framed by Hamilton, however. Since Jefferson's departure he had dominated not only the Treasury, but also the State Department.

Jay was instructed to "repel war," while at the same time seeking compensation for American losses at sea for which the British were responsible. Jay was also to try to bring the British into compliance with the peace treaty of 1783 by having their troops depart the posts they still occupied on the American frontier. In addition, the instructions allowed for a commercial treaty with Great Britain that would result in the recognition of the neutral rights of the United States.[18]

Randolph managed to give Jay an important bargaining chip, inserting in his instructions that he could approach Sweden and Denmark about joining in a pact to defend with arms the rights of neutral ships. Hamilton decided that pressing such a point might complicate negotiations and passed word to Lord Grenville that the United States had no intention of becoming entangled in European alliances. Thus he gave the British reason to harden their stance—and made Jay's task more difficult.[19]

Meanwhile, former senator James Monroe; his wife of eight years, the former Elizabeth Kortright; and their seven-year-old daughter, Eliza, were settling into a furnished hotel on the Rue de Richelieu.[20] With them was Joseph Jones Jr., whose birth fifteen years before had caused Monroe so much angst. Now Joseph Jones Sr. had charged him with the Sisyphean task of civilizing the teenager.

George Washington had appointed Monroe, a known friend of France, as U.S. envoy to allay the consternation that Jay's appointment was causing to the French government. Monroe knew that he had not been the president's first choice. Robert Livingston of New York, whose politics mirrored Monroe's, had turned the post down, explaining that "differing so much as I do from the . . . administration, I am satisfied that I would either be compelled to violate my own principles by yielding to theirs or risk my reputation by incurring their resentment."[21] Monroe would come to see the wisdom of this advice, but unpersuaded at the time, he had accepted the president's appointment.

The Monroes arrived in Paris less than a week after the National Convention, the governing body of France, had arrested and executed revolutionary leader Maximilien Robespierre. The result was to end the Reign of Terror, but violence lingered. Robespierre's associates were guillotined, as were eighty-seven members of the Paris Commune.

Envoys were required to present their diplomatic credentials, but amid the turmoil, Monroe could not get the attention of the Committee of Public Safety, which had served as the executive of the French government for more than a year. He decided to write directly to the National Convention to announce his presence and was quickly invited to attend the Convention's proceedings in the Tuileries Palace. On August 15, 1794, he was escorted into the Salle des Machines, an enormous space that had once been a royal theater fitted out with elaborate stage machinery. The three-story hall was lined with statues of ancient lawgivers and surrounded by graceful balconies, which in the days before the Revolution had been the purview of the aristocracy. Now they were crowded with citizens from the Paris streets.[22]

Monroe and the Americans who accompanied him were greeted with wild applause and shouts of "Live the Convention! Live the United States of America, our brave brothers!" A Marylander in Monroe's party noted, "We were in fact received more like beings of a superior nature than men."[23]

Monroe's remarks lavished praise on the French, even commending their troops, who were having remarkable success in a war in which enemies now included England, Spain, Austria, Prussia, and the Netherlands. Monroe assured Convention delegates that the government of the United States was not an "unfeeling spectator" of their war with Europe's monarchies and proved his point by submitting letters that conveyed the warm best wishes of Congress and declared the affection of the United States. In a covering note, Secretary of State Randolph had written, "The successes of those who stand forth as [liberty's] avengers will be gloried in by the United States and will be felt as the successes of themselves and the other friends of humanity." The president of the United States, Monroe told the delegates, shared these warm sentiments.[24]

In his response, the president of the Convention, Merlin de Douai, took a swipe at England, dubbing it "now debased Albion," and called the alliance of France and the United States "the sweetest and most honest fraternity." To signify the close relationship, Douai bestowed the *accolade* upon Monroe, an embrace and kiss that sent the audience into paroxysms of joy.[25]

Monroe suspected that his Convention appearance would cause a stir back home, but Secretary of State Randolph's response to it stung nonetheless. Randolph criticized the address's "extreme glow" and all-too-public presentation. Why had Monroe failed to keep in mind the American policy of neutrality, Randolph asked, or the impact his words would have on England? "You have it still in charge to cultivate the French Republic with zeal," Randolph wrote, "but without any unnecessary éclat, because the dictates of sincerity do not demand that we should render notorious all our feelings in favor of that nation."[26]

Monroe was convinced his remarks had been no more glowing than Secretary Randolph's note. As he saw it, his speech was also in tune with the instructions Randolph had given him before he had sailed for France: to cultivate the French, show confidence in the Republic, and even promise "that in case of war with any nation on earth, we shall consider France as our first and natural ally." Had he been expected to smuggle in such professions of friendship and whisper them in a few ears? To do that, Monroe rationalized, would be duplicitous.[27]

Randolph had also instructed him to allay French concerns about Jay's mission to England. He should say that Jay had a very narrow assignment, mainly to seek reparations and the return of American posts. He should declare that Jay was forbidden from weakening in any way engagements the United States had with France. Monroe did as Randolph instructed, although probably with some uneasiness. He had not been told that Jay had permission to negotiate a commercial treaty, but the idea was in the air. Such an agreement could easily weaken the treaties that the United States had signed with France during the Revolution. Monroe was wary: Was he being used deliberately to mislead the French?[28]

Monroe's duties extended beyond cultivating goodwill. He had hardly arrived in Paris when he began to receive letters from Thomas Paine, who had been born in England but had immigrated to America, fought in the Revolution, and sworn allegiance to the United States. His wildly popular pamphlet *Common Sense*, published early in 1776, had convinced many an American that it was time for the United States to become independent. *The American Crisis*, another of his works, had inspired the men who crossed the Delaware. A slender man who wore his dark brown hair in a ponytail, Paine had subsequently become so committed to the cause of the French Revolution that he was made an honorary citizen of France and even chosen to serve as a delegate to the National Convention. But when Robespierre came to power, Paine had been expelled from the Convention for being an Englishman, arrested, and thrown into Luxembourg prison. He had been there for more than seven months, watching as hundreds of his fellow prisoners were led to the guillotine. He had developed an abscess on his side that made him so ill he nearly died.

Monroe convinced French authorities that Paine was a citizen of the United States, and since that country was allied to France, he should be freed. When Paine was released in November 1794, he was both too poor and too sick to live on his own, and Monroe took him to the American legation. He was not an easy houseguest. In February he wrote a reproachful letter to Washington, whom he thought was his friend, for not intervening to get him out of prison. "In the progress of events," Paine wrote, "you beheld yourself a president in America and me a prisoner in France: you folded your arms, forgot your friend, and became silent." Monroe managed to get the letter suppressed, and when he and Mrs. Monroe purchased (with borrowed money) a small but elegant residence known as the Folie de la Bouexière, Paine moved with them—and brought his indignation along.[29]

In September 1795, Monroe discovered that Paine was writing another letter to Washington, and he and Paine agreed that Paine should move out. He did so and included the letters he had written while Monroe's guest in a bitter and lengthy denunciation of Washington that he published in pamphlet form. Washington was not a great military leader, Paine wrote, except for his "constancy." Horatio Gates was responsible for Saratoga, Nathanael Greene for victories in the South, and the French for Yorktown. Washington was nonetheless highly regarded, and for that Paine had a succinct explanation: "By the advantage of a good exterior he attracts respect, which his habitual silence tends to preserve."[30]

Chastising Washington for not having helped him while he was in prison, Paine observed:

It has some time been known by those who know him that he has no friendships; that he is incapable of forming any; he can serve or desert a man or a cause with constitutional indifference; and it is this cold hermaphrodite faculty that imposed itself upon the world and was credited for a while by enemies as by friends, for prudence, moderation, and impartiality.

France's chargé d'affaires Louis Otto wrote a similar description. Washington had everything a man could want, wrote Otto, "except the sweetnesses of friendship."[31]

When Paine's pamphlet appeared in the United States, the president wrote to a friend that his enemies wanted to see "his character reduced as low as they are capable of sinking it, even by resorting to absolute falsehoods."[32] The pamphlet thoroughly aggravated Washington—exactly as Paine had intended.

Early in his time in Paris, Monroe also heard from Adrienne de Noailles, wife of the Marquis de Lafayette. As Monroe knew, the marquis, who early on had been a central figure in the French Revolution, was now imprisoned in Olmütz, then a part of Austria. After the radicals had risen to power in France and ordered him to trial, he had fled the country, but was soon arrested at an Austrian post in Belgium. Adrienne, still in France, had been arrested not long after, and by the time of Monroe's arrival in August had been confined nearly two years. Her grandmother, mother, and sister, who had also been imprisoned, had been sent to the guillotine. Since the downfall of the radicals, just days before Monroe reached Paris, Adrienne had thought she would be spared, but she wanted her "irons broken," she wrote to Monroe, so that she could be with her children.[33]

When other prisoners were released and Madame Lafayette was not, Monroe and his wife, Elizabeth, decided to draw attention to her plight. Not much is known about Elizabeth Monroe. Her beauty was often remarked upon. She was a native of New York City, who had not yet adopted soft southern ways. A "little too much New York" was the judgment of one of Monroe's friends. She had excellent taste in furniture and clothing and, to judge from her participation in the effort to highlight the injustice visited upon Madame Lafayette, a brave heart as well.

Accompanied by a few servants, Mrs. Monroe rode in a fine carriage to Plessis, a college that had become a prison, where Adrienne was confined in the attic. Mrs. Monroe's arrival excited great interest from the crowd gathered around the prison gate, as did her emotional meeting with the nearly hysterical Adrienne. As James Monroe described the scene in his autobiography:

> The sensibility of all the beholders was deeply excited. The report of the interview immediately spread through Paris and had the happiest effect. Informal communications took place in consequence between Mr. Monroe and the members of the Committee [of Public Safety] and the liberation of Madame Lafayette soon followed.

Upon her release, Madame Lafayette began making arrangements for her son, sixteen-year-old George Washington Lafayette, to travel to America, and for her and her two daughters, Anastasie, eighteen, and Virginie, thirteen, to join her husband in Olmütz. From October 17, 1795, until September 19, 1797, when the entire family was freed, the three women stayed in the prison with him.[34]

Monroe had been instructed to press commercial claims with France. Like the British, only less enthusiastically, France had been seizing American ships, taking their cargoes, and imprisoning their sailors. Monroe argued for a return to terms set forth in the Treaty of Peace and Amity that both countries had signed in 1778, which required that goods on board ships of noncombatant countries be regarded as off-limits. In early January 1795, the Committee of Public Safety decreed that ships of neutral parties, as well as the goods and passengers they carried, could henceforth "sail in all security."[35] The French government also committed to compensation for damages caused by the French navy.

Monroe brought off this diplomatic achievement after he had been in France less than four months, but his job, which would last another year and a half, was about to grow very difficult. The problem began when reports reached Paris that John Jay had completed a treaty with England—exactly what Monroe had told the French government would not happen. He hurried to assure the Committee that such reports could not be true; Jay's mission was a decidedly narrow one. He also expressed disbelief to the secretary of state: Given the professions of friendship that he, Monroe, had been instructed to offer the French government, a treaty with Britain that would come between the United States and France "would be an act of perfidy, the example of which was perhaps never seen before."[36]

Then he heard from Jay. Yes, he had completed a treaty, Jay wrote, but it was not cause for concern, because it did not affect provisions of the 1778 treaty with France. Monroe passed these reassurances along to the Committee and, no doubt embarrassed at how two-faced he had been made to seem, promised that he would provide specifics as soon as he learned of them.[37]

When Jay learned of Monroe's commitment, he objected. The United States should not reveal details of a treaty that had not been ratified. Jay refused to provide Monroe information unless he agreed to keep it confidential. Monroe, for his part, felt honor bound to refuse to receive details of the treaty unless he could share them with the French.[38]

During the impasse, the Jay Treaty was shipped from London to Philadelphia. What would have been a time-consuming journey in any case turned out taking four months. The first ship, transporting two copies of the treaty, was attacked and the treaties thrown overboard lest they fall into the wrong hands. A second ship carrying a copy encountered strong headwinds. When it finally reached North America, it did not land in the expected port, and the treaty had to be carried overland by a messenger whose horse foundered. By the time he reached the capital by stagecoach, it was March 7, 1795. Congress was not in session, nor would it be for another three months.[39]

Madison had suspected the treaty would be unfavorable to the United States. He had observed to Jefferson that Jay would give up a great deal "to avoid returning with his finger in his mouth." The treaty was surrounded with secrecy once it reached Philadelphia, but Madison soon had the broad outlines of it, and once the Senate convened, he began receiving a leaked copy in installments. Once or twice a week a post rider delivered pages of the document to Montpelier until Madison had the entire treaty.[40]

Article 1 was an innocuous profession of friendship, and article 2 a commitment on the part of the British to return the western posts, a good thing, but they were delaying the handover until June 1796. The more Madison read, the worse matters grew. One article opened trade with the West Indies, but on unacceptably harsh terms. Another undercut established U.S. policy that all goods in neutral ships must be considered neutral by setting out a program for searching for and seizing enemy goods, including foodstuffs, being carried by neutral ships. With a drought going on in Britain, Lord Grenville had seen the usefulness of diverting grain being carried to France by American ships to the hungry citizens of England.

Article 15, which forbade the United States from imposing trade restrictions on Great Britain for twelve years, would have made it impossible for Madison and Jefferson to achieve something they had long thought justice demanded, which was for trade restrictions imposed by Britain on the United States to be matched by American restrictions on British trade. The prohibition in article 15 also meant that the United States could not use trade as a weapon against British aggression on the seas. For the United States to give up such powers for a decade, Madison later wrote, was among the treaty's many "shameful concessions."[41]

The treaty passed by a vote margin of 20 to 10, exactly the two-thirds needed and no more. Madison reported to Monroe on the secrecy that had surrounded the Senate's debate and recounted how Virginia senator Stevens Mason had defied the policy of secrecy by sending a copy of the treaty to the *Aurora,* a Republican-leaning newspaper, "from whence," Madison wrote, "it flew with an electric velocity to every part of the Union" and was "universally and simultaneously" assailed. In Boston, a crowd boarded a British privateer, chopped down its masts, dismantled the cabin, and burned the hull. In New York, Alexander Hamilton, trying to defend the treaty before a hostile crowd in Broad Street, was struck in the head by a rock.[42]

Washington had thought from first reading that the treaty was weak, a judgment underscored by historians. Few contemporaries stood up for it, historian Henry Adams noted, and in later years he wrote, "No one would venture on its merits to defend it." The president was nonetheless taken aback by the public outcry. In a letter marked "Private and perfectly confidential," he sought Hamilton's advice, even though the New Yorker had retired from the administration six months before. Hamilton responded promptly and at length, pointing out faults, but arguing that merits outweighed them. The treaty, Hamilton opined, would preserve peace for the United States.[43]

Before Washington signed the document the British returned to their bad behavior, seizing grain cargoes from American ships sailing to France. How could he sign? asked Secretary of State Randolph, who was often the voice of caution. When Hamilton had urged the president to send troops into western Pennsylvania, Randolph's recommendations had delayed the invasion for more than a month. He put one obstacle after another in front of the Jay Treaty, but for all the frustration he caused, his advice to delay made good sense. The president took Randolph's recommendation even though the rest of the cabinet was urging him to sign.[44] He trusted a man he had known since the beginning days of the Revolution, when he had appointed the young Randolph as one of his aides-de-camp.

Later Washington had entrusted personal legal affairs to Randolph and sent two of his nephews to study law with him. The president wrote to Madison that he preferred Randolph "to any person I am acquainted of not superior abilities, from habit of intimacy with him."[45] It was a bit of backhanded compliment to note that there were better lawyers, but still an endorsement for the president to place his trust in Randolph.

When he had needed a new secretary of state, Washington had pressed the departing Jefferson for his opinion of Randolph, drawing from him an observation that the younger man's financial situation was so dire that people had begun to worry about "his character of independence." Jefferson was unhappy with Randolph, whose vote he could never be sure of in the cabinet. In a letter to Madison, he called him "the poorest chameleon I ever saw, having no color of his own and reflecting that nearest him." But Jefferson's analysis of his financial affairs was correct. Randolph had been stretched thin since early manhood, when his father John "the Tory" had disinherited him for his loyalty to the American cause.[46]

Washington had nevertheless chosen Randolph as Jefferson's successor. The new secretary of state tried faithfully to do what he believed the president wanted (which was not always what Jefferson wanted) and soon was a trusted adviser. But as Washington was deciding whether to sign the Jay Treaty, Secretary of War Timothy Pickering, a stern-faced New Englander, showed him a dispatch that the British had captured. In it, Jean-Antoine Fauchet, France's departing minister to the United States, reported on the political situation in America and attributed much of what he communicated to Randolph. One could conclude from Fauchet's letter that the secretary of state had been remarkably indiscreet. One could also conclude—though it was not necessary to do so—that he had solicited a bribe, a charge to which Jefferson's warning about his financial distress lent credence.

The letter was amateurishly translated and incomplete, referring to other dispatches that were not at hand.[47] Fauchet also seemed to be puffing his own importance, which should have made Washington wary, as should the conspiratorial air the French minister assumed, seemingly in an effort to make himself seem worldly and sophisticated.

Despite these warning signs, Washington did not pause to order an investigation or even a formal hearing. Instead, he quickly reversed himself on the Jay Treaty, signing it even as the British continued seizing American ships. Randolph, although disappointed, worked tying up loose ends, and when he was finished, Washington called him in. The president handed him the dispatch (about which Randolph knew nothing) and asked him to explain it, as Secretary of War Timothy Pickering and Oliver Wolcott, who had succeeded Hamilton as secretary of the Treasury, looked on. Angered at what he called this "tribunal of inquiry," Randolph departed and sent in his letter of resignation.[48]

Benjamin Bache's newspaper, the *Aurora*, said that the president had reversed himself on the treaty "in a fit of bad humor occasioned by an enigmatical intercepted letter." Madison, writing to Monroe, questioned the connection. How could an intercepted dispatch make the Jay Treaty any better or excuse Britain's seizing provisions headed to France? It was a reasonable question, but perhaps irrelevant to the president's decision. Washington may have been driven by anger at the inside picture of his administration that he believed Randolph had painted for Fauchet: the divisions within, the dominance of Hamilton, and Washington's acceding to him in raising troops and invading Pennsylvania. The best way to undercut these unflattering descriptions was to discredit the man who had ostensibly made them—which was also the best way to distance himself from a subordinate who might possibly be accused of treason. Not waiting for charges or judicial determinations was uncharitable to Randolph, but Washington was not the first leader—nor would he be the last—to ignore the welfare of an underling in service to a cause he believed more important.[49] It may also be that Washington had little tolerance for those whom he perceived as weak.

Randolph thought that Washington prejudged the case against him because of a temperament "which under the exterior of cool and slow deliberation rapidly catches a prejudice and with difficulty abandons it." He offered this description in *A Vindication of Edmund Randolph,* a pamphlet he wrote to clear his name. He included in it the documents that Fauchet's dispatch referred to. He tracked down Fauchet, who was departing for France, and obtained from him a denial that Randolph had been indiscreet or possibly traitorous. His contemporaries as well as modern scholars have judged that Randolph exonerated himself, but he went down too many side paths and was too often self-pitying. He also bitterly insulted Washington, suggesting, for example, that he had been led astray by aides who "insidiously pampered" him with "lavish assurances of an affectionate attachment." When *A Vindication* reached Mount Vernon and Washington read it, he exploded. An eyewitness reported that "he threw the pamphlet down and gave way to a terrific burst of denunciation."[50]

Madison wrote to Monroe that Randolph's "greatest enemies will not easily persuade themselves that he was under a corrupt influence of France, and his best friend can't save him from the self-condemnation of his political career." Pickering and Wolcott, whom biographer Irving Brant labeled "two of the most malevolent men who ever decorated a presidential cabinet," made sure that Randolph never recovered his good name by hunting down and holding him responsible for State Department expenditures over which he had no control. Randolph would be haunted by debt for the rest of his life.[51]

Madison knew the risk of taking on the president, but found it impossible to avoid. To his surprise and chagrin, Congressman Edward Livingston of New York, an opponent of the Jay Treaty, introduced a resolution that the president turn over to the House of Representatives the instructions given to John Jay as well as all related papers. Livingston's resolution assumed that the House had a role in treaty making. Although the Constitution laid out no such role, it did reserve certain powers to Congress, assigning to the House specifically the power of the purse. If a treaty required appropriations to put it into effect, as the Jay Treaty did, the House had a role in passing judgment on it, or so the argument went.

Madison agreed that the House had this prerogative, but had hoped to make the point in a more conciliatory way and avoid a direct confrontation with the president. Madison tried to soften Livingston's resolution with an amendment to give the president discretion about what he turned over, but the amendment failed. Livingston's resolution passed 62 to 37.[52]

Washington was determined to protect executive power. In addition, he had been warned by Hamilton that there were things in

Jay's instructions "inexpedient to communicate."[53] Was Hamilton concerned, perhaps, that the papers would expose his overarching role?

The president refused to turn over the papers and sent a sharp message. "The power of making treaties is exclusively vested in the president, by and with the advice and consent of the Senate," he wrote. The House had no role in treaty making, he said, and no reason to demand the papers—unless members wished to impeach him. Should anyone doubt where authority for treaty making lay, he had deposited the official journal of the Constitutional Convention with the State Department. In it one could clearly see that the convention had voted down a proposition requiring that treaties be ratified by laws.[54]

Chief Justice John Marshall, who knew Washington, Jefferson, and Madison, later wrote that this message "appeared to break the last cord of that attachment which had theretofore bound some of the active leaders of the opposition to the president personally." Madison was certainly one of those leaders. The president's constitutional disagreement with him was one thing, but the imperious tone of his message was "improper and indelicate," he wrote to Jefferson, and he bridled at the reference to the Constitutional Convention. It was off point, for one thing. The House had not asserted a right to assent to or deny *all* treaties, only those that required legislation to put them into effect. Moreover, the president had not been entrusted with the official journal of the convention so that he might do what he wished with it. The convention had declared that he act only on the order of Congress.[55]

Federalists were less concerned with accuracy than with making a political point. They seized on the president's reference to show that Madison had been disingenuous to argue that the House had a role in the treaty process. Wrote Federalist Fisher Ames, "Madison is deeply implicated by the appeal of the president to the proceedings of the General Convention, and most persons think him irrevocably disgraced as a man void of sincerity and fairness."[56]

The House nevertheless passed resolutions affirming the institution's prerogatives and did so by a substantial margin. When members moved on to take up consideration of appropriations to fund the treaty, Madison took to the floor to strike out at those who argued that it had to be put into effect to prevent war with Britain. How could that be? he asked. The French had been remarkably successful in battling Europe's monarchies, while Great Britain, struck by drought and hobbled by war, was torn by bread riots. "Was it conceivable," he asked, "that Great Britain, with all the dangers and embarrassments which are thickening upon her, would wantonly make war on a country which was the best market she had in the world for her manufactures?" It would require "a degree of madness," Madison declared.[57]

Few historians have teased out this line of thought and examined its merits. An exception is Joseph Charles, who argued:

We may seriously question whether Great Britain would have wished to acquire another enemy. To bring about war with us in 1795 or 1796, she would have had to take the initiative in a way in which she did not have to either in 1775 or in 1812. This war would have been against her heaviest debtor and her best customer at a time when she was on the verge of bankruptcy, against the country which was her one certain source of food at a time when provisions were desperately scarce and very expensive.

The consensus has been that had the treaty failed, the country would have found itself at war, and that bad as the treaty was, it served, in Samuel Flagg Bemis's words, "to postpone hostilities to another remove and to give the United States in the meantime an opportunity to develop in population and resources."[58]

Certainly the war argument was used to great effect at the time, particularly by Fisher Ames, who predicted "tempest and war" if the treaty failed. He painted a dramatic picture of carnage in the Northwest Territory, where British-occupied posts had been centers for Indian unrest and would continue to be unless the treaty went forward:

> In the daytime, your path through the woods will be ambushed; the darkness of midnight will glitter with the blaze of your dwellings. You are a father: the blood of your sons shall fatten your cornfield! You are a mother: the war-whoop shall wake the sleep of the cradle!

So sustained was the onslaught that Madison's majority melted away, and the House approved appropriations for the treaty 51 to 48. Wrote Madison to Jefferson, "The people have been everywhere made to believe that the object of the House of Representatives in resisting the treaty was—*War;* and have thence listened to the summons 'to follow where Washington leads.'"[59]

Madison also told Jefferson that the treaty fight was "the most worrying and vexatious that I ever encountered," and it took a visible toll. Madison looked "worried to death," John Adams observed. "Pale, withered, haggard." The treaty loss had one benefit, Madison explained, and that was the effect of "riveting my future purposes."[60] He had been thinking of retiring from Congress, but now he was certain.

Madison knew that his personal relationship with the president, long strained, was at an end, but he had no idea of the depths of Washington's anger. The president had begun work on his Farewell Address, and he was determined to use it to point out what he believed was Madison's hypocrisy. When he had thought of retiring at the end of his first term, he had asked Madison to write a farewell for him. Now at the end of his second term, he wanted to quote the earlier address in its entirety to show that Madison, who had fervently opposed extensions of federal power as "monarchical," knew that he, Washington, had not sought to become a king. Quite the opposite, he had tried to give up the presidency in 1792.[61]

Hamilton convinced the president to take another route and wrote an entirely new address in which he took care to condemn ideas that Madison advanced, such as the legitimacy of the democratic societies. Washington urged Americans to "discountenance irregular oppositions to [government's] acknowledged authority."[62] Although his strong condemnation of the societies in 1794 had spelled the end of them, Washington wanted to drive home the point that citizens should not organize in opposition to the duly elected government.

Washington's address is often remembered for its recommendation that the United States "steer clear of permanent alliances with any portion of the foreign world" and seek instead "harmony

[and] liberal intercourse with all nations." Madison could not help but note how much these sentiments were at odds with the bias toward England and disdain for France that the president had shown in his second term. Madison tried as he usually did to shift the blame from the president to those who influenced him. "He [is] completely in the snares of the British faction," he wrote to Monroe. He did wonder how the president had brought himself to "adopt some parts of the performance," so glaringly inconsistent were they with the past.[63]

Washington had no interest in shifting blame away from Republicans. Madison and his ilk, the president wrote, "not only brought the Constitution to the brink of a precipice, but the peace, happiness, and prosperity of the country into eminent danger." Madison had not been invited to Mount Vernon since 1791, and never again would he be. Washington tried to forget Madison's very existence. As historian Stuart Leibiger has noted, Washington, once he had retired to Mount Vernon, "never again even mentioned Madison's name in his letters or writings."[64]

Like Madison, Jefferson described Washington as a good man misled into bad measures, and he observed that the president was extraordinarily effective at advancing those measures because his character was so widely admired. During the fight over the Jay Treaty, Jefferson used a line from *Cato*, the president's favorite play, to describe his frustration with Washington: "Curse on his virtues, they've undone his country."[65]

Jefferson distinguished between public and private criticism of

Washington—once in a letter to the commander in chief himself. Hearing that someone was trying to "sow tares" between him and Washington, he wrote to assure the chief executive that he was not engaged "in turbulence and intrigue against the government." He went on to add that he had never conceived that in private he had any requirement "to belie my sentiments nor even to conceal them. When I am led by conversation to express them, I do it with the same independence here which I have practiced everywhere and which is inseparable from my nature."[66] When it came to sowing tares, Jefferson set the example. The letter essentially admitted that he had criticized Washington in private—and asserted his right to do so.

Washington's response, like his letter to Joseph Reed many years before, was, in the beginning at least, utterly polite on the surface but throbbing with anger underneath. Now that Jefferson had mentioned it, he wrote, people had told him that the former secretary of state described him as "under a dangerous influence." He told those people that such a thing was impossible, because unless Jefferson was a hypocrite, he would have come to him with his concern. Besides, Jefferson had only to review the years he had been secretary of state to see that Washington had yielded his decision making to no one: "Abundant proofs would occur to him that truth and right decisions were the *sole* objects of my pursuit."[67]

Washington dropped the mask of politeness when he turned to the subject of political parties, which Jefferson had helped Madison create and lead. Partisans had gone to unimaginable lengths, Washington said, criticizing him while he was trying to keep the nation from a devastating war. He had never imagined, he said, "that every act of my administration would be tortured, and the grossest and most insidious misrepresentations of them be made (by giving one side *only* of a subject and that too in such exaggerated and indecent terms as could scarcely be applied to a Nero, a notorious defaulter, or even to a common pickpocket)."[68]

This exchange of letters was one of the last between Washington and Jefferson. They would cross paths when Washington's successor was inaugurated, but once the president retired to Mount Vernon, they never saw one another again.[69]

At about the same time that Washington dressed down Jefferson, he recalled Monroe from Paris. Secretary of State Timothy Pickering, unusually skilled at intercepting letters, had gotten his hands on one written by Monroe, in which America's envoy to France offered to write about U.S. policy in France for a Republican newspaper—anonymously, of course.[70] Washington, not surprisingly, decided it was time for a new envoy.

Monroe knew nothing about his letter being intercepted. His only hint of the reason he was being relieved of his post was a letter from Pickering saying that the president was dissatisfied that he had not done a better job of persuading the French government to accept the Jay Treaty.[71]

Monroe was furious. How could the Directory, now the official government of France, be content with an agreement that exposed French property on board U.S. ships to British seizure, while the 1778 treaty between the United States and France protected British property on U.S. ships from French seizure? How could the Directors accept the double-dealing of the United

States, in which he had been made to play an unwitting part? And given that French aid had rescued the American Revolution, how could they not resent the United States turning against them and toward England? Monroe made plain the bitterness he felt toward Washington in a letter to Madison. "Most of the monarchs of the earth practice ingratitude in their transactions with other powers ... but Mr. W. has the merit of transcending not the great men of the ancient republics, but the little monarchs of the present day in preaching it as a public virtue."[72]

Monroe was eager to vindicate himself, but soon after arriving back in the United States, he was diverted by a very angry Alexander Hamilton. James Callender, a driven, misanthropic, and very talented writer from Scotland, had published a pamphlet reviving the old charge that Hamilton had speculated while he was Treasury secretary. Hamilton was convinced that Monroe, who had been one of the members of Congress who had inquired about the matter five years before, had leaked information to Callender about payments he had made to James Reynolds. Letters flew back and forth until a duel seemed imminent, and Monroe asked a friend to intervene. That friend, Aaron Burr, who would kill Hamilton in a duel seven years later, succeeded in averting one between Monroe and Hamilton.[73]

Hamilton, meanwhile, put the charges of speculation behind him by writing a pamphlet of his own, one in which he made public what he had confessed to the congressmen. Instead of being a speculator, he wrote, he was an adulterer. He did have the grace to say that the confession made him blush.[74]

SIX

Interregnum

∞

The President from Braintree

The two men stepped out of the President's House into a cold March wind. It was shortly after the inaugural of 1797, and they had dined with former president George Washington, who had not yet left Philadelphia. As the two headed east on Market Street, backs to the wind, they were an oddly matched pair. The one walking next to the townhouses was as short and round as the other, walking next to the street, was tall and lanky.[1]

They were mismatched politically as well as physically. The framers of the Constitution had made no provision for political parties to field tickets listing candidates for both president and vice president. Every elector cast two votes, and the presidency and vice presidency went to those who finished first and second, no matter their party. And so it happened that the shorter of the men, recently inaugurated president John Adams, was a Federalist. His companion, the new vice president, Thomas Jefferson, was a Republican. Their administration would be the only one in American history in which the president and vice president were of different parties.[2]

Jefferson's supporters had intended him for the top slot, with New Yorker Aaron Burr to be his number two. But when Jefferson finished second (and Burr fourth), he had graciously accepted the outcome, composing a letter to Adams in which he declared, "I leave to others the sublime delights of riding in the storm, better pleased with sound sleep and a warm berth below, with the society of neighbors, friends, and fellow laborers of the earth than of spies and sycophants." After wishing the president-elect an administration "filled with glory and happiness," Jefferson sent the letter not to Adams but to his friend James Madison for review. Madison worried that rather than improving the relationship between the two men, the letter could worsen it. Adams was a prickly sort, Madison observed, and might take Jefferson's commentary about "the sublime delights of riding in the storm" as a slap at his ambition. Moreover, wrote the politically savvy Madison, Republicans were likely to oppose Adams during his time in office, leading to "real embarrassments from giving written possession to him of . . . compliment and confidence."[3] The letter never made it to the president-elect.

Jefferson, who had spent the last three years at Monticello, did not think it was necessary for him to travel to Philadelphia to be sworn in as vice president, but he decided to go anyway. He wanted to reach out to Adams, with whom he had served on the committee to draft the Declaration of Independence in 1776. They had been diplomats in Europe together and enjoyed one another's company despite political differences. Jefferson remained convinced, he wrote Madison, "of the rectitude of his heart."[4]

Jefferson called on Adams as soon as he reached Philadelphia, and the president-elect returned the favor the next day. In a private conversation, he talked to Jefferson about his concerns over a rupture with France. The Directory seemed to be looking for ways to punish the United States for concluding the Jay Treaty with England, and Adams sought advice on sending a delegation to Paris. Would Madison agree to be part of it? Jefferson told Adams that the former congressman had turned down a similar opportunity, and although he did not tell the president-elect the reason for Madison's refusal, he knew that Madison worried that during one of his seizures he would fall overboard. He assured Adams that he would ask.[5]

Now as they walked along Market Street after dining with former president Washington, Vice President Jefferson told President Adams that Madison would refuse an assignment to France. The president said that it made no difference. He had changed his mind. He had kept the Federalists who had served in Washington's cabinet, including Timothy Pickering and Oliver Wolcott, and they had objected to a Madison appointment, even threatened to resign.[6] Adams had put aside his interest in reaching across party lines.

The two men parted when Jefferson turned off on Fifth Street toward his lodgings. The president continued on Market Street, headed for the hotel where he would stay until Washington left for Mount Vernon. Adams, Jefferson reported, "never after that said one word to me on the subject or ever consulted me as to any measures of the government."[7]

∞

The four-year period from 1797 to 1801 was the only time in the first thirty-six years of the Republic that the presidency was not held by a Virginian. Jefferson's vice presidency, being a cipher, did little to advance the influence of the Virginia dynasty on the governance of the country, and it left Jefferson with few official duties. Free from politics, he indulged his many interests. During his short stay in Philadelphia, he paid fifty cents to see a Bengal elephant on Market Street and bought a nautical atlas. He directed a meeting of the American Philosophical Society, of which he had recently become president, and listened as a member read aloud a paper Jefferson had written on the *Megalonyx*. On the basis of bones discovered in what is now West Virginia, he had concluded (mistakenly) that clawed carnivores three times the size of lions had once roamed North America.[8]

Eleven days after arriving in Philadelphia, he departed for Monticello, but only after paying seventy-five cents to see an elk. He arrived home in time to admire his cherry and peach trees in full bloom and to enjoy the first asparagus and spinach from the garden. Over the next weeks, his correspondence shows, he exchanged grains of barley and kernels of corn with friends, sketched a plan for a prison that provided solitary confinement (considered an enlightened reform), and looked for information to defend his scholarship in *Notes on the State of Virginia*. He also worked on *A Manual of Parliamentary Practice for the Use of the Senate of the United States*. As vice president, he was president of the Senate, and he wanted to set down on paper the rules by which that

body should abide. And never far from his mind was the recon-
struction of Monticello. In order to construct a dome such as he
had seen in France, he was making plans to tear off the roof.[9]

Little more than a month later, Madison arrived at his Piedmont home. He had retired from Congress, "wearied with public
life," he later wrote, and concerned that Montpelier, in his absence, was in decline. Albemarle County lawyer William Wirt
noted that Madison was unwell: "His constitution had received a
serious shock." Wirt's report suggests that Madison had suffered
in severe form one of the "sudden attacks, somewhat resembling
epilepsy," to which he had long been subject.[10] The natural beauty
of the Piedmont—dogwoods and sweet spire in bloom—would be
a powerful antidote to the pressures of Philadelphia.

Meanwhile, James Monroe was still seething over having been
recalled from his post. He suspected he had been played for a fool,
used to divert the French government while Jay concluded a treaty
with England, and he worried about his prospects. Could he clear
his name? Would the recall plague him for the rest of his days?

Someone trying to predict in the early months of 1797 whether
Jefferson, Madison, and Monroe would play significant national
roles in the years ahead could easily have gotten it wrong. Not
only were the Virginians at a remove from the national scene, the
Republican Party that Madison and Jefferson had created and that
Monroe enthusiastically supported had made little progress, causing a disconsolate Jefferson to observe, "Republicanism must lie
on its oars."[11]

In addition to failing to gain the presidency in 1796, Republicans lost seats in Congress, even from Virginia, where three

Federalists had been elected. John Beckley, a political operative upon whom Republicans depended, had been ousted as clerk of the House of Representatives.[12]

Jefferson complained about a call for a special session of Congress in May but returned to Philadelphia and dutifully listened as President Adams reported on the deteriorating relationship with France. The president recounted how the five-man Directory had refused to receive Charles Cotesworth Pinckney, Monroe's successor as minister of the United States, and had even forced him to leave the country. He also described Monroe's leave-taking, at which the president of France had offered "sentiments . . . studiously marked with indignities towards the government of the United States." These insults, said the president, were a deliberate effort to make the American government unpopular with its own people. He also spoke of a new decree that made American ships fair game for the French navy and privateers. While the administration would continue to try to deal with such threats "by amicable negotiation," defensive measures were also required, said Adams, particularly a reformed militia and a naval establishment.[13]

Adams had a catalog of injuries he could have cited, including the French seizure of more than three hundred American merchant vessels in less than a year, but beating the war drums louder would have made negotiations harder. As far as Thomas Jefferson was concerned, however, the president had gone too far. He was soon writing that Adams "was disposed or perhaps advised to proceed in a line which would endanger the peace of our country." Someone showed Jefferson's letter to a supporter of Adams, who subsequently made notes of what he could recall and sent them to the president. Adams declared Jefferson's statements to be "evidence of a mind soured yet seeking for popularity and eaten to a honeycomb with ambition, yet weak, confused, uninformed and ignorant." At about the same time Jefferson described Adams as "vain, testy, given to excessive self-love, and disinclined to listen to anyone."[14] Gone was the comity of former times.

Jefferson offered his description of Adams to Philippe-André-Joseph de Létombe, the French consul general in Philadelphia, with whom he had several meetings during May and June. He talked to Létombe about the American delegation that President Adams was sending to Paris and recommended that the French government welcome the delegates, prolong the negotiations, and treat the Americans courteously.[15] He assumed that the negotiations would not succeed, but he did not want the Directory to be abrupt and rude. As the case of Charles Cotesworth Pinckney had shown, ill-mannered treatment of U.S. envoys excited American hostility toward the French. Jefferson offered good advice that would be spectacularly ignored.

While he was in Philadelphia, Jefferson also wrote to Aaron Burr, whom Republicans had wanted to be vice president in 1796. At forty-one, Burr was thirteen years younger than the fifty-four-year-old Jefferson. He was five years younger than Madison, whom he had known at Princeton. In his letter to Burr, Jefferson declared his esteem, took up the subject of the president's "war address," and lamented the current state of the national Republican Party. He thought he saw hopes of a revival in New York and said he believed that if they were realized, the nation might avoid the return of British domination.[16]

The special session of May and June 1797 and the letter to Burr marked Jefferson's return to national politics.[17] If Republicans were going to defeat Adams in 1800, Burr needed to be brought along. He had distinguished himself in the Revolution. He was brilliant, charismatic, and, Jefferson knew, irritated that Virginia's electors had given Jefferson twenty electoral votes in 1796, while awarding him just one.

But the darkly handsome Burr was quick to respond to Jefferson's overture. He arrived in Philadelphia within the week so that he and Jefferson could talk about "the gauntlet" that Federalists had thrown down. The two visited with James Monroe before he left for Virginia, and heard his complaints about the impossibility of maintaining good relations with France while the Washington administration had seemed intent on creating a rift. Conversation between Burr and Monroe must have been personal at times. Burr had married Theodosia Prevost, under whose spell both he and Monroe had fallen, but she had died at forty-seven and now he was a widower. The two men surely recalled the lovely and accomplished Theodosia and the long summer days at the Hermitage.[18]

Monroe traveled home to Virginia, where he planned to write a vindication of his time in France. He had been demanding papers from the State Department relating to his recall, thereby signaling his intentions to Washington. After Monroe passed through Alexandria, not far from Mount Vernon, the former president noted sarcastically that Monroe "did not honor me by a call."[19]

∞

In the late summer of 1797, the Madisons and Monroes visited Vice President Jefferson at Monticello. The rebuilding of his home, Jefferson himself admitted, had made it a scene of "noise, confusion, and discomfort." It was also hazardous. His eighteen-year-old daughter, Maria, had fallen through a floor and landed in the cellar—an accident, Jefferson reported, "from which she escaped miraculously without hurt." Madison, who was reconfiguring Montpelier, and Monroe, who planned to build what he called a "cabin castle" on land he had purchased adjacent to Monticello, witnessed home renovation on a grand scale. Jefferson was doubling the size of Monticello. He would soon take off much of the roof to replace it with a dome. Enslaved people were doing most of the work, chipping at mortar in walls Jefferson wanted to come down and packing clay into brick molds for walls Jefferson wanted to put up. They ripsawed logs in a sawpit along Mulberry Row. Nearby was a shop where joiners carved fine decorative work for Monticello.[20]

Jefferson and his guests had business to discuss, including what Jefferson called Monroe's "affair." For a month Monroe had been working on a book-length defense of his service in France, and he wanted advice from both Jefferson and Madison, which they were eager to give.[21]

In a letter after their meeting, Monroe tried out a title for his book on Jefferson: *A View of the Conduct of the Executive of the United States in the Management of the Affairs of those States for the Years 1794, 5, and 6. By an Appeal to the Official Instruction and Correspondence of James Monroe Late Minister*

Plenipotentiary of the United States to the French Republic, to which is Prefixed an Introductory Narrative by the same James Monroe. Jefferson recommended that Monroe revise the title to take out the word "executive" lest people think he was criticizing Washington. Monroe rejected this advice but did have the good sense to pick up on a suggestion from Jefferson that the title was a little long. Monroe cut it from some sixty words to closer to forty.[22]

When *A View* was published in December, Jefferson gave it high marks, writing to Monroe, "It works irresistibly." To Madison he reported that the book was considered "as masterly by all those who are not opposed in principle." Madison responded that those who had read the book inevitably remarked, "If this did not open the eyes of the people, their blindness must be incurable." The problem was that it was almost impossible to get a copy. When he had been in Richmond in January, Madison wrote, "A single copy only had reached that place." In February he told Jefferson that Monroe himself had not seen a printed copy.[23]

Former president Washington was anxious to read the book and twice asked Secretary of State Pickering to send him a copy. He inquired of his correspondents about the book's reception. "What is said of it?" he wrote to Oliver Wolcott, who responded, no doubt to Washington's disappointment, "I [am] sorry to say that *many* applaud it." After he had received a copy, Washington at first denied reading it, which was one way to avoid commenting on it. Sometime in the early months of 1798, he read *A View* carefully and made extensive comments in the page margins. The editors of his papers describe these notes as "the most extended, unremitting, and pointed use of taunts and jibes, sarcasm, and scathing criticism in all of his writings." The former president called Monroe "a mere tool in the hands of the French government." He had been "cajoled—flattered—and made to believe strange things." Washington's Federalist leanings are evident in the notes. He described the controversy over the Jay Treaty as being entirely manufactured by the Republicans: "There was nothing in the treaty which *ought* to have embroiled this Country with France," he wrote. Opposition to it had been fomented by "the French party" in the United States, which had war with Great Britain as a goal. "This and this only was the source of all the discontents."[24]

On one point, Washington had Monroe dead to rights. As envoy to France, Monroe had, indeed, promoted "the views of a party," though Washington's description of that party as "obstructing every measure of the administration" was not accurate.[25] The Republicans had tried mightily, but failed to obstruct the Jay Treaty. Their influence had reached a nadir.

What Washington did not see was that he himself promoted Federalist policies. As Joseph Charles wrote, he should not be blamed "for allying himself with a party, but for not knowing that he had done so."[26]

As for Monroe, he considered getting a wider readership for his book by having it excerpted in newspapers, but in the end he comforted himself, as has many a disappointed author, by saying that popularity had not been his goal. "The book will remain and be read in the course of fifty years, if not sooner," he wrote to Jefferson, "and I think the facts it contains will settle or contribute to settle the opinion of posterity."[27]

Jefferson thought it was foolish to wait on posterity to clear one's name. Believing that Monroe ought to run for office again, he reminded him of the insults that President Adams was tossing his way and emphasized how damaging they were to his reputation. The solution, Jefferson said, was for Monroe to take a seat in the U.S. House of Representatives. There he could make himself known rather than let others define his character. But Monroe declined. He needed the income from his law practice and saw little appeal in serving in a body controlled by Federalists, whose arrogance seemed to increase by the day.[28]

Although Jefferson failed to get Monroe to run for Congress, he did succeed in riling him up. In letters to Madison and Jefferson, Monroe talked about challenging the president to a duel, but he finally concluded that would be unseemly given Adams's age and position. In notes to himself, he even considered challenging Washington, who, in his view, had ultimate responsibility for Adams's insult since he was the one who had recalled him from France. The incident tore open old wounds, and Monroe fulminated against Washington in much the way he had a decade earlier, when he had become convinced that Washington's character was contrived. Now, in a letter that he never sent, Monroe addressed the former president: "If I were to select out from the general and comprehensive roll of your fellow citizens the person who had done most harm to his country for eight or ten years past, it would be yourself."[29]

When President Adams's delegation to France arrived in Paris in October 1797, they found a new foreign minister in place:

Charles Maurice de Talleyrand-Périgord, a brilliant and calculating man who had successfully maneuvered his way through the various permutations of the French Revolution. Although once a bishop of the Catholic Church, Talleyrand had never met a vice he did not relish, and greed came to the fore when the American commissioners appeared in Paris. Through agents, dubbed X, Y, and Z in official dispatches, Talleyrand demanded a bribe. Only after he had the money in hand, the delegation was given to understand, could negotiations begin.

When news of the attempted extortion reached the United States, James Madison could scarcely believe it. "I do not allude to its depravity," he wrote to Jefferson from Montpelier. "Its unparalleled stupidity is what fills one with astonishment." Talleyrand had lived in Philadelphia for two years. He must have known that his venality would come to light and that public exposure would energize France's enemies.[30]

The image of decadent Frenchmen demanding a payoff from upright Americans did indeed lead to a surge of anti-French feeling in the United States—and the lionization of John Adams. The pro-French crowds of five years before were replaced by swarms of young Federalists, their hats adorned with black cockades, flower-shaped ribbons resembling those worn by Washington's army. One Monday afternoon some eight hundred of them marched to the President's House to cheer Adams on. The president, who had long yearned to be a soldier, welcomed them in military uniform, complete with a sword at his side. Two days later, Republicans joined in, wearing tricolor cockades to honor the French Revolution. A punch was thrown, someone was knocked in the head, and the ensuing riot caused Adams to send to the war office for "chests of arms" so that he could defend himself and his family.[31]

Federalist sentiment ruled the day. Congress, slow to improve the nation's military posture, suddenly became busy, not only increasing the size of the regular army, but also creating a provisional army of ten thousand men to be used by the president in case of foreign invasion. Republicans objected to the buildup, as they did to the Department of the Navy, which was created on April 30, 1798. As they saw it, an established military could all too easily devolve into what Madison called "instruments of tyranny."[32]

Congress also authorized the use of force against France, but stopped short of a war declaration. Thus, the nation found itself in an undeclared war, a "Quasi War," or a "half war," as John Adams called it.[33]

Life for Republicans in Federalist-dominated Philadelphia became increasingly uncomfortable. Jefferson long remembered the "brow beatings and insults," as well as the "personal indignities" that came his way. He said that he was "dogged and watched in the most extraordinary manner." To evade Federalist spies along main thoroughfares, he took back roads. When he visited Deborah Logan, whose husband, George, was on a personal peace mission to France and suspected by Federalists of encouraging a French invasion, Jefferson took a roundabout route to the Logan farmhouse, one that took him by the Falls of Schuylkill and down a road to Germantown. When he reached the farmhouse, he passed by the front entrance and entered via a road on the side.[34]

Matters only grew worse as Congress turned attention to the enemy within. Federalists first targeted immigrants, particularly from France, who, it was thought, had foreign allegiances and in any case had shown an unbecoming preference for the Republican Party. Among the laws passed was the Alien Act, giving the president authority to expel any alien of any nation at any time if he thought the person dangerous. As it turned out, only one person was deported, because many who would have been charged leased ships and sailed for France.[35]

On July 14, 1798, John Adams signed a sedition bill criminalizing "false, scandalous, and malicious" statements against the government of the United States, the president, or the Congress. The vice president was unmentioned, meaning that it remained perfectly legal to malign him.[36]

To Jefferson the Sedition Act was clearly part of a political war. "The batteries of slander are fully opened for the campaign to decide the presidential election," he wrote to his sister. The Federalists could attack without worrying about Republican counterattacks, since the Sedition Act made them illegal. On the other side, supporters of the act claimed that at a time of crisis with France, criticism of the government was dangerous. Former president Washington wrote from Mount Vernon that Republicans were trying "to set the people at variance with their government." Unless such activity was "arrested," he wrote, civil discord would ensue, and the Union be destroyed.[37]

Washington's support of the Sedition Act is sometimes overlooked, perhaps because it seems so improbable that the first among the founders would be in favor of suppressing speech. He

was more than an approving observer of the act; he worked behind the scenes to hearten advocates and turn around opponents—
although his efforts did not always turn out as he had hoped.

He leaned hard on a tall, dark-haired Richmond attorney
named John Marshall to run for Congress, no doubt assuming
that a stalwart Federalist such as Marshall would be committed to
the Alien and Sedition Acts. Shortly after announcing for Congress, however, Marshall declared in the Richmond *Virginia Gazette* that if he had been in Congress when the Alien and Sedition
Laws came up, he would have opposed them.[38]

Washington wrote to Marshall, enclosing a pamphlet by Judge
Alexander Addison in which Addison declared the Sedition Act
"not only expedient but necessary." Without such restraint, Addison wrote, it would be "impossible to prevent the corruption of
public opinion or to preserve any government against it." People
might say that they wanted "to hear both sides" in pursuit of the
truth, Addison wrote, but "truth has but one side, and listening to
error and falsehood is indeed a strange way to discover truth."
Washington suggested that Marshall read Addison's pamphlet
and decide whether it cast any light upon the Alien and Sedition
Laws. Marshall's reply, like Washington's letter, was a model of
tact. He did not directly say that he opposed the Sedition Act, but
instead wrote, "However I may regret the passage of one of the
acts complained of, I am firmly persuaded that the tempest has
not been raised by them." He deflected attention from his own
actions by blaming the press. When newspapers were attacked,
Marshall wrote, they flooded the public mind with lies.[39]

Caught up in the Federalist sweep was Benjamin Bache, the

editor of the influential Republican newspaper the *Aurora*. Arrested for statements that tended "to excite sedition," he defended himself in a pamphlet that detailed the many attempts to silence him, including beatings and attacks on his home. He never came to trial because at age twenty-nine, less than three months after his arrest, he died of yellow fever.[40]

Bache's successor at the *Aurora*, William Duane, was arrested for seditious rioting, and when he was found not guilty, a charge of seditious libel was brought. Former president Washington approved the Adams administration's persistence, writing about Duane to Secretary of State Timothy Pickering, "There seems to be no bounds to his attempts to destroy all confidence that the people might and . . . ought to have in their government." When the second attempt to silence Duane failed, the Federalist-controlled Senate weighed in and declared him guilty of "malicious assertions." Only after John Adams left office could Duane breathe easy.[41]

Among the others fined and sentenced for criticizing the president was Congressman Matthew Lyon of Vermont, who had made not-so-veiled references to Adams's "continual grasp for power" and his "unbounded thirst for ridiculous pomp, foolish adulation, and selfish avarice." A homeless man in Massachusetts ran afoul of the law for preaching Republican doctrine in his wanderings about the countryside. A drunken garbage-scow driver in New Jersey was fined and locked up for two months for an opinion he expressed in a bar. Listening to cannon boom as the president and Mrs. Adams passed through Newark, he announced that he did not care if a cannonball were "fired through [the president's] arse."[42]

❧

As the jailings continued, Jefferson and Madison discussed how to respond. Both had hoped that what Jefferson called "the reign of witches" would pass away, but the threat to liberty along a front crucial to freedom had grown so great that they could wait no longer.[43]

With the Federalists controlling the executive and legislative branches, as well as the Supreme Court, there was but one place to turn: the states. By fall 1798, Jefferson and Madison had agreed to write resolutions protesting the acts. They would have others introduce them in state legislatures, not only in Virginia, but also in a neighboring state (which turned out to be Kentucky), thus emphasizing that opposition to the laws spread beyond the Old Dominion. They also agreed to proceed with great secrecy. Jefferson, the sitting vice president, could be impeached for acting against laws passed by Congress and signed by the president. Both men could be punished under the Sedition Act, the very law they were protesting. For more than a decade, their authorships would remain unknown.

The resolves that the two men drafted are a case study in their differences and an example of their influence on one another. Jefferson's Kentucky Resolutions declared that when the federal government promulgated an unconstitutional act, every state had a natural right to "nullify" it. Some prudent soul in the Kentucky legislature struck out the nullification language, making Jefferson's document less inflammatory, though it was still far from mild. It declared, for example, that laws such as the Sedition Act, "unless arrested at the threshold may tend to drive these states into revolution and blood" and furnish "new pretexts for those who wish it to be believed that man cannot be governed but by a rod of iron."[44]

In drafting the Virginia Resolutions, Madison avoided the idea that a state could void an unconstitutional federal law, writing instead that it had the obligation to "interpose," a general term that could simply mean "to protest." Jefferson saw Madison's resolutions as they were on their way to the Virginia legislature and, judging them insufficiently forceful, had them changed to include the language of nullification. Madison likely caught wind of Jefferson's meddling, because shortly before the vote on the resolutions, the words "utterly null, void, and of no force or effect" were stricken. Madison did not rebuke Jefferson for his high-handedness (just as he had not rebuked him when Jefferson had gone behind his back during the states' ratifying conventions), but he did explain the political reality. There was "a reason of great weight" for temperate language. The resolutions were to be sent to other states in hopes they would agree that the Alien and Sedition Acts were unconstitutional. Specifying a remedy for an unconstitutional federal law as controversial as nullification would lessen the chances of getting consensus. Jefferson seemed impressed by Madison's explanation. For the moment, at least, he began to advocate "firmness on our part, but a passive firmness," as well as studied avoidance of "anything rash or threatening."[45]

The states' responses to the Virginia and Kentucky Resolutions began to arrive during the late winter and early spring of 1799 and were overwhelmingly negative. In opposing the Kentucky and Virginia Resolutions, New Hampshire's legislature declared the Alien and Sedition Acts "constitutional and, in the present critical situation of our country, highly expedient." Like New Hampshire, New York folded Virginia's more moderate approach into Kentucky's more radical one, declaring both to be "inflammatory and pernicious."[46] Jefferson and Madison had a steep hill to climb to defend free speech against long-prevailing opinion that it was dangerous, particularly in a time of crisis.

Jefferson recommended to Madison that the Virginia and Kentucky legislatures issue a second set of resolutions to emphasize their disagreement with the criticism leveled against the first set. The new resolutions, Jefferson wrote, should declare "in affectionate and conciliatory language our warm attachment to union," but he also recommended that if the federal government continued to overreach its constitutional powers, Virginia and Kentucky should "sever" themselves from the Union.[47] As Jefferson and Madison began a second year of battling against the Alien and Sedition Acts, Jefferson was ready to push matters to the extreme—and beyond.

Madison made the daylong trip to Monticello, arriving in the afternoon heat, and began yet once again to counsel moderation. Jefferson listened. When he sent a friend who was headed for Kentucky suggestions for that state's second set of resolutions, he wrote that in deference to Madison's judgment, he had "reced[ed] readily" from the idea of separation.[48]

James Monroe, whose nearby house, Highland, was by now habitable, if not finished, attended the Monticello meeting as well. Although he had not been part of devising or promulgating the Kentucky and Virginia Resolutions, he quickly recognized the dangerous territory that his fellow Virginians had entered. When Jefferson proposed a trip to Montpelier to consult with Madison,

Monroe warned him off. A meeting between public figures of the highest profile could not be kept secret and "would certainly compromit you both." The visit was canceled.[49]

Prudence was not enough to ensure the success of their plan. When the legislators of Kentucky issued a declaration in 1799, they chose to use the word "nullification," which together with the idea of dissolving the Union would echo down the years to the Civil War—and beyond.[50]

In 1798 and 1799, while Madison and Jefferson were fighting the Alien and Sedition Acts, George Washington was again commander in chief. President Adams had appointed him to head "all the armies raised or to be raised for the service of the U.S." in connection with the Quasi War, and although Adams did so without asking, the sixty-six-year-old Washington accepted. He spent five weeks in Philadelphia engaged in military planning that included everything from how many artillery companies should be stationed at New York, Boston, and Cape Fear, to what uniforms soldiers should wear. The commander in chief's coat was to be blue "with yellow buttons and gold epaulets each having three silver stars." He would be further distinguished by "a white plume in the hat."[51]

One of the pleasures of Philadelphia for Washington was the company of Eliza Powel, who was fifty-five years old and a widow now. She and Washington had stayed in touch since his presidency ended. In one exchange of letters, she told him that inside a writing desk that she had purchased from him, she had discovered "love letters of a lady addressed to you." She then confessed that the letters were ones Martha had written him. Washington tried to respond with humor, writing that he would have been troubled to learn that he had left love letters lying around—if he had any love letters to leave lying around. Then came a remarkable statement. Should Martha's letters to him have "fallen into more inquisitive hands," he wrote, "the correspondence would, I am persuaded, have been found to be more fraught with expressions of friendship than of *enamored* love."[52] Even if his relationship with Martha was more friendship than romance, it is doubtful that she would have appreciated his telling Eliza Powel.

Mrs. Washington had not been educated in the niceties of letter writing. She had a friendly way of putting her thoughts on paper that paid little attention to punctuation, and she spelled words with even more abandon than was usual in the eighteenth century. During his presidency, Washington had begun to draft her letters to important persons, including Eliza Powel, and Martha copied them to send. The practice continued into his retirement. Mrs. Powel had promised not to read the letters she found in the desk, and Washington surely hoped she would not. For the elegant Eliza to encounter the unvarnished Martha was something he wanted to avoid.[53]

Washington saw Eliza several times while he was in Philadelphia. They had breakfast and tea together, though he entered neither event in his diary. She bought him a set of prints and at his request presents for him to take back to Mount Vernon: a $7.00 thread case for Martha; a $65.00 piece of muslin for Martha's nineteen-year-old granddaughter, Nelly Custis; and a doll costing $2.50 for Martha's great-granddaughter, almost-two-year-old Eliza Law.[54]

As the time of his departure neared, Eliza lost her usual good cheer. Life was unlikely to bring them together again, and that prospect filled her with sadness. "My heart is so sincerely afflicted and my ideas so confused that I can only express my predominant wish—that God may take you into his holy keeping and preserve you safe both in traveling and under all circumstances, and that you may be happy here and hereafter is the ardent prayer of your affectionate, afflicted friend."[55]

His response to her emotional outpouring was gracious and formal: "For your kind and affectionate wishes, I feel a grateful sensibility and reciprocate them with all the cordiality you could wish, being my dear Madame your most obedient and obliged humble servant."[56]

She invited him to dinner, but he courteously declined, citing the press of business. He had promised to call on her before he left for Mount Vernon, but he did not. They never saw one another again.[57]

The Philadelphia visit reminded Washington that he was subordinate to President Adams, a fact that he found irritating. When he wanted Hamilton to be his second-in-command, Adams, who had lost all trust in the New Yorker, refused. Washington, spurred on by Hamilton, wrote an outraged letter to Adams that never quite said but made perfectly clear that unless Hamilton received the top appointment, Adams would have to find himself another commander in chief.

Adams gave in, and since Washington had said that he had no

intention of taking to the field until the army was "in a situation to require my presence," Hamilton became de facto commander. He had many grand ideas for how to use his power, including against southern enemies. When arch-Federalist Theodore Sedgwick, a senator from Massachusetts, called the resolutions of Virginia and Kentucky "little short of a declaration of war," Hamilton agreed. "When a clever force has been collected," he wrote to Sedgwick, "let them be drawn towards Virginia." And that was just the beginning. There were European colonies to be liberated in both Americas. Louisiana and East and West Florida were ripe for seizure.[58] The army could be put to many a splendid purpose.

But these glittering dreams came crashing down. In February 1799 President Adams announced that he would send another peace mission to France. Napoleon Bonaparte had suffered a disastrous defeat at the Battle of the Nile, and the French government was sending signals that it wanted an accommodation. There was even greater change after Adams's announcement. Napoleon ran a coup, dismissed the Directory, and named himself First Consul. The government that had provided the rationale for Federalist war preparations no longer existed. In May 1800, Congress gave John Adams authority to disband the provisional army, which he soon did.

About the time of Adams's announcement, prominent Republicans, including Jefferson, began pressuring Madison to stand for the Virginia House of Delegates. George Washington, looking to strengthen the Federalist Party, had urged Patrick Henry to be a candidate, and Henry agreed. A deeply religious man, he was against the separation of church and state, a principle that Jefferson and Madison believed essential. He opposed initiatives that

Republicans favored and would likely continue to do so, this, as Republican John Taylor wrote, at "the exact moment proper for an effort to manufacture the opinion of Virginia with an eye to the election of president." Madison, who had proved that he could go toe to toe with Henry, agreed to be nominated. Both men were elected, but Henry died before the legislature convened. A strong dose of mercury prescribed by his doctor killed him.[59]

Even without Henry to oppose, Madison had his hands full during the legislative session. He had not yet written Virginia's response to criticism of its 1798 resolutions, and his Richmond lodgings were so disagreeable that they did not ease the work to be done. He felt duty bound to warn Dolley: "Lower your expectations," he wrote. Soon and, one suspects, not coincidentally with boarding at Watson's, Madison was suffering from dysentery.[60]

He worked through his illness to finish a twenty-thousand-word document explaining the Virginia Resolutions of 1798 and defending them from charges that they would lead to disunion. As he had before, he took issue with the general government's assuming powers not explicitly delegated by the Constitution, and he once again made the case for freedom of expression and the danger of government suppressing it:

> May it not be asked of every intelligent friend to the liberties of his country whether the power exercised in . . . an act [such as the Sedition Act] ought not to produce great and universal alarm? Whether a rigid execution of such an act, in time past,

would not have repressed that information and communication among the people, which is indispensable to the just exercise of their electoral rights? And whether such an act, if made perpetual, and enforced with rigor, would not, in time to come, either destroy our free system of government or prepare a convulsion that might prove equally fatal to it.

By mid-January 1800, both houses of the Virginia legislature had approved Madison's *Report of 1800*, and Jefferson was anxious for an official copy. He had a draft and from it had concluded that Madison's calm and careful work would rally Republicans in a cause to which he was now fully committed: his own election to the presidency of the United States. Eventually the legislature ordered five thousand copies printed and distributed.[61]

A second mission for Madison was to change the way Virginia's electors were chosen. The district system currently in place had resulted in Jefferson's winning twenty out of twenty-one electoral votes in 1796. Republicans were confident that even if they did not hold majorities in every district, they had a majority in the commonwealth, meaning that a statewide ballot would likely give Jefferson all the state's electoral votes in the presidential election of 1800.

Madison reported to Jefferson that a general ballot was a hard sell, not because voters disliked it, but because the plan was "so novel."[62] Still, the general ballot passed the House of Delegates by five votes and made it through the Senate as well.

Madison's third undertaking was getting James Monroe elected governor of Virginia. When Republicans had urged him to run, he readily acquiesced. If he won, they told him, he would not be part of a beleaguered minority as he would be in Washington City, which would soon become the seat of government.

Predictably, the Federalists attacked Monroe as soon as he was nominated, but Madison was there to defend him. He took to the floor of the House of Delegates, creating such a stir that a reporter taking notes observed that for several minutes, he "could not hear one word which he said." When the crowd settled down, the reporter took note of Madison's dismissal of Federalist demands to investigate Monroe's tenure as minister to France. "Such a step was entirely superfluous," Madison said. "Every fact, every argument, every circumstance, every insinuation had already been brought forward, explained, and sifted." He declared that Monroe's mission had been successful "in the most delicate and important points." And according to the reporter, "Mr. Madison spoke highly of [Monroe's] private character as pure and of his public character as unimpeachable." When the legislature voted, Monroe defeated his Federalist opponent by 111 votes to 66.[63]

Several days later Washington was reading recently arrived newspapers in the parlor at Mount Vernon with his personal assistant, Tobias Lear. Whenever he came to an interesting story, he would read it aloud, but he had been out riding in hail, rain, and blowing snow and grew hoarse as evening advanced. He asked Lear to read to him reports of debates in the Virginia General Assembly. As Lear later told it, "On hearing Mr. Madison's observations respecting Mr. Monroe, [Washington] appeared much affected and spoke with some degree of asperity on the subject." As Lear was used to doing, he tried to calm "the General," as he called him, and Washington went to bed.[64]

He woke well before dawn, struggling to breathe. Dr. Craik, his longtime neighbor, appeared, but the struggle to save the former president was futile. "I die hard," Washington said to Craik, "but I am not afraid to go." Between ten and eleven o'clock that night, Washington's breathing eased, and he felt for his own pulse. Then his hand dropped, and the great Washington was no more.[65]

The three remaining members of the Virginia dynasty each responded to Washington's death in his own way. James Monroe learned that the president had died as he was traveling to be sworn in as governor:

> I heard of the death of the late General Washington as I entered [Richmond] and felt my resentment calmed and done away in an instant. From the dead we have nothing to fear or hope, and the good a man has done ought to survive him; in this principle I acted on that subject.

Monroe emphasized himself more than Washington, but he was not alone in self-referential mourning. Hamilton linked his sorrow to his loss of the great man's support and protection. "He was an aegis very essential to me," he wrote.[66]

Madison's brief eulogy in the House of Delegates was about what George Washington had meant to the people of Virginia, the nation, and the world, and how they had loved and honored him:

Death has robbed our country of its most distinguished ornament and the world of one of its greatest benefactors. George
Washington, the hero of liberty, the father of his country, and
the friend of man is no more. The general assembly of his native state were ever the first to render him, living, the honors
due to his virtues. They will not be the second to pay to his
memory the tribute of their tears.[67]

Madison had his objections to Washington's policies and actions,
but his eulogy rose to a larger appreciation of his life.

Jefferson learned of Washington's death at Monticello and did
not arrive in Philadelphia in time for national ceremonies honoring the former president. Contemporaries suspected that his late
arrival was purposeful, that Jefferson wanted to avoid the proces-
sions and eulogies honoring Washington, and Jefferson's biographer Dumas Malone thought that as well. Malone further noted
that Jefferson said nothing publicly—or apparently privately—
about Washington at the time of his death. In January 1801, before the outcome of the election of 1800 was known, he would pay
a call on Martha Washington at Mount Vernon. A friend recalled
her saying of his visit, "Next to the loss of her husband it was the
most painful occurrence of her life."[68]

Years later Jefferson wrote a description of Washington that
seems honest and perceptive:

His mind was great and powerful, without being of the very
first order; his penetration strong, though not so acute as that
of a Newton, Bacon, or Locke; and as far as he saw, no judgment was ever sounder. It was slow in operation, being little

aided by invention or imagination, but sure in conclusion.
Hence the common remark of his officers, of the advantage he
derived from councils of war, where hearing all suggestions, he
selected whatever was best; and certainly no General ever
planned his battles more judiciously. But if deranged during
the course of the action, if any member of his plan was dislo-
cated by sudden circumstances, he was slow in re-adjustment.
The consequence was, that he often failed in the field, and
rarely against an enemy in station, as at Boston and York. He
was incapable of fear, meeting personal dangers with the calm-
est unconcern. Perhaps the strongest feature in his character
was prudence, never acting until every circumstance, every
consideration, was maturely weighed; refraining if he saw a
doubt, but, when once decided, going through with his purpose, whatever obstacles opposed. His integrity was most
pure, his justice the most inflexible I have ever known.[69]

So beloved had Washington been that he had lifted the Federalists, helping them maintain political dominance. His death boded
ill for their prospects, as did the determined effort that Republicans undertook to get their message out. Because eighteenth-
century presidential candidates did not campaign personally,
Jefferson stayed at Monticello during the summer and fall, but he
had advocates anxious to praise him. Political operative John
Beckley wrote a pamphlet extolling him and found ways to get
five thousand copies distributed in at least four states. Scandal-
monger James Callender (with financial support from Jefferson)

wrote a pamphlet praising Jefferson and calling President Adams, among other things, a "hoary headed incendiary."[70] *The Prospect Before Us,* as the pamphlet was called, increased its audience when Callender was jailed for sedition. Never one to miss an opportunity, Callender wrote a second volume from behind bars.

The most sustained Republican effort was establishing party newspapers. In 1795 there were about eighteen Republican newspapers; in 1800 the number had reached eighty-five. In August of that year Federalist senator Uriah Tracy reported that in a trip across Pennsylvania he found Republicans establishing "presses and newspapers in almost every town and county," while "Federal presses are failing for want of support." Jefferson, firmly believing that the press was the "engine" for triumphing over the Federalists, had contributed to this phenomenon. He was tireless in urging friends that "every man must lay his purse and his pen under contribution."[71]

Since Jefferson had reached out to Aaron Burr in June 1797, the two had been corresponding regularly. In January 1800, Burr had news he wanted to deliver in person and took a "flying trip" to Philadelphia. There he told Jefferson that the New York House of Representatives had an excellent prospect of receiving an influx of Republican members in the upcoming election.[72] Since the New York legislature chose New York's electors, there was every possibility that there would be a Republican slate.

Burr had accomplished this by organizing what may well be the first modern campaign. Realizing that the outcome of legislative elections in Manhattan was likely to decide the matter, he concentrated on seeing to it that top-notch candidates were fielded there. In his Manhattan house, he organized what would today be called a "war room." He sent out teams to identify Republican voters. He and the leader of the New York Federalists, Alexander Hamilton, made stump speeches across the city. Jefferson kept Madison up to date by sending him a state-by-state rundown that included New York.

Republicans made a clean sweep of the city's legislative seats. New York electors, crucial to Adams's victory in 1796, would be Republican in 1800. When the news reached Philadelphia, Republicans were so exuberant that Senate business could not proceed.[73]

On May 11, the Republican caucus nominated Jefferson for president. Burr, praised for his "generalship, perseverance, industry, and execution" in the New York elections, became the nominee for vice president. Burr had a price for joining the ticket. He wanted Republicans to pledge that "the southern states will act fairly." He did not want a repeat of his humiliating defeat in 1796, when all but one of Virginia's Republican electors voted for Jefferson but not for Burr. Assurances that this would not happen again were forthcoming.[74]

Virginia Republicans had good reason to be optimistic in the summer of 1800, but late in August came a stark reminder of how precarious the Virginia way of life was and of the brutality that sustained it. Gabriel, a skilled blacksmith who had learned to read and write, organized an army of five to six hundred enslaved men to attack Richmond, burn the warehouse district, and seize arms. With their ranks augmented by others who wanted freedom, they would then move on to counties as far afield as Albemarle and Princess Anne, killing and looting, sparing only "the Quakers, the Methodists, and the Frenchmen," who were believed to be "friendly to liberty."[75]

But the rebellion was doomed before it began. On the day planned for the march on Richmond, one of the men in Gabriel's ranks told a member of the family for which he labored about the uprising. In addition, a thunderstorm flooded creeks and washed out bridges, making it impossible for the rebels to gather.[76]

After ten men had been caught, condemned, and hanged, Monroe wrote to Jefferson, "Where to arrest the hand of the executioner is a question of great importance." Jefferson agreed, telling him, "There is a strong sentiment that there has been hanging enough." Gabriel himself was captured and brought to the governor's mansion in Richmond on September 27. Perhaps there, but more likely in the penitentiary to which Gabriel was moved, Monroe met with the tall, determined man. "He seemed to have made up his mind to die," Monroe wrote.[77]

On September 28, the day after Gabriel had been brought to the governor's mansion, Monroe's sixteen-month-old son, James Spence Monroe, who had been sick for weeks, died, plunging both his parents into grief. Mourning one death, Monroe tried to prevent others, proposing to the Council of State that rebels "less criminal in comparison" be reprieved until the state legislature was in session. He anticipated that legislators would pass a law allowing the state to transport some convicted rebels rather than hanging them, but the council was unable to reach a decision, and there were more hangings, until twenty-six men, including Gabriel, had been executed.[78]

Federalists hastened to blame Jefferson and his allies for the uprising. Wrote one, "I doubt not that the eternal clamor about liberty in Virginia . . . has matured the event which has happened."

It was a point well taken. One of the conspirators, asked to defend himself, compared his deeds to those of a Virginia hero:

> I have nothing more to offer than what General Washington would have had to offer had he been taken by the British and put to trial by them. I have adventured my life in endeavoring to obtain the liberty of my countrymen and am a willing sacrifice in their cause.[79]

People who had learned about the glories of freedom wanted it for themselves.

As part of a bruising attack on Jefferson in the election of 1800, Federalists claimed that he was an atheist. They cited his support of the French Revolution as evidence. One of the first acts of the National Assembly had been to seize the churches of France. The same could be expected of Jefferson, his enemies said—and more. An editorial in a Federalist newspaper claimed that Jefferson's election would bring "murder, robbery, rape, adultery, and incest." So strong was the rhetoric that a woman who met Jefferson in her parlor had to pinch herself. "Is this the violent democrat, the vulgar demagogue, the bold atheist, and profligate man I have so often heard denounced by the Federalists?" she asked. "Can he be that daring leader of a faction, that disturber of the peace, that enemy of all rank and order?"[80]

Jefferson was publicly silent about the campaign, as was the custom, and Republicans (often at his behest) defended him. One of their most effective tactics was to celebrate his authorship of the Declaration of Independence. They brought it forward as a "deathless instrument" come from the pen of "the immortal Jefferson."[81]

Because each state could determine when to have the elections leading up to the meeting of the Electoral College on December 3, 1800, the contest went on for months. After five states voted, it appeared that Republicans Thomas Jefferson and Aaron Burr and Federalists John Adams and Charles Cotesworth Pinckney all had about the same number of electoral votes. The order of candidates changed in the weeks ahead, but the election remained close.

Then came a stunning October surprise. Alexander Hamilton was furious with John Adams for having hesitated to make him second-in-command of the army intended for the Quasi War, and he had become angrier still when Adams had not promoted him to command of the army upon Washington's death. Adams had also fired two Federalist cabinet members to whom Hamilton was close and had dared to send a peace mission to France. Hamilton poured out his complaints in a long letter that became public. He accused Adams of "disgusting egotism" and "distempered jealousy." He was unsuited for the presidential office, Hamilton wrote, because of "paroxysms of anger" that caused him to lose control. The letter seemed to show Hamilton himself out of control. For confirmation, one had only to turn to the end of the diatribe, where despite his devastating criticism of the president, Hamilton urged Federalists to vote *for* him. The letter was a "thunderbolt," one of Jefferson's correspondents observed. Surely it would cost Adams votes.[82]

In early November, Monroe urged Madison to meet with George Erving, a young man concerned that a victory over the Federalists might not be enough for Jefferson to win the presidency. What if the two Republicans, Jefferson and Burr, tied? After meeting with Erving, Madison wrote to Monroe that even if there was a tie, the decision would be made in the House of Representatives, "where the candidates would certainly, I think, be arranged properly even on the recommendation of the secondary one." Burr supporter David Gelston wrote Madison of his confidence that there would be no tie. He had good information from three states that electors voting for Jefferson would not give their second vote to Burr. Burr himself wrote that he would yield the presidency to Jefferson should there be a tie.[83]

On December 3, 1800, electors gathered in their state capitals to cast their votes. Madison, a Virginia elector, traveled to Richmond, where he voted for Jefferson and Burr—as he felt honor bound to do. But in a grave error, he helped persuade seventy-four-year-old George Wythe to do likewise. Wythe, who had been Jefferson's beloved teacher, was determined to throw away his second vote, but Madison showed him David Gelston's reassuring letter, and Wythe changed his mind.

The electors in other states who were to vote only for Jefferson never materialized. On February 11, 1801, Jefferson, presiding in the Senate, broke the red wax seals on state tallies and announced the electoral vote: seventy-three for Jefferson and seventy-three for Burr. If Madison had let Wythe have his way and all else remained the same, Jefferson would have prevailed at that moment by seventy-three to seventy-two. Burr, although he had said he would yield to Jefferson, was not heard from.

Because of the 1790 compromise struck by Madison and Hamilton and brokered by Jefferson, the capital had moved from Philadelphia to Washington City in 1800. Unfinished marble buildings rising from the Potomac wilderness resembled nothing so much as crumbling ruins. Years later, they still reminded Henry Adams of "white Greek temples in the abandoned gravel pits of a deserted Syrian city."[84]

Near the Capitol were boardinghouses where congressmen and senators stayed, but there was not much else in Washington City. Abigail Adams, living in the unfinished President's House, told her sister that Georgetown, where the only nearby market was located, was "the very dirtiest hole I ever saw for a place of any trade." She did allow that the President's House was beautifully situated, offering views of a wild and romantic landscape.[85]

The Capitol also had a grand setting on Jenkins Hill, but so far there was a single wing that had a chamber for the Senate but none for the House. There was space for the Library of Congress, a huge room measuring eighty-six feet by thirty-five with a ceiling thirty-six feet above the floor. It was there, during snowy February days, that representatives gathered to choose the next president of the United States.[86] The Constitution provided the rules by which they would proceed. Each state would have one vote (which would be determined by that state's delegation). There were sixteen states, and for either Jefferson or Burr to prevail, he had to win nine, or a majority. The lame-duck House, which was controlled by Federalists, would be voting, but even though the Federalists had more members, they were distributed in such a way that the Republicans controlled more state delegations.

Being without a candidate, the Federalists had to choose between two Republicans. Although Hamilton entered the debate again to argue against Burr, they decided to cast their votes for the New Yorker, whom they deemed malleable, rather than for Jefferson, whom they despised. The first ballot showed Jefferson with eight states, Burr with six, and two states split so that neither candidate received the necessary votes. In order for Burr to emerge victorious, he had to turn three states, a daunting task. Jefferson had to turn just one, but if the Federalists held fast, they could prevent that, and keep him from winning the presidency. Hold fast they did through ballot after ballot, all of which had the same result: Jefferson eight states, Burr six, and two states split.

As the balloting went on around the clock, food and blankets were brought in. An ill Republican was carried two miles through the February cold so that he could vote. Meanwhile, Jefferson spent his time in the Federalist-controlled Senate, presiding whenever it was in session. Federalists had a scheme to block his election through Inauguration Day, March 4, when the offices of president and vice president would become vacant. In that circumstance, the president pro tempore of the Senate would become president—if there were a president pro tempore. In February 1801, there was none because the office was filled only when the president of the Senate (that is, the vice president) was absent.

Jefferson was determined never to be absent and thus never to let the Federalists succeed with their plan.[87]

Jefferson also threatened that if Federalists tried to usurp the election, "the middle states would arm." Virginia and Pennsylvania were, in fact, gathering arms and preparing to mobilize their militias. A fire in the Treasury Building caused apprehension. Was it part of a plot? According to one rumor, should the Federalists try to inaugurate a usurper, fifteen hundred men from Maryland and Virginia stood ready to march on Washington and assassinate him on March 4.[88]

In a meeting with President Adams, Jefferson hammered home what would happen if the Federalists tried to put the president pro tempore of the Senate into the president's office. "Such a measure would probably produce resistance by force," he said. Adams responded by telling Jefferson that he had the solution to the problem in his own hands. He could become president by making commitments to the Federalists that he "would not turn out [Federalist officeholders], nor put down the navy, nor spunge the national debt." They wanted him, in other words, to govern like a Federalist. Jefferson, according to his notes, changed the subject.[89]

For thirty-five ballots, Federalist James Bayard of Delaware had voted for Burr, but the tall, blond, thirty-three-year-old finally became convinced that the election had gone on long enough. As the sole member of his state's delegation, Bayard had it within his power to bring matters to an end. By casting his ballot for

Jefferson instead of Burr, he could make Jefferson president. But there was a less painful way to accomplish the same end, one that spread the blame around and did not require voting for Jefferson. Federalists who had supported Burr in states divided between the two candidates could tip their states to Jefferson simply by not voting. Bayard and congressmen from divided states agreed that before doing this they should seek "terms of capitulation."[90] Whether they secured them or not has been a cause of controversy for nearly two centuries.

In a deposition several years later, Bayard said that he first approached Representative John Nicholas of Virginia, a friend of Jefferson's, with what had become Federalist talking points: Would Jefferson support the navy and public credit and keep non-cabinet-level Federalist officeholders in place? Nicholas told him that what he had outlined conformed to Jefferson's intentions, but Bayard wanted more—confirmation from Jefferson himself. That Nicholas could not offer and would not seek.

Bayard next approached Republican Samuel Smith, a distinguished, gray-haired representative from Maryland. Bayard wanted a private conversation, and in an empty committee room in the Capitol he expressed the concerns that he had laid out for Nicholas. He particularly emphasized that Federalist officeholders below cabinet level not be routinely dismissed and offered Allan McLane, port collector at Wilmington, Delaware, as a case in point.

As Smith told it, he replied to Bayard that within the last few days Jefferson had said he intended to protect the navy and public credit. As for keeping lower-level Federalist officeholders such as Allan McLane in place, Smith said that he did not know

Jefferson's thinking, but was willing to find out. He took Bayard's concerns to Conrad and McMunn's, a Capitol Hill establishment where he and Jefferson both boarded. The next day he told Bayard that Jefferson had said he planned no political firings of lower-level government employees and that he had received such good reports on Allan McLane that his job was safe. After telling Bayard that he could be "assured . . . that Mr. Jefferson would conduct as to those points agreeably to the opinions I had stated as his," Smith said that Bayard offered an assurance of his own: "We will give the vote on Monday."[91]

It was Tuesday, on the thirty-sixth ballot, that Bayard abstained from voting, thereby reducing Burr's total from the six states he had received on previous ballots to five. He was reduced to four states when Federalists from South Carolina, a state previously in his column, cast blank ballots. A Federalist congressman from Vermont withdrew, and four Maryland Federalists cast blank ballots, allowing Republicans in those delegations to move two votes into Jefferson's column, which had previously had just eight. The final result: ten for Jefferson, four for Burr, and two states with no results. With Bayard leading the way, the Federalists had broken the logjam and elected Jefferson.

Did Jefferson cut a deal with Bayard? Bayard certainly thought so. After the final ballot was cast, he wrote "I have taken good care of you" to port collector McLane, who would, in fact, stay in that office for twenty-eight years. Some have said this letter proves there was a bargain. But Jefferson did not intend to displace all Federalists. He specifically said that "good men, to whom there is no objection but a difference of political principle practiced only as far as the right of a private citizen will justify are not proper subjects of removal." McLane, a hero of the Revolution, who had impoverished himself in the cause, fit this category.[92]

As was his wont, Jefferson did not defend himself publicly, but he wrote in his diary, "Neither [Smith] nor any other Republican ever uttered the most distant hint to me about . . . giving any assurances to anybody; and still more certainly was neither he nor any other person ever authorized by me to say what I would or would not do."[93]

After Jefferson died in 1826, his denial became public. Four years later, with controversy over the statement still churning, Smith, now age seventy-seven, gave an account of his part in the negotiations that was much more modest than the one he had given earlier. He no longer implied that he had questioned Jefferson, but instead stated clearly that he had introduced Bayard's concerns as topics of casual conversation. No longer did he represent himself as offering assurances on behalf of the president; the commitments he made, he wrote, were his own.[94]

Smith had exaggerated the role he had played in the 1800 election. Albert Gallatin, Jefferson's wise secretary of the Treasury, believed that something such as this had happened. Late in his life, obviously referring to Smith, he wrote: "One of our friends . . . undertook to act as an intermediary, and, confounding his own opinions and wishes with those of Mr. Jefferson, reported the result in such a manner as gave subsequently occasion for very unfounded surmises."[95]

While overstating one's role is not recommended behavior, Smith, by doing so, may well have changed history. Bayard had already rejected reassurances from a colleague who refused to confirm them with Jefferson. If Smith hadn't persuaded him that he was Jefferson's agent, Bayard might well have pulled his offer and walked away. The result could have been a government incapable of action and even, as was said often during the turmoil, the end of the Republic.

The election of 1800 gave rise to another controversy worthy of note. John Adams had eight fewer votes in the Electoral College than Jefferson, and many scholars have written that had it not been for the three-fifths clause in the Constitution giving advantage to the South—and to the southerner Jefferson—Adams would have emerged the winner. But there has not been a definitive analysis of the vote in 1800 and may never be one, since there are so many uncertainties. Without the three-fifths clause, for example, district lines would have been different. Who can know how they might have been drawn and to whom they would have given advantage? Moreover, if one reconfigures one element of the past, surely others are fair game. What if there had not been a party row in Pennsylvania in 1800? Jefferson might have gained enough votes to win even without the three-fifths clause.[96]

The clause did give Jefferson an advantage, but he had others as well, including the impressive political skills deployed in New York on behalf of Republicans by none other than Aaron Burr.

SEVEN

The Spirit of '76

∞

The Virginians Return

On March 4, 1801, a day that hinted at spring, fifty-seven-year-old Thomas Jefferson, plainly dressed, walked from his lodgings at Conrad and McMunn's to the United States Capitol. For him there was no elegant carriage, no sword, no silver buckles. His would be a simple inauguration.[1]

But the military could not resist marking the occasion. A signal gun announced Jefferson's departure from his lodgings. Alexandria militia officers in blue and buff uniforms led him toward the flat-roofed building that made up the whole of the Capitol in 1801. As Jefferson knew, the sandstone structure would someday be the north wing of the Capitol. A south wing would mirror it, and from a central building connecting the wings, a dome would rise.[2]

Jefferson entered the building to the sound of cannon fire and walked the short distance to the Senate chamber, a handsome, semicircular room that stretched upward more than forty feet. The gallery was full on this day, as was the floor of the chamber, where senators had claimed seats in half the crowded room and representatives found places to stand, having gallantly turned seats in their half of the room over to the ladies. According to Margaret Bayard Smith, whose husband published one of Washington City's first newspapers, "Every inch of ground was occupied."[3]

Aaron Burr, who had been sworn in as vice president, was presiding when Jefferson entered. As the audience stood to recognize the president-elect, Burr, whom Jefferson had not forgiven for prolonging the election, left the president of the Senate's chair, which was arranged in front of the chamber's principal window, so that Jefferson could assume it.[4]

After a few moments of silence, Jefferson rose to make his address. In a low, soft voice, difficult to hear, he began on a modest note, declaring that the post to which he had been elected was above his talents: "I shrink from the contemplation and humble myself before the magnitude of the undertaking," he said. He paid tribute to the legislators in the chamber for being "resources of wisdom, of virtue, and of zeal on which to rely under all difficulties." Their guidance and support, he said, would help him "steer with safety the vessel in which we are all embarked." In the most famous passage of his address, he spoke of harmony and appealed to Americans to come together after a time of bitter partisanship. "Every difference of opinion is not a difference of principle," he said. "We are all republicans, we are all federalists."[5]

His words were uplifting and the sentiments appropriate, but hardly had he uttered them when Chief Justice John Marshall stepped forward to administer the oath of office. John Adams had nominated Marshall, a Federalist, to be chief justice in January, and he had been sworn in just a month before Jefferson. He was now in a position from which he could bedevil Jefferson and from which Jefferson could not remove him. Marshall was an early reminder, as was Burr, that despite the sentiments of the inaugural address, some differences were hard—if not impossible—to reconcile.

Jefferson's antipathy for the vice president and chief justice (and theirs for him) did not dampen the celebratory spirit of the occasion. This was the first time a president had taken the oath of office in Washington City and the first time that an election had resulted in a turnover of power from one ideology to another, from one party to another. Margaret Bayard Smith wrote to her sister-in-law:

> I have this morning witnessed one of the most interesting scenes a free people can ever witness. The changes of administration, which in every government and in every age have most generally been epochs of confusion, villainy, and bloodshed, in this our happy country take place without any species of distraction or disorder.[6]

Other outcomes had seemed possible during the course of the election, but on March 4, 1801, in the first of many peaceful regime changes, Thomas Jefferson became president of the United States. Together with Madison, he would dramatically expand the power of the presidency—though things did not start out that way.

Jefferson's inaugural address, widely admired over the years, had come from the heart. He truly wanted to bring Republicans and Federalists together. He truly wanted people to reach across to those of different opinion. He truly wanted the United States to overflow with "that harmony and affection without which liberty and even life itself are but dreary things."[7]

At the same time, it rankled that Federalists had made him president by abstaining or casting blank ballots. Not one had voted for him, which was, he told Madison, "a declaration of war on the part of this band."[8]

Jefferson was determined to restore "the spirit of '76." He believed that the Federalists had frightened Americans into laying aside the love of liberty that had marked the Revolution's beginnings. By repeatedly predicting a French invasion and stoking fears about immigrants and dissenters, they had created "rawhead and bloody bones," a bogeyman that made many yearn for a large and powerful government to protect them. In Jefferson's mind, a controlling central government was exactly what the Revolution had allowed him and his fellow countrymen to escape, and he was determined to reduce its power.[9]

A restoration of the spirit of '76 meant changing Federalist policies for Republican ones, a reversal unlikely to inspire the "harmony and affection" that he spoke about so felicitously in his inaugural address. Federalists who thought they had a deal with him before his election must have been beside themselves when among the first matters to which he turned were cutbacks in the navy, reduction of the nation's debt, and removal of some Federalist officeholders—the three actions they had tried to prevent.[10]

The President's House was a lonely place for a widower whose daughters were still in Virginia. Apart from a dozen servants, free and enslaved, who lived in the basement, Jefferson was the only occupant. Neither dinner companions nor good conversation, both of which he enjoyed immensely, was in the offing.

He wrote to an acquaintance from Albemarle County, a young man whom he admired for his courage and honesty, to offer him the job of being his secretary. The pay was low, Jefferson admitted, but he would supplement it with room and board at the President's House. Captain Meriwether Lewis, a tall twenty-six-year-old, formal in manner and given to moods, accepted and promised to get to Washington City "with all possible dispatch." By the time he arrived, however, Jefferson, after just thirteen days in the President's House, had departed for Monticello. When the president returned to Washington, he found Lewis ensconced in the yet-to-be plastered Audience Room, where Abigail Adams had hung laundry. A partition at the south end of the room created space for a bedroom and office. Jefferson wrote his daughter that he and Lewis in the large mansion were "like two mice in a church."[11]

Jefferson had hired Lewis not only for his knowledge of the army, but also for what he knew about the West, which Lewis had explored during frontier postings. Jefferson had long been fascinated by the land beyond the Appalachians. His library shelves were packed with books on the subject, some speculating that woolly mammoths and live volcanoes could be found in the West. Jefferson was convinced by reports that there was an enormous mountain of salt.[12]

Despite his fascination with natural curiosities, Jefferson thought the freedom and possibility that the West represented were more important. The West could reanimate Americans, restoring the energy and aspiration of the Revolution. It could bring back the spirit of '76 and direct the country's citizens to the noble goal Jefferson described in his inaugural address: "a rising nation, spread over a wide and fruitful land . . . advancing rapidly to destinies beyond the reach of mortal eye."[13]

While Jefferson and Lewis studied maps in Jefferson's light-filled office, fifty-year-old Secretary of State James Madison; his wife, Dolley; her son, John Payne Todd; and her sister, Anna Payne, were in a carriage headed toward the federal city. The road, treacherous at first, finally smoothed out, and the travelers could enjoy the beauty of tulip poplars shooting bright green leaves a hundred feet and more into the sky and of wild azaleas in bloom. Nearer the President's House the scene was different. Tulip poplars were dying from having had a ring of bark removed. "Girdling" was a cheap and easy way for poor residents of the federal city, who needed wood, to bring them down. Weeds were the only green in the area surrounding the President's House, which one visitor described as a "stony unfenced waste." Kilns still dotted the grounds, as did shacks that had housed enslaved and free tradesmen who had labored to build the mansion.[14]

The Madisons stayed with Jefferson for three weeks. There were pleasant dinners that included Meriwether Lewis, and there was work, much of it concerned with rebalancing a government weighed down by Federalists. John Adams had made dozens of appointments toward the end of his administration. Some appointed after Jefferson's election the new president considered "nullities," and he named his own appointees to those positions, which made Federalists furious. When Jefferson, ignoring an Adams appointee, named a Republican to the port collectorship at New Haven, eighty angry merchants wrote him to protest. In response he noted that upon becoming president, he had found government offices almost entirely filled by Federalists. "Was it to be imagined that this monopoly of office was still to be continued?" The voters had expressed their opinion about the direction they wanted the government to go, and those who agreed with what the people wanted should hold their fair share of offices.[15]

Adams and the lame-duck Federalist Congress had also passed the Judiciary Act of 1801, which created sixteen new circuit court judgeships just in time for Adams to fill them with what came to be called "midnight judges." The Republicans replaced the Judiciary Act of 1801 with the Judiciary Act of 1802, which canceled the new judgeships.[16]

Adams had also nominated forty-two justices of the peace who were confirmed by the Senate on the very eve of the inauguration. In the frantic hours before the change of administrations, the Federalists had been unable to deliver all the commissions required for the new justices to take office, and as soon as he was sworn in, Jefferson ordered Secretary of State Madison to hold the undelivered commissions.

One commission was meant for William Marbury, a wealthy financier and active Federalist, who lived in a handsome brick home on Bridge Street (M Street today) in Washington City. A man used to getting his way, Marbury filed a suit in the Supreme Court for a writ of mandamus compelling Secretary of State Madison to hand over his commission. The court handed down an opinion a little over a year later. In *Marbury v. Madison,* Marshall declared that Marbury had a right to his commission but that the court could not compel Madison to turn it over because the law that would have permitted the court to make such a decision was unconstitutional.[17]

This outcome was initially regarded as a win for Jefferson and Madison. They had succeeded in preventing the Federalist Marbury from becoming a justice of the peace, but soon it became clear that the decision had really been a triumph for Marshall. Regarded today as a basis for judicial review, *Marbury* conveyed enormous power to the court, an unelected body, by setting a precedent for it to declare laws passed by the Congress and signed by the president unconstitutional. Jefferson later wrote that the opinion made the Constitution "a mere thing of wax in the hands of the judiciary, which they may twist and shape into any form they please."[18]

Sorting out aspirants for government jobs was as difficult as displacing incumbents. Some office seekers seemed desperate, others entitled, and their numbers were legion. The applicant with the greatest sense of entitlement was James Callender, the inflammatory writer who had supported Jefferson with his pen before the 1800 election, while Jefferson, in turn, had provided him with financial support. *The Prospect Before Us,* the pamphlet in which he called President Adams a "hoary headed incendiary," had triggered the Sedition Act and landed Callender in jail. He was out by Jefferson's inauguration, but the president granted him a pardon, as he did to others whom the Federalists had used the Sedition Act to punish. The pardon absolved Callender of a two-hundred-dollar fine he had paid, and in early March Jefferson promised the money would be remitted promptly. But days passed, then months, and Callender, destitute and with two young sons to support, grew agitated. He also decided that his work for the Republican Party entitled him to a sinecure, specifically to the postmaster's job in Richmond.[19]

Jefferson turned to Virginia colleagues. He sent Meriwether Lewis to give Callender fifty dollars and an explanation that the money was a gift to tide him over. Callender, outraged rather than placated, called the gift "hush money," saying that it was meant to keep him quiet about certain Jefferson secrets to which he was privy. Jefferson, who had also arranged for Monroe to give Callender money, tried to cut his losses. "Make no use of the order I enclosed," he instructed the governor of Virginia.[20]

Madison, in Washington, tried to insulate the president. He took on the disagreeable task of informing Callender that he would not be Richmond's postmaster. He hoped that what he called his "plain dealing" would calm Callender, but that was not the result. Madison wrote to Monroe, "Callender's irritation, produced by his wants, is whetted constantly by his suspicion that the difficulties, if not intended, are the offspring of indifference in those who have interposed in his behalf."[21]

Finally, on June 20, 1801, Callender received the two-hundred-dollar remission of his fine and seemed to be mollified. Madison and Monroe breathed a sigh of relief and Jefferson likely did, too, although he had put on a brave face throughout. There was nothing to fear, he wrote to Monroe. There was nothing that Callender knew "which I am not willing to declare to the world myself."[22]

Meantime, at Monticello, an enslaved woman named Sally Hemings nursed a newborn baby. The tiny girl, named Harriet, had been conceived during the summer of 1800, the campaign summer during which Jefferson had been in residence at Monticello.[23]

In his inaugural address, Jefferson had emphasized "peace, commerce, and honest friendship with all nations," but the Barbary states were another matter. For years the United States had paid tribute to keep them from attacking American ships, and for years Jefferson had protested. "Why not go to war with them?" he had asked Monroe in 1784. The United States would be hard pressed to find a "weaker foe."[24]

The rulers of the Barbary states not only demanded bribes, they also seemed to delight in humiliating nations that paid them tribute. Not long before the election of 1800, the USS *George Washington* arrived off the coast of Algiers, carrying tribute for the dey of Algiers. As the captain, William Bainbridge, was off-loading everything from sugar to chinaware, the dey made a demand. He had his own tribute to pay to the sultan of the Turks, and he wanted the *George Washington* to transport it to Constantinople. Bainbridge thought the demand outrageous, but refusing it could mean that he and his crew would be thrown in prison or sold into slavery. After acquiescing, Bainbridge discovered that the cargo he was to transport included enslaved Africans, the Algerian ambassador and dozens of hangers-on, and $800,000 in coins, as well as parrots, ostriches, lions, and tigers. To deepen the insult, the dey ordered Bainbridge to sail under the Algerian flag.[25]

Not long after Jefferson's inauguration, word arrived from the pasha of Tripoli, who demanded an immediate payment of $225,000 and $25,000 a year going forward for allowing American ships to sail unmolested in Mediterranean waters. Jefferson, who had no inclination to pay further bribes, decided to send three frigates and a sloop of war to the Mediterranean. He saw no contradiction in using American naval power at the same time he was making severe cutbacks to the navy. From his point of view, this affair was exactly the limited kind of conflict for which the United States could use a few warships. But there was no need for a large navy, he believed, since the United States was not going to be battling great powers on the high seas anytime soon.[26]

Jefferson had not sought Congress's approval of the mission because neither the Senate nor the House was in session. Besides, the ships were simply a "squadron of observation," Jefferson wrote to the pasha. As Secretary of State Madison explained it to American diplomats, matters were a little more complicated.

Should the squadron's commodore arrive to find that war had been declared, he had orders to use force. Having moved at the Constitutional Convention that Congress—not the executive— had the power to declare war, Madison now described a circumstance in which the executive could order military action—when it was needed for defense. His explanation took up a question that has been fiercely debated since. How much power does the president have to commit the American military?[27]

As it happened, the pasha had already declared war by ordering the flagpole in front of the American consulate in Tripoli cut down. It was an efficient method and an act not easily reversed since trees suitable for making flagpoles did not grow in the rocky plateaus and hot sands of the Sahara Desert.[28]

War in the Mediterranean, which both Jefferson and Madison thought would be over quickly, continued into Jefferson's second term. Notable for accident and mischance, the conflict nonetheless produced an American hero, Lieutenant Stephen Decatur, a tall man and a brave one, with a shock of curly brown hair. He and his well-armed men undertook the dangerous task of sailing into the harbor of Tripoli while most of the Tripolitan fleet was anchored there. Under the cover of night, they boarded and blew up the USS *Philadelphia*, which the Tripolitans had captured after it had embarrassingly run aground. Decatur's successful mission ensured that the USS *Philadelphia* would not be used to fight Americans.[29]

The action in Tripoli also led to an enduring patriotic song. Marines conducted a land and sea operation at the Battle of Derna that inspired the opening lines of the "Marines' Hymn": "From the Halls of Montezuma / To the shores of Tripoli, / We fight our country's battles / On the land as on the sea."[30]

In the end the United States negotiated a treaty that required no payment for ending hostilities and no tribute. It did provide that the Americans would pay sixty thousand dollars for the return of some three hundred prisoners who had been captured with the *Philadelphia*.[31]

Of greater consequence was the purchase of Louisiana, an accomplishment in which Jefferson, Madison, and Monroe would all play a part. They would seize upon a world-changing opportunity that had its origin in an historic revolution in the French colony of Saint Domingue (Haiti today).

A slave uprising brought Toussaint Louverture, once himself enslaved, to power. The French Directory appointed him commander in chief, a title that understated his total control of the island and overstated his allegiance to France. When Napoleon seized power in 1799, he determined to reassert French authority. He had no intention of letting the colony's thriving sugar and coffee plantations slip away. He sent an army of twenty thousand under the command of Charles Leclerc, who had reached high rank by way of marriage to Bonaparte's free-spirited sister Pauline. Napoleon insisted that Leclerc take the bright, beautiful, and often inconvenient Pauline to Saint Domingue with him.[32]

As dozens upon dozens of French ships under Leclerc's command sailed into Samana Bay in late January 1802, Louverture, watching from high ground nearby, was momentarily filled with dread. How could he and his fellow countrymen overcome such might?[33]

In Washington City, the reaction to Napoleon's expedition was shock. Already worried that the rebellion in Saint Domingue might inspire like efforts in the United States, Republican lawmakers now had to consider what Napoleon's goal might be. There were rumors that France once again owned Louisiana. If Spain, which had acquired Louisiana from France in 1762, had ceded it back, might Napoleon use the army he had sent across the Atlantic not only to subdue Saint Domingue, but also to take control of Louisiana and thus the port of New Orleans? Should that happen, the ambitious and bellicose French would have a stranglehold on the Mississippi River—and on the American economy.[34]

Secretary of State Madison, in charge of official correspondence, wrote Robert Livingston, the wealthy, self-confident New Yorker whom Jefferson had appointed U.S. minister to France. A man of striking appearance, with one blue eye and one brown, Livingston had a long résumé. He had been a member of the committee assigned to draft the Declaration of Independence, the highest judicial officer in New York, and secretary for foreign affairs under the Articles of Confederation. He was also, as Abigail Adams observed, a man of "insatiable ambition."[35]

Madison instructed Livingston to let the French government know that taking control of Louisiana would disrupt French and American relations. Be "candid and friendly" while delivering a tough message, he wrote. If France were to take possession of New Orleans, "the worst events are to be apprehended."[36]

Jefferson, unable to stay out of the mix, wrote a private letter to Livingston. He wanted the French government to understand that New Orleans was the port "through which the produce of three-eighths of our territory must pass to market." It was of such value to the United States that should Napoleon take control of it, France would become America's enemy, and Britain, with whom France was expected soon to be at war, would become America's ally. The French would find the United States "a belligerent power."[37]

Madison, too, knew the value of back channels, and in a pointed conversation with Louis-André Pichon, the French chargé in Washington, he described the high price France would pay for possessing Louisiana. "France cannot long preserve Louisiana against the United States," he said. Pichon noted that Madison had delivered this message with "much coolness, much method, and as if he had been prepared." Particularly in times of crisis, Madison was not given to off-the-cuff remarks.[38]

In October 1802, Juan Ventura Morales, a high-ranking Spanish official at New Orleans, escalated the crisis by closing the port to American shipping. Madison turned his tough-minded diplomacy on Spain, instructing Charles Pinckney, the U.S. minister (and cousin to Charles Cotesworth Pinckney), to impress upon the Spanish government how inflammatory the closure was. To farmers in the West, who floated their harvests down the Mississippi and deposited them at New Orleans, the river meant everything. "It is the Hudson, the Delaware, the Potomac, and all the navigable rivers of the Atlantic states formed into one stream," he wrote.[39]

Livingston wrote a long, well-reasoned memorandum to twenty French notables setting forth the disadvantages to France of taking control of Louisiana. While not belaboring the point that a war between France and England seemed inevitable, he asked whether it was wise to invest in a colony when money might be needed for a war. He also brought up "the hardships, expenses, and loss of lives that result from the establishment of new colonies in a marshy country and warm climate," as well as the risk of further insurrection.[40]

Napoleon's extensive propaganda campaign regularly changed bad news coming from the Caribbean into good, but Livingston's mention of insurrection and disease hinted that the truth was getting through. Although Leclerc and his forces had captured Louverture and exiled him to an unheated cell high in Europe's Jura Mountains where he would die, French troops had been dying for months in bloody fighting. By May, four thousand to five thousand had been lost. Meanwhile, yellow fever struck. In the end it would kill more than fifteen thousand French soldiers and sailors.[41]

Matters worsened for Napoleon in the first week of January 1803, when he received a notice that struck a personal blow. Among those dead from yellow fever was his brother-in-law Charles Leclerc. "Damn sugar, damn coffee, damn colonies!" he raged. When he also learned of hawkish threats coming from the United States Senate, he let go his ambition for a French empire in the Americas and called in Finance Minister François Barbé-Marbois. "It is not only New Orleans that I will cede," he told him, "it is the whole colony without any reservation."[42]

Lucien Bonaparte, Napoleon's brother, later added a comic sidebar to Napoleon's very serious decision. When Lucien and his brother Joseph learned of Napoleon's intentions, they confronted him at the Tuileries Palace, where he was taking one of his regular two-hour baths. They hammered away at the idiocy of selling Louisiana, but Napoleon, wanting to hear none of it, half stood in the bathtub and shouted at Joseph, "You are insolent!" Then he threw himself back into the tub, sending up a wave of perfumed water that drenched both brothers. Napoleon's valet, witnessing the scene, fell over in a dead faint.[43]

Foreign Minister Talleyrand met with Livingston on April 11 and asked whether the United States wished to have the whole of Louisiana. "No," Livingston responded. His brief was to acquire New Orleans and perhaps East and West Florida. There had been no discussion about the United States buying the entire Louisiana Territory.[44]

Soon realizing what he had turned down, Livingston spent the day of April 12 trying to get Talleyrand to follow up. He was aware that Napoleon made decisions quickly and unmade them just as fast. He also knew that April 12 was the day that James Monroe, recently retired from his third term as Virginia's governor, would arrive in Paris. Jefferson had sent him as a minister extraordinaire, not only because he wanted someone he knew and trusted at the negotiations, but also because Monroe's appointment would help placate the West, where outrage over the closing of the Mississippi was leading to talk of war and secession. Monroe had traveled in the West, bought land there, and was known to be sympathetic to western concerns.[45]

Monroe had not sought a government position. After three terms as Virginia governor, he was broke and wanted to repair his finances by working as a lawyer. Moreover, although neither Jefferson nor Madison seemed aware of it, Monroe felt estranged from the administration. They had not sought his advice on important matters and made many errors, he wrote in a memorandum he kept secret. Their personnel policy was not stringent enough, their actions toward France were insufficiently conciliatory. And on went the list.[46]

Jefferson told him that by taking the ministerial post, he could earn a place in history. "On the event of this mission," he wrote, "depends the future destinies of this republic." Monroe accepted. Madison helped with Monroe's cash crisis by agreeing to pay the interest on his debts in exchange for silver and china that Monroe had purchased on his previous posting to France. The signatures of both Jefferson and Madison on Monroe's appointment letter showed the harmony in which the three Virginians were working.[47]

Monroe's appointment did not sit well with Livingston. After working the Louisiana portfolio for more than a year, he now saw his efforts coming to a conclusion more splendid than he had ever imagined, and he was in no mood to share the limelight. Monroe wrote to Madison in April complaining that Livingston was trying to make it appear that everything of significance had been done before he arrived, but Monroe did not send the letter, somewhat surprising behavior for a man so intent on advancing himself. In fact, during negotiations for Louisiana and for some time afterward, Monroe was relatively modest, never claiming that he had persuaded the French government and even praising Livingston for his "zeal and industry."[48]

On May 2, 1803, Monroe and Livingston rode to the Hôtel Tubeuf, an imposing brick-and-stone structure that dated to the reign of Louis XIII. It had become the headquarters of the French Treasury and the office of the head of the Treasury, Barbé-Marbois, and it was there that the three men signed the treaty providing that the United States for fifteen million dollars would acquire land that contained more square miles than Great Britain, France, Germany, Italy, Portugal, and Spain added together.[49]

During the handshakes after the signing, Livingston struck just the right note. "We have lived long," he said, "but this is the noblest work of our whole lives."[50]

In the immediate aftermath of the treaty signing, Monroe continued to avoid taking credit, but he was keen on seeing that Livingston did not get it, and by the middle of May Livingston's self-promotion became too much for him. In a letter to Madison, Monroe wrote, "The most difficult, vexatious, and embarrassing part of my labor has been with my associate."[51]

Madison was irate when the long memo that Livingston had sent to French notables appeared in newspapers as evidence that its author had driven the French decision to sell Louisiana. Jefferson, trying to defuse the competition, publicly stated that both Livingston and Monroe deserved praise, but in truth he and Madison had grown suspicious of Livingston and privately stood with Monroe. Livingston continued his frenetic efforts to garner credit, even changing dates on documents to make his role seem more important. But with Madison and Jefferson aligned with Monroe,

Livingston stood little chance of becoming the ministerial hero of the Louisiana Purchase.[52]

As Monroe saw it, many factors had contributed to the success of the negotiations, among them "the pressure of England, . . . the temper of our country, . . . our government in putting the question fairly at issue by sending me here." The last was a fair point. Jefferson had been determined throughout, and by delegating a political dignitary to whom he was known to be close, he had made his commitment to guarding U.S. interests clear.[53]

Absent from Monroe's list of the forces behind the purchase was a group to which historian Henry Adams later called attention. "The prejudice of race alone," Adams wrote, "blinded the American people to the debt they owed to the desperate courage of five hundred thousand Haitian Negroes who would not be enslaved."[54]

For Jefferson, the Louisiana Purchase was a vision realized. Even before the American Revolution had ended, he had written about adding "an extensive and fertile country" to America's "empire of liberty." And even before he learned that the Louisiana Treaty had been signed, he had asked Congress for an appropriation to fund an expedition to explore the land beyond the Mississippi. Upon receiving it, he chose his secretary, Meriwether Lewis, to lead the Corps of Discovery.[55]

Jefferson believed that Lewis had the persistence and bravery to command the expedition, and he saw to it that he had the knowledge as well. He lent him books and maps. He wrote to Andrew Ellicott, a renowned surveyor, who agreed to recommend measuring instruments for the expedition and teach Lewis how to use them. He prevailed upon Dr. Benjamin Rush to provide medical knowledge that Lewis might need and asked other friends in Philadelphia to tutor him in botany and paleontology. Between lessons, the indefatigable Lewis purchased equipment and provisions for the journey ahead.[56]

Toward the middle of June, Jefferson received Lewis in Washington City, where he was putting a final polish on instructions for the journey. Jefferson had been working on them for months, but as historian Donald Jackson observed, "They embrace[d] years of study and wonder."[57]

On July 4, while Lewis was still in Washington, the *National Intelligencer* brought news of the purchase to the public: "The United States have obtained the full right to and sovereignty over New Orleans and the whole of Louisiana." Since becoming president, Jefferson had thrown open the doors of the President's House on the Fourth of July, and the crowd that gathered in 1803 had, as a participant described it, a "mighty event" to celebrate. Military units marched outside, parading and firing guns, until the president appeared and received their marching salute.[58]

The next day, Meriwether Lewis set out for Pittsburgh and from there, on a keelboat he had designed, traveled down the Ohio River to Clarksville, Indiana, where he met with William Clark, whom he had recruited to lead the expedition with him, and a group of sturdy young men Clark had enlisted for the journey. After wintering over, the Corps of Discovery headed up the Missouri River on the way to the West. Reports of the journey, few though they were, would lift Jefferson's spirits during his second term. The safe return of Lewis and his party to St. Louis brought Jefferson "unspeakable joy," he wrote. He proudly displayed the Native American artifacts that Lewis presented to him—shields, quill work, a painted buffalo robe—in the entrance hall at Monticello, where visitors were amazed by their strangeness and beauty, as was he.[59]

The Louisiana Purchase fired many an imagination. General Horatio Gates, a man not known for his poetic soul, wrote, "It has the air of enchantment!" More predictable but elegant, nonetheless, was the oration delivered by Dr. David Ramsay, a noted speaker, that set the purchase in the context of American history: "The establishment of independence and of our present Constitution are prior both in time and importance, but with these two exceptions, the acquisition of Louisiana is the greatest political blessing ever conferred on these states."[60]

Despite the widespread enthusiasm for the purchase, the Federalists grumbled. The United States should not have paid "a large sum for a vast wilderness world," Senator William Plumer of New Hampshire wrote. It could "prove worse than useless to us." Other New Englanders saw the treaty as an instrument for increasing the power of the South at the expense of the North. "Is Virginia to be our Rome?" asked Massachusetts congressman Fisher Ames. A contingent of Federalist newspapers found amusement in claims that Jefferson made in a report to Congress that included the enormous salt mountain. Why not "an immense lake of molasses"? asked one. Why not "a considerable lake of pure whiskey"? queried another. Jefferson, who had a limited sense of humor, would not have found these jokes amusing.[61]

The most serious attack was that Jefferson had acted unconstitutionally in acquiring Louisiana. He had overseen a vast acquisition, when nowhere in the Constitution did it say that the U.S. government had the right to acquire property.

Secretary of State Madison and Secretary of the Treasury Albert Gallatin, clear-eyed men both, advised that there was no constitutional issue. The United States, like every other nation, had an inherent right to acquire property, and the Constitution provided the means to do it, such as the power to make treaties. Jefferson, who had long argued that the powers of the central government were restricted to those laid out by the Constitution, was unconvinced and decided that a constitutional amendment was necessary. He was working on drafts with Madison and Gallatin when word came that Napoleon was getting cold feet. Faced with the practicality of events, Jefferson abandoned the idea of amending the Constitution and wrote to Madison, "The less we say about constitutional difficulties respecting Louisiana the better." When Congress convened, the treaty was rushed through in a week.[62]

The constitutionality of the United States acquiring territory would be affirmed in 1828 by the U.S. Supreme Court in *American Insurance Company v. Canter*, but at the time Jefferson decided to present the treaty to the Senate, he doubted that he was following the strict letter of the law. Still, he was convinced that he was doing the right thing. He wrote to his ally Senator John Breckenridge on August 12, 1803:

> The Constitution has made no provision for our holding foreign territory. . . . The executive in seizing the fugitive occurrence, which so much advanced the good of their country, have done an act beyond the Constitution. The legislature . . . must ratify and pay for it and throw themselves on their country for

doing for them unauthorized what we know they would have done for themselves had they been in a situation to do it. It is the case of a guardian, investing the money of his ward in purchasing an important adjacent territory and saying to him when of age, "I did this for your good."

He had come a long way from 1798 when he had written in the Kentucky Resolutions that the Constitution "delegated to [the] government certain definite powers, reserving, each state to itself, the residuary mass of right to their own self-government, and that whensoever the general government assumes undelegated powers, its acts are unauthoritative, void, and of no force." The presidency had changed his perspective, which in this instance, or so generations of Americans have believed, resulted in the correct outcome.[63]

The Louisiana Purchase, without doubt the high point of Jefferson's presidency, occurred at the same time that a personal scandal threatened his reputation. James Callender reappeared, convinced that Jefferson had turned his back on him and intent on bringing the president down. In the *Richmond Recorder*, he wrote, "It is well known that the man *whom it delighteth the people to honor* keeps and for many years past has kept as his concubine one of his own slaves. Her name is Sally." He reported that Sally had five light-skinned children. The story was picked up by newspapers and commemorated with salacious doggerel. Federalists, who saw their power declining, used the story to assault the president's character.[64]

Jefferson had no comment then or afterward. Family members denied that Sally Hemings's children were his, as did generation after generation of historians and intellectuals. Few even allowed the possibility until Annette Gordon-Reed's 1997 book, *Thomas Jefferson and Sally Hemings: An American Controversy.* In 1998, DNA evidence was published linking Eston Hemings, one of Sally Hemings's children, with the Jefferson line, and the consensus changed. As historian Joseph Ellis, who once found the possibility of a liaison remote, wrote, "The likelihood of a long-standing sexual relationship . . . can never be proven absolutely, but it is now proven beyond reasonable doubt."[65]

Despite Jefferson's public pillorying, there is no indication that he ever regretted his connection with Sally Hemings. After the scandal that Callender provoked, she bore two more children, Madison in 1805 and Eston in 1808. Jefferson saw to it that they, along with the other two Hemings children who reached adulthood, lived their mature lives free.[66]

Two weeks after word of the Louisiana treaty reached Washington, forty-five-year-old James Callender was found dead, drowned in three feet of water in the James River. The Richmond coroner ruled the death an accident, caused by Callender's being in a drunken stupor.

I have ever considered diplomacy as the pest of the peace of the world," Jefferson wrote, and at times he brushed it away, as one might a gnat. One such moment was occasioned by a

British minister's arrival in Washington. Anthony Merry was a long-serving diplomat who seemed perpetually sunk in gloom. Toujours Gai, he was sarcastically called behind his back. Elizabeth Merry was a "large, tall, well-made woman," according to Margaret Bayard Smith, and reportedly "of fine understanding." She studied botany, wore dramatic gowns and splendid diamonds, and on social occasions took attention away from her dour husband.[67]

Jefferson invited the Merrys to dine at the President's House, but when dinner was announced, instead of leading Mrs. Merry in, as both Merrys had expected, the president took Mrs. Madison's hand. The secretary of state rescued Mrs. Merry, leaving the minister on his own. He found a chair at the table, but before he could sit down, a congressman slipped into it, and he had to scramble for another. Several days later, when the Merrys attended a dinner at the F Street home of the secretary of state, they also found rules of precedence ignored. Madison escorted Mrs. Gallatin, wife of the Treasury secretary, to her seat. When no one came forward to take Mrs. Merry's hand, Minister Merry did so himself.[68]

Jefferson had a rationale for acting as he did. He explained to a friend:

> The principle of society with us, as well as of our political constitution, is the equal rights of all; and if there be an occasion where this equality ought to prevail preeminently, it is in social circles collected for conviviality. Nobody shall be above you, nor you above anybody.

Merry thought he had been deliberately insulted, and he may well have had a point. The Madisons knew that the Merrys would be affronted. Dolley Madison had tried to persuade Jefferson to escort Mrs. Merry to the dining table, and the secretary later told Monroe that he had not wanted to offend the British minister and his wife, but felt he should show solidarity with the president. If the Madisons, who had never traveled to Europe, knew the Merrys would be offended, certainly Jefferson, with his diplomatic experience, would have been aware.[69]

As the dinner incidents grew into a diplomatic crisis, Jefferson wrote down the rules to be followed, and Madison explained them to Merry. The minister quite understandably complained that he should have been told of the change before he encountered it.[70]

The treatment of the Merrys had consequences. The minister and his wife turned down future invitations to dine at the President's House and became estranged from the Jefferson administration. Merry formed an anti-administration alliance with Spanish minister Carlos Martínez de Yrujo, and later both would lend a sympathetic ear to Aaron Burr as he outlined his grandiose plans for the American West. Martínez de Yrujo would even provide modest funding for his project. Jefferson, totally misreading Merry, declared, "We believe him to be personally as desirable a character as could have been sent us." Elizabeth Merry, on the other hand, was "an opposite character in every point." She was "a virago," he wrote, and if she continued to stir up trouble, "She must eat her soup at home."[71]

For Jefferson to place the blame for the social contretemps on

Mrs. Merry is somewhat surprising. He had met well-educated, forceful women before and corresponded with many of them. He noted that Mrs. Merry had "disturbed our harmony extremely," and since he hated disharmony, he may have been irritated by the way she roiled the waters. Elizabeth Merry also challenged his authority, which the salonnières of Paris had never done.[72]

It should also be noted that at the dawn of the nineteenth century, wife blaming was unremarkable behavior. Indeed, the *Gazette of the United States* painted the wives of Jefferson's cabinet members as crude and silly creatures, who had set the stage for the social crisis.[73]

At the beginning of 1804, Jefferson was even more optimistic than usual. The Republicans, who overwhelmingly controlled both the House and Senate, had nominated him for a second term, and he had every reason to look forward to winning in a landslide. Not only had he nearly doubled the size of the United States, he had, thanks to his brilliant secretary of the Treasury, Albert Gallatin, overseen a decline in the national debt and the end of internal taxes.

All too soon grief intruded. About the time of his nomination, Jefferson received a letter from Maria, his beautiful and fragile younger daughter. Nearing the end of her third pregnancy, she told her "dear Papa" of being "low in spirits and health." Jefferson worried about her as he worked on a project to extract the teachings of Jesus from the New Testament. Using a blade, he cut "morsels of morality" from two Bibles he had purchased and pasted them to blank pages that he subsequently had bound. In the forty-six-page document he created, miracles were absent as was anything that failed the test of reason. What remained, Jefferson believed, was the essence of Jesus's most admirable philosophy.[74]

When Jefferson learned that Maria had given birth to a daughter, he wished her "a thousand joys," but she continued to decline. He arrived at Monticello in early April to find that she could barely stand, was unable to eat, and suffered from an abscess on her breast. Her sister Martha, who had recently had a baby, nursed Maria's along with her own.[75]

On April 17, Maria died. Jefferson's granddaughter remembered her mother, Martha, telling her that on the day of Maria's death, she came upon Jefferson holding a Bible. The story would be easy to dismiss as a daughter's or granddaughter's attempt to protect Jefferson from accusations that he was an unbeliever. He had, after all, recently rejected all but small portions of Scripture. Maria's death, however, seemed to turn his thoughts toward what he had dismissed. In a letter to John Page, an old friend, Jefferson lamented his daughter's death and the deaths of so many whom he and Page had known:

> When you and I look back on the country over which we have passed, what a field of slaughter does it exhibit! Where are all the friends who entered it with us, under all the inspiring energies of health and hope? As if pursued by the havoc of war, they are strewed by the way.

But a source of comfort remained:

> We have, however, the traveler's consolation. Every step short-
> ens the distance we have to go; the end of our journey is in
> sight, the bed wherein we are to rest and to rise in the midst of
> the friends we have lost. "We sorrow not then as others who
> have no hope."

The quotation, a paraphrase from Paul's First Epistle to the Thes-
salonians, concerns the greatest of Christian miracles—the resur-
rection of the dead.[76] For a time, at least, Jefferson may have embraced
the Bible as a whole.

Jefferson delayed his return to Washington from "a desire to
see my family in a state of more composure before we separate."
Once back in the federal city he immersed himself in work. On
his agenda was West Florida, where converging rivers flowing
into the Gulf of Mexico held great promise for American commerce. The United States viewed West Florida as part of the Louisiana Purchase, a claim that Spain disputed, arguing that the land
had belonged to Spain rather than France at the time the treaty
was executed. Secretary of State Madison vigorously supported
the American position, as did James Monroe, still in Europe,
whom Jefferson had delegated to negotiate with Spain and France.
Efforts to strike an agreement were tedious and ultimately futile,
though not without drama. The Spanish minister, Martínez de
Yrujo, was so outraged by the American claim to West Florida

that he appeared in the secretary of state's office and berated Madison. Lest this performance failed to make his displeasure clear, he packed bags and took up residence in Philadelphia.[77]

The Twelfth Amendment to the Constitution, ratified in the summer of 1804, required that electors distinguish between votes cast for president and those for vice president, thus preventing another election of 1800 in which a party's presidential and vice-presidential nominees ended up running against each other. The Republican caucus unanimously chose Jefferson as their presidential nominee and selected New York governor George Clinton to be vice president. Clinton had earlier written to Jefferson that his age (sixty-four) and his ill health (which he blamed on "the incessant care and confinement" of the governorship) had made him decide not to run for governor again, but he found the vice presidency attractive. Jefferson, for his part, seemed satisfied. The Virginia dynasts took care of their own, and a young and vigorous vice president might emerge as a candidate against Madison in 1808.[78]

Burr turned his eye to New York, where he launched a campaign to succeed Clinton as governor. The contest was a nasty one, with many a broadside taking up Burr's well-known sexual profligacy. Burr was certain that Alexander Hamilton, who had opposed him in 1801, was behind the charges, and after he had been crushed at the polls he demanded that Hamilton disavow words that he had reportedly uttered, which Hamilton refused to do. The two men met on the dueling field at Weehawken, New Jersey. Shots were fired, Hamilton fell, and the next day he was dead.[79]

Jefferson and Clinton won fifteen of the Union's seventeen states, an overwhelming victory. Aaron Burr, his reputation in tatters, set out for the West, hoping that fame, fortune, and power could still be his. Jefferson heard reports that Burr had plans to split the West from the Union, but was not alarmed, in part because they came from sources he did not trust. In the fall of 1806, however, both he and Madison began to think that Burr was serious about establishing a separate confederacy—and not necessarily by peaceful means. "We learn that he is actually building ten or fifteen boats able to take a large gun and fit for the navigation of [the Ohio River]," Jefferson wrote to Thomas Mann Randolph, who was married to his daughter Martha. There had been no legal action, he explained: "As yet we have no legal proof of any overt act." Article 3, section 3 of the Constitution required two witnesses to an "overt act" for a person to be convicted of treason.[80]

In late fall, Jefferson received a dispatch from General James Wilkinson, the senior officer of the United States Army. Unbeknownst to Jefferson, Wilkinson, widely thought to be a scoundrel, was part of the western conspiracy, but concerned that he would soon be exposed, the general had turned on Burr and was trying to recast himself as the discoverer of the plot. His October 21 letter to the president, full of ominous warnings about a huge and desperate enterprise, prompted Jefferson to send a proclamation to military and civilian authorities to watch for evidence of criminal conspiracies and stop them from moving forward. He did not name Burr, nor had Wilkinson.[81]

In January 1807, Jefferson received another letter from Wilkinson, this one containing a sworn affidavit from the general as well as a decrypted copy of a ciphered letter, which was purported to be from Burr, though, in fact, it was not. It portrayed Burr declaring that he had the necessary funding in place and that boats were being built to bring five hundred to one thousand armed men gathered on the Ohio River down the Mississippi. The goal now was to seize money and military stores in New Orleans and use them to invade Mexico—or so the ciphered letter had Burr saying. Jefferson sent the affidavit containing the ciphered letter to Congress, as well as a message. Burr was guilty "beyond question" of "this scene of depravity," he declared—even though the federal government had not yet arrested Burr, much less put him on trial. Jefferson would be accused of prejudging Burr, as indeed he had. Luther Martin, a lawyer for Burr, said of the president, "He has let slip the dogs of war, the hell hounds of persecution, to hunt down my friend."[82]

Burr was arrested in the Mississippi Territory and brought to Richmond, Virginia, to face charges of treason. Jefferson's nemesis, Chief Justice John Marshall, presided as a circuit court judge. Burr often argued on his own behalf and had a skilled defense team to back him up. Two of the three prosecutors, perhaps coincidentally, had close ties to James Monroe. Lead attorney George Hay would become his son-in-law within the year. William Wirt was Monroe's good friend. Wirt would deliver a riveting speech toward the end of the trial that for generations would be considered a model of American oratory.[83]

The venue at the Eagle Tavern became so crowded that grand jury proceedings were moved to the chamber of the House of Delegates in the Virginia state capitol. When the trial for treason began, even the House chamber proved too small and many would-be spectators had to be turned away. Jefferson did not attend the trial but worked on it with such intensity from Washington City that Burr's conviction seems to have become an idée fixe with him. He personally interviewed a key witness while Secretary of State Madison took notes. He barraged George Hay with elaborate instructions, even sending him presidential pardons with the name of the beneficiary left blank and advice on how best to use them.[84] The scene remains one of the most arresting in American history: the president of the United States, supported by his secretary of state, directing from behind the scenes the prosecution of his former vice president.

One of Burr's gambits was to ask the court to issue subpoenas for letters that General Wilkinson had sent to the president. Marshall allowed the subpoenas to go forward on the grounds that the president was not a king, he was a citizen, subject like other citizens to the law. Jefferson responded to the news that a subpoena was on its way with a letter to Hay, which Hay subsequently read in court. In it, Jefferson asserted the "right of the President of the United States to decide independently of all other authority what papers coming to him as president the public interests permit to be communicated and to whom." He promised to cooperate fully, "to do what was right," but unfortunately, Jefferson wrote, the letter was not in his possession. He was trying to find it, he said, but at least during Burr's legal difficulties, he did not. Burr complained, but neither he nor Marshall pressed the issue.[85]

Jefferson had the benefit of Madison's counsel when he responded to a second subpoena for communications with Wilkinson. The secretary of state was visiting Monticello when Jefferson wrote to George Hay, instructing him to present a copy of a letter to the court that he, Jefferson, had redacted, along with a signed certificate from him attesting that the redactions were not material to the trial. Although Marshall had previously ruled that a copy would not be admitted, the letter was received and not discussed again.[86]

Neither Jefferson nor Marshall pushed the matter of presidential prerogative to a resolution, but their disagreement was significant. It was an early skirmish over a controversial matter that would later be called executive privilege.

Not long before Burr's trial, Marshall had broadly construed the concept of treason: "If a body of men be actually assembled for the purpose of effecting by force a treasonable purpose, all those who perform any part, however minute or however remote from the scene of action and who are actually leagued in the general conspiracy, are to be considered as traitors." The prosecution in the Burr trial repeatedly brought up Marshall's interpretation, believing that it covered Burr's actions. He was the instigator of a gathering upward of thirty men "armed and arrayed in a warlike manner" on Blennerhassett Island in the Ohio River, and although he was not present when they raised their muskets on Ohio militiamen, Burr was as guilty as if he had been. He was "leagued in the general conspiracy," or so the prosecution maintained.[87]

The prosecution planned on calling more than a hundred witnesses to make their case, but after few more than a dozen, Marshall granted a defense motion to exclude the others on the grounds that their testimony would be irrelevant. None of the potential witnesses could describe Burr participating in an "overt act" of "levying war," as the Constitution required, because he had left the island by the time the men brandished their muskets. By thus suppressing the prosecution's evidence, Marshall made it impossible for jury members to convict. After short deliberation, they declared Burr "not guilty," but only after explaining their verdict: "We of the jury say that Aaron Burr is not proved to be guilty under this indictment by any evidence submitted to us."[88]

Marshall's ruling, hewing close to the Constitution, was very different from what he had declared before about participants in a general conspiracy sharing guilt, even if they were "remote from the scene of action." Jefferson, on the other hand, who had seemed to embrace a close reading of the treason clause when he wrote to his son-in-law about the need for evidence of an "overt act," favored a latitudinarian interpretation of the clause during the trial.[89]

It is tempting to see both men favoring victory over consistency, given how thoroughly they had come to detest one another. But each had a larger purpose. Marshall's was to strengthen the idea that the judicial branch was not only the equal of the legislative and the executive, but also the final expositor of the Constitution. Jefferson's goal was to maintain and strengthen the executive against what he called "the engulfing power" of the courts.[90]

At the same time that Jefferson was contending with Burr and Marshall, he faced a growing crisis with Britain. Warring with France and finding themselves short of seamen, British sailors were stopping American ships, seizing men on board that they suspected of being British, and impressing them into the Royal Navy, although many were, in fact, American. The U.S. government viewed impressment as an insult, a refusal on Britain's part to recognize the independence the United States had won nearly a quarter century before. Madison and Jefferson, neither wanting war, placed their first hope in diplomacy, particularly after Charles James Fox, an amiable, corpulent, longtime supporter of the United States, became Britain's foreign secretary. Fox firmly secured the goodwill of the president and secretary of state with one of his first acts, the recall of minister Anthony Merry.

Monroe, now minister in England, was optimistic about reaching an agreement with the new ministry, but his mood soured when he learned that the administration was sending an envoy extraordinaire to London to assist in negotiations. He viewed the appointment of William Pinkney, a Maryland attorney of commanding demeanor, as an affront, and he vented his disappointment by writing to Jefferson that the appointment conveyed to the world that the administration had lost confidence in him. It was even a breach of friendship, he wrote, since no one had bothered to consult him. "At no period of my life was I ever subjected to more inquietude," he lamented. Then he set aside the sheets of paper on which he had laid out his feelings, neither sending them nor burning them.[91]

Madison instructed Monroe and Pinkney to consider impressment the most important of the maritime wrongs that Great Britain had inflicted on the United States. Jefferson and Madison informed Congress (and, thereby, the public) that they had emphasized with Monroe and Pinkney the necessity of a treaty halting the practice, but after the death of Charles James Fox in September 1806, British negotiators flatly refused to take up the subject. Unable to consult with either the secretary of state or the president (a letter from England to the United States could take two months to arrive, as could an answer back), Monroe and Pinkney signed a treaty that made no mention of impressment. When the new British minister to the United States, David Erskine, received the treaty and rushed to Madison's office with it, the secretary of state was astonished. When Jefferson, who was suffering from a migraine that debilitated him for most of March, learned that the treaty did not address impressment, he refused to submit it to the Senate. It was a decision that left Monroe deeply resentful, angrier than either Jefferson or Madison realized.[92]

Jefferson and Madison were hit hard by the Federalist press. According to the *Columbian Centinel*, Jefferson's rejection of the treaty was political. He knew that Monroe had supporters in Virginia who wanted him to run for president, but Jefferson wanted Madison to succeed him, which Madison wanted as well. "*Therefore,*" according to the *Centinel*, "it could not be expected in these evil times that Mr. Madison would let slip so favorable an opportunity of blasting the reputation of his *rival* as not to advise the president to muster up all his *energies* and condemn the treaty-copy off hand."[93]

The Federalist press had called Jefferson a coward, a double-dealer, an infidel, and a libertine, among other things, but the charge that he had rejected the Monroe-Pinkney Treaty because of a political scheme especially bothered him. He was also simultaneously being condemned for his aggressive pursuit of Burr, particularly for declaring him guilty before he had been tried. Asked *The Salem Gazette*, "If our great men can thus pronounce upon a man's guilt or innocence, what need have we of juries?"[94]

As Jefferson's anger mounted, he received a polite letter asking for advice on creating a good newspaper. John Norvell, the young man wanting guidance, was no doubt surprised by the strong response he got. Wrote Jefferson:

It is a melancholy truth that a suppression of the press could not more completely deprive the nation of its benefits than is done by its abandoned prostitution to falsehood. Nothing can now be believed which is seen in a newspaper. Truth itself becomes suspicious by being put into that polluted vehicle.

One way to improve newspapers, he suggested to Norvell, was to reserve in them a special section for lies.[95]

Twenty years earlier Jefferson had written: "Were it left to me to decide whether we should have a government without newspapers or newspapers without a government, I should not hesitate a moment to prefer the latter." He had lost his faith in a free press.[96]

On June 22, 1807, the captain of the HMS *Leopard*, a fifty-two-gun warship, demanded to search the USS *Chesapeake,* a thirty-eight-gun frigate sailing out of Hampton Roads, in order to remove British deserters. When the American commodore denied there were deserters on board and refused to allow a search, the British ship fired two broadsides into the *Chesapeake,* then a third as the ship lowered its colors. The assault killed three and injured eighteen. The British impressed four sailors, three of whom, it turned out, were American.[97]

The attack on the *Chesapeake* catalyzed American anger against the British. "This country has never been in such a state of excitement since the battle of Lexington," Jefferson wrote to James Bowdoin, a Massachusetts philanthropist who was in Spain negotiating on behalf of the United States. Even the normally cool and collected Madison caught the fever, drafting a proclamation for the president that denounced the *Leopard*'s "avowed and insulting purpose of violating a ship of war under the American flag" and the "lawless and bloody" intent of the British attack. Usually it was Madison who restrained Jefferson, but in a role reversal, Jefferson edited out much of Madison's aggressive prose—though, to be sure, the proclamation was still sharp-edged.[98]

Neither the president nor the secretary of state wanted war. The United States was ill-prepared for hostilities, and as Republicans saw it, war gave unconscionable power to the federal government. Madison, who had long believed that commercial policies could compel a foe to change, urged Jefferson to turn to such measures after Napoleon declared a blockade of Britain and King George ordered a blockade of France, its allies, and its colonies. Adding insult to injury, Great Britain announced that far from being ended, the practice of impressment would be expanded. "The whole world is thus laid under interdict by these two nations," wrote a frustrated Jefferson, "and our vessels, their cargoes, and crews are to be taken by the one or the other for whatever place they may be destined out of our own limits." Following Madison's lead, he made a decision that would dog him for the rest of his presidency. He asked Congress to pass an embargo that would keep all American ships in port, which the House and the Senate, both about 80 percent Republican, promptly did, and when he requested supplements to strengthen the embargo, Congress approved those as well.[99]

Madison wrote essays for the *National Intelligencer* to justify the embargo to the public. It was a protective measure, he wrote, meant to keep American ships safe. It would avoid war while putting heavy pressure on enemies to stop ship seizures and impressment. It would bring privations, to be sure, but he asked, "What are these compared with [the embargo's] effects on those who have driven us into the measure?" National honor was also at stake, he advised. Standing fast by the embargo would show the world that the United States would "flinch from no sacrifices which the honor and good of the nation demand from virtuous and faithful citizens."[100]

Madison's calls for sacrifice and patriotism could not overcome the realities of the embargo. When the spring ice melted and ships that normally carried goods to overseas markets stayed in harbor, thousands of merchants, sailors, fishermen, and farmers saw their livelihoods slipping away. New Englanders organized petition drives, and in a single month, more than five thousand citizens of Massachusetts signed the protests. Jefferson was flooded with letters. James Lewis, a Revolutionary War veteran, wrote that he could no longer support his wife and seven children. John Lane Jones, addressing Jefferson as "You infernal villain," was furious that he had been forced to steal bread to feed his family. Jefferson later wrote that amid the rage he had "felt the foundations of the government shaken under my feet by the New England townships." As had happened in other times of crisis, he succumbed to a migraine, this one lasting nearly two weeks.[101]

Once recovered, Jefferson doubled down, firm in the belief that the embargo was the only alternative to either war or being under the British thumb. As smugglers ran rampant, particularly along the Canadian border, he requested an Enforcement Act that would allow him extraordinary powers. Even as Congress debated suspending the embargo, he declared the Champlain valley to be in a state of insurrection and ordered state and federal authorities to suppress the uprising. After the Enforcement Act became law, he used the United States Navy and the regular army to enforce the embargo.[102]

Having begun his presidency opposing the expansion of federal power, he had, at the end, exercised more power in the presidency than either of his predecessors. The results were far from what he had hoped. The U.S. economy took a mighty blow. Exports dropped from $108 million in 1807 to $22 million in 1808. There were reports that the embargo was also hurting England—but not so much that it drew them into serious negotiations. In his last message to Congress, Jefferson admitted that the embargo—"this candid and liberal experiment," he called it—had failed.[103]

Not long into his retirement, Jefferson offered justification for the powers he had exercised as president:

A strict observance of the written laws is doubtless *one* of the high duties of a good citizen, but it is not *the highest*. The laws of necessity, of self-preservation, of saving our country when in danger are of higher obligation. To lose our country by a scrupulous adherence to written law would be to lose the law

itself, with life, liberty, property and all those who are enjoy-
ing them with us.

He set out examples, including one that resembled the Louisiana
Purchase. His decision in that case had so obviously benefited the
country that it had garnered wide support. The embargo was
quite different, causing more pain and outrage than the government of a republic could endure.[104]

EIGHT

Securing Independence

∞

War Under the Constitution

The Senate chamber of the U.S. Capitol, so grand at Jefferson's first inauguration, began to fall apart in his second term. Columns cracked and timbers rotted, but Congress refused to fund a renovation, not even when a piece of the ceiling fell next to the president of the Senate's chair. Makeshift measures, such as wrapping cracked columns in whitewashed linen, did little good. Columns continued to split, pieces of the plastered ceiling continued to fall, and the timbers holding up roof and floor continued to rot and weaken.[1]

Under circumstances that would prompt an evacuation today, the Republican caucus met in the Senate chamber on the evening of January 23, 1808, to choose their candidate to succeed Jefferson. Members filled out their ballots by candlelight, and when the counting was over, Secretary of State James Madison, President Jefferson's choice, was the victor, winning 83 of 89 votes cast.[2]

Madison's win was impressive, but seventy-nine Republican officeholders did not attend the meeting in the Senate chamber, and many of them had other candidates in mind. In New York, Republican political leaders, tired of Virginia's dominance of the presidency, were coalescing around George Clinton, Jefferson's jowly, white-haired vice president during his second term. Clinton received just three votes on the presidential ballot in the Senate chamber, but on a subsequent vote, members nominated him to be Madison's running mate, hoping to keep him from an independent run for president.

In Virginia, Madison's base and the motherlode of electoral votes, conservatives looked at his support of Jefferson's policies, and concluded that he had abandoned faith in limited government. These "Old Republicans," as they called themselves, persuaded James Monroe, the youngest member of the Virginia dynasty, to take up their banner. They wrote to him while he was in London, portraying every action of the administration as calculated to give Madison the advantage in the upcoming presidential contest. Political operative John Beckley told him that Madison was "deemed by many too timid and indecisive as a statesman." Monroe, with far more energy and determination, should be Jefferson's successor, Beckley wrote.[3]

Virginia congressman John Randolph of Roanoke wrote Monroe that Republican ideals were dead: "Everything is made a business of bargain and traffic, the ultimate object of which is to raise Mr. M[adiso]n to the presidency." Randolph was a brilliant eccentric, who, probably for medical reasons, perhaps a childhood disease, had a boyish face, an excruciatingly thin body, and a high-pitched voice. He was a master of sarcasm, a tool he often used to eviscerate his enemies. Although most people disgusted him, he was fond of Monroe, who had been kind to Randolph's nephew. Monroe took the boy, who was deaf, into his London home, found him a well-recommended school, and faithfully reported on his progress.[4]

As long as he was in Europe, Monroe did not succumb to the siren song of those who wanted him to run, but after he returned home, he let his name be put forward. In the Republican caucus for president in the Senate chamber, he, like Clinton, got just three votes, and he also came up short when Virginians caucused in Richmond. Jefferson, trying to avoid a split between Madison and Monroe, wrote to Monroe that he dreaded an internecine conflict: "I see with infinite grief a contest arising between yourself and another, who have been very dear to each other and equally so to me." He explained the decisions that had offended Monroe and assured him that no personal animus had been behind them. Monroe, who remembered that Jefferson had set him on a new path when he despaired of moving forward at all, declared that he was "perfectly satisfied by the explanations and assurances."[5]

Monroe did not take his name out of the running, partly out of pride, but also because he resented Madison, who, he believed, had blocked his upward rise for twenty years, going back to the Constitutional Convention. Likely, too, he was jealous of Madison's relationship with Jefferson, in which an intellectual parity existed that Monroe would never achieve. In his autobiography, which covered the years 1743 to 1790, Jefferson wrote nothing about Monroe that approached his praise of Madison for "a habit

of self-possession which placed at ready command the rich resources of his luminous and discriminating mind." For his part,
Madison felt no obligation to extend the hand of friendship to a
man running against him for the second time. The payments of
interest he had made on Monroe's loans, which had helped under-
write Monroe's time in Paris, also smarted, especially since Madison was borrowing money to pay his own rent. For at least two
years, Madison and Monroe would neither see nor correspond
with one another.[6]

Following custom, neither man actively campaigned for the
nomination, depending instead upon local Republican organiza-
tions and supporters writing newspaper editorials and letters extolling their candidate's qualifications. Madison, savvy politician
that he was, no doubt offered campaign suggestions, but he left no
paper trail. Among Monroe's papers are long letters to John Taylor of Caroline, one of his strongest supporters, in which he set
forth "hints" for conducting his campaign. Jefferson and Madison
should not be attacked, but the rejection of the Monroe-Pinkney
Treaty ought to be, he wrote. His own impressive experience in
foreign policy should be emphasized, including that "the cession
of Louisiana was due to me"—several steps beyond what he had
claimed before.[7]

George Clinton, the current vice president and nominee to be
Madison's as well, confirmed the dim view that most Republicans
had of him by deciding to run for president as an independent at
the same time he was running for vice president as a Republican.
He urged Federalists to join his campaign, but, buoyed by the failure of the embargo, they nominated their own candidate, Charles
Cotesworth Pinckney of South Carolina. An official Federalist

candidate made it unlikely that Clinton would peel off Federalist votes—an advantage for Madison, but hardly his only one. As it became increasingly clear that he would win, Monroe's friends fell away. One was the tall, curly-haired William Wirt, who became Madison's ardent and eloquent defender. When Monroe supporters accused Madison of "want of energy," Wirt demanded to know exactly when Madison had shown a lack of drive and vitality. Was it when he led the way to replace the Articles of Confederation with the U.S. Constitution? Was it when he threw himself into debate with Patrick Henry to get the Constitution ratified, or when he fought to defeat the Alien and Sedition Acts?[8]

Madison also grew in favor by inviting senators and congressmen to his F Street home. Dolley Madison served southern comfort food, ensured lively conversation, and provided cards and gambling chips for guests, which they enjoyed, although newspaper publisher Samuel Harrison Smith confessed that he was embarrassed to put Mrs. Madison's money in his pocket.[9]

In a town where congressmen had little to do in off-hours except continue the political debates they had been having all day, evenings at the Madisons were a welcome relief. They also showed Madison to his best advantage. A British minister found him "a social, jovial, and good-humored companion, full of anecdote." Senator Samuel Mitchill of New York, a Republican, wrote to his wife that because of Dolley Madison, James Madison was "going greatly ahead" of George Clinton.[10]

Electoral votes would not be officially counted until early February 1809, but tallies in the states revealed the result well before the president of the Senate announced it. Madison lost the states in which anger about the embargo ran high—New Hampshire, Massachusetts, Connecticut, Rhode Island, and Delaware—but with the exception of a few scattered electors, he swept the rest, for a total of 122 electoral votes. Pinckney won 47 votes, and George Clinton, 6. The former New York governor had decisively lost the presidency, but topped the voting to serve as vice president. Monroe received several thousand votes in Virginia, but won not a single elector.[11]

In a letter combining ambition and naïveté, Monroe wrote to Jefferson on January 18, 1809, and suggested that he be sent on a mission to England and France to try to avert war. He offered to leave right away and not take his family, which was for him a true sacrifice. He was a doting husband and father, accustomed to having his wife and daughters with him everywhere—even on foreign assignments.[12]

The difficulties with Monroe's plan were obvious. Madison would not become president until March, but Monroe's mission would extend beyond that, making Madison's foreign policy hostage to his recent rival. Virginia's regular Republicans would be furious at Jefferson advancing Monroe. They had already begun to exact political revenge from those who had backed him. Jefferson told Monroe that there was simply no support in Congress for the mission he had in mind, but Monroe pressed the case in a second letter, which there is no record of Jefferson answering. Later in the year, Monroe told Francis Baring, a British merchant banker, "I am now withdrawn altogether from public life and may remain so for years if not forever."[13] Nearly thirty years before, he had said the same thing.

On March 4, 1809, Madison was inaugurated in the recently completed chamber of the House of Representatives, a grand room that Jefferson had played a part in designing. His inspiration was the light-filled Halle aux Blés, where he had met Maria Cosway more than two decades before. Publisher Samuel Harrison Smith declared the chamber to be "the handsomest room in the world occupied by a deliberative body."[14]

Men and women in formal dress crowded into the chamber, as did Washingtonians who made no pretense to social distinction. All found it difficult to hear the new president as he expressed gratitude for his election by a free people, but as he continued, his voice grew stronger. They could hear him emphasize the importance of seeking peace while also being mindful of the very real possibility of war. Should that come, he said, the country would find its "bulwark" in well-trained militia rather than a standing army and so avoid the danger to liberty that a large and permanent military force posed. He set forth the principles that his opponents had accused him of abandoning: support of the Constitution, recognition of the limited authority of the federal government, and the preservation of individual rights. He concluded by acknowledging "that Almighty Being whose power regulates the destiny of nations, whose blessings have been so conspicuously dispensed to this rising republic, and to whom we are bound to address our devout gratitude for the past, as well as our fervent supplications and best hopes for the future."[15]

That evening there was an inaugural ball at Long's Hotel. Mrs.

Madison, wearing a buff-colored velvet gown, looked like a queen, observed Margaret Bayard Smith, though, she noted, her neckline was shockingly low. Unselfconscious about being taller than her husband, Dolley wore a turban topped with bird-of-paradise plumes that dramatically increased her height. Thomas Jefferson attended and was in high spirits that he would soon be returning to Monticello, but President Madison seemed "spiritless and exhausted," wrote Smith. The room was hot and crowded, but the new president's listlessness was probably also due to the concerns that had weighed on him the last few months.[16]

Jefferson had essentially retired as soon as the result of the 1808 presidential election was known. Determined not to limit Madison's options as Adams had tried to limit his, he stopped providing guidance to the Congress about the direction the United States should take. It was a time of looming war, and Madison and Gallatin urged him to steer members toward "some precise and distinct course," but he was quite content with being passive. He described himself to his friend George Logan as "chiefly an unmeddling listener."[17]

In the absence of presidential leadership, Madison worked behind the scenes on a proposal with Wilson Cary Nicholas, a Virginia congressman who thought that war was the only honorable step, but recognized that such a measure would not make it through Congress. Madison suggested repealing the embargo except for Britain and France and granting the president authority to resume trade with either nation should it recognize the right of the United States to sail the seas unmolested. It was a face-saving way of ending the embargo (and quieting discontent in New

England), as well as staving off war. After lengthy debate, legislation close to Madison's suggestions passed the Senate and the House and was signed by Jefferson just days before his presidency ended.[18]

The Non-Intercourse Act, as it was called, soon looked like a brilliant move. Just weeks into Madison's presidency, British minister David Erskine hurried to the State Department, a dormered, redbrick building to the west of the President's House, with word that the British Foreign Office had offered not only to withdraw the Orders in Council that endangered American shipping, but also to make reparations for the death and destruction caused by the bombardment of the *Chesapeake*. When this news was carried to the president, Madison agreed to reopen trade with England, and a national celebration followed. Jubilant citizens rang church bells and fired off cannon. In suddenly busy harbors sailors readied and loaded ships with everything from salted cod and wheat to pine, tar, and turpentine. During five days in June, seventy-two American merchant vessels landed in Liverpool.[19]

The thirty-two-year-old Erskine was a genial man, and although Frances Few, Albert Gallatin's nineteen-year-old niece, found him to have "some of the twirls and twitches of English manners," he had a lovely American wife and was kindly disposed toward the United States. Perhaps that was why he made the British offer appear more favorable than it was. He had presented demands that he knew the United States would never accept as though they were negotiating points. He dropped some requirements himself and assented to the Americans dropping others. When the agreement with the United States reached London, Foreign Secretary George Canning was aghast. Where, for example, was the requirement that the United States allow the British to seize American ships that violated the American ban on French trade? Canning reported to the House of Commons that Erskine had violated his instructions, formally disavowed him, and ordered his recall.[20]

Madison was at Montpelier when he learned of the British repudiation. "I find myself under the mortifying necessity," he wrote to Jefferson, "of setting out tomorrow morning for Washington." He arrived in two and a half days and immediately found himself in a disagreement with his secretary of state, Robert Smith. Madison had put Smith into the State Department post when it became apparent that a faction in the Senate, which included Robert's brother, Senator Samuel Smith, would block confirmation of Madison's first choice, Albert Gallatin. Robert Smith had no talent for diplomacy—or for much of anything, according to John Randolph of Roanoke, who noted that at least "he can spell." Smith's loyalty was also in question since he frequently aligned himself with his brother rather than with the administration. Madison dismissed Smith's advice that he had a constitutional obligation to get authorization from Congress to reimpose the embargo. Congress was out of session, matters could not be left to drift, and Madison, though often said to be tentative, signed the authorization and was back in Montpelier eight days after he had left.[21]

The Eleventh Congress proceeded in what President Madison described to Jefferson as an "unhinged state." Many members were uncertain about what should come after the embargo, but absolutely positive about what should not, a state of affairs that escalated tempers already high. Isaac Coles, Madison's private secretary, became so infuriated by a fellow Republican congressman that he slapped him in the face, or perhaps slugged him, depending on who told the story. Congressman John G. Jackson, Dolley Madison's brother-in-law and a strong defender of the president, fought a duel with arch-Federalist Joseph Pearson, which left Jackson with a hip wound that would trouble him for the rest of his life.[22]

The measure that passed Congress at the end of the session, known as Macon's Bill Number 2, lifted trade restrictions entirely for three months and provided that if either France or England recognized American rights at sea, the United States would cease to trade with the other country. David Erskine's successor as British minister was the haughty Francis James Jackson, whose view of the United States was the opposite of Erskine's. He saw Macon's Bill Number 2 as evidence that the U.S. government deserved the disdain in which he held it. "They have covered themselves with ridicule and disgrace," he wrote.[23]

Madison tried to find something positive in the bill. Since the British commanded the seas, they stood to profit more than France from the lifting of trade restrictions, so Napoleon might be tempted to recognize American rights in order to shut down British trade. This theory seemed like prophecy when Madison received a letter from Napoleon's foreign minister, the Duc de Cadore, saying that Napoleon would relax strictures on American trade as soon as the United States caused "their rights to be respected by the English." The president put the British on notice that the United States would reimpose sanctions unless England, like France, recognized American rights at sea. He also wrote to Jefferson that should an agreement come about, it would give the United States "the advantage at least of having but one contest on our hands at a time." John Randolph of Roanoke had another interpretation, calling the arrangement "a bargain which credulity and imbecility enter into with cunning and power."[24]

Madison's management of a simultaneous crisis belied Randolph's caricature. In West Florida, Spanish authority had begun to collapse and American settlers decided it was time to free themselves from Spanish rule. They organized a convention that Madison expected would bring a request for American occupation, but instead the West Floridians sent a motley contingent to capture the Spanish fort at Baton Rouge, issued a declaration of independence, and demanded a loan of one hundred thousand dollars from the American government as their price for joining the Union. There were also threats to turn to the British if the United States did not meet their demands.[25]

As Madison saw it, West Floridians had made themselves a ripe target for a British takeover, an event that would prove dangerous to the United States. He wrote to Jefferson that he realized the crisis in West Florida presented "serious questions as to the authority of the executive," but on the other hand, "Being our own [it] may be fairly taken possession of if it can be done without violence."[26]

Rather than engage with the convention and negotiate, Madison designated its proceedings part of an emergency that required American action. On October 27, he issued a proclamation citing the crisis that had occurred under Spanish rule, as well as the claim that West Florida had been part of the United States since the Louisiana Purchase, to deem it "right and requisite that possession should be taken of the said territory in the name and behalf of the United States." He ordered the proclamation to be published in Florida, but otherwise did not make it public.[27]

Congress was not in session at the time of Madison's proclamation, and only when members returned did they learn what he had done. Federalists accused him of operating outside the law, as he had expected they would, but by this time the occupation of West Florida was a fait accompli. Madison had done what he had earlier speculated about with Jefferson, "taken possession of [West Florida] . . . without violence."[28] His political opponents might complain about presidential overreach, but there was little they could do besides accept Madison's action. And there was little Spain could do besides deny the American claim.

In mid-October 1809, Meriwether Lewis died. Those who knew him were aware that he fell into melancholic moods and had financial problems, but they were nonetheless stunned at news of his apparent suicide. He had shot himself twice and, still alive, stabbed himself repeatedly.[29]

Lewis had been governor of the Louisiana Territory, and Madison heard that Monroe was interested in the position. He did not believe the rumor, but asked Jefferson to visit Monroe to see if it were true. On a cold November day, Jefferson rode to Monroe's home at Highland, where the two men first talked about Lewis's recent death. Jefferson then inquired about Monroe's interest in governing the Louisiana Territory, and expressed his regret "at the curtain which seemed to be drawn between him and his best friends." He suggested that Monroe's "going into any post would be a signal of reconciliation," not only with Madison, but also with Republicans who were still irritated about his presidential run. Monroe replied that the governorship of Louisiana was "incompatible with the respect he owed himself." His attention for the next few years was going to be on "the liberation of his pecuniary embarrassments." Jefferson reported the conversation back to Madison and said he was left with the impression that Monroe would accept a cabinet position.[30]

Jefferson's visit may have encouraged Monroe to think about restoring his relationship with Republicans. He ran successfully for the House of Delegates and on Election Day gave a speech emphasizing his fidelity to the Republican Party and his support for the president. Early in 1811, the general assembly made him the state's governor once more, but his shift—from the dissident Republicans who had convinced him to run against Madison to the mainstream of the party—caught the attention of John Randolph of Roanoke. He accused Monroe of yielding to ambition, of abandoning "the ground which you took after your return from England" in order to become governor. But remembering Monroe's kindness toward his nephew led him to write another letter.

"Be assured," he wrote to Monroe, "that I can never be rendered by any circumstance whatsoever less sensible of my personal obligations to you (through my nephew) than I have uniformly demonstrated myself to be; that I shall ever rejoice to hear of your personal prosperity and to promote it should it ever be in my power so to do."[31]

In March 1811, Monroe heard from Madison, who could bear Secretary of State Robert Smith no longer. Smith was telling all who would listen how misguided he thought Madison's policies were. He had even told the British chargé. There were other failings, such as Smith's correspondence, which was often so "crude and inadequate" that Madison had to rewrite it, but the unforgivable offense was disloyalty.[32]

Madison asked Monroe in a most conciliatory fashion that if there were an opening in the State Department, would he be interested. Madison expected him to say yes. The post of secretary of state was, after all, a stepping-stone to the presidency. But getting Monroe's agreement took a second letter. In it the president indicated that the Jefferson administration's refusal to seek ratification for the Monroe-Pinkney Treaty had been no fault of Monroe's, but a result of "different understandings of certain facts and constructive intentions." Within a week Monroe was on the road to Washington.[33]

The ever-practical Madison, who had obtained Robert Smith's resignation, suggested that Monroe consider moving into Smith's Capitol Hill residence. It was the best available in Washington and "not yet out of reach." Moreover, the president helpfully added, Smith intended "to dispose of certain portions of his furniture, which might suit your purposes." Monroe, instead, rented

a fine house on I Street, where he and Mrs. Monroe would enter-
tain with an elegance they could not afford.[34]

B<small>y</small> the time Monroe assumed office on April 2, 1811, the president had reinstated sanctions on the British, as Macon's Bill Number 2 required him to do if they did not join France in recognizing
American rights at sea. But the French navy continued to prey
upon and plunder American ships, leading Federalists to charge
that Napoleon's offer was a ploy aimed at creating a face-off between the United States and England. The emperor wanted to ensure enmity between his enemies.

One interpretation of these events is that Madison was duped,
manipulated by the French into giving them exactly what they
wanted. But Madison also got what he wanted. Having done all he
could to avoid war, except submitting to adversaries, he now had
the advantage he had described to Jefferson of having a single ad-
versary, and the contest would be with the right one. French
abuses were one thing, but English abuses were part of a long pattern of humiliation, of ignoring the nationhood and national
honor of the United States. For Americans to suffer British insults was to pretend that the Revolution had been repealed.

T<small>he</small> elections of 1810 increased the prospect of war. New congressmen from the South and West brought a frontier sense of
honor to the Twelfth Congress. Full of energy and bravado, these

young men would not stand by while the British insulted American rights at sea. They were also in a fury about Indian raids, in which they had lost grandmothers, brothers, aunts, uncles, cousins. They blamed the British for fomenting these attacks, a justified claim, but the war hawks, like generations to come, failed to acknowledge what underlay Indian rage. The Shawnee, Cherokee, and people of other nations regarded frontier settlers as brutal usurpers, intent on taking away their homelands and destroying ancient ways.[35]

Thirty-four-year-old Henry Clay, a slender man with a wide smile, had left the Senate, a body of "solemn stillness," he called it, for the "turbulence" of the House, where he became the leader of the war contingent. A charismatic Kentuckian famous for his oratory, Clay had impeccable credentials as a Madisonian Republican, having once fought a duel in defense of the embargo. He also knew how to charm. He arrived in Washington with a gift for the president—a bottle of Madeira, Madison's favorite, made from grapes grown in Kentucky. Soon he would be politely flirting and sharing snuff with Dolley Madison.[36]

On November 4, 1811, the first day of the Twelfth Congress and Clay's first day as a representative, he was elected Speaker of the House. The next day, President Madison sent an annual message that recommended an aggressive course. Rather than arguing about whether the French had withdrawn their decrees on American commerce, he assumed they had, as he would continue to do in the months ahead. He condemned Britain for not doing likewise, and urged preparations for war. "With this evidence of hostile inflexibility in trampling on rights which no independent nation can relinquish," his message read, "Congress will feel the duty of putting the United States into an armor and an attitude demanded by the crisis and corresponding with the national spirit and expectations."[37]

The president further aligned himself with the war hawks by pointing to the Northwest, where warriors of Indian nations were gathering, as he put it, "under the influence and direction of a fanatic of the Shawanese tribe." A Shawnee warrior named Tecumseh was creating a confederacy, but he was not a fanatic. He reasonably saw that the nations needed to combine if they were to resist successfully the encroachment of white soldiers and settlers. He used his powerful oratory in the cause of bringing them together. His brother, the Prophet, added a spiritual dimension, urging a separation from white culture and a return to ancestral ways.[38]

William Henry Harrison, the ambitious governor of Indiana, decided to destroy the Prophetstown settlement founded by Tecumseh and the Prophet. He marched with an army up the Wabash, camping on November 6 near the mouth of the Tippecanoe River. In the dark hours before dawn on November 7, an assault force of Kickapoo and Winnebago attacked. Within a few hours, 61 of Harrison's men were dead and 127 wounded, a toll greater than suffered by his attackers. The next day, Harrison decided on a counterassault, but when he and his army reached the Indian settlement, it was empty. They burned it and left the area as quickly as they could.[39]

Tippecanoe proved their case, the war hawks declared. "War is not to commence by sea or land," thundered Felix Grundy of Tennessee on the floor of the House. "It is already begun, and some of the richest blood of our country has already been shed."[40]

Clay used his power as Speaker to appoint fellow supporters of war, such as Felix Grundy and South Carolina's John C. Calhoun, to the Foreign Affairs Committee. As they took up the president's message, they worked with Secretary of State Monroe, who was Madison's liaison to the Congress and entrusted with the most sensitive matters. When committee members worried about going out on a limb, Monroe met with them late into the night and pledged that if the British did not change their policies by spring, the president would support a declaration of war. The president's message and Monroe's pledge set the nation on a path from which the administration would not waver.[41]

The committee members had given the president what he wanted, but in the Senate, Virginian William Branch Giles tried to sabotage the House's plans. A man of high temper, known for quick leaps from support to animosity, Giles, once Madison's friend, was now his foe. Instead of acquiescing in a ten-thousand-man expansion of the army, Giles set the number at twenty-five thousand for five years, which he thought the House unlikely to accept. But Henry Clay, rather than argue, took to the House floor and, with all the skill one would expect, declared that Giles's number was what he had wanted all along. Observing this behavior, Madison complained to Jefferson that while many in the Congress wanted war, they seemed unwilling to provide the measures needed. Replied Jefferson, "That a body containing one hundred lawyers in it should direct the measures of a war is, I fear, impossible."[42]

A proposal from South Carolina's Langdon Cheves to build twenty frigates was defeated in the House, where many members thought a navy a threat to freedom because it could not be quickly disbanded. Then came proposed taxes, "very chokey meat," a

Federalist called them, but after two weeks, there was a positive vote—though members stipulated that taxes were not to be imposed until war began. Madison was satisfied, writing to Jefferson, "The House of Representatives have got down the dose of taxes. It is the strongest proof they could give that they do not mean to flinch from the contest to which the mad conduct of Great Britain drives them."[43]

Madison and Monroe believed they had found a way to stiffen spines further when Monroe was approached by the Comte de Crillon, who came recommended by the French minister to the United States. Crillon represented John Henry, an American citizen who had served the British as a secret agent in New England and was willing to sell papers documenting his story to the United States. After reading a sample, Monroe agreed to buy them. They included a letter to Henry from Canadian governor-general Sir James Craig sending him on a secret mission to Boston, where antiwar sentiment was strong, to assess how far leading Federalists were willing to go. Would they attempt to secede from the Union? Craig provided a cipher for sending information back to him and a credential certifying Henry's mission, which he was to use if he came across Federalist leaders wanting to communicate with the Canadian government.[44]

After returning from his mission to Boston, Henry had written to Lord Liverpool, British secretary of state for war and the colonies, describing the five months he had spent encouraging Federalists to defy the American government and letting them know they would have British support if they did. A copy of this letter was in Henry's papers, as well as Lord Liverpool's response— a recommendation that Henry be appointed to a substantial post in Canada.[45]

When Madison transmitted the Henry papers to Congress in early March, Federalists vehemently objected that they were being used to libel their party, but upon finding that no names were named, they joined Republicans in condemning the British for sending a spy into New England. As Henry Adams described it, "The halls of Congress, as well as the columns of every Republican newspaper in the country, were filled with the denunciations of England's conduct." Federalist newspapers went on the attack when it came to light that Monroe had paid Henry $50,000, an immense sum, but Republican papers, more numerous and influential, advanced a different view. One editorialized that if $500,000 were the price for the John Henry letters, obtaining them would still be *"one of the cheapest bargains ever made."*[46]

Historians have often described the affair of the Henry papers as a fiasco, and there were farcical aspects. Crillon, for example, turned out to be a con man rather than a count. This was not known at the time, however, and in any case does not invalidate Henry's documents or take into account the use that Madison made of them to shame the British ministry.

The law of nations, in which Madison was well versed, was an enormously influential concept of the time. Based on universal principles, it deemed violations of its tenets to be dishonorable, a blot on a nation's reputation. Madison knew well the work of Emmerich de Vattel, one of the chief expositors of the law of nations. He also knew that the English held Vattel in particularly high esteem, and he used his concepts in the short message transmitting the Henry papers to Congress. Vattel had written that nations were to deal honestly with one another. Madison emphasized that the British had not. While claiming to be negotiating amicably, they had sent a spy into the United States. Vattel had written that natural law forbade "nations to practice any evil maneuvers tending to create *disturbances in another state* [or] *to foment discord.*" Madison described Henry's spy mission as intending exactly that. He had been sent for the purpose of "fomenting disaffection to the constituted authorities." He was to involve himself "in intrigues with the disaffected for the purpose of bringing about resistance to the laws," and ultimately "destroying the Union and forming the Eastern part thereof into a political connection with Great Britain." According to Vattel, "No state has the smallest right to interfere in the government of another," or "to authorize odious machinations against the internal tranquility of states." The thrust of Madison's transmittal message was that the British were guilty on both counts.[47]

The significant store that European nations set on eighteenth-century theories such as Vattel's is evident in the strong response to Madison's use of them. Opposition members in the House of Lords, who were Whig, immediately struck the theme that the ministry of Spencer Perceval, which was Tory, had violated the law of nations and brought dishonor to England. On the grounds of "the general relations of all civilized states," Lord Holland, Whig Party leader, demanded a parliamentary investigation. Earl Grey noted that "communicating with the disaffected subjects of a state with whom we were not at war . . . was a proceeding which all writers on the law of nations condemned." The Earl of Darnley rose to declare the government's action "utterly indefensible upon every principle, whether that of the law of nations or that of common honor and honesty. . . . Even were it not against the declarations of Grotius and Vattel, it would be against the dictates of common sense."[48]

Lord Liverpool, secretary of war and a signatory on one of the letters in the Henry file, offered a strained and lengthy defense, a "sidewind justification of treachery and perfidy," Holland called it. The connections were too many and international law too clear for Liverpool to make a convincing case that he and the Perceval ministry had acted honorably.[49]

The opposition lost a motion for the government to provide Henry's correspondence from official archives but would have brought the subject up again had not tragedy struck. On May 11, less than a week after the debate in the House of Lords, Prime Minister Spencer Perceval was assassinated in the lobby of the House of Commons. Lord Liverpool began forming a new government rather than justifying past government actions.[50]

On June 16, 1812, the British suspended the vexatious Orders in Council. Tory exasperation at having their honor called into question (and not having an effective response) played a part in the British suspension and subsequent repeal of the Orders in Council, according to Henry Adams. There were other factors, including growing public discontent with the domestic economic consequences of the orders and having a new and unproven ministry in place, but the embarrassment caused by the upstart Americans lingered. How much easier to be rid of their complaints.[51]

Madison, operating on more than one track, had in the mean-time sent an aggressive message to Congress. He set forth the hostile acts of the British, including their incitement of Indian nations, and listed the futile attempts of the United States to negotiate an end to the violations. He charged the Congress with considering "whether the United States shall continue passive under these progressive usurpations and these accumulating wrongs or, opposing force to force in defense of their national rights, shall commit a just cause into the hands of the Almighty disposer of events."[52]

The president did not mention in his message that the nation was unprepared. Secretary of the Treasury Gallatin had tried to raise eleven million dollars through subscription to support the war, but he got no more than six million dollars. Secretary of War William Eustis had scoured the nation for men and matériel, but was far from having created an adequate army. Secretary of the Navy Paul Hamilton ought to have had an easier job overseeing the ocean-going fleet of the U.S. Navy, which had just sixteen vessels in service, but with the United States facing a British navy of six hundred vessels, he faced hard questions about the deployment of America's small naval force.[53]

John Randolph did not hesitate to raise the question of preparedness. How, he demanded to know on the floor of the House, could his colleagues go to war "without money, without men, without a navy!" He also observed a lack of public enthusiasm for the war, a point to which Tennessean Felix Grundy replied, "It is only while the public mind is held in suspense, it is only while there is doubt as to what will be the result of our deliberations, it is only while we linger in this hall that any manifestations of uneasiness will show themselves. Whenever war is declared, the people will put forth their strength to support their rights." This was the president's opinion as well. Later, when the war was long behind, he told historian George Bancroft, "He esteemed it necessary to throw forward the flag of the country, sure that the people would press onward and defend it."[54]

Secretary of State Monroe had another reason for going to war before preparations were complete: Canada. Even without full ranks, he believed, an American army could subdue the sparsely populated colonies and use them as leverage to negotiate an end to hostilities.[55]

On June 18, 1812, two days after Parliament suspended the Orders in Council, Congress approved a declaration of war according to Article I, Section 8, of the Constitution and President Madison signed it. As he began to receive hints of British suspension of the Orders, he made clear that he was not dealing. He had no intention of changing the course the United States was on for assurances that could easily be withdrawn.

Being the first president to take the nation to war under the Constitution, he had no precedent for the symbolic acts that ought to accompany such an occasion. He visited the offices in the Departments of War and the Navy, and although he wore a cockade on his hat that one observer noticed was too large for a man of his stature, the president delivered firm and inspiring remarks.[56]

Jefferson cheered him on from Monticello and suggested how to deal with domestic opposition to the war. Southern Federalists were "poor devils," he wrote. "A barrel of tar to each state south of the Potomac will keep all in order." As for the North, "You may there have to apply the rougher drastics of . . . hemp and confiscation." Madison did not take him literally, nor had Jefferson meant him to, but the former president was serious when he encouraged the "conquest of Canada." He did not think it would be hard. He told newspaper publisher William Duane that it would be "a mere matter of marching."[57]

Belief in an easy conquest of Canada soon proved false. In the middle of August, Brigadier General William Hull had barely begun to invade Canada when he retreated to Detroit. Ill and terrified of being attacked by Indian allies of the British, Hull surrendered Fort Detroit and his army of two thousand without a fight. At about the same time, Captain Nathan Heald evacuated Fort Dearborn (Chicago today). A mile and a half from the fort, the evacuees were set upon by hostile Potawatomi, who killed and mutilated most of the ninety men, women, and children trying to make their way to safety. In October, the bad news compounded. A thousand Americans were killed, wounded, or captured at Queenstown Heights on the Niagara Escarpment. An attack on Montreal was foiled by Federalist governors in Massachusetts, Connecticut, and Rhode Island who refused to send militia.[58]

Nearly everyone from the president on down had believed that American strength would show itself on land, but it was the neglected navy that excelled. On August 19, 1812, Isaac Hull, nephew of the disgraced general and a veteran of the Tripolitan War, lifted the spirits of the nation when the frigate he captained, the superbly built USS *Constitution*, defeated the HMS *Guerriere*. The battle, wrote Henry Adams, "raised the United States in one half hour to the rank of a first-class power in the world."[59]

The *Constitution*'s victory bolstered Madison's prospects for a second term. Vice President George Clinton had died in April 1812, and a Republican caucus under Madison's sway chose Elbridge Gerry of Massachusetts, sixty-seven, to take Clinton's place. Gerry's age would not have escaped Madison's notice. Neither he nor Jefferson was anxious to set up a rival for a possible fourth member of the Virginia dynasty.

Madison and Gerry handily defeated DeWitt Clinton, George Clinton's nephew, who ran as a dissident Republican, and Jared Ingersoll, a Federalist from Pennsylvania. Before their inaugural came word of another naval victory, the triumph of the USS *United States* over the HMS *Macedonian*. Stephen Decatur, captain of the *United States*, who was already a hero from the Tripolitan War, decided on a dramatic gesture. He sent the flag of the *Macedonian*, a red ensign with a Union Jack in the canton, to Washington. Decatur's messenger arrived as the navy was being celebrated at a grand ball and laid the 9-by-16-foot flag at Dolley Madison's feet.[60]

Madison, who would make an unusual number of cabinet changes, began his second term trying to strengthen the departments charged with the war. Despite dramatic naval victories, Secretary of the Navy Paul Hamilton had to go. A decent man, he drank too much, and despite efforts to help him, he could not stay sober. He was replaced by former congressman William Jones. Secretary of War William Eustis, who understood that the army's dreadful performance dictated that he leave, handed in his resignation. The president asked Monroe to replace him temporarily, although he knew well that Monroe preferred an army command. The question of a military assignment would be taken up later.[61]

Monroe in the War Department, temporarily or not, infuriated Federalists, as well as prominent Republicans in New York. In a speech on the House floor so impassioned that it veered into language that had to be edited, Josiah Quincy declared that Virginia had been too powerful for too long: "Out of twenty-eight years since our Constitution was established, the single State of Virginia has furnished the president for twenty-four years." The Virginians wished to continue their dynasty, he said, to make sure that "James the First" was succeeded by "James the Second," and one way of doing that was to give Monroe military power. If he ran for president backed by an army of thirty thousand, who would challenge him? Who would object to his becoming president for life?[62]

Monroe settled back into the State Department, and the president chose John Armstrong Jr., who had been a soldier in the Revolution and minister to France, to be secretary of war. Besides his military and diplomatic experience, Armstrong had the advantage of being a New York Republican, whose appointment might help mollify the party in that state. Also important was that everyone else to whom Madison had offered the post had turned him down.[63]

Even as he sent Armstrong to the War Department, Madison was uneasy. Although thirty years had passed, who could forget that Armstrong was part of the Newburgh conspiracy, a plan from late in the Revolution to rouse the army to challenge, even threaten, Congress to produce overdue military pay? A man of haughty bearing, Armstrong was known as a schemer and a bully and was rude in his dealings with others. He rubbed Virginians the wrong way and did not seem to care.[64]

Monroe had been suspicious of Armstrong since both had been ministers in Europe. He had written a letter to Jefferson questioning Armstrong's principles but did not mail it. When he learned shortly after Armstrong's appointment to the War Department that the secretary wanted to lead the northern army's assault on Canada, he adopted a similar course, writing a long letter to Madison filled with objections, which he apparently did not send.[65]

Armstrong was emerging as a possible candidate for the presidency, and Monroe's frustration grew. He finally sent a letter, this one to Jefferson, noting the many times that Madison had changed his mind about an assignment for him and his own repeated offers to the president to accept a military posting or, failing that, to move to the War Department permanently. He wanted Jefferson to know that he had tried and tried again, and what had come of it? Armstrong had become secretary of war and placed him on the list of potential major generals, a rank Monroe would not accept. Jefferson, instead of addressing Monroe's complaints, showered him with praise for a report on the military that he enclosed with his letter. "Every line of it," Jefferson wrote, "is replete with wisdom."[66]

When the Thirteenth Congress gathered in the spring of 1813, Madison reported yet another "signal triumph" by the navy. Off the coast of Brazil, the sloop of war USS *Hornet* had destroyed the brig HMS *Peacock* in just fifteen minutes. The president also reported that the army had attacked and captured York (Toronto today) in what he declared was "a presage of future and greater victories." He did not mention that in celebrating their victory, American troops had burned down York's government buildings. That, too, was a portent.[67]

Madison's most significant announcement was that Czar Alexander I of Russia had offered to mediate a peace between the United States and Great Britain. Before Congress met, Madison had commissioned and sent three envoys to negotiate, one of them being Albert Gallatin. Madison had a personal as well as political interest in Gallatin's voyage to St. Petersburg. Dolley's dashing son, Payne Todd, had sailed with him. Payne, twenty-one, was a young man without direction or any real interest in finding one, and the Madisons probably thought that being with the sensible, grounded Gallatin would be good for him. As it turned out, Payne abandoned Gallatin's traveling party to spend time in Paris and returned home with his sights set low as ever.[68]

Madison had surely learned that when it came to Gallatin, the United States Senate would be uncooperative, but when senators threatened to reject his nomination as envoy, it came as a hard blow. Before he could meet with senators about their objections, he fell deathly ill. Monroe described Madison's ailment to Jefferson as "a bilious fever, of that kind called the remittent." So sick was he for a time that he could not drink the infusion of bark that doctors recommended for malaria, migraines, and epilepsy. His foes did not ease off. Federalist newspapers predicted his demise. A new, beetle-browed Federalist congressman named Daniel Webster barged into his sickroom to present papers accusing him of having duped the nation into war by misrepresenting French intentions. The Senate joined in, rejecting Gallatin's nomination even though he was already in Europe.[69] Madison added him to the list of Americans charged with negotiating a treaty with the British at Ghent.

As Madison recovered, he learned that British warships, which had been terrorizing and burning towns around the Chesapeake Bay, had been spotted near the mouth of the Potomac. Secretary Armstrong led two infantry battalions (about six hundred men) on a scouting mission to Fort Washington, twelve miles down the Potomac. Secretary Monroe, back in his element, led a troop of dragoons and a company of Virginia light infantry on his own scouting trip, a day's ride farther downriver to Cedar Point, from which he could see British ships. He sent back a count of two frigates and two brigs accompanied by smaller vessels and passed on a report of another squadron off Ragged Point. When Monroe discovered three to four hundred British soldiers digging wells for fresh water on Blackstone's Island, he was sure that he and his men could take them if Armstrong would just send one of his battalions. Secretary Armstrong, irritated by the secretary of state's derring-do, wrote to the president to explain how misguided Monroe's project was. Madison quashed it, but Monroe knew who had soured his plans, and his resentment deepened. For his part, Armstrong no doubt rode back to the capital thinking the episode was much ado about nothing. He was sure the British would never attack Washington.[70]

His health not completely recovered, Madison took the advice of his doctors and left for Montpelier. Several weeks after he and Dolley arrived, she pronounced him "perfectly well but will be the better for another month on the mountain." The house was crowded around the clock, but one visitor was especially welcome. Jefferson arrived on September 24, one day after an express rider had brought official news to Montpelier of a singular victory. An American fleet commanded by twenty-eight-year-old Oliver Hazard Perry, a veteran of the Tripolitan War, had defeated and captured a British fleet on Lake Erie. The details were thrilling. After Perry's flagship was hopelessly damaged, he rowed under fire to another brig and led his men to victory. After the battle, he penciled a note to General William Henry Harrison: "We have met the enemy and they are ours."[71]

If the two old friends, drinking Madeira in Montpelier's dining room, did not yet know all the particulars, they understood the overarching significance of Perry's victory. With American control of the lake, the way was open for an attack on Detroit to take back the American territory that the British had captured early in the war. Upon hearing the news, John Adams, long a proponent of naval power, celebrated in Quincy and wrote, "Perry's triumph is enough to revive Mr. Madison, if he was in the last stage of a consumption."[72]

Monroe did not share in the memorable evening at Montpelier. Jefferson told him that he planned to be there on September 24, and warned him off making a visit at the same time. Word might get out, he wrote, and the newspapers would report it "as portending some great conspiracy." Jefferson was right to be suspicious. It had happened before that when the Virginians got together, they were thought to be plotting and planning—which they often were. Monroe, though likely irritated at being the odd man out, would have seen the wisdom of Jefferson's warning. He was ever more aware that calling attention to the Virginia dynasty did not bode well for his prospects. "Jealousy of Virginia," he wrote his son-in-law, was likely to figure in the presidential contest of 1816.[73]

Just before he left Montpelier for Washington, President Madison learned of William Henry Harrison's victory in the Battle of the Thames. Perry's squadron had transported most of Harrison's men across Lake Erie, and from there they pursued the retreating British and their Indian allies north along the Thames River. In the encounter that followed, the Americans won a decisive victory, one that broke the British hold on the Northwest. In the battle Tecumseh had been killed, and the Indian nations he had drawn together separated once more.[74]

Madison also knew of Napoleon's victory at Dresden. When the emperor won, so did the United States, because as long as he was in the field and the British were fighting him, they could not turn their full force on North America.

The president had much to savor as he made his way through Virginia hills ablaze with fall colors. He was in good spirits as he arrived back in the capital city, but that evening he was visited by Daniel Parker, the chief clerk of the War Department. Parker reported that while the president had been at Montpelier and

Secretary of War Armstrong on his way to Sacket's Harbor on Lake Ontario to take charge of the northern campaign, Monroe had moved all military correspondence from the War Department to the State Department. Monroe's rationale was probably that during the prolonged absences of the president and secretary of war from Washington, he might have to make a decision that would render the correspondence crucial. The difficulty of this explanation was that the State Department shared a building with the War Department. If Monroe needed occasional access to the correspondence, he could simply walk across the hall or take the stairs. Constant access, on the other hand, would provide a way to keep close track of what John Armstrong was up to.[75]

An angry Madison personally went to the State Department and ordered the correspondence returned to the War Department. "He was more in a passion, than [I] had ever [seen] him at any other period of his life," Parker reported, "and gave it very distinctly to be understood that he thought that Mr. Monroe had been meddling with the affairs of the War Department more than was proper."[76]

The northern campaign failed miserably. Armstrong returned from the front convinced that militia, whom he watched flee before firing a shot, could not be depended upon to win a war. He recommended conscription, which Monroe saw as a political disaster. That was just one reason to fire Armstrong, Monroe wrote to Madison. His errors of command on the northern front and his attempt to make young officers loyal to him rather than the president were others. "It is painful for me to make this communication to you," Monroe wrote, "nor should I do it if I did not most conscientiously believe that this man if continued in office will ruin not you and the administration only, but the whole Republican Party and cause." Monroe's hatred of Armstrong had grown white hot, and Armstrong returned the favor. Later he would accuse Monroe of "crimes against the state." He had aimed "to render the war disastrous or inefficient," Armstrong claimed, for the purpose of destroying his reputation.[77]

Madison did not fire Armstrong. Grating as he was, he knew how to organize and work within budget constraints. He had a talent for picking young generals to replace older men who were unfit and had never been properly trained. But keeping Armstrong would mean ongoing warfare within Madison's cabinet in the months ahead and personal aggravation for him.[78]

On December 30, 1813, the British packet *Bramble* landed at Annapolis with French newspapers headlining Napoleon's defeat at Leipzig—and prompting anxiety. When Napoleon lost, the United States lost, because the British could then turn troops to the American conflict.

The *Bramble* also carried an offer from the British. While they declined to negotiate with the czar mediating, they offered to negotiate directly. Madison named three commissioners already in Europe—John Quincy Adams, James Bayard, and Albert Gallatin, and to this list added Speaker Henry Clay and Jonathan Russell, a Massachusetts Republican recently returned from a diplomatic posting in London.

Certain that months would pass before he heard from the commissioners, Madison went to Montpelier. He wrote to both Monroe and Jefferson that his wheat fields were flourishing but under attack by the Hessian fly. Worries about his farm were cut short when a messenger arrived to report that the allied coalition had captured Paris. With Napoleon gone, the tens of thousands of British forces that had fought his armies in Europe had little to occupy them—but the United States could give them plenty to do.[79]

Monroe wrote to the president that there were doubts about the threat. "There is cause to infer that the situation of Bonaparte is not so desperate as first appearances indicated." He cited unconfirmed reports that the Duke of Wellington had been set back at Rabastens and British general Thomas Graham repulsed in the Netherlands. Still, Madison set out for Washington. He set a cabinet meeting for June 7, and amid uncertainties about France, the secretaries agreed to resume offensive operations on the Canadian front. If a large number of British troops, say ten thousand or more, crossed the Atlantic, they would likely land in eastern Canada and from there follow the natural route of Lake Champlain to invade the United States.[80]

Later in June, Secretary of State Monroe received a letter that he delivered to the president, which put the worst fears of both into words. Two of the American peace commissioners in Europe, Albert Gallatin and James Bayard, confirmed that Napoleon had abdicated and been exiled to Elba, that the French had signed a peace treaty with coalition allies, and that the United States could expect to be attacked by Britain's now "disposable force." As for peace negotiations, there was a sticking point: The British would not agree to end impressment. Unless the United States wanted to continue the war, American negotiators would have to give way on "the principal remaining object of the war." In a cabinet meeting on June 27, all present agreed to authorize a treaty, setting aside impressment for a future negotiation. As he voted, Monroe surely remembered that when he and Pinkney had proposed a treaty in 1806 that failed to deal with impressment, Jefferson and Madison had summarily rejected it. Perhaps he reminded himself that times had changed. Napoleon's defeat meant that the British would no longer be frantic about putting as many men into as many ships as possible.[81]

Madison was struck by Gallatin's and Bayard's descriptions of vindictiveness in England—a desire to seek a revenge that would humiliate the United States in the eyes of the world. Secretary of War Armstrong maintained that Washington was safe because it was of so little strategic importance, but Madison was not so sure. The British might attack the capital simply for the "éclat" that would accompany it. He convened the cabinet again on July 1 and told the secretaries that if the British were to send men to operate on the Atlantic coast, "the capital would be marked as the most inviting object of a speedy attack." He laid out defensive measures, including a force of ten thousand, mostly militia, to protect the city and caches of weapons to arm them. With little discussion and no vote, the meeting adjourned.[82]

Madison may have avoided debate because Armstrong was not the only skeptic in the cabinet. Most members believed Washington to be in less danger than the president did. But in avoiding a vote, Madison may have failed to convey a sense of urgency. Armstrong seemed quite relaxed in mid-July when he authorized Brigadier General William Winder, commander of the military district that included Washington, to have nearby states ready militia for the capital's defense. Armstrong did nothing to ensure that the authorization reached Winder in a timely manner, and it was three weeks before he received it, too late, it would turn out, to ready militia.[83]

Armstrong's sins of omission were not the worst of it. The

president started a list of the secretary's exceeding his authority and on August 13 presented it to him along with stern commentary. He itemized everything from Armstrong's taking it upon himself to determine which regiments to consolidate and which officers to retain, to his hastily advising Andrew Jackson that he would become a major general when Madison had wanted to tell Jackson himself. He was additionally irritated that he had learned of these decisions from newspapers. Madison stressed the president's supremacy over the heads of departments, charged the secretary of war with ignoring it, and set out ten rules for him to follow in the future. "They will give a more suitable order and course to the business of the department," he concluded.[84]

On Thursday, August 18, Secretary of State Monroe learned from the president that a British squadron was sailing up the Patuxent River, and he rode out from the city to reconnoiter. Finding the enemy in a large area was difficult, but after two days Monroe and his cavalrymen spied British troops debarking at Benedict, Maryland. Monroe wrote to Madison that it was "almost certain" that Washington was the object.[85]

On August 22, the president and part of his cabinet rode to Long Old Fields, eight miles from the capital, where General Winder was camped with an army he had hastily assembled. The presidential party encountered an enthusiastic Monroe, who was delighted at being in the field again, even as a scout. The dignitaries stayed the night, and the next morning, the president wrote to Mrs. Madison that the troops were "in high spirits and make a good appearance." He assured her that "the last and probably truest information [on the British] is that they are not very strong and are without cavalry and artillery, and of course that they are not in a condition to strike at Washington." Subsequent reports changed his mind, and he penciled her a second note. "The enemy seemed stronger than had been reported," he wrote. She should "be ready at a moment's warning to . . . leave the city."[86]

Madison returned to the President's House and received a string of visitors. An exhausted William Winder arrived to report that his army had retreated into the city. A civilian visitor offered to booby trap the Capitol so that it would blow up when the British entered. All he needed, he said, was "a corporal's guard, a few miners, and the necessary quantity of powder." The president declined.[87]

The next morning, the president and cabinet members met at Winder's quarters in the Navy Yard. Armstrong was late, and an impatient Monroe galloped off to Bladensburg, Maryland, where the British were thought to be heading. There was a bridge just outside the village that would take them across the Eastern Branch of the Potomac and put them on the road to Washington. The president ordered Winder and his men to follow Monroe, and then, accompanied by Attorney General Richard Rush, he set out himself, armed with a pair of dueling pistols that his Treasury secretary, George Campbell, gave him at the last minute.[88]

At Bladensburg, Winder's army joined militia and volunteers already in place, bringing the American force to about six thousand. Rather than defend the village, the Americans occupied higher ground to the west from which they could target troops trying to cross the bridge. Madison, unaware that British troops were marching into the town, rode toward it until an alert scout warned him off.

If Madison had not thought before of the consequences of his being killed or captured, he did now, and sensibly decided that he, James Monroe, and John Armstrong should view the battle from the rear.[89]

The fighting started while the Americans were still deploying into lines. The British fired Congreve rockets, which though not very dangerous were terrifying to the untrained militia. Redcoated soldiers, six abreast, started across the bridge, but they made easy targets and fell back. Rallied by their officers, they started across again, this time faster, and came pouring out the western side. Although outnumbered, they were battle hardened, and the Americans on the hill were no match for them. The lines collapsed, the battle was lost, and as the president described his reaction, "I fell down into the road leading to the city and returned to it." In the hard days ahead, people would be struck by his calm.[90]

Dolley Madison, not easily intimidated, waited for her husband at the President's House. A letter that she addressed to her sister Lucy on August 23 describes her packing up official papers and discouraging a servant ("French John") who wanted to blow up the cannon at the gate. On August 24 (the letter goes over two days), she describes peering through a spyglass hoping to see James, hearing of the battle at Bladensburg, and, most famously, making sure that a full-length portrait of President Washington was off to a safe place. The letter is invaluable not only for its details but for what it reveals about the author. In a time when women commonly avoided recognition, Dolley Madison created a record of what she had done at a memorable time. And she kept it, intending to have her place in history.[91]

When friends finally persuaded her to flee, Mrs. Madison crossed the Potomac into Virginia with the family of Navy Secretary William Jones, and the group stayed that night at Rokeby farm, in the newly built home of her friend, twenty-three-year-old Matilda Lee Love. Set on a rise of land, Rokeby provided a view of the capital, now burning with fires set by the British.[92]

President Madison arrived at the President's House shortly after Mrs. Madison left and departed after a brief stay. As the French minister described the scene, "He coolly mounted his horse, accompanied by some friends, and slowly reached the bridge that separates Washington from Virginia."[93]

Accompanying the president as he rode up the Virginia side of the Potomac was Richard Rush, who described what they saw: "columns of flame and smoke ascending throughout the night of the 24th of August from the Capitol, President's House and other public edifices, as the whole were on fire, some burning slowly, others with bursts of flame and sparks mounting high up in the dark horizon." The president and Rush spent that sad night at Salona, the redbrick home of the Reverend William Maffitt.[94]

The next day the president and Mrs. Madison were reunited at Wiley's Tavern, sixteen miles above Georgetown. James Monroe was also at Wiley's. He had spent most of the last several days on horseback and many more would pass before he had the luxury of changing clothes. After conferring with the president, Monroe crossed the Potomac to join Winder and what was left of the army. Madison and Attorney General Rush followed that evening and on August 27 met up with Monroe in Brookeville, Maryland. News that the British had withdrawn from the capital soon put them on the road to Washington. Both were aware of how crucial it was not only to get the government up and running, but also to show people that it was.[95]

They returned to a devastated city. The interior of the President's House was in ashes and its exterior blackened by flames. The Capitol's walls were charred and cracked, and the chamber of the House of Representatives, where Madison had been inaugurated, was open to the rain. Margaret Bayard Smith wrote to her sister, "The roof, that noble dome, painted and carved with such beauty and skill, lay in ashes in the cellars beneath the smoldering ruins."[96] The *National Intelligencer* was also targeted. Admiral George Cockburn, commander of the British naval forces, had taken offense at the news coverage he had received and ordered its offices plundered and presses destroyed.

Most residents returning to Washington found their homes intact, but looters were everywhere, stealing anything they could carry. Inhabitants who were worried that the British would return delegated William Thornton, superintendent of the Patent Office, to tell Madison and Monroe that they wanted to capitulate. Thornton caught up with the two Virginians near the Capitol and delivered the message. The president adamantly opposed any surrender and was convincingly seconded by Monroe. "If I saw any of them proceeding to the enemy," he threatened, "I would bayonet them."[97]

Armstrong returned to Washington a few days later to find that the militia blamed him for the city's lack of preparation. Some spoke in strong terms, saying that "every officer would tear off his epaulets" rather than take an order from Armstrong. On an evening ride, the president stopped at Armstrong's lodgings and told him what he was hearing. He also told the secretary of war that in his absence Monroe's acting as military commander had worked well. Not about to let anyone take over any of his duties, Armstrong offered to resign. Madison suggested that he take some time to visit his family in New York. Armstrong agreed, but he got only as far as Baltimore before he sent in his resignation.[98]

On September 25, 1814, the day that Secretary Armstrong's resignation became official, Monroe wrote an unusual letter to the president. He ordinarily framed any aim he had in mind by saying that it was not his idea, but something others thought he should do, but this message was straightforward. "The department of war ought to be immediately filled," he wrote. "I think also that I ought to take charge of it."[99]

The direct approach worked. The next day the president sent Monroe's name to the Senate and the day after he was confirmed as secretary of war. He continued to act as secretary of state, making him unique in United States history in holding two cabinet posts at once. He and Madison did not govern as seamlessly as Jefferson and Madison during Jefferson's presidency, but the third and fourth members of the Virginia dynasty were now in tandem.

In the roller coaster that was the War of 1812, the humiliation of the burning of Washington was followed by consequential successes. British infantrymen were repulsed by well-trained militia as they attacked Baltimore, and their attempt to knock out the guns at Fort McHenry failed. The night spectacle of flaming Congreve rockets and exploding mortar shells was followed by a dawn that revealed "broad stripes and bright stars" flying over the fort. These were the sights that inspired Georgetown lawyer Francis Scott Key to write the words for America's anthem.[100]

When Congress gathered in mid-September, members met in the Patent Building, the only official building left, and listened to a presidential message not only about Baltimore but also about Lake Champlain, where, as the president explained, a squadron of American ships led by Captain Thomas Macdonough and his "intrepid comrades" captured "the whole of the enemy's ships." The thirty-year-old master commandant had rigged his ship, the *Saratoga*, with kedge anchors and cables so that his crew could rotate it 180 degrees. When the *Saratoga*'s starboard guns were empty, Macdonough ordered the ship turned, presented the portside, and pounded the enemy's flagship with fresh firepower. By defeating the British squadron and gaining control of the lake, Macdonough convinced an invading British land force, the largest, most experienced ever sent into the United States, to turn back to Canada. Theodore Roosevelt, in his book *The Naval War of 1812*, wrote of Macdonough: "Down to the time of the Civil War, he is the greatest figure in our naval history."[101]

In his message to Congress, Madison quickly passed over painful subjects. He wrote of the need for "filling the ranks of the regular army," reported that the U.S. Treasury was down to its last five million dollars, and left it up to cabinet members to fill in the details. Thus Monroe, less than a year after he had demanded that Armstrong be fired for proposing conscription, was trying to persuade Congress to enact it. He failed, as did Alexander J. Dallas (Madison's third secretary of the Treasury), who tried to convince Congress to get the nation's finances in order. One result of congressional intransigence was that Monroe had to make the rounds of Washington banks asking for loans to support Major General Andrew Jackson in his defense of the Gulf Coast. The banks asked Monroe to sign for them, and he did, despite his own empty coffers.[102]

Madison had New England much on his mind. In 1812 he had worried that opposition in Massachusetts and Connecticut had "so clogged the wheels of the war" that an American victory on the frontier of eastern Canada was impossible. Now his concern was that discontented New Englanders would secede and destroy the Union. William Wirt visited the president at the Octagon House, a striking redbrick structure in which the Madisons were living, and found the usually imperturbable president looking "heartbroken," scarcely able to talk of anything but "New England sedition."[103]

Within a week of Wirt's visit, Massachusetts invited the New England states to attend a convention in Hartford, Connecticut, where delegates would "lay the foundation for a radical reform in the national compact." Republicans pressed Madison for a strong response. Vice President Elbridge Gerry, who believed that Massachusetts Federalists had gone insane, recommended a scathing manifesto and fifteen thousand troops to free Maine, then part of Massachusetts, from British occupation. Wilson Cary Nicholas, soon to be Virginia governor, advocated "an immediate exertion of the force of the general government." Philadelphia publisher Mathew Carey agreed that federal action was necessary, but since the beginning of the war, he had been urging a "calm and philosophical tranquility" on the president. Shortly after the announcement of the Hartford Convention, he gave up, writing to Madison that he was closing their correspondence.[104]

Madison, who had lived through the Alien and Sedition Acts, would not suppress speech about secession, but action was a different matter. Behind the scenes, he and Secretary Monroe sent an agent in the guise of a recruiter into New England. Colonel Thomas Jesup reported back to Monroe that opposition to the general government was moderate in Connecticut, but so fervent in Massachusetts that it was likely to lead to "open acts of hostility." Should that happen, Jesup recommended, the power of the opposition "should be instantly crushed." Madison and Monroe were prepared to do that with a detachment of troops stationed just over the Massachusetts border in Greenbush, New York.[105]

Madison's firmness would have gratified Elbridge Gerry, but he did not live to see it. The vice president died on November 23, 1814; Madison did not nominate a replacement.

Monroe was struggling to draw Major General Andrew Jackson's attention to New Orleans, a vexing problem given slow communications and Jackson's stubbornness. Between October 10 and October 21, Monroe received a letter that Jackson had written on September 9, 1814, threatening an attack on Pensacola. Monroe had warned Jackson in letters of September 7 and September 27 that the British were headed for Louisiana and he should be too. But Monroe had no idea whether Jackson had received his letters in time. Had he attacked Pensacola, thereby delaying defense preparations in New Orleans? As it turned out, Jackson had received the letter of September 27 in a timely fashion, but decided to attack Pensacola anyway. He told the secretary of war that he would have time for New Orleans afterward—and he did. He drove the British out of Pensacola, and since its fort had been destroyed, returned the town to Spanish authority.[106]

By January 8, 1815, Jackson had assembled a force near New Orleans of U.S. Army regulars; militia and volunteers from Kentucky and Tennessee; black soldiers, both enslaved and free; Creoles; Choctaw; and a few pirates; and his army had laboriously built an eight-foot-high wall of mud between an impassable cypress swamp and the Mississippi. Although outnumbered by the British, Jackson and his men dealt them a mighty blow as they advanced in solid columns toward the earthworks and kept advancing even over the bodies of their killed and wounded.[107]

The next day, Jackson described the battle and the bravery of both Americans and British in a letter to Secretary of War Monroe:

> Early on the morning of the 8th, the enemy, after throwing a heavy shower of bombs and Congreve rockets, advanced their columns. . . . I cannot speak sufficiently in praise of the firmness and deliberation with which my whole line received their approach. . . . For an hour the fire of the small arms was as incessant and severe as can be imagined. The artillery, too, directed by officers who displayed equal skill and courage did great execution. Yet the columns of the enemy continued to advance with a firmness which reflects upon them the greatest credit. Twice the column which approached me on my left was repulsed . . . and twice they formed again and renewed the assault. At length, however, cut to pieces, they fled in confusion from the field, leaving it covered with their dead and wounded.

Jackson estimated the enemy's loss as at least "1500 in killed, wounded, and prisoners." Present-day historians suggest he undercounted and that British casualties were about two thousand. Jackson's own losses, he reported, were fewer than twenty killed and wounded.[108]

By Friday, February 3, 1815, four and a half weeks after the battle, Monroe had Jackson's letter in hand and sent the "account of a victory truly glorious" to Madison. The president was no doubt as elated as his secretary of war, but neither man lost sight of the practicalities. Monroe suggested that the president leak the letter to Joseph Gales, who had succeeded Samuel Harrison Smith as publisher of the *National Intelligencer*, and there it appeared on the following Monday. Gales had not let the British destruction of his presses keep him out of newspaper publishing for long.[109]

Candles shone in windows up and down Pennsylvania Avenue in happy tribute to Jackson's victory, and the next week brought more cause for celebration. Henry Carroll, secretary to Henry Clay, arrived in Washington with a leather-wrapped wooden box containing a treaty signed by British and American commissioners in Ghent on December 24, 1814. Earlier in the negotiations the British had made unreasonable demands, such as American cession of lands that the British occupied in Maine, but the treaty that Carroll brought simply restored the relationship between the two countries to what it had been before the war. The president studied the document and sent it to the Senate, where it was quickly ratified. Four days after the treaty's arrival in Washington, Madison signed it in his second-story office at the Octagon. Declared *Niles' Weekly Register*, "PEACE IS SIGNED IN THE ARMS OF VICTORY." It was a worthy headline. Peace was ratified and signed against the backdrop of Jackson's triumph.[110]

The war restored the status quo ante, but that did not make it meaningless, as delegates from the Hartford Convention realized when they arrived in Washington. Amid the celebration, their demands, such as keeping federal tax money and using it to conduct their own defense, seemed like unpatriotic relics, as they did themselves and as their party soon did. As the delegates left Washington bound for New England, the Federalist Party headed into oblivion.

Public pronouncements one after another addressed how the war had changed the United States in the eyes of the world and its own citizens. On the floor of the House, Speaker Clay described "the scorn of the universe, the contempt of ourselves" that had characterized the country before the war and asked, "What is our present situation?" The United States now had "respectability and character abroad, security and confidence at home. . . . Our character and Constitution are placed on a solid basis, never to be shaken."[111]

Less than two years before, John Adams had anticipated charges that the war was of no consequence. "A more necessary war was never undertaken," he wrote. "It is necessary against England; necessary to convince France that we are something and above all necessary to convince ourselves that we are not nothing." In the wake of the Battle of New Orleans and the Treaty of Ghent, people cheered that their country had refused to be bullied, cheered that their army and navy had held their own against the might of Great Britain, and cheered that they were Americans.[112]

The usually reserved Madison was "much elated," Senator William Barry of Kentucky observed to his wife. "The glad tidings of peace, procured by the glory of the American arms under his management, has inspired him with new life and vigor." Mrs. Madison, or "Queen Dolley," as he called her, "is in high spirits." But after several weeks of company crowding into the Octagon, Dolley was exhausted. "In truth ever since the peace my brain has been turned with noise and bustle. Such overflowing rooms I never saw before—I sigh for repose."[113]

Dolley wanted to visit Europe, but hobnobbing with strangers would not have appealed to James. He had also been long reluctant to cross the Atlantic because one of his "sudden attacks" could be dangerous on an ocean voyage. The Madisons headed for the Piedmont on March 21, where they planned to stay eleven weeks.[114]

Madison visited Monticello, where Jefferson had turned his nine-foot-tall pine bookcases into packing crates. He was shipping his library of some 6,500 books to Washington to replace the congressional library lost in flames when the British burned the Capitol. Madison, sixty-four, was thin, but looking relaxed and genial; Jefferson, seventy-two, his reddish hair disorderly, was stooping a little. Sending the books away was surely an occasion for nostalgia. More than thirty years before, in Mrs. House's comfortable boardinghouse, they had talked about establishing a congressional library. Neither could have imagined that it would consist of Jefferson's lovingly chosen books.

Jefferson used the payment for his library, $23,950, to pay some of his more pressing debts, but that did not prevent him from incurring more. Even before the wagons containing his former books crossed the Rappahannock River, he was ordering new ones, including *The Life of George Washington*, written by Chief Justice John Marshall. Jefferson had often tangled with Marshall and was not inclined to let his Federalist version of the 1790s pass unremarked. He took up his pen, set out his views, and supported them with notes taken at the time. He arranged for these papers and others known as *Anas* to be published after his death. Many of them were sure to cause controversy, which he had always tried to avoid—but he would not have to deal with it.[115]

At Montpelier, Madison learned that Napoleon had escaped from the island of Elba, raised an army, and marched triumphantly into Paris. It was stunning news that raised questions about American plans to dissuade the new dey of Algiers from demanding tribute just as one of his predecessors had. Monroe urged Madison to delay sending a flotilla to the Mediterranean until the European situation was better understood. Madison decided otherwise and sent orders to naval hero Stephen Decatur to sail with a squadron of ten ships to Algiers.[116]

Three months later, Alexander Dallas, secretary of the Treasury, told the president of a dreadful battle between Napoleon's army and British forces: "The carnage must have exceeded anything in the history of battles," he wrote. The number of killed and wounded at Waterloo exceeded twenty thousand on the side of the allies, but forty thousand among Napoleon's troops. He had fought his last battle.[117]

At the same time that Madison and Monroe were learning about Waterloo, they were receiving word that Decatur had triumphed in the Mediterranean in what became known as the Second Barbary War. (The Tripolitan War became the First Barbary War.) In a demonstration of naval prowess, Decatur had quickly captured two ships, one of them commanded by the legendary corsair Rais Amidon, who died in the battle. The dey, suitably impressed, agreed to end piracy, release prisoners, and cease demanding tribute. Decatur became the toast of the nation. He and his much-admired wife, Susan, built an imposing redbrick home on Lafayette Square. Five years after his second Mediterranean triumph, he was dead, killed in a duel at age forty-one.

An account of Decatur's victory was an upbeat start to Madison's seventh annual message to Congress. He praised Decatur's bravery and "high character," as well as the "accustomed gallantry of all the officers and men."[118] The president also spoke of treaties arrived at with Indian nations as a most positive occurrence, and so it was for settlers moving west, but not so for the Shawnee, Ojibwa, Potawatomi, and others, who were pushed farther west, away from the lands that were their home.

Some of Madison's proposals no doubt surprised Congress. He was reducing the size of the army, but he recommended creating an army general staff and expanding the navy, proposals he would once have vehemently opposed. The biggest surprise was that he recommended the Congress consider a national bank. During George Washington's first term, Madison had been firmly opposed to Alexander Hamilton's proposal for such a bank, arguing that there was no provision in the Constitution that gave the federal government the authority to establish one.

John Randolph of Roanoke would not let Madison's about-face escape without notice. Madison "*out-Hamiltons* Alexander Hamilton," he observed. Madison argued that a precedent had been established for a bank, and certainly the need for it had been demonstrated by the difficulty of borrowing money during the war.[119]

The charge of inconsistency still lingers over Madison's reputation, but he and the other creators of the American nation were doing what had not been done before. They had theories that had not been tested as they built a large republic: that a standing army was a threat to liberty, that a large navy was an unneeded expense. The war showed both ideas to be wrong, and Madison followed the evidence.

The Federalist Party, in tatters, posed little threat to Republicans for the 1816 presidential election, on which Monroe had his eye. The crucial fight was for the Republican nomination, and that was complicated by the "clamor," to use Monroe's word, against electing another Virginia president. Former New York governor Morgan Lewis, a Republican, opposed another Virginian, but if there were going to be one, he preferred a third term for Madison to the election of Monroe. "Madison is quick, temperate, and clear," he wrote. "Monroe slow, passionate, and dull."[120]

Republican William Crawford, a burly, affable Georgian who had replaced Dallas as Treasury secretary, making him Madison's fourth appointment to that cabinet position, emerged as Monroe's chief opponent. After considerable maneuvering and scheming on both sides, Monroe narrowly won the caucus vote.

With Monroe having the Republican nomination safe in hand, James and Dolley Madison left for Montpelier, where they stayed four months. On a cool July afternoon, they had an outdoor meal for ninety people. All sat at a single table "fixed on the lawn under a thick arbor," as Dolley described it to her sister. "The dinner was profuse and handsome," she wrote—and only six guests stayed the night. This was a golden time that the Madisons surely hoped would last until the end of their days.[121]

Dolley's son, Payne Todd, was likely among those dining under the thick arbor. A dark-haired, good-looking twenty-four-year-old who had acquired a worldly air during his sojourn in Paris, Payne had not returned on the ship his mother had expected, causing her great worry, particularly after she learned that his luggage was on the ship. When he did appear she was thrilled, but the president less so. Payne had borrowed sixty-five hundred dollars from British bankers in his stepfather's name, and Madison, though not happy about the debt, repaid it.[122]

Monroe won the presidency, 183 electoral votes over Senator Rufus King of New York, who would be the last Federalist nominee for president. The Madisons were back in Washington in time to see the last member of the Virginia dynasty assume that office, and they, like Monroe, were celebrated. The mayor of Washington paid the former president a fine tribute. "Power and national glory, sir, have often before been acquired by the sword, but rarely without the sacrifice of civil or political liberty." Madison had wielded the sword of war "without infringing a political, civil, or religious right."[123]

When they finished packing their belongings and sending them to Montpelier, the Madisons left Washington for the last time. They made part of the journey by steamboat. A passenger reported that the former president "talked and jested with everybody on board and reminded me of a schoolboy on a long vacation."[124] Madison's leavetaking from the presidency was a happy one."

NINE

Dynasty's End

~

Gathering Storm Clouds

On March 4, 1817, James Monroe, graying and dressed in old-fashioned breeches, took the presidential oath of office outdoors. The ceremony had been planned for the brick building in which Congress met while the Capitol was being repaired, but a quarrel between the Senate and the House intervened. The senators wanted to bring their elegant red chairs into the House chamber for the occasion, and Speaker Henry Clay was having none of it. The impasse led to the hasty construction of a portico for the swearing in.[1]

The day was sunny and the crowd large, as many as eight thousand people, reported the *National Intelligencer*. Sally Foster Otis, the wife of Massachusetts senator Harrison Gray Otis, a Federalist, tried not to be impressed, but had to marvel at the crowd. "The view was beautiful," she wrote:

The broad Pennsylvania Avenue, three miles in length, crowded as far as the eye could extend with carriages of every description, the sidewalks with foot passengers, men, women and children, fiddles, fifes, and drums altogether presented a scene picturesque and animating.

Since hardly anyone could hear Monroe's inaugural address, a marshal waved a white flag in a circle to show the crowd when to cheer. After the speech was published in newspapers, readers described it as plain in style. *The National Register,* a weekly Washington publication, declared simplicity to be just fine: "It forms no objection with us that there are no flowers of rhetoric scattered through it." A Marylander thought the speech's "homespun character . . . well-calculated for . . . common understandings."[2]

Monroe's first presidential project was to tour the nation, which Washington had done in the early days of his presidency. President Washington had divided his tour into two parts, traveling through New England in the first half and being wildly celebrated. Monroe also headed north; his intention, he told Jefferson, was to inspect "fortifications, dockyards, etcetera." The tour, which lasted sixteen weeks, turned into more than an evaluation of the nation's defenses. Jubilant crowds gathered at every stop along the route. Most Americans had never seen a president before, not even a printed image of one, and they waited in the hope of catching a glimpse of Monroe. Dignitaries greeted the new president and feted him with speeches, banquets, and ceremonies. Over one bridge he crossed, citizens had built nineteen triumphal arches, one for every state in the Union, and tethered live eagles atop. In Boston, where federalism had once been powerful, the *Columbian Centinel* celebrated a new age, an "Era of Good Feelings."[3]

From Sacket's Harbor, his eleventh stop on the tour, Monroe wrote a letter to his son-in-law George Hay. Trying not to seem to brag, he recounted the huge crowds, the worshipful enthusiasm, and the difficulty of what he was doing. But something was nagging at him, and in an indignant postscript, he added, "In the course of this tour, I have been compelled to answer four or five addresses in a day, . . . not one of which I had seen or heard till read and in some instances have had cause to presume that I had been peculiarly successful. How does this fact, if true, correspond with the dullness and slothful operation of faculties imputed to me by Mr. Wirt."[4]

William Wirt, a talented writer as well as orator, had published *The Letters of the British Spy* anonymously, but the author's identity was an open secret. Everyone knew that it was Wirt who had written of Monroe, "Nature has given him a mind neither rapid nor rich; and therefore he cannot shine on a subject which is entirely new to him." Wirt had gone on to write that Monroe was "endued with a spirit of generous and restless emulation, a judgment solid, strong, and clear, and a habit of application which no difficulties can shake; no labors can tire." But Monroe fixed on the comments about his intellect. As was his habit, however, he gave no public indication of feeling insulted. He chose Wirt to be his attorney general, and Wirt remained in that office for Monroe's two terms as well as serving a third term under Monroe's successor.[5]

Wirt was not the only one to note Monroe's lack of intellectual agility nor to observe his praiseworthy qualities. The descriptions of him are so consistent that is hard to doubt their accuracy. British diplomat Henry Vassall-Fox, Lord Holland, wrote that Monroe was "somewhat slow in his apprehension, but he was a diligent, earnest, sensible, and even profound man." He was also unafraid of having men around him whose skill and knowledge exceeded his, Secretary of State John Quincy Adams being a case in point. Monroe added the sagacity of others to his own by consulting widely and listening carefully.[6]

Back in Washington at the end of his sixteen-week tour, Monroe called his new secretary of state to the President's House. Fifty-year-old Adams, the balding son of the former president, was a man of Yankee stringency and mordant humor. He once confided to his diary that he knew his "cold, austere and forbidding manners" were a character defect, but he lacked "the pliability to reform it." He began many a day with a bracing swim. British minister Stratford Canning reported that Adams could be seen "floating down the Potomac with a black cap on his head and a pair of green goggles," and that might well be the extent of his wardrobe.[7]

Adams was brilliant, studious, and had impressive foreign policy credentials. He had spent years in Europe with his father while the elder Adams served as a diplomat, and he had taken on numerous assignments himself: minister to the Netherlands, to Prussia, and to Russia. After he served on the mission that negotiated the Treaty of Ghent, James Madison appointed him U.S. minister to Great Britain. His being from Massachusetts was also an asset. That four of the first five presidents were Virginians had become a political issue, and Monroe wanted his administration to represent other parts of the country.

Adams visited Monroe at the President's House, gleaming white from paint that covered char marks left by the British burning. The president and the secretary of state talked in general terms about American relations with Great Britain, Spain, and France, but there was no time for in-depth discussion. The president told Adams that he was leaving for Virginia within a few days. He was concerned about the fumes of fresh paint and plaster that lingered in the President's House, he said, and anxious to see his family. There may have been a third reason: He wanted to consult with James Madison about how to deal with Andrew Jackson.[8]

While Madison was in office, the War Department had given an assignment to one of Jackson's topographical engineers without routing it through the general, which, Jackson wrote Monroe on his Inauguration Day, was "a violation of all military etiquette and subversive of every principle of subordination." When the matter was left unsettled, Jackson took it upon himself to forbid his officers to obey any order that did not pass through him. Monroe wrote Jackson from his tour, "The principle is clear, that every order from the department of war, to whomever directed, must be obeyed." Monroe softened the note with praise for Jackson and a promise to "communicate further and fully on this subject."[9]

What Monroe needed was an explanation of the principle on which he founded his opinion, and after conversing with Madison, he had one. He wrote to Jackson:

This order involves the naked principle of the power of the executive over the officers of the army . . . for the department of war cannot be separated from the president. . . . He is vested with the power and made responsible according to the Constitution and laws of the United States for the wise direction and government of the military and naval force of the nation in both war and peace. Under these circumstances I cannot perceive on what ground an order from the chief magistrate, within the limitation stated, can be disobeyed.

The letter suggested that in instances when it was necessary for an order from the executive to be given to a subordinate, the commanding officer ought to be promptly advised, and on this basis the conflict with Jackson would be defused. As he was leaving Highland, Monroe wrote to Madison, "I have written a private letter to General Jackson, in the spirit of our conversation, of which I send you a copy."[10]

Monroe also sought Madison's opinion on internal improvements, specifically federal funding to build roads, canals, and bridges. Madison's last act in office had been to veto an internal improvements bill, and Monroe, agreeing that federal funding was unconstitutional, had made that point to Congress in an effort to forestall improvements legislation. His opponents accused him of inconsistency. The government had improved the Cumberland Road under both the Jefferson and Madison administrations, so why should there be strictures on financing further projects? Wrote Monroe to Madison, "Be so good as give me in detail the reasons which justify the Cumberland Road."[11]

Madison's response was unusual in seeming to criticize Jefferson. The former president's assent to the Cumberland Road legislation, Madison suggested, "was doubtingly or hastily given." He blamed himself as well for continuing appropriations "with less of critical investigation perhaps than was due to the case." He provided points for arguing that the Cumberland Road was not a precedent for a program of internal improvements, none of which were particularly convincing, but they bolstered Monroe in his opposition. The prospect of internal improvements would prove irresistible, however, and by the end of his term, Monroe would be signing bills to fund them.[12]

Monroe frequently corresponded with Jefferson as well as Madison, often about Jefferson's overriding interest, the college that he dreamed of building near Charlottesville. The Virginia legislature called it Central College at first, but in 1819 it became the University of Virginia, the beloved project of Jefferson's retirement years. Monroe and Madison, who shared his belief in the power of education, joined him on the Board of Visitors.

Monroe tried to keep Jefferson up to date on world affairs, but it had been eight years since he left the presidency, and he was almost seventy-four when Monroe assumed office. He had put the clamor of politics behind. "I read no newspapers now but Ritchie's," he wrote Monroe, "and in that chiefly the advertisements, as being the only truths we can rely on in a newspaper." As a result he had little context for congressional documents that Monroe sent in early 1819 about a boundary dispute with Spain and simply suggested that they be published.[13]

Monroe consulted with his cabinet more than any of his predecessors. Meetings could go on for hours and extend over days. One
such series occurred in the summer of 1818 after Andrew Jackson
seized Pensacola (again) and effectively occupied Florida by
transporting the Spanish governor to Cuba. Seminole warriors
in Florida had been making raids into Georgia, and Jackson had
clear authority to pursue them when they crossed back over the
border. He did not have authority to rid Florida of Spanish authority
nor to execute British citizens. He had one hanged and another
shot for inciting Seminole attacks on the United States.

In meetings that began on July 15 and went on for four days,
the president and most of the cabinet (John Quincy Adams being
the exception) agreed that the seizure of Pensacola amounted to an
act of war against Spain and violated the Constitution since declaring war was a congressional prerogative. Restoring Pensacola
to the Spanish was a necessity; the issue was how to handle Jackson, who was as volatile as he was popular. Adams advanced theory after theory justifying Jackson's actions, none of which were
accepted, but he noted in his diary, "The president heard with candor and good humor all that I said." In the end, Monroe wrote a
letter to Jackson telling the general that he had exceeded his orders
and acted on his own authority—based on facts and circumstances
unknown when the orders were given. Thus, the United States had
not declared war nor had the administration acted unconstitutionally. Jackson had only exceeded his orders, Monroe wrote, when
he encountered a situation that the orders did not address.[14]

Jackson was not grateful for Monroe's legerdemain. On August

19, he wrote back that he had not exceeded his orders and never would. He had acted because the War Department had told him to "be prepared to concentrate your forces and [to] adopt the necessary measures" to terminate the Seminole conflict. Being ordered to prepare for action was different from being ordered to act, and Jackson cited no authority from the president for seizing Florida. Monroe would manage to mollify him in the short run, but Jackson never gave up entirely. After he became president and the question of whether he had disobeyed orders surfaced again, he claimed that Monroe had sent him a secret letter ordering him to occupy Florida. Monroe was on his deathbed, but at the recommendation of William Wirt, who was acting as his lawyer, the former president signed an affidavit saying that no such letter had ever existed.[15]

Throughout the Florida crisis, Monroe proceeded slowly, which irritated Secretary Adams, but the task was complicated. Monroe had to judge the right degree of censure for Jackson. Too much and the general would resign and create a political firestorm. Too little and Spain would be alienated. With the Spanish empire crumbling, King Ferdinand VII was looking on Florida as a burden, but negotiations for the United States to acquire it were unlikely to succeed if the Spanish government thought that the United States had declared war. Monroe calibrated with enough precision to keep Jackson in the army and make it possible to reach an agreement with Spain. The Spanish government, once assured that Jackson's attack was not an act of war, looked upon the U.S. incursion as one more example of Spanish vulnerability in Florida, one more reason why Spain should cede it to the United States.[16]

For Spanish officials to take this view greatly assisted Secretary of State Adams, who was negotiating a treaty with Spain's minister, Luis de Onís. Patiently, brilliantly, Adams persuaded Onís to agree that the United States would acquire Florida and take responsibility for paying up to five million dollars for claims against Spain. The treaty also established a boundary between U.S. and Spanish territories that extended to the Pacific Ocean, thereby making the United States a transcontinental power.

On the day that he and Onís signed the treaty, Adams exulted, noting in his diary that the line reaching to the Pacific had been his idea. "It was perhaps the most important day of my life," he wrote. Justified as his pride was, he kept it to himself. His deference to the president was one reason that they worked well together. Adams's diary is full of references to his receiving instructions from the president and rewriting documents to conform to the president's suggestions. Monroe struck out passages in Adams's reports so often that Adams tried putting in passages that he believed the president would take out in an effort to preserve others that he hoped to maintain. Whether the tactic worked is uncertain.[17]

Monroe began his second tour, this one of the South, in March 1819, and as had happened on his northern tour, crowds gathered and dignitaries competed to hold banquets in his honor. But reports of financial distress began coming in. Credit had dried up and prices plummeted. The pain was affecting everyone from manufacturers in New England to farmers in the West. Jefferson wrote from Monticello, "Lands in this state cannot now be sold for a year's rent." The United States had never seen the like. This was the country's first depression, and while no one was certain how it had come about, banks came in for most of the blame. The president, whose main response was trying to talk the crisis down, was scarcely faulted. Few thought it was the business of the government to try to control the economy. The Panic of 1819, as it came to be called, ended three years later, but not before setting many on their way to financial ruin.[18]

A far worse crisis was building, centered on the slaveholding territory of Missouri. Should it be admitted as a state only if its constitution forbade the importation of persons held in slavery and contained a plan for gradual emancipation? When an amendment in the Fifteenth Congress made such a proposal, the reaction was an apocalyptic confrontation of South and North. Thomas Cobb of Georgia warned that proposing to put restrictions on Missouri's admission threatened the Union. It had "kindled a fire which all the waters of the ocean cannot put out, which seas of blood can only extinguish." James Tallmadge Jr. of New York, the author of the amendment, responded that he worked for "a great and glorious cause, setting bounds to a slavery the most cruel and debasing the world ever witnessed." Addressing Cobb he declared, "If a dissolution of the Union must take place, let it be so!"[19]

By the time the Sixteenth Congress convened in December 1819, the issue had national attention. People thronged to town meetings, signed petitions, and distributed pamphlets. Rowdy crowds burned effigies of congressmen whose views offended them. Even as battle lines hardened, the president was optimistic.

On January 8, 1820, he told Secretary of State Adams that "he apprehended no great danger. . . . He believed a compromise would be found and agreed to which would be satisfactory to all parties." Adams, much less sanguine, perceived the "Missouri slave question" to be one of many divisive issues facing the administration, all of them made more difficult by "the rankling passions and ambitious projects of individuals." One individual riling him was Georgian William Crawford, who had been secretary of the Treasury under Madison and continued in that position under Monroe. Crawford, who still had presidential ambitions, frequently attacked the administration through surrogates, prompting Adams to describe him as "a worm preying upon the vitals of the administration within its own body."[20]

The debate in Congress on the Missouri question brought a sentiment to light that was usually whispered in the dark. Southern slaveholders commonly described slavery as an evil that could be remedied at some future time, but William Smith of South Carolina defended slavery on the floor of the Senate. "All the nations of the East held slaves in abundance," he declared. "The Greeks and the Romans at the most enlightened periods of those republics. Athens, the seat of the muses, held slaves." Slavery was acceptable in the eyes of God, he said, and Thomas Jefferson was wrong to have declared it immoral. Senator Benjamin Ruggles of Ohio was dumbfounded. "This was taking entirely new ground," he said of Smith's speech. "It was going farther than he had ever heard any gentleman go before." Like Smith, Ruggles was a Republican, but the Missouri crisis put them on opposite sides.[21]

Monroe, Madison, and Jefferson believed that splitting Republicans was the point of the Missouri question, that those behind it intended, as Monroe wrote to Madison, "to form a new party division." Madison agreed, writing to Monroe, "The real object is, as you intimate, to form a new state of parties founded on local instead of political distinctions," *local* meaning issues heretofore regulated by each state—such as slavery. The Missouri crisis caught Jefferson's attention. From Monticello he wrote to Monroe, "This Missouri question by a geographical line of division is the most portentous one I have ever contemplated."[22]

Bringing Maine, which was seeking statehood, as well as Missouri into the Union would balance the number of free and slaveholding states, but pairing them was not enough. The Senate insisted that Missouri be treated as other states had been—that is, admitted with no restrictions. The House, on the other hand, was adamant that Missouri be required to cease importing enslaved persons and to set a plan in place for gradual emancipation. A breakthrough came when Senator Jesse Thomas of Illinois offered an amendment to a bill linking Maine and an unrestricted Missouri that proposed a line extending westward from the southern border of Missouri at thirty-six degrees and thirty minutes north latitude. Missouri was north of that line, but going forward no other slaveholding state would be. Speaker Henry Clay now had the bargaining chip he needed. He cajoled and blustered, used his extraordinary charm and a parliamentary maneuver or two to bring the House into agreement. After President Monroe signed the bill on March 6, 1820, southerners had an unrestricted Missouri, as they had demanded, and northerners had a guarantee that in the future only free states would be formed north of 36°30'.

It did not go unnoticed, however, that southerners gained an immediate benefit, while northerners would have to wait for theirs.

Within months it appeared that the compromise would not hold. Missouri presented a constitution to Congress that would "prevent free negroes and mulattoes from coming to and settling in this state," a proviso unacceptable to the North. Once again Speaker Clay came to the fore, devising a condition that would allow Missouri to maintain its proviso, but only if it passed legislation that it would never be used, "never be construed to authorize the passage of any law, and that no law shall be passed in conformity thereto, by which any citizen of . . . the states of this Union shall be excluded from the enjoyment of any of the privileges and immunities to which such citizen is entitled under the Constitution of the United States." Using this language, Monroe proclaimed the admission of Missouri "to be complete."[23]

John Quincy Adams realized early on in the Missouri debate that a compromise might delay catastrophe, but could not prevent it. He wrote in his diary, "I take it for granted that the present question is a mere preamble—a title page to a great tragic volume." Jefferson pondered the line drawn between North and South and saw it as a much greater threat than the schism between Federalists and Republicans had ever been. That division "existed in every state," he wrote, but the new demarcation, by setting free states against slaveholding states, would "kindle . . . mutual and mortal hatred." He had been trying to stay out of politics, he wrote, "but this momentous question, like a fire-bell in the night, awakened and filled me with terror. I considered it at once as the knell of the Union."[24]

❦

Neither the Federalists nor the Republicans nominated a presidential candidate in 1820. The Federalists thought doing so was hopeless, and the Republicans decided that since Monroe had no opponent, it was unnecessary. Both were correct. Vice President Daniel Tompkins of New York, who had no national profile when he became Monroe's vice president in 1817 (and would still have none after eight years in office), announced the results in the new Senate chamber. They showed Monroe receiving every electoral vote but one. William Plumer of New York, a foe of Monroe, had cast a protest vote for John Quincy Adams.

Personal debt plagued Monroe during his time in the President's House, as it had for most of his career. He had returned to Virginia after diplomatic assignments in France and England with obligations that continued to grow as he became governor of Virginia, secretary of state, and secretary of war. The presidency was one more public office that he could not afford. His salary was twenty-five thousand dollars a year, a handsome sum, but he paid for his national tours and was responsible for all entertaining, a considerable expense since attending large events at the President's House often required little more than showing up. Monroe wrote to Fulwar Skipwith, who from his own diplomatic postings knew how costly public office could be: "No saving that I can make will rescue me."[25]

Monroe had assets, but they were illiquid. He owned thousands of acres at Highland, in Albemarle County, where he had built his "cabin castle"—a substantial wood-and-brick farmhouse with a stone foundation. He also owned thousands of acres at Oak Hill, a Loudoun County property with a farmhouse that he had purchased with his uncle Joseph Jones. After Jones died in 1805, his half of the property went to his son, Joe, whose wild youth ended only when he became very ill. He died without heir in 1808, whereupon Monroe, according to a will Jones had signed in 1795, became the owner of the whole estate. Despite the trauma of some forty years before, he became his uncle's heir.[26]

Monroe had been trying since 1809 to sell Oak Hill in order to pay down his debts, but had still not succeeded when he became president. By 1820 he had decided not to sell, and using a sketch that Jefferson drew began construction on a spacious manor. The new house, just a half day's ride from Washington, would be much more convenient than the old one at Highland, but Jefferson seems not to have contemplated that Monroe would actually leave Highland until January 1823, when he received a letter from Monroe telling him that he needed to sell some of his Highland acreage. He hoped that he could continue to live there, he told Jefferson, but perhaps he would have to leave:

Should that be the result, it will form one of the most painful occurrences of my life. In the one country I shall leave those to whom I have been long and affectionately attached, while in the other I shall find myself an entire stranger and at a period of life when new friends are rarely formed. Wherever I may be, I beg you to be assured that I shall always recollect with the kindest and most grateful feelings the relation which was formed between us in my youthful days and the many good offices which I have received from you through the whole intervening time.

Jefferson, seeming taken aback, began his response began in a scolding tone:

I had had great hopes that while in your present office you would break up the degrading practice of considering the President's House as a general tavern and economize sufficiently to come out of it clear of difficulties. I learn the contrary with great regret.

Jefferson softened the letter by observing that Monroe's "society during the little time I have left would have been the chief comfort of my life."[27]

Monroe intended his Oak Hill home as a residence to which an ex-president could retire, and he built accordingly. He probably had Mount Vernon, Monticello, and Montpelier in mind, and although he did not achieve their scale or elegance, he constructed a handsome brick dwelling. A seven-columned portico provided a view of Oak Hill's lush acreage. Inside were tall-ceilinged rooms of fine proportion. Added to expenses for White House upkeep (for which there was no allowance), the building of Oak Hill left him $35,000 in debt.[28]

That the president's finances were precarious would have been the last thought to occur to most White House visitors. The usual reaction was awe at the sumptuous state rooms the Monroes had created with funds appropriated by Congress. The Oval Room (the Blue Room today) gleamed with gilded chairs and sofas from France. The State Dining Room was a treasure house of French ormolu: a clock, candelabras, and a fourteen-foot "plateau" with a mirrored surface that graces the formal dining table of the White House still today.

One White House guest, Mrs. Tuley of Virginia, recorded details of the gowns worn by the Monroe women at a New Year's Day reception. The older daughter, Eliza, who was married to George Hay, wore a dress of "crimson velvet, gold cord and tassel around the waist." The younger daughter, Maria, "rich white satin, trimmed with a great deal of blonde lace, embroidered with silver thread." Loveliest of all was Mrs. Monroe, wearing "superb black velvet, neck and arms bare and beautifully formed . . . around her neck an elegant pearl necklace." No federal appropriation underwrote these expensive gowns, and although Monroe could ill afford them, he would not have regretted going further into debt for finery for his daughters and his wife. He doted on Eliza and Maria, "the delight and consolation . . . of their mother's and my own life," he said, and he spoke openly to others about his love for Elizabeth. In 1803, a dinner companion wrote of the "fine conjugal feelings" that Monroe had for his wife, and that did not change with the passage of years.[29]

Mrs. Monroe missed many public events because she was ill, and her health was of deep concern to the president. Eliza, tall and graceful, stood in for her. But Eliza was contentious. She quarreled bitterly with her uncle Joseph Monroe; her brother-in-law, Samuel Gouverneur; and nearly all of Washington society. As a substitute for her mother, she was expected to make the first visit to diplomatic wives, which she refused to do. They, in turn, refused to visit her, and when Maria was married in the President's House, Eliza forbade the diplomatic corps from calling on the newlyweds. Difficult as she was, Eliza often had a point. The custom of the president's wife (or her stand-in) riding through the dusty streets of Washington in search of diplomatic wives to call on made little sense.

The Monroes shrugged off criticism of Eliza. They understood that she not only stood in for her mother, she ran the household, a task so burdensome that Monroe believed it made her ill. Eliza was beautiful, intelligent, and sophisticated, speaking French fluently, as did the others in her family. But her presence did not bring calm to a residence that could have used it, particularly as Mrs. Monroe's health continued to decline.[30]

In his second term, Monroe declared the policy that most firmly established his legacy. The Monroe Doctrine, as it came to be known, like the acquisition of Florida and the extension of the American border to the Pacific, was a consequence of the diminishing power of Spain. Colonies from Chile to Mexico, seeing a chance for independence, launched revolutions to attain it. Since the opening months of his administration, Monroe had been discussing with his cabinet the possibility of recognizing independent republics, but he wanted to be sure that they were able to stay independent rather than follow the example of Venezuela, where a republic that was declared in 1811 collapsed in 1812, leaving the country again under the influence of Spain. Also standing in the way was the Transcontinental Treaty that Adams and Onís had negotiated. King Ferdinand VII had delayed approving it, and for the United States to recognize Spain's former colonies might persuade him not to. Ferdinand finally agreed to let the treaty go forward, and in February 1821 the two nations exchanged ratifications.[31]

Monroe moved carefully. It was more than a year before he announced his intention to recognize Buenos Aires, Columbia, Chile, Peru, and Mexico. They had declared their independence, and Spain, acting on its own, could not regain them. But a question remained: What if European powers decided to help Spain reclaim her former colonies? British foreign minister George Canning, interested in protecting British trade with South America, suggested that his country and the United States join in declaring "the recovery of the colonies by Spain to be hopeless," and stating that the two countries "would not see any portion [of the former colonies] transferred to any other power with indifference."[32]

Monroe sought counsel from his predecessors. Jefferson wrote that he considered the question of cooperating with the British the most momentous since the Revolution. The United States and Great Britain acting in concert, he wrote, could "emancipate a continent at one stroke." Madison thought that British motives ought to be examined, but observed that an alliance could shield the interests of the United States by adding "the power and the fleets of Great Britain" to its own.[33]

Jefferson and Madison no longer had the last word with Monroe. Without revealing the advice of his predecessors, the president led a discussion of the pros and cons of Britain's proposal at a November 7 cabinet meeting. The British offer would likely result in a pledge from the United States not to acquire any part of Spain's American possessions, and Secretary of State Adams pointed out that such a promise could backfire. What if Texas or Cuba should ask to join the United States? After the president observed that he wanted to avoid any action that would make the United States appear subordinate to Britain, the secretary of state spoke up again: "It would be more candid as well as more dignified to avow our principles explicitly . . . than to come in as a cockboat in the wake of the British man-of-war." Heads nodded around the room.[34] Pride as well as pragmatism entered into the decision that America would act alone.

At the president's instruction, Adams drafted a response turning down Canning's proposal, and it was discussed at a four-hour cabinet meeting on November 21. The president's suggestions made it more tactful, but Adams was satisfied at the end of the discussion. He wrote in his diary, "The final paper though considerably varied from my original draft, will be conformable to my own views."[35]

The president also read aloud draft passages for his seventh annual message to Congress, which he was to transmit on December 2, 1823. The subjects addressed made clear that he did not intend his foreign policy decisions to be tucked away in diplomatic dispatches, as cabinet members had presumed, but publicly set forth to the nation and the world. Adams was alarmed at the harsh tenor of the president's draft passages, and in a private meeting persuaded Monroe to keep his legacy in mind. His administration, now drawing to an end, would likely be remembered as "the golden age of this Republic," Adams said, but a confrontation with all of Europe could upend that. To make the close of his time in the President's House consistent with the rest, the message should be an "earnest remonstrance against the interference of the European powers, by force with South America." It was advice Monroe took to heart.[36]

But South America was not the only attraction for monarchs wanting to extend their empires. Alexander I, czar of Russia, had issued an edict asserting claims to the Pacific Northwest, which led Adams to advise and Monroe to agree that the United States needed a comprehensive approach to foreign powers casting covetous eyes on either North or South America. Adams drafted a statement that Monroe included verbatim in the December 2 message to Congress: "The American continents, by the free and independent condition which they have assumed and maintain, are henceforth not to be considered as subjects for future colonization by any European power."[37]

A second statement in the message that came to define the Monroe Doctrine went a step further and was of even greater consequence. Not only should there be no colonizing, Monroe wrote, there should also be no interference: "We owe it . . . to candor and to the amicable relations existing between the United States and [European] powers to declare that we should consider any attempt on their part to extend their system to any portion of this hemisphere, as dangerous to our peace and safety." Like the first passage, this one emphasized that the New World, based on freedom, differed from the Old and wanted no part of its monarchical "system." Monroe addressed a variety of other subjects, from the "condition of the public finances" and "the state of the army" to "the transportation of the mail." But it was his assertion of a new world order that would live on.[38]

When John Quincy Adams made a list of his accomplishments as secretary of state, he recorded many items, but nowhere did he mention what has become known as the Monroe Doctrine, although in the back-and-forth with Monroe, his contribution had been enormous. Adams knew that Monroe's interest in the independent republics to the south was the initiating force for the development of the doctrine. He knew that it was Monroe who determined to proclaim it. Moreover, in Adams's view, the president made the final decisions, and if he accepted good advice, he should get the credit.[39]

President James Monroe's last years in office were caught up in the election of 1824. With no successor from Virginia on the horizon, Republicans from other states imagined themselves as president. Secretary of State John Quincy Adams of Massachusetts was one, as was Secretary of the Treasury William Crawford of Georgia, even though he had been devastated by a stroke in the summer of 1823. A third member of Monroe's cabinet, John C. Calhoun, a South Carolinian with piercing eyes, was more than willing to take up residence in the President's House, although he and his wife already lived on a fine estate that would one day be known as Dumbarton Oaks. Congressman Henry Clay from Kentucky, as shrewd as he was charming, and war hero Andrew

Jackson, now a senator from Tennessee, were also in the running, although following the campaign etiquette of the day, they did not publicly admit it.

There were no political parties in the 1824 election, but factions surrounding the candidates made the run-up to it as divisive as if there had been. Congressional allies of Crawford and Jackson pushed the idea that Monroe's handling of a twenty-thousand-dollar appropriation for White House furniture was scandalous. Although it became clear that Monroe had not supervised his accounts carefully, no wrongdoing was found. A "malignant effort," Monroe called it.[40]

Adams and Monroe, despite their amicable relationship, had a confrontation when Adams realized that Clay ally Massachusetts representative Jonathan Russell had provided the State Department with a supposed copy of a letter that had somehow vanished from its files. The copy had been changed from the original to cast Adams's work at the Ghent negotiations in a bad light, and when Monroe found the original letter in his personal files, Adams expected that the truth would soon come out. The president, however, not wanting to look as if he favored Adams over the other candidates, hesitated to release either the original letter or the copy, and the two men argued, Monroe raising his voice in "sharp anger" and Adams barely restraining himself. The politically created division was not permanent, and the two worked together as Monroe told Congress about the letters but did not submit them, and Adams was busy behind the scenes trying to get a friendly representative to ask for them. In the end Adams was vindicated, and Representative Russell's career in Congress was over.[41]

❧

A rift with Jefferson was more serious. In February 1824, Jefferson wrote a letter to Monroe asking him to appoint Bernard Peyton, a Richmond commission merchant, as either postmaster or port collector in Richmond, whichever position opened first. Both were currently filled by aged men "thought near their exit," as Jefferson put it. Jefferson reminded Monroe that when he had previously passed on recommendations for office, he had done so in a dutiful manner so that Monroe would not think he had an interest in the case, but this was different, "one single case and but one in the whole world into which I should go with my whole heart and soul." For years, Peyton, a genial man with a fine military record, had assisted Jefferson in buying everything from schoolbooks to eight tons of plaster of Paris to six gross of the finest wine corks. Struggling to make ends meet himself, Peyton understood Jefferson's situation and found credit for him when he needed it. Jefferson had ties with other members of the Peyton family: John, Bernard's brother, worked for Jefferson as an attorney. Craven Peyton, from another branch of the family, had business dealings with Jefferson and was married to his niece. "Grant me this [appointment]," Jefferson wrote to Monroe, "and as I never have, so I never will again, put your friendship to the trial." Jefferson was not merely asking, he was pleading.[42]

Six months later, when the Richmond postmaster died, Jefferson wrote Monroe again, stressing Peyton's qualifications and the hope that Monroe "will pardon my laying your friendship under contribution in this single case." He sent a copy of this letter to Peyton with a covering note: "You will see that I place the request on ground which must prevail, if I am anything at Washington." But Monroe chose James Patton Preston, a former governor of Virginia, who, seriously wounded during the War of 1812, had spent time recovering at Monroe's house in Washington. Monroe explained that he had promised then to use his good offices on Preston's behalf and obliquely remarked on the former governor's superior credentials.[43]

None of this satisfied Jefferson. He described himself as "sorely and deeply wounded" by Monroe's decision. "I . . . shall better understand my place hereafter," he wrote to Peyton. He had been deeply humiliated by a man whom he had raised up when the world had pushed him down and with whom he had been friends for half a century.[44]

On October 18, 1824, Monroe wrote to Jefferson saying his "warmest desire" was to visit him, but the next month he missed one of the most important events of Jefferson's life, a "patriotic banquet" in Charlottesville, where the University of Virginia, Jefferson's brainchild, was nearly finished. The dome of the spectacular Rotunda had yet to be completed, but the campus already served as a tribute to Jefferson's vision. Jefferson, Madison, and President Monroe were to attend the dinner to honor the Marquis de Lafayette, dear friend of them all, who was touring the United States, but Monroe dropped out when the marquis was several days late, writing from Highland that he had to leave for Washington immediately to prepare his annual address to Congress. The address was five weeks away, a long time to ready a presentation, but Monroe was meticulous and reviewed draft after draft with his cabinet.[45]

The Charlottesville dinner was long remembered by those who attended. Lafayette seated at the head table between Jefferson and Madison was a sight wonderful to behold. The toasts were excellent, particularly Madison's, but when it came time for the eighty-one-year-old Jefferson to read his response, he was too weak, and the presiding officer, a Mr. Southall, read it for him. After dinner, riding in Jefferson's elegant landau, Lafayette and Jefferson toured Jefferson's "academical village." The Rotunda, designed after the Pantheon in Rome, defined the north end of an open rectangle. Two rows of pavilions running south and separated by a wide lawn formed the sides. Professors would live and teach in the pavilions and students reside in lower structures connecting them. Laid out in orderly, classical fashion, the academical village accommodated variation, with each of the pavilions in a different style.[46] The village evidenced Jefferson's lifelong study of classical architecture and his conviction, shared with Madison and Monroe, that knowledge was essential to freedom.

Over the next nine months, Monroe wrote to Jefferson several times saying he would like to visit Monticello, and Jefferson invited him to. But even though Monroe was often at Highland, just thirty minutes away from Jefferson's home, if one judges from their letters nothing seems to have worked out. It was as though each man felt a duty to reconcile, but neither could quite bring himself to do it.

In August 1825, Lafayette, about to leave for France, wanted to see Jefferson once more, and Monroe joined them at Monticello. The event focused on the reunion of Jefferson and Lafayette, leaving little time for a visit between Jefferson and Monroe, but they surely exchanged courtesies.

In a letter of June 15, 1826, Monroe described the difficulty he was having in selling land. He hoped soon to be successful, he wrote to Jefferson, and have "the pleasure to be more frequently with you." But that visit, like so many before, was not to happen. Jefferson died a little over two weeks later.[47]

Andrew Jackson won the popular vote for president and prevailed with electors, winning 99 votes to 84 for Adams, but because he did not win a majority, the election went to the House of Representatives. Henry Clay took up Adams's cause, and was credited for the secretary of state's winning the vote in the House by a bare majority and his ascension to the presidency. Adams's subsequent appointment of Clay to be secretary of state caused outcries of a "corrupt bargain" that Jackson and his allies would use against Adams for the next four years.

In the weeks before Adams's inauguration, William Crawford, recovered sufficiently to try to prove that he still had influence, visited the President's House and insisted that Monroe appoint certain friends of his to government positions. Monroe's objections to a number of the friends brought forth a petulant remark from Crawford, to which Monroe angrily responded. Crawford, in turn, as John Quincy Adams recorded it, "raised his cane, as in the attitude to strike, and said, 'You damned infernal old scoundrel!'" Continued Adams:

> Mr. Monroe seized the tongs at the fireplace for self-defense, applied a retaliatory epithet to Crawford, and told him he would immediately ring for servants himself and turn him out of the house, upon which Crawford, beginning to recover

himself, said he did not intend and had not intended to insult him and left the house.

The Era of Good Feelings proclaimed at Monroe's entrance into the presidency was not obvious at the end.[48]

Monroe left office deeply concerned about Mrs. Monroe's health. His debts weighed on him, and he probably regretted his estrangement from Jefferson. But as he watched his successor deliver his inaugural address, Monroe's mood must have brightened for a moment. President John Quincy Adams paid tribute to the expansion of the nation under his presidency and to the spread of freedom in the Western Hemisphere. "The Floridas have been peaceably acquired," Adams said, "and our boundary has been extended to the Pacific Ocean; the independence of the southern nations of this hemisphere has been recognized, and recommended by example and by counsel to the potentates of Europe."[49]

Monroe was not one to forget the questions about his intellect that had plagued him over the years, and he might well have thought of his accomplishments as a refutation. In truth, however, he lacked the brilliance of his immediate predecessors. He had neither Jefferson's soaring imagination nor Madison's profound knowledge. He was not Washington. No one was Washington. But in age as in his youth, he shared a characteristic with that great man. Call it stubbornness, perseverance, or tenacity, none of them the same as brilliance, but all of them useful for rising in the world and creating a distinguished presidency.

Epilogue

In his retirement, which lasted less than three years, George Washington knew times of contentment. He was finally able to devote attention to Mount Vernon and his farms. He enjoyed the wedding of Nelly Custis, his lovely step-granddaughter, and always there was Martha, who brought him comfort and love. There were annoyances: Nelly's brother Washy, whose indolence was maddening, crowds of strangers who came unbidden to Mount Vernon, and the difficulty of making his income from farming match his expenses. And politics followed him. At a time when he had imagined resting under his "vine and fig tree," he felt obliged to keep his fellow Federalists from destroying themselves and Jefferson and the Republicans from destroying the nation.[1]

These were the years when Washington (albeit with caveats) agreed to President Adams's request that he organize an army to fight the French, only to have Adams announce a peace mission to France.

These were the years during which he supported the Sedition Act, believing that in a crisis it would be a good thing to silence political (that is, Republican) opposition. These were also the years in which he enjoyed the company of Elizabeth Powel and wrote a letter to Sally Fairfax, whom he had loved in his youth. He could not forget, he wrote, "those happy moments—the happiest of my life—which I have enjoyed in your company."[2]

He was deeply troubled by the condition of the people enslaved at Mount Vernon, and as he wrote his will in 1799, setting that to right was in the forefront of his mind. His first bequest was to his "dearly beloved wife," to whom he left the "use, profit (an)d benefit" of his estate for her lifetime. Upon her death, the 123 persons he held as property would be free. The young, the old, and the infirm would be cared for, as Virginia law required. In addition he directed that the young be taught to read and write and learn a useful skill. Washington could not free 153 enslaved persons who were part of Martha's dower and would upon her death revert to the Custis family. His will, though far from a perfect remedy, was a fine model, though few of his fellow Virginians emulated his deed.[3]

After his death at Mount Vernon in 1799, he was entombed in the family vault after a small and dignified service. In the nineteenth century he would be apotheosized. A sixty-five-foot fresco by Constantino Brumidi in the dome of the U.S. Capitol shows him transformed into a god, encircled by Roman deities, heroic goddesses, and thirteen maidens representing the thirteen original states—more glory than is usually accorded to mere mortals.

For all his complaints about the productiveness of his farms, Washington was a man of means. If his expenses outran his income (and they usually did), he sold some of the tens of thousands of acres he owned. He explained to Lawrence Lewis in 1799 that for four or five years, he had depended on fifty thousand dollars in proceeds from land sales to balance his books. On occasion he got a bank loan, but he hated to do it.[4]

Matters would be very different for Washington's successors. They experienced the Panic of 1819, during which European markets for American produce collapsed and the price of land dropped precipitously. Far from being able to sell land, Jefferson, Madison, and Monroe were hard put to mortgage it. When James Madison applied for a loan, he was turned down by Nicholas Biddle, who informed him that the Bank of the United States was avoiding "all loans on the security of real estate."[5]

Jefferson left the presidency in 1809. He had been in debt most of his life but believed that his assets exceeded what he owed and took this optimistic view into the early years of his retirement. His estate, he wrote, was worth fifty times a debt he owed of $4,500. With worries about money set aside, he could delight in the joys of domesticity. Margaret Bayard Smith, who visited Monticello in the first summer of Jefferson's return, described coming across her graying, slightly stooped host arranging races on the lawn for his grandchildren and being sure that the smallest got a head start. At the end of the course, the children ran into his open arms for a hug. "I saw him in the scenes for which his heart had panted," Smith wrote.[6]

As time passed, family became a concern. Thomas Mann Randolph, husband of Jefferson's daughter Martha, was volatile, particularly when he drank too much, as he often did. The same was true of Charles Bankhead, husband of Ann, Jefferson's oldest, much-loved granddaughter. The family knew that Bankhead became violent with her, but she loved her husband, with whom she had three children, and would not leave him. When the birth of a fourth child left her gravely ill, Jefferson visited her and, realizing she would die, "shed tears and abandoned himself to every evidence of intense grief."[7]

In 1819, as the Panic was hitting with full force, Jefferson's financial situation was brought home to him. He received devastating news from Wilson Cary Nicholas, a friend and real estate speculator for whom he had guaranteed a note of twenty thousand dollars. Nicholas could not pay it, and the debt became Jefferson's. Such an amount was a huge blow, "a clap of thunder," Jefferson called it.[8]

Even as his debts drove him into despondency, Jefferson remembered the happiness life had brought him. He had begun a correspondence with John Adams, from whom he had been long estranged, and late in 1825 a question arose: Would you choose to live life over again? Adams recalled those he had lost—father, mother, Abigail, children, and friends. "Instead of suffering these griefs again, I had rather go forward and meet my destiny." Jefferson acknowledged the grief they had both suffered but wrote,

"The pleasures surely outweigh the pains of life. Why not then taste them again?"[9]

In February 1826, Jefferson thought he had found a way out of his extreme financial difficulties. He wrote to Madison that he would hold a lottery for his lands, which would be priced at fair valuation rather than depreciated prices. The proceeds would pay his debts and perhaps allow him to keep Monticello. Even on his last day, Jefferson believed that something would remain for his family, but the lottery on which he relied was abandoned. After his death, his family paid down his debts by selling the Monticello mansion, land Jefferson had owned, and 133 enslaved men, women, and children. In accordance with his will, five members of the Hemings family were freed.[10]

Jefferson was eighty-three when he died at Monticello on July 4, 1826, the fiftieth anniversary of the nation's independence. On the same day, five hundred miles away in Quincy, Massachusetts, ninety-year-old John Adams died. For ages to come, one eulogist said, Americans who gathered to celebrate independence would "tell of the wonders of that day on which our illustrious countrymen were summoned together to appear before their God."[11]

Some months before his death, Jefferson wrote to Madison, his friend of more than a half century. "To myself you have been a pillar of support through life," he wrote. "Take care of me when dead and be assured that I shall leave you with my last affections." Replied Madison, "You cannot look back to the long period of our private friendship and political harmony with more affecting recollections than I do. If they are a source of pleasure to you, what ought they not be to me?"[12]

Madison, who left office in 1817, did take care of his friend. Jefferson had become agitated near the end of his life by proposals for the government to finance internal improvements such as roads and canals, and he declared in a private letter that such unconstitutional seizures of power by the federal government might require "the dissolution of our union." After Jefferson's death the letter became public, and the Resolutions of 1798 that Madison had written for the Virginia legislature came to the fore. Before the resolutions had been introduced, Jefferson, thinking them too mild, had inserted the words "null" and "void," which raised the red flag of dissolution. The words had been stripped from the resolution before passage, but no matter. Madison had to defend himself as well as Jefferson from being labeled a disunionist. Madison might have been able to clear his name by pointing out that "null" and "void" were Jefferson's words, but instead he took care of his friend's reputation and trained his sights on the principle of nullification. It would end with the Union being "broken up and scattered to the winds," he wrote, an idea "more painful than words can express."[13]

Madison had the comfort of family in his old age, particularly Dolley, who brought joy to his life. Likely it was she who turned their walks on the Montpelier veranda into foot races and she who arranged food and accommodation for the many visitors who appeared at Montpelier. As time passed and his eyesight grew weak, Dolley read to him and almost certainly took a hand in inviting guests whom he particularly wanted to see. One was English feminist and abolitionist Harriet Martineau, who visited on "a sweet day of early spring," in the 1830s. She found Madison to be "a wonderful man of eighty-three, lively and pleasant," although his rheumatism confined him to a single room. Martineau observed that the former president often turned the conversation to slavery, as though he wanted to explain himself before he died. Yes, he said, slavery was an abomination, but if the enslaved were freed, where would they go? A Virginia law of 1806 would not permit them to stay in the commonwealth for more than a year, and other states were hardly welcoming. "Africa," he said, "is their only refuge." Both he and Monroe had been leaders in the American Colonization Society, which encouraged emancipation by underwriting the transportation of freed people to Liberia. It was not a practical solution, Madison acknowledged. Many of the formerly enslaved had little interest in living in Africa. Virginia was their home. But the American Colonization Society, he said, was the only thing that kept him from complete despair.[14]

Reassuring as family was, it also brought a fair measure of distress. Dolley's brother-in-law Richard Cutts seemed perpetually in need of a bailout: $11,500 here, $4,000 and $6,000 there. But even worse was Payne Todd. For all James's and Dolley's efforts to set him on the right path, Payne remained a ne'er-do-well. He would disappear for weeks, even months, fast acquiring debts that Madison had to pay. Once Madison had to borrow $300 to bail him out of jail. Madison had receipts showing that the debts he had paid off for Payne amounted to $20,000—about half, Madison judged, of the whole amount.

This was for Madison what Wilson Cary Nicholas's default was for Jefferson, a coup de grâce that made a mockery of his struggle to pay off his own debts. He wrote his will in the expectation that his papers, which he and Dolley had arranged and edited during his retirement, would sell for around one hundred thousand dollars. Even after bequests to relatives and institutions—Princeton, the University of Virginia, and the American Colonization Society—he assumed Dolley would be able to live in comfort. But when the papers were sold to Congress, they brought less than he had counted on, and his creditors grew more aggressive. Meanwhile Payne, determined as ever to live well without working, was pilfering valuable items from Montpelier.

Madison died at Montpelier in 1836. After his death, Dolley sold the estate and the enslaved people who lived there. She spent her last years in Washington, a poor widow, but a celebrated personality.

Monroe stayed in Washington nearly three weeks after his successor, John Quincy Adams, was sworn in. Mrs. Monroe was too ill to travel, and over the next years she would seldom be well. The Monroes' older daughter, Eliza, her husband, George Hay, and their teenage daughter, Hortensia, were usually with the Monroes at Oak Hill, and Eliza managed the household. The Monroes' other daughter, Maria, and her husband, Samuel Gouverneur, moved to New York, at least in part, one suspects, because Eliza and Samuel despised each other.

Monroe managed to ride at least once a day and worked, without much success, to increase his crop yield with up-to-date methods, such as planting clover in fields that lay fallow. But most of his time and attention was devoted to his finances. "With accumulated loans and interest, compound added to simple," he wrote, his debts "have become immense." The reason for his extensive borrowing, he told almost anyone who would listen, was that he had been forced to pay expenses during his years as a diplomat that the government should have covered. For example, when he had been recalled from France in 1796, he received neither salary nor expenses for the months it had taken him to get back home. He provided Congress with an accounting going back thirty years of what he was owed: $23,570 plus interest of $30,000. Disallowing some of his claims and most of his interest charges, Congress granted him $29,513 in 1826.[15]

The money from Congress staved off creditors for a time, but by 1829, the last of his land in Albemarle had been seized for debt. Oak Hill was mortgaged, and he would have lost it but for the kindness of a person in Charlottesville who volunteered to pay the interest. All the while, Monroe persisted in pressing his claims. His friends joined in, citing his distinguished public service, during which he had been forced to borrow. They also noted that Congress had recently voted two hundred thousand dollars to Lafayette.[16]

The year 1830 was Monroe's annus horribilis. His son-in-law George Hay died, followed shortly by Elizabeth Kortright Monroe, his much-loved wife of forty-four years. Judge E. R. Watson, who was at Oak Hill when Mrs. Monroe died, later remembered the aged Monroe's grief. "With trembling frame and streaming eyes, [he] spoke of the long years they had spent happily together."[17] Monroe, frail with age, and the widowed Eliza moved to New York to live with the Gouverneurs, which cannot have made for a happy household.

In February 1831, Congress voted the seventy-two-year-old Monroe thirty thousand dollars for "public services, losses and sacrifices."[18] It was enough to save Oak Hill, but Monroe was too ill to visit his home. He died in New York in 1831—on July 4, as Jefferson and Adams had done.

Before his death, Monroe wrote to Madison: "I deeply regret that there is no prospect of our ever meeting again, since so long have we been connected and in the most friendly intercourse in public and private life, that a final separation is among the most distressing incidents that could occur." Madison also disregarded past strife: "Closing the prospect of our ever meeting again afflicts me deeply, certainly not less so than it can you. The pain that I feel at the idea, associated as it is with a recollection of the long, close, and uninterrupted friendship which united us amounts to a pang which I cannot well express."[19]

Jefferson, Madison, and Monroe died in financial straits, which none of them would have chosen, but that surely mattered less to them than the opportunity offered by time and place to be of consequence, to create something wholly new, and to change the world for the better. Like Washington, his successors knew they were historical figures. All four attended to their letters and documents, certain that future generations would want to read them. But they could not be certain what the context would be. Would the United States be regarded as a noble effort that failed or one that endured and inspired lovers of freedom everywhere? Nothing was set in stone, the members of the Virginia dynasty knew. Men and women in centuries to follow would determine the destiny of what they had created, the fate of what George Washington called "the last great experiment for promoting human happiness."[20]

ACKNOWLEDGMENTS

The idea for this book has been percolating for more than fifty years, starting when my husband and I began spending time in Northern Virginia, he to work for Gerald Ford and I to use the amazing resources of the Library of Congress to finish my dissertation. When I finally raised my head from books about British poetry, I was struck at being surrounded by so many icons of the creation of the United States. Some were official, such as the gleaming monuments of Washington, D.C., but others were more personal. George Washington's Mount Vernon was just up the road, Monticello, lovingly built by Thomas Jefferson, was a few hours away, and James Madison's Montpelier was less than an hour from there. I was hooked.

I began writing history—and I would like to thank the editors of *Smithsonian* and *American Heritage,* in particular, for giving an English Ph.D. a chance. I am most grateful to the exuberant Philip Merrill, who decided that *Washingtonian,* a very successful city magazine that he published until his untimely death, should have a monthly essay on history that would be paired with the work of fine photographers. Phil gave me a license to dig into the stories behind everything from the

ACKNOWLEDGMENTS

classical Greek columns that distinguish Washington, D.C., to the oft-disputed design (and redesign and redesign) of the Capitol Dome. The last essay I wrote was about the Constitution, the document encased in titanium at the National Archives that provides the framework for the nation.

What I was doing, though I didn't think of it this way at the time, was circumventing the academic study of history and going right to the thing itself—a pleasant occupation, but it didn't last long. President Ronald Reagan appointed me chair of the National Endowment for the Humanities in 1986, and I entered the job as the cultural wars were in full fury. The worthy idea that history should be more inclusive had become a mandate for focusing on America's failings and pushing everything else to the margin. I was hardly alone in objecting, and I'd like to thank the stalwarts who worked alongside me at the endowment, including Celeste Colgan, Jerry Martin, Marguerite Sullivan, and Anne Neal Petri. In 1987, the bicentennial year of the Constitution, we had the wind at our backs. Among other worthy NEH projects were grants to libraries across the nation to purchase books about our nation's founding document.

I kept at history while my husband was vice president, writing books for children, the most important audience of all. I'd like to acknowledge the talented illustrators and artists who helped make these books a success, beginning with the fabulous Robin Preiss Glasser, who depicted the joy of our national story in *America: A Patriotic Primer, A is for Abigail: An Almanac of Amazing American Women,* and *Our 50 States: A Family Adventure Across America.* Peter Fiore's paintings caught the peril and triumph of the Christmas night described in *When Washington Crossed the Delaware,* and Greg Harlin's gorgeous watercolors captured as well as anything I have seen of the world-historical event described in *We the People: The Story of Our Constitution.*

ACKNOWLEDGMENTS

So there it was again. No matter where I started I seemed to end up at the Constitution, and it only made sense that when I decided to write a full-length biography, it was *James Madison: A Life Reconsidered*, the story of the brilliant, politically savvy fellow at the center of it all. It was impossible to write about Madison without noting how consequential were the relationships between him and his famous neighbors, not only George Washington and Thomas Jefferson but also James Monroe, the last of the four presidents of the Virginia dynasty. Monroe has not received the attention that Washington, Jefferson, and Madison have, but that is changing, thanks to the work of Daniel Preston and his team at the University of Mary Washington, who recently published the seventh volume of *The Papers of James Monroe*. In a fine new biography, *James Monroe: A Life*, author Tim McGrath provides an example of the fresh insights that this multivolume comprehensive edition of Monroe's papers helps make possible.

My gratitude to Washington attorney Bob Barnett for matching me once again with an excellent publisher, Viking, a storied imprint. Bob knows what he is about, which is why so many authors show up on his doorstep. His political sympathies are different from mine, illustrating that friendship can reach across the aisle. I've even forgiven him for twice playing my husband's opponents for the vice presidency in practice debates—with Joe Lieberman in 2000 and John Edwards in 2004.

At Viking I would like to thank president and publisher Brian Tart, editor in chief Andrea Schulz, associate publisher Kate Stark, and director of publicity Lindsay Prevette. I am most fortunate to have had Wendy Wolf as my editor once again. She gave me a nudge from time to time, usually when I fell behind, but I cannot imagine a kinder, more understanding, more intelligent person to have in charge of my book. Thanks too to associate editor Terezia Cicel; production editor Bruce Giffords; copy editor Jane Cavolina; Brianna Harden, who designed the jacket; Cassandra Garruzzo, who designed the page layout; publicists Shelby Meizlik and Sara Delozier; and marketing director Mary Stone.

I would like to thank the American Enterprise Institute, where I am a senior fellow, for supporting my work and acknowledge President Robert Doar for his leadership and imagination. Yuval Levin, the talented director of Social, Cultural, and Constitutional Studies, also has my gratitude. AEI attracts very smart recent college graduates, and during the six years I worked on this book, I have had some of the best as research assistants: Paul Bartow, Nicole Penn, and Katherine Quigley. Nicole managed to find for me the exact Paris building where the Louisiana Purchase was signed. Katherine found confirmation in John Quincy Adams's diaries for my impression that President Monroe often edited Adams's work. I have also had wonderful interns: Chris Grimaldi, Andrea Marshall, Meghan Pradko, Hugh Ramlow, Rebecca Marquis, Elizabeth Patten, Michael Marrow, Nicholas Couto, and Brigid Wolf.

M̲y deep gratitude to the secretary of the Smithsonian Institution, Lonnie G. Bunch III, for guiding me through the newest museum on the mall, the National Museum of African American History and Culture. Starting with few resources besides his own firm commitment, Bunch was the force behind bringing this remarkable museum into being. Housed in a striking, three-tiered building inspired by a Yoruban crown, the NMAAHC has given millions of visitors the opportunity to learn about slavery and freedom from a most appropriate place: the heart of our nation's capital. I would like to acknowledge Fleur Paysour for making my visit possible, as well as Barbara Paca, OBE, indomitable champion of underappreciated artists.

Another institution that should be acknowledged is the University of Virginia Press, which has produced digital editions of the papers of the founders, including those of Washington, Jefferson, and Madison. They are invaluable research tools. I would particularly like to recognize Holly Shulman, editor of *The Dolley Madison Digital Edition*, whose pioneering work has advanced the concepts and methods of digital editing.

A longtime debt that I would like to acknowledge is to the Library of Congress, where I have been a grateful researcher since that institution was presided over by Daniel Boorstin. Carla Hayden, the current librarian of Congress, brings deep knowledge and experience to managing the world's largest library and working to open its priceless collection to the public. I'd like particularly to thank her for her commitment to digitization. Library staff members Patrick Kerwin, Julie Miller, Mary Yarnall, Signe Carey, and Yujung Park were most helpful as I gathered materials for my research on *The Virginia Dynasty*.

The Massachusetts Historical Society, ably overseen by Catherine Allgor, is a digital stop that anyone writing about the founding period and nineteenth-century America must make, particularly to visit the Adams Family Papers, a treasured source for historians. I would like to thank the staff at the society for their generous assistance and cite Tim Minty as a good example.

Bill Garner, president of the George Washington Foundation, kindly guided me through George Washington's birthplace at Ferry Farm, Virginia. I'd like to thank Suzanne Whitmore for arranging that visit. I owe a special debt to Mary V. Thompson, research historian at the Fred. W. Smith National Library for the Study of George Washington. I will remain ever grateful to Gay Gaines, past regent of the Mount Vernon Ladies' Association, for helping me better understand Mount Vernon and the women who saved it from ruin.

Andrew O'Shaughnessy, vice president of Monticello, and members of the wonderfully skilled staff graciously provided guidance and information. I'd like to thank Gary Sandling, Sofia Spidalieri, Endrina Tay, Anna Berkes, and Lisa Francavilla.

Montpelier, James Madison's home, has been well served by the dynamic leadership of former president and CEO Kat Imhoff. My thanks as well to Elizabeth Chew, Hilarie Hicks, and Ellen Wessel.

James Monroe's Highland home has benefitted immensely from the creativity of executive director Sara Bon-Harper and Nancy Stetz, education programs manager. Through their efforts visitors can see the synergy between archaeological and historical scholarship, as James Monroe's home—the real one—is unearthed. For many years the guest house at Highland was presumed to be where he lived.

At Highland, as at Mount Vernon, Monticello, and Montpelier, research and educational projects give a central place to the experiences of the men, women, and children who were held in slavery at these presidential homes. The descendants of those who were enslaved provide advice, guidance, and leadership for the interpretation of the *whole* community of people who lived on these historic properties.

James Monroe built a second home at Oak Hill in Loudoun County, Virginia. Today it is owned by Tom and Gayle DeLashmutt, who are committed stewards of this historical treasure. I am most grateful to Mrs. DeLashmutt for guiding me around the lovely house and grounds.

The James Monroe Museum in downtown Fredericksburg, Virginia, is required for anyone studying Monroe. Furniture that he and Mrs. Monroe purchased in Paris and took to the White House is there. So is jewelry that belonged to Mrs. Monroe and some of her elegant dresses. Director Scott Harris, head curator Jarod Kearney, and public programs coordinator Lynda Allen could not have been more generous in showing me some of the more than sixteen hundred artifacts at the museum.

Others I would like to acknowledge for their assistance are Coxey Toogood, historian, Independence National Historical Park; Terrance Rucker in the Office of the Historian of the United States House of Representatives; and Page Knox at the Metropolitan Museum of Art, who guided me to the wonderful collection of George Washington portraits in the museum as well as to the magnificent painting *Washington Crossing the Delaware*.

No debt I owe is greater than the one to my family. Dick, Liz, and Mary, thank you more than I can say for your love and support. And thanks to my dear grandchildren, Kate, Elizabeth, Grace, Philip, Richard, Sam, and Sarah, for being a wellspring of joy.

NOTES

ABBREVIATIONS

∞

Repositories and Collections

LC	Library of Congress
LC-AJ	Library of Congress, Andrew Jackson Papers
LC-BC	Library of Congress, Burr Conspiracy Collection
LC-JMa	Library of Congress, James Madison Papers
LC-JMo	Library of Congress, James Monroe Papers
LC-TJ	Library of Congress, Thomas Jefferson Papers
MIS	Missouri Historical Society
NYPL	New York Public Library

Abbreviated Titles

ASP-FR *American State Papers, Foreign Relations.* Edited by Walter Lowrie, Matthew St. Claire Clarke, Walter S. Franklin, Asbury Dickins, and James C. Allen. 6 vols. Washington, D.C.: Gales and Seaton, 1833–1858.

ASP-MA *American State Papers, Military Affairs.* Edited by Walter Lowrie, Matthew St. Claire Clarke, Walter S. Franklin, Asbury Dickins, and John W. Forney. 7 vols. Washington, D.C.: Gales and Seaton, 1832–1861.

PMHB   *Pennsylvania Magazine of History and Biography*
VMHB   *Virginia Magazine of History and Biography*

Published Papers from the Founding Period

DHRC   *Documentary History of the Ratification of the Constitution*
PAH   *Papers of Alexander Hamilton*
PAJ   *The Papers of Andrew Jackson*
PDM   *Papers of Dolley Madison, Digital Edition*
PJA   *The Papers of John Adams*
PJJ   *Papers of John Jay*
PJM   *The Papers of James Monroe*
PMC   *Papers of James Madison, Congressional Series*
PMP   *Papers of James Madison, Presidential Series*
PMR   *Papers of James Madison, Retirement Series*
PMS   *Papers of James Madison, Secretary of State Series*
PTJ   *Papers of Thomas Jefferson*
PTJR   *Papers of Thomas Jefferson, Retirement Series*
PWCE   *Papers of George Washington, Confederation Series*
PWD   *Papers of George Washington, Diaries*
PWP   *Papers of George Washington, Presidential Series*
PWR   *Papers of George Washington, Revolutionary War Series*
PWRT   *Papers of George Washington, Retirement Series*

PROLOGUE

1. Washington, *Writings*, 26:485, "Circular to the States," June 8, 1783.

2. Witherspoon, *Selected Writings*, 189–204.

3. Clark, "Provincialism," in *Moments of Vision*, 50–62; Bailyn, *To Begin the World Anew*, 3–36.

4. Fischer, *Albion's Seed*, 207–418.

5. Sydney Smith, review of *Statistical Annals of the United States of America*, by Adam Seybert, *Edinburgh Review, or Critical Journal*, 79; *PWCE*, 1:127, to Elias Boudinot, Feb. 18, 1784; Jefferson, *Notes on the State of Virginia*, 17, 22.

6. Mowry, *The Territorial Growth of the United States*, 5, 8, 28–29, 39; *DHRC*, 9:608–9, Hugh Williamson to John Gray Blount, June 3, 1788; Malone, "The Great Generation," 109–10; Force, *American Archives*, ser. 4, 1:1194.

7. 1790 Census figures include Kentucky, which was part of Virginia until 1792; "Constitution for the United States," We the People, http://constitutionus.com/. For further discussion of the Three Fifths Compromise and the Election of 1800, see page 213.

8. Coolidge Collection of Jefferson Manuscripts, to Ellen Wayles Randolph Coolidge, Aug. 27, 1825; *Collected Works of Abraham Lincoln*, 3:376, to Henry Pierce and others, April 6, 1859; Goldwin, *Why Blacks, Women, and Jews Are Not Mentioned in the Constitution*, 15; *Frederick Douglass Papers: Digital Edition*, ser. 1, 3:361, "The American Constitution and the Slave," March 26, 1860.

9. Wirt, "Eulogy," in *A Selection of Eulogies*, 381.

10. *PTJ*, 14:188, to Madison, Nov. 18, 1788.

11. *Republic of Letters*, 3:2002, "Advice to My Country," 1834.

ONE

THE WARRIORS

1. Douglas Southall Freeman, *Washington*, 3:473, 483; Thacher, *Military Journal During the American Revolutionary War*, 37; Adams, *Letters of John Adams*, 1:195, March 16, 1777; Greene, *Life of Nathanael Greene*, 1:101.

2. *PWR*, 3:357, "General Orders," Feb. 24, 1776; 3:362, "General Orders," Feb. 26, 1776.

3. Puls, *Henry Knox*, 14.

4. Gordon, *History of the Rise, Progress, and Establishment of the Independence of the United States of America*, 2:25–27; Douglas Southall Freeman, *Washington*, 4:34–37 and n66; Nash, *Journal of Solomon Nash*, 7–8.

5. Gordon, *History of the Rise, Progress, and Establishment of the Independence of the United States of America*, 2:27; Archibald Robertson, *His Diaries and Sketches in America*, 74.

6. *PWR*, 3:545, to Landon Carter, March 27, 1776; 4:16–17, from Hancock, April 2, 1776.

7. *PTJR*, 7:101, to Walter Jones, Jan. 2, 1814; "Dancing with General Washington," George Washington's Mount Vernon, http://www.mountvernon.org /george-washington/colonial-life-today/dancing/.

8. *Adams Family Papers: An Electronic Archive*, Abigail Adams to John Adams, July 16, 1775.

9. Schutz and Adair, eds., *The Spur of Fame*, 97, Adams to Benjamin Rush, Nov. 11, 1807.

10. *PWCE*, 3:149, to David Humphreys, July 25, 1785.

11. Moore, ed., *George Washington's Rules of Civility and Decent Behaviour*.

12. For examples of commentary on Washington as "disinterested patriot," see James Thacher and Thomas Burke in Thompson, "Statements Regarding the Physical Appearance, Traits and Personal Characteristics of George Washington," 2, 9; Moore, ed., *George Washington's Rules of Civility and Decent Behaviour*, 21; *Annals*, 3rd Cong., 2nd sess., 796, Nov. 22, 1794.

13. Royster, *A Revolutionary People at War*, 35; *PWR*, 3:89, to Joseph Reed, Jan. 14, 1776.

14. Van Tyne, *The Founding of the American Republic*, 2:243, 246; Troyer Steele Anderson, *The Command of the Howe Brothers During the American Revolution*, 69; Douglas Southall Freeman, *Washington*, 4:148.

15. Lengel, *General George Washington*, 142–46; Fithian, *Journal*, 218–19.

16. Symonds, *A Battlefield Atlas of the American Revolution*, 27; *PWR*, 6:199, to Hancock, Sept. 2, 1776.

17. Adams, *Letters of John Adams*, 1:170, Oct. 8, 1776.

18. *PWR*, 6:248–49, to Hancock, Sept. 8, 1776; *Plutarch's Lives*, trans. Langhorne and Langhorne, 2:53–90. Washington had a copy of *Lives of the Noble Greeks and Romans* in his library at Mount Vernon. See Carroll and Meacham, *The Library at Mount Vernon*, 153.

19. *PWR*, 6:249–53, to Hancock, Sept. 8, 1776. For varied interpretations see, for example, Douglas Southall Freeman, *Washington*, 4:186–89; McCullough, *1776*, 207; Ellis, *His Excellency George Washington*, 95–96; Chernow, *Washington*, 249.

20. *PWR*, 6:250–51, to Hancock, Sept. 8, 1776.

21. *PWR*, 6:308, to Hancock, Sept. 14, 1776.

22. Monroe, *Autobiography*, 23; Ammon, *James Monroe*, 7–8; Douglas Southall Freeman, *Washington*, 4:190.

23. Martin, *A Narrative of a Revolutionary Soldier*, 30–31.

24. Force, *American Archives*, ser. 5, 2:1252; 2:1013; *PWR*, 6:313, to Hancock, Sept. 16, 1776; Heath, *Heath's Memoirs of the American War*, 70; George Weedon Papers, George Weedon to John Page, Sept. 20, 1776.

25. Thacher, *Military Journal During the American Revolutionary War*, 70; Reed, *Life and Correspondence of Joseph Reed*, 1:236.

26. De Luzancy, *A Panegyrick to the Memory of His Grace Frederick*, 12.

27. Douglas Southall Freeman, *Washington*, 4:159.

28. Hanser, *The Glorious Hour of Lt. Monroe*, 70; Reed, *Life and Correspondence of Joseph Reed*, 1:237.

29. Hanser, *The Glorious Hour of Lt. Monroe*, 70–71.

30. Ammon, *James Monroe*, 2, 7, 576n2.

31. Bacon, *The Essays or Counsels Civil and Moral of Francis Bacon*, 210; Jefferson, *Works*, 11:128, to James Madison, Nov. 30, 1809.

32. *PWR*, 5:180, "General Orders," July 2, 1776.

33. Reed, *Life and Correspondence*, 1:238; *PWR*, 6:331–33, to Hancock, Sept. 18, 1776.

34. *PWR*, 6:348, "General Orders," Sept. 20, 1776; 6:445, "General Orders," Oct. 1, 1776.

35. *PWR*, 6:493–96, to Lund Washington, Oct. 6, 1776.

36. *PWR*, 6:394–97, to Hancock, Sept. 25, 1776.

37. *PWR*, 2:449, to Reed, Nov. 28, 1775; 3:172, to Reed, Jan. 23, 1776.

38. *PWR*, 2:449, to Reed, Nov. 28, 1775; Graydon, *Memoirs*, 148; *PWR*, 2:551–52, to Reed, Dec. 15, 1775.

39. *PWR*, 6:441–42, to Lund Washington, Sept. 30, 1776.

40. Adams, *Warren-Adams Letters*, 1:61, Adams to James Warren, June 20, 1775; Warren, *History of the Rise, Progress, and Termination of the American Revolution*, 1:291–92.

41. Gibbes, *Documentary History of the American Revolution*, 2:4, Pinckney to his mother, June 15, 1776; John Adams, *The Adams Papers*, 1:335, Abigail Adams to John Adams, Dec. 10, 1775.

42. Alden, *General Charles Lee*, 9.

43. Caesar Rodney, *Letters to and from Caesar Rodney*, 112, from Haslet, Sept. 4, 1776.

44. Force, *American Archives*, ser. 5, 2:1095; *PWR*, 6:535, to Hancock, Oct. 11–13, 1776; 6:239, to Jonathan Trumbull Sr., Sept. 6, 1776; 6:344–47, to the Massachusetts General Court, Sept. 19, 1776; 6:380–82, to Jonathan Trumbull Sr., Sept. 23, 1776.

45. *PWR*, 3:37, from John Adams, Jan. 6, 1776; 22:225, to Reed, Aug. 22, 1779; 6:552–53, "General Orders," Oct. 13, 1776.

46. Lee, *The Lee Papers*, 2:261–62, to General Gates, Oct. 14, 1776.

47. *PWR*, 6:575, to Jonathan Trumbull Sr., Oct. 15, 1776; 6:507 and 508–9n8, to John Hancock, Oct. 8–9, 1776; 6:576, "Council of War," Oct. 16, 1776.

48. *PWR*, 6:594–95, to Robert Livingston, Oct. 20, 1776; Martin, *A Narrative of a Revolutionary Soldier*, 46.

49. Reed, *Life and Correspondence of Joseph Reed*, 1:244; Heath, *Heath's Memoirs of the American War*, 88.

50. Heath, *Heath's Memoirs of the American War*, 93; *PWR*, 7:96–97, to Hancock, Nov. 6, 1776.

51. *PWR*, 7:97–98, to Hancock, Nov. 6, 1776; Douglas Southall Freeman, *Washington*, 4:241.

52. *PWR*, 7:135, "Instructions to Major General Charles Lee," Nov. 10, 1776; 3:379–81, "General Orders," Feb. 27, 1776; 4:83–84, "General Orders," April 19, 1776; 5:112–13, "General Orders," June 27, 1776.

53. Moore, ed., *George Washington's Rules of Civility and Decent Behaviour*, 10.

54. *PWR*, 7:115–16, to Greene, Nov. 8, 1776.

55. Golway, *Washington's General*, 1, 21–29; Thayer, *Nathanael Greene*, 24, 45; Force, *American Archives*, ser. 5, 2:870.

56. *PWR*, 22:225, to Reed, Aug. 22, 1779; Heath, *Heath's Memoirs of the American War*, 97.

57. *PWR*, 7:187, from Lee, Nov. 19, 1776.

58. *PWR*, 7:103–4, to John Augustine Washington, Nov. 6–19, 1776; 7:47–48, from Greene, Oct. 29, 1776.

59. *PWR*, 7:194, to Lee, Nov. 21, 1776; Lee, *The Lee Papers*, 2:291, to General Heath, Nov. 21, 1776.

60. *PWR*, 7:187, from Lee, Nov. 19, 1776; 7:210, from Lee, Nov. 24, 1776; 7:224–25, to Lee, Nov. 27, 1776; 7:249, to Lee, Dec. 1, 1776; 7:257, to Lee, Dec. 3, 1776; 7:276–77, from Lee, Dec. 8, 1776; 7:288–89, to Lee, Dec. 10, 1776; 7:301, to Lee, Dec. 11, 1776.

61. *PWR*, 6:394–97, to Hancock, Sept. 25, 1776; 3:172, to Reed, Jan. 23, 1776.

62. Lee, *The Lee Papers*, 2:305–6, to Reed, Nov. 24, 1776; *PWR*, 7:237, to Reed, Nov. 30, 1776.

63. Monroe, *Autobiography*, 24.

TWO
RIVER CROSSING

1. LC-TJ, from Peale, Aug. 21, 1819; Peale, *The Selected Papers of Charles Willson Peale*, 5:50, "The Autobiography of Charles Willson Peale."

2. *PWR*, 7:352, to John Hancock, Dec. 16, 1776.

3. Wilkinson, *Memoirs*, 1:108.

4. Force, *American Archives*, ser. 5, 3:1247; Thomas Rodney, *Diary*, 19; *PWR*, 7:290, to Lund Washington, Dec. 17, 1776.

5. *Journals of the Continental Congress*, 6:1027, Dec. 12, 1776; *PWR*, 7:382, to Hancock, Dec. 20, 1776.

6. *PWR*, 7:317–318, from Joseph Reed, Dec. 12, 1776; 7:414–15, Joseph Reed, Dec. 22, 1776.

7. Fischer, *Washington's Crossing*, 195–96; *PWR*, 7:415–16, from Reed, Dec. 22, 1776.

8. *PWR*, 6:251, to Hancock, Sept. 8, 1776.

9. Fischer, *Washington's Crossing*, 140.

10. *PWR*, 7:423, to Reed, Dec. 23, 1776; Chernow, *Washington*, 272.

11. Ammon, *James Monroe*, 11–12; Monroe, *Autobiography*, 25; Fischer, *Washington's Crossing*, 221; *PWR*, 7:436, "General Orders," Dec. 25, 1776.

12. W. W. H. Davis, "Washington on the West Bank of the Delaware," *PMHB*, 1880, 153.

13. Stryker, "No. 37. From Diary of an Officer on Washington's Staff," in *The Battles of Trenton and Princeton*, 363; W. W. H. Davis, "Washington on the West Bank of the Delaware," *PMHB*, 1880, 153; Monroe, *Autobiography*, 26.

14. Wilkinson, *Memoirs*, 1:130.

15. Monroe, *Autobiography*, 26. In portraits of Washington with this horse, named Bluestone, the charger appears nearly white, with bluish gray mane and tail. See John Trumbull, *George Washington at Trenton*, 1792, oil on canvas, 92½ in. x 63 in., Yale University Art Gallery, New Haven, Conn.

16. Becker, "Smallpox in Washington's Army," 381–93; *PWR*, 8:264, to Shippen, Feb. 6, 1777.

17. Sellers, "The Common Soldier in the American Revolution," in Stanley J. Underdal, ed., *Military History*, 154, 164; *PJM*, 2:4, to John Thornton, July 3, 1777; Jones, *Letters of Joseph Jones*, 1, to Washington, Aug. 11, 1777.

18. Monroe, *Autobiography*, 26–27; Royster, *A Revolutionary People at War*, 92 Cresson, *James Monroe* 32.

19. Nelson, *William Alexander, Lord Stirling*, 3, 39, 87, 118; Field, *The Battle of Long Island*, 525.

20. Symonds, *A Battlefield Atlas of the American Revolution*, 53; Nelson, *William Alexander, Lord Stirling*, 114.

21. Symonds, *A Battlefield Atlas of the American Revolution*, 57; Monroe, *Autobiography*, 28; *PJA*, 5:151, to Nathanael Greene, April 13, 1777.

22. Wright Jr., *The Continental Army*, 118; Paine, *Life and Writings*, 2:277; Nelson, *William Alexander, Lord Stirling*, 117.

23. Monroe, *Autobiography*, 29.

24. *PWR*, 13:109-10, "General Orders," Jan. 2, 1778; 13:127, "General Orders," Jan. 3, 1778; 13:143, "General Orders," Jan. 5, 1778.

25. *PAH*, 2:34, to John Laurens, April 1779.

26. Allan McLane Hamilton, *The Intimate Life of Alexander Hamilton*, 245.

27. Bodle and Thibaut, *Valley Forge Historical Research Report*, 3:134; Flexner, *George Washington in the American Revolution*, 401; Symonds, *A Battlefield Atlas of the American Revolution*, 51; *PWR*, 13:160, from Craik, Jan. 6, 1778.

28. *PWR*, 12:684–85, to Henry Laurens, Dec. 23, 1777; 14:578, to John Banister, April 21, 1778.

29. *PWR*, 12:683, to Henry Laurens, Dec. 23, 1777; 13:552–53, to Clinton, Feb. 16, 1778.

30. Lossing, *Mary and Martha*, 168–72; Lafayette, *Lafayette in the Age of the American Revolution*, 1:225, to Adrienne Lafayette, Jan. 6, 1778; Fraser, *The Washingtons*, chap. 3; *The Adams Papers Digital Edition*, 1:385, Warren to Abigail Adams, April 17, 1776.

31. Du Ponceau, "Autobiographical Letters of Peter S. Duponceau," *PMHB*, 1916, 181; Ridley Papers, Sarah Vaughan to Kitty Livingston, Oct. 10, 1784.

32. *PJM*, 2:46, 54, 117, 176, to Mercer, Sept. 12, 1782, March 8, 1783, Aug. 8, 1784, Feb. 20, 1785; Du Ponceau and Whitehead, "Notes and Documents: The

Autobiography of Peter Stephen Du Ponceau," *PMHB*, April 1939, 192; *PJM*, 2:8–9 and n6, to Peter Duponceau, April 11, 1778.

33. Waldo, "Valley Forge, 1777–1778. Diary of Surgeon Albigence Waldo, of the Connecticut Line," *PMHB*, 1897, 313; Greene, *Life of Nathanael Greene*, 1:563.

34. *PWR*, 15:38–39, "General Orders," May 5, 1778; Laurens, *The Army Correspondence of Colonel John Laurens*, 169, to Henry Laurens, May 7, 1778.

35. Humphrey, ed., "Document 3: Letter from William Bradford Jr. (May 14, 1778)," in *Voices of Revolutionary America*, 98–99; Longmore, *The Invention of George Washington*, 174.

36. *PWR*, 15:268, to Landon Carter, May 30, 1778.

37. McBurney, *Kidnapping the Enemy*, 124–39; Boudinot, *Journal*, 77–78.

38. *PJM*, 2:25, from Charles Lee, July 18, 1780.

39. Lafayette, *Memoirs*, 1:50–51.

40. Washington had specifically been given the power to override more than a year before. See *Journals of the Continental Congress*, 7:196–97, March 24, 1777.

41. *PWR*, 15:578, to Henry Laurens, June 28, 1778; Lee, *The Lee Papers*, 3:12, 18–19, 78. It was a matter of dispute whether Lee had some four thousand men, as he claimed, or nearer to five thousand. See Lee, *The Lee Papers*, 3:178.

42. Lee, *The Lee Papers*, 3:16, 81, 134–35.

43. Ibid., 199–200; Clinton, *The American Rebellion*, 93.

44. Martin, *A Narrative of a Revolutionary Soldier*, 110; Lee, *The Lee Papers*, 3:184, 186–87.

45. Lee, *The Lee Papers*, 3:205, 112; Scheer and Rankin, *Rebels and Redcoats*, 330.

46. H. Robertson, "Washington at Monmouth," 1190; Lee, *The Lee Papers*, 3:191, 206.

47. Lee, *The Lee Papers*, 3:112, 201; 2:469; Lafayette, *Memoirs*, 1:54.

48. Nelson, *William Alexander, Lord Stirling*, 130; *PJM*, 2:10, to Washington, June 28, 1778; Lafayette, *Memoirs*, 1:54.

49. *PWR*, 16:25, to John Augustine Washington, July 4, 1778.

50. *PWR*, 15:594–95, from Lee, June 30, 1778.

51. *PWR*, 15:595–96, to Lee, June 30, 1778.

52. *PWR*, 15:596, from Lee, June 30, 1778; 15:596, from Lee, June 30, 1778; 15:597, to Lee, June 30, 1778; 16:1, "General Orders," July 1, 1778; Lee, *The Lee Papers*, 3:2.

53. *PWR*, 15:578, to Henry Laurens, June 28, 1778; 15:596, to Lee, June 30, 1778; Lee, *The Lee Papers*, 3:9–10, 54–56, 205.

54. Alden, *General Charles Lee*, 238–40; *Revolutionary Diplomatic Correspondence of the United States*, 1:280, "Introduction"; Isenberg, *Fallen Founder*, 46.

55. Du Ponceau, "Autobiographical Letters of Peter S. Duponceau" *PMHB*, 1916, 181; *PJM*, 2:11–12, to Prevost, Nov. 8, 1778; Ammon, *James Monroe*, 25–26; "George Washington's Visits," Hermitage Museum, https://web.archive.org

/web/20170501022012/http://thehermitage.org/history/history_people_prevost
_george.html.

56. Nancy was an eighteenth-century nickname for Anne, which was Miss Brown's given name. Her lineage can be seen at frenchfamilyassoc.com/FFA/, where she appears in the fifth generation. The romance between Brown and Monroe lived on in social lore, but accounts became distorted and exaggerated. Monroe was even said to have jilted Brown at the altar: Van Rensselaer, "Our Social Ladder," 14–15. Susannah Livingston's and Lord Stirling's quarrel, which was brought to Washington's attention, probably by Mrs. Livingston, occurred in the spring of 1777: *PWR*, 9:358, to Lord Stirling, May 6, 1777; 9:359–60, from Lord Stirling, May 6, 1777; *PJM*, 2:13, to William Woodford, May 26, 1779.

57. Sparks, *Life of Gouverneur Morris,* 1:177; Rush, "Excerpts from the Papers of Dr. Benjamin Rush," *PMHB*, 1905, 18.

58. *Journals of the Continental Congress,* 12:1195, Dec. 5, 1778; Monroe, *Autobiography,* 29; Garnett, "John Francis Mercer," 194. Neither Monroe nor Mercer nor any of their contemporaries knew that Lee, while held by the British, presented them a plan for putting a quick end to the American rebellion. It involved cutting the southern states off from the middle ones and sailing the British fleet into the Chesapeake. The plan was not discovered until seventy years after Lee's death, and historians argue about it today. Was Lee a traitor or was he trying to help the American cause by sowing confusion among the British? In any case, the plans he advanced seemed to have had little effect. See Alden, *General Charles Lee,* 174–79; and Troyer Steele Anderson, *The Command of the Howe Brothers During the American Revolution,* 226.

59. Shaw, *The Journals of Major Samuel Shaw,* 55–56; Lee, *The Lee Papers,* 4:151, 3:283–84.

60. Lee, *The Lee Papers,* 3:322; *PWR*, 21:501 and n2, "Enclosure," 1779; 21:500 and n2; from Joseph Reed, July 15, 1779.

61. *PWR*, 21:501, "Enclosure," 1779; Adams, *Letters of John Adams,* 2:15; Tudor, *An Oration Delivered March 5, 1779,* 8–9.

62. Papas, *Renegade Revolutionary,* 277; *PWR*, 21:504, "Enclosure: Newspaper Publication," 1779; Lee, *The Lee Papers,* 4:314.

63. *PWR*, 20:574–75, to Archibald Cary, May 22, 1779; *PJM*, 2:14, to Lee, June 13, 1779.

64. *PJM*, 2:14, to Lee, June 13, 1779.

65. George Harrison Sanford King, comp., *The Register of Overwharton Parish, Stafford County, Virginia,* 244, indicates that Joseph Jones Jr. was born "circa 1780." Monroe's letters of June 13, 1779 (to Charles Lee), and Sept. 1779 (to William Woodford) indicate a birth date in the summer of 1779. In 1795, Jones Sr. wrote a will confirming that Joseph Jones Jr. and his "heirs and assigns" were to inherit all his estate, "real and personal." He added that should Joseph Jones Jr. die "before he arrives to lawful age or being of lawful age shall die without a child or children to inherit the estate hereby given to him, it is my will that the same shall after his death be divided between the children of my late sisters . . . allowing my nephew Colonel James Monroe the first choice." Historic Records

& Deed Research, *Will Book G,* 437. Jones Sr. died in 1805 and Jones Jr., unmarried and childless, around 1808, and thus Monroe ultimately became one of the heirs of Joseph Jones Sr. Monroe, *Autobiography*, 29; *PJM*, 2:16–17, from Joseph Jones, March 1, 1780; Ammon, *James Monroe*, 29–32.

66. *PJM,* 2:25, from Lee, July 18, 1780.

67. *PJM,* 2:26, to Jefferson, Sept. 9, 1780.

68. Washington, *Writings*, 22:103–4, to Chevalier de La Luzerne, May 23, 1781; 22:105–7, "Conference with Comte de Rochambeau," May 23, 1781.

69. Doniol, *Histoire de la participation de la France à l'établissement des États-Unis d'Amérique,* 5:475, Rochambeau to de Grasse, May 28, 1781.

70. Washington, *Writings*, 22:143, to Lafayette, May 31, 1781; Thacher, *Military Journal During the American Revolutionary War*, 315–16; Mackenzie, *Diary of Frederick Mackenzie*, 2:536, 698; *PWD*, 3:375 and n8, May 31, 1781; Washington, *Writings*, 22:109, "Circular to the New England States," May 24, 1781; *Annual Register*, 123.

71. *PWCE*, 6:413–14, to Noah Webster, July 31, 1788.

72. *PWR*, 1:227, to Hancock, Aug. 4–5, 1775; Watson, *Men and Times of the Revolution*, 20; Van Doren, *Secret History*, 262–64.

73. *PWCE*, 6:413–14, to Webster, July 31, 1788; *PWR*, 8:437, to Patrick Henry, Feb. 24, 1777.

74. Flexner, *George Washington in the American Revolution*, 439; Grainger, *The Battle of Yorktown*, 37; "Grand Strategy," George Washington's Mount Vernon, http://www.mountvernon.org/digital-encyclopedia/article/grand-strategy; Chernow, *Washington*, 401.

75. LC-TJ, to Walter Jones, Jan. 2, 1814; Paine, *An Eulogy on the Life of General George Washington*, 9. A few of many examples of Washington being "fixated on victory": Washington, *Writings*, 22:103–4, to Chevalier de La Luzerne, May 23, 1781; 22:105–7, "Conference with Comte de Rochambeau," May 23, 1781; 22:143, to Lafayette, May 31, 1781; *PWD*, 3:369, May 22, 1781; 3:378, June 5, 1781; 3:404–5, Aug. 1, 1781; Washington, *Writings*, 22:208–9, to Rochambeau, June 3, 1781; 22:7–8, to de Grasse, Aug. 17, 1781.

76. Trumbull Jr., "Minutes of Occurrences Respecting the Siege and Capture of York in Virginia," 332.

THREE
THE INTELLECTUALS

1. Quotations are from the opening of the declaration as it was reported by the Committee of Five to the Continental Congress. Benjamin Franklin may have substituted *self-evident* for the phrase *sacred and undeniable,* which appeared in the draft Jefferson sent to Franklin. Members would change *inherent and in-alienable rights* to *certain inalienable rights,* which in the course of printing the

document became *certain unalienable rights.* Maier, *American Scripture,* 136, 144; *Pennsylvania Gazette,* June 12, 1776.

2. Fliegelman, *Declaring Independence,* 5–10. Jefferson's marks are also indicated by errors in what is known as the proof copy of the Dunlap broadside of the declaration. The printer mistook Jefferson's pause marks for quotation marks.

3. Jefferson, *Works,* 12:409, to Henry Lee, May 8, 1825.

4. *PMC,* 9:318, to Jefferson, March 19, 1787; 9:384–85, to Washington, April 16, 1787; 9:370, to Edmund Randolph, April 8, 1787.

5. *PMC,* 10:16, "Resolutions Proposed by Mr. Randolph in Convention," May 29, 1787.

6. "Constitution for the United States," We the People, http://constitutionus.com/.

7. John Quincy Adams, *Jubilee of the Constitution,* 111.

8. LC-JMa, to Samuel H. Smith, Nov. 4, 1826.

9. Dabney, "Jouett Outrides Tarleton," 690–94; Kranish, *Flight from Monticello,* xi, 283, 296, 316.

10. *PMC,* 4:333, to Edmund Randolph, June 11, 1782; *PTJ,* 6:183, from Monroe, May 11, 1782; 6:185–86, to Monroe, May 20, 1782.

11. *PTJ,* 6:185–86, to Monroe, May 20, 1782; Randall, *The Life of Thomas Jefferson,* 1:382.

12. *PMC,* 5:151, from Edmund Randolph, Sept. 20, 1782; 5:170, to Edmund Randolph, Sept. 30, 1782.

13. *PMC,* 6:63–65, "Report on Books for Congress: Editorial Note"; 1:105, to William Bradford, Jan. 24, 1774.

14. *PMC,* 6:65, 97, "Report on Books for Congress," Jan. 23, 1783; *Jefferson Papers: An Electronic Archive,* "1783 Catalog of Books," 166, 242; *PTJ,* 39:461–62, "Jefferson's Volumes of the Encyclopédie Méthodique [Enclosure]."

15. Jefferson, *Notes on the State of Virginia,* 157, 174–75.

16. *PTJ,* 8:184, to Marquis de Chastellux, June 7, 1785.

17. Harris and Kidd, eds., *The Founding Fathers and the Debate over Religion in Revolutionary America,* 133–36; Jefferson, *Notes on the State of Virginia,* 170.

18. Locke, *Works,* 5:9–10; *PMC,* 1:170–79 and n7, "Declaration of Rights and Form of Government of Virginia," May 16–June 29, 1776; Garrison, "Characteristics of American Organized Religion," 15–16.

19. *PMC,* 8:300, "Memorial and Remonstrance against Religious Assessments," ca. June 20, 1785; 8:399–401 and n1, "An Act for Establishing Religious Freedom," Oct. 31, 1785; 8:474, to Jefferson, Jan. 22, 1786.

20. Cheney, *Madison,* 4, 29, 51–52, 87–88, 113; De Coppet Collection, Madison to Delaplaine, memo, Sept. 1816; Jefferson, *Autobiography,* 2; *PMC,* 12:466, to Washington, Jan. 4, 1790.

21. *PTJ,* 6:262, to Madison, April 14, 1783; 6:335–36, to Madison, Aug. 31, 1783.

22. Malone, *Jefferson,* 1:399–400.

23. Jefferson, *Autobiography*, 70; Peterson, *Thomas Jefferson and the New Nation*, 276–77.

24. Wood, *Empire of Liberty*, 116, 122, 361–62; Stilgoe, *Common Landscape*, 87–88, 99, 102–3; Peterson, *Thomas Jefferson and the New Nation*, 285.

25. *PTJ*, 6:412, "III. Washington's Address to Congress Resigning His Commission," Dec. 23, 1783; *Letters of Delegates to Congress*, 21:228, David Howell to William Greene, Dec. 24, 1783; Rufus King, *Life and Correspondence*, 3:545.

26. *PJM*, 2:96–97, "Thomas Jefferson: List of Books Sold to James Monroe," May 10, 1784; 2:98–99, to Jefferson, May 14, 1784; 2:55–56, to John Francis Mercer, March 14, 1783; *PTJ*, 7:234, to Madison, May 8, 1784.

27. Jefferson, *Memorandum Books*, 1:560 and n79.

28. De Chastellux, *Travels in North-America*, 2:41–42, 47.

29. *PTJ*, 10:157–59, from Madame de Tessé, July 20, 1786.

30. *PTJ*, 2:196, to Giovanni Fabbroni, June 8, 1778; 15:375–77, "List of Baggage Shipped by Jefferson from France," ca. Sept. 1, 1789.

31. *PTJ*, 10:445–46, to Maria Cosway, Oct. 12, 1786; Kaminski, ed., *Jefferson in Love*, 48–49.

32. Malone, *Jefferson*, 2:71–72; *PTJ*, 10:443, to Cosway, Oct. 12, 1786.

33. *PTJ*, 10:443–52, to Cosway, Oct. 12, 1786.

34. Colin Jones, *The Smile Revolution*, 1; Poulet et al., *Jean-Antoine Houdon*, 18.

35. *PTJ*, 11:271, to de Tott, April 5, 1787; *PTJR*, 11:525, to Paul Clay, ca. July 12, 1817.

36. *PTJ*, 11:226, to de Tessé, March 20, 1787.

37. Coolidge Collection of Jefferson Manuscripts, from Cosway, April 7, 1819.

38. *PMC*, 9:382, from John Dawson, April 15, 1787.

39. *PTJ*, 7:558, to Madison, Dec. 8, 1784.

40. *PMC*, 9:78–79, to Jefferson, June 19, 1786.

41. *PMC*, 9:51, to Jefferson, May 12, 1786; 8:265, to Jefferson, April 27, 1785; 8:11, to Jefferson, March 16, 1784; 8:501, March 18, 1786; Taylor Diary, March 2, 1786.

42. *PMC*, 9:247–48, from Jefferson, Jan. 30, 1787.

43. *PMC*, 9:163–64 and n1, "Bill Providing for Delegates to the Convention of 1787," Nov. 6, 1786; Washington, *Writings*, 26:486, "Circular to the States," June 8, 1783.

44. *PMC*, 9:199, to Washington, Dec. 7, 1786; 9:315, to Washington, March 18, 1787.

45. Farrand, ed., *Records*, 3:94, William Pierce, "Character Sketches of Delegates to the Federal Convention."

46. Farrand, ed., *Records*, 1:35–38, Madison's notes, May 30, 1787; 1:38–40, Yates's notes, May 30, 1787; 1:40–43, McHenry's notes, May 30, 1787.

47. Farrand, ed., *Records*, 1:50, Madison's notes, May 31, 1787; 2:318, Madison's notes, Aug. 17, 1787; Adair, "'That Politics May Be Reduced to a Science,'" 349–60.

48. *PMC*, 10:163, to Jefferson, Sept. 6, 1787.

49. *PMC,* 10:232, to Archibald Stuart, Oct. 30, 1787; 10:208, to Jefferson, Oct. 24, 1787.

50. Farrand, ed., *Records,* 1:299, Yates's notes, June 18, 1787.

51. *PMC,* 10:268–69, *Federalist* 10, Nov. 22, 1787.

52. *PMC,* 10:477, *Federalist* 51, Feb. 6, 1788.

53. *PTJ,* 12:440–41, to Madison, Dec. 20, 1787; *PMC,* 10:208, to Jefferson, Oct. 24, 1787.

54. LC-JMa, to Nicholas Trist, May 15, 1832; *PMC,* 11:28, to Jefferson, April 22, 1788.

55. *PTJ,* 12:351, to Adams, Nov. 13, 1787; 12:356, to Smith, Nov. 13, 1787.

56. *PTJ,* 12:425–26, to William Carmichael, Dec. 15, 1787.

57. *PTJ,* 12:476–79, to Uriah Forrest, Dec. 31, 1787; *PMC,* 11:64, from Daniel Carroll, May 28, 1788.

58. Ford, ed., "Letter by Edmund Randolph," in *Pamphlets on the Constitution of the United States,* 274–75.

59. *PMC,* 10:290, to Edmund Randolph, Dec. 2, 1787; 10:354–55, to Edmund Randolph, Jan. 10, 1788; 11:25–26, from Edmund Randolph, April 17, 1788.

60. *DHRC,* 9:933, Debates, June 4, 1788.

61. *PMC,* 11:77, to Washington, June 4, 1788.

62. *DHRC,* 9:953, 963, 962, Debates, June 5, 1788.

63. *DHRC,* 9:996, Debates, June 6, 1788; *PWCE,* 6:316, from Bushrod Washington, June 7, 1788.

64. *PTJ,* 12:571, to Alexander Donald, Feb. 7, 1788; *DHRC,* 9:1096–97, Debates, June 10, 1788.

65. *DHRC,* 9:1035, Debates, June 7, 1788; LC-JMa, to Jonathan Elliot, Nov. 1827.

66. *DHRC,* 9:1051, Debates, June 9, 1788; 10:1223, Debates, June 12, 1788; *PTJ,* 12:568–70, to Madison, Feb. 6, 1788; 10:1651, Stuart to John Breckinridge, June 19, 1788.

67. *PMC,* 11:196–97, to Jefferson, July 24, 1788; *PTJ,* 14:188, to Madison, Nov. 18, 1788.

68. *PJM,* 2:391, to Jefferson, July 27, 1787.

69. *PJM,* 2:444, "Some Hints Directing the Measures to Be Taken to Form a Monarchy Out of Several Confederate Democracies," June 1788; Wood, *Revolutionary Characters,* 41.

70. *PJM,* 2:444, "Some Hints Directing the Measures to Be Taken to Form a Monarchy Out of Several Confederate Democracies," June 1788.

71. Ibid., 444–47.

72. Gilman, *James Monroe,* 219–20.

73. Hunt, *The Life of James Madison,* 164; *PMC,* 11:404–5, to George Eve, Jan. 2, 1789.

74. Hunt, *The Life of James Madison,* 165.

75. *PMC,* 12:37, to Jefferson, March 29, 1789; Jefferson, *Works,* 11:128, to Madison, Nov. 30, 1809.

76. *PTJ,* 7:559, to Madison, Dec. 8, 1784.

FOUR
UNTRODDEN GROUND

1. *PMC*, 11:446–47 and n1, from Washington, Feb. 16, 1789; 12:120–23, "Address of the President to Congress: Editorial Note."

2. "President-Elect George Washington's Journey to the Inauguration," George Washington's Mount Vernon, https://www.mountvernon.org/george-washington/the-first-president/inauguration/; Maclay, *Journal*, 9, April 30, 1789.

3. Fisher Ames, *Works*, 1:35–36, to George Minot, May 3, 1789.

4. *Annals*, 1st Cong., 2nd sess., 451–52, June 8, 1789.

5. *PMC*, 12:402, to Edmund Pendleton, Sept. 14, 1789.

6. *PTJ*, 15:111, to John Jay, May 9, 1789; 15:116, to John Adams, May 10, 1789; 15:305, to Cosway, July 25, 1789.

7. *PTJ*, 15:118, to Washington, May 10, 1789; "Declaration of the Rights of Man—1789," Avalon Project, https://avalon.law.yale.edu/18th_century/rightsof.asp.

8. *PTJ*, 15:153, from Madison, May 27, 1789; 15:369, to Madison, Aug. 28, 1789.

9. *PTJ*, 15:392, to Madison, Sept. 6, 1789; 15:118, to Washington, May 10, 1789.

10. *PMC*, 13:18–21, to Jefferson, Feb. 4, 1790.

11. *PMC*, 13:18, "Madison's Rebuttal to 'the Earth Belongs to the Living' Precept 4 February 1790: Editorial Note."

12. *PTJ*, 16:92–93, to Madison, Jan. 9, 1790.

13. *PTJ*, 16:182, to Madison, Feb. 14, 1790.

14. Jefferson, *Works*, 1:175, "The Anas, 1791–1806"; 7:224, "The Assumption," Feb. 1793.

15. Jefferson, *Works*, 7:226–27, "The Assumption," Feb. 1793; Riley, "Philadelphia," 362.

16. *PMC*, 13:375–76, "The Bank Bill," Feb. 2, 1791.

17. *PMC*, 10:422–24, *Federalist* 44, Jan. 25, 1788.

18. Humphrey, *The Press of the Young Republic*, 42–47.

19. *PTJ*, 19:351, to Philip Freneau, Feb. 28, 1791; Chernow, *Hamilton*, 395–96; *PMC*, 14:23, to Jefferson, May 12, 1791.

20. Wulf, *Founding Gardeners*, 89–91; *PTJ*, 20:463–64, to Martha Jefferson Randolph, May 31, 1791.

21. *PAH*, 2:563–67, to Schuyler, Feb. 18, 1781.

22. *PTJ*, 20:558–59, to Washington, June 20, 1791; *PMC*, 14:43, to Jefferson, July 10, 1791.

23. *PMC*, 14:180, to Henry Lee, Jan. 1, 1792.

24. *Annals*, 2nd Cong., 1st sess., 388, Feb. 6, 1792; *PMC*, 14:371, "A Candid State of Parties," *National Gazette*, Sept. 22, 1792.

25. *PTJ*, 14:650, to Francis Hopkinson, March 13, 1789; *PMC*, 14:197, "Parties," ca. Jan. 23, 1792.

26. Fisher Ames, *Works*, 1:127, to Thomas Dwight, Jan. 1793.

27. *PMC*, 14:299–304, "Memorandum on a Discussion of the President's Retirement," May 5, 1792.

28. Ibid.

29. *PTJ*, 24:317, from Washington, Aug. 23, 1792; 24:353, 358, to Washington, Sept. 9, 1792; *PAH*, 12:347–49, to Washington, Sept. 9, 1792.

30. *PTJ*, 26:101–2, "Notes of a Conversation with George Washington," May 23, 1793; *PTJR*, 2:272, to Walter Jones, March 5, 1810.

31. *PTJ*, 24:433–34, "Notes of a Conversation with George Washington," Oct. 1, 1792.

32. Maxey, *A Portrait*, 30–31; *PWCE*, 5:279–80, to Powel, July 30, 1787.

33. Maxey, *A Portrait*, 17–32; *PWP*, 11:395–97, from Powel, Nov. 17, 1792.

34. *PWP*, 12:30, to Lee, Jan. 20, 1793.

35. Schauffler, ed., *Washington's Birthday*, xx; *National Gazette*, Feb. 27, 1793; *Annals*, 2nd Cong., 2nd sess., 905, Feb. 28, 1793.

36. Maclay, *Journal*, 374, Jan. 20, 1791.

37. Jefferson, *Complete Anas*, 114.

38. Ludlum, *The Weather Factor*, 112.

39. Bizardel and Rice Jr., "'Poor in Love Mr. Short,'" 531.

40. *PTJ*, 25:14, to Short, Jan. 3, 1793; Shackelford, *Jefferson's Adoptive Son*, 122–23.

41. *PTJ*, 25:402, to Joseph Fay, March 18, 1793.

42. *PTJ*, 16:293, to Lafayette, April 2, 1790.

43. *PMC*, 15:29, to Jefferson, June 13, 1793; *PTJ*, 26:444, to Madison, July 7, 1793.

44. Irving, *Life of George Washington*, 5:147–49.

45. *PTJR*, 6:254, from Adams, June 30, 1813.

46. *PTJ*, 26:652, to Madison, Aug. 11, 1793.

47. *PTJ*, 26:729, from Madison, Aug. 20, 1793; *PMC*, 15:65, "Madison's 'Helvidius' Essays, 24 August–18 September, 1793: Editorial Note."

48. *PTJ*, 27:20, "Enclosure: Resolutions on Neutrality and Friendships with France," from Madison, ca. Aug. 27, 1793; 27:16–18, from Madison, Sept. 2, 1793.

49. Jefferson, *Complete Anas*, 158–59.

50. *PTJ*, 27:102, to Madison, Sept. 12, 1793.

51. Drinker, *Extracts*, 190–95; *PTJ*, 27:62, to Madison, Sept. 8, 1793.

52. *PTJ*, 24:434, "Notes of a Conversation with George Washington," Oct. 1, 1792.

53. *PJM*, 2:710, to Washington, April 8, 1794; 2:710–11, from Washington, April 9, 1794; 2:711–12, to Washington, April 11, 1794.

54. Allgor, *Perfect Union*, 28; *PDM*, from Coles, June 1, 1794.

55. Ketcham, *Madison*, 381.

56. *PWD*, 6:193–94, Oct. 19, 1794.

57. *PMC*, 15:379, to Jefferson, Nov. 16, 1794; *PTJ*, 28:205, to William Branch Giles, Nov. 20, 1794; 28:182, to Madison, Oct. 30, 1794.

FIVE
SCHISM

1. "Notes and Queries," *PMHB,* June 1884, 226.

2. Ibid.

3. *PWP,* 17:181–86, "To the United States Senate and House of Representatives," Nov. 19, 1794.

4. *PMC,* 15:396, to Jefferson, Nov. 30, 1794; Hollitz, *Contending Voices,* 1:98, "Resolutions of the Pennsylvania Democratic Society (1794)"; Foner, ed., *The Democratic-Republican Societies,* 8–15.

5. *PMC,* 15:396–97, to Jefferson, Nov. 30, 1794.

6. Foner, ed., *The Democratic-Republican Societies,* 3, 136–37, 93–96, 29–30, 263.

7. *PTJ,* 28:228, to Madison, Dec. 28, 1794; *PMC,* 15:406–7, to Monroe, Dec. 4, 1794.

8. *PMC,* 15:406–7, to Monroe, Dec. 4, 1794.

9. *Annals,* 3rd Cong., 2nd sess., 934, 947–50, Nov. 27, 1794, Nov. 28, 1794.

10. *PWP,* 16:723, to Burgess Ball, Sept. 25, 1794; *PMC,* 14:371, "A Candid State of Parties," *National Gazette,* Sept. 22, 1792.

11. Jefferson, *Complete Anas,* 39–40; Barratt and Miles, *Gilbert Stuart,* 152, 166, 147.

12. Barratt and Miles, *Gilbert Stuart,* 152; Ring, "John Greenwood," 849 and f3; "The Trouble with Teeth," George Washington's Mount Vernon, https://www .mountvernon.org/george-washington/the-man-the-myth/the-trouble -with-teeth.

13. Link, *Democratic-Republican Societies,* 21; *PAH,* 14:371, "Enclosure," May 2, 1793; Foner, ed., *The Democratic-Republican Societies,* 3–4.

14. "Washington's Farewell Address 1796," Avalon Project, http://avalon.law .yale.edu/18th_century/washing.asp.

15. Washington, *Writings,* 35:30–31, to Charles Carroll, May 1, 1796.

16. *PAH,* 16:275, 278–79, to Washington, April 14, 1794; Barratt and Miles, *Gilbert Stuart,* 120–21.

17. *ASP-FR,* 1:519, John Jay to Edmund Randolph, March 5, 1795; *The Manuscripts of J. B. Fortescue,* 2:578, Lord Auckland to Lord Grenville, June 22, 1794; *PJJ,* 4:304–5 and n1, to Diego de Gardoqui, March 1, 1786; 4:305–6 and n1–2, to Charles Thomson, March 3, 1786; *PWP,* 1:349 and n1, from Jay, March 1, 1789.

18. Jay, *The Correspondence and Public Papers of John Jay,* 4:11–21, from Edmund Randolph, May 6, 1794.

19. Reardon, *Edmund Randolph,* 266; Bemis, *Jay's Treaty,* 337.

20. Boucher and Huard, *American Footprints in Paris,* 107.

21. *PJM,* 2:724, from Livingston, May 16, 1794. James Madison was also approached about being minister to France.

22. Jean Duplessi-Bertaux, *Assassinat du député Ferraud (ou Feraud) à la Convention nationale. La tête du député présentée à Boissy d'Anglas le 20 mai 1795, 1793–1803,*

19.7 cm. x 25.4 cm., Musée Carnavalet, Histoire de Paris, http://parismuseescol lections.paris.fr/fr/musee-carnavalet/oeuvres/assassinat-du-depute-ferraud -ou-feraud-a-la-convention-nationale-la-tete-du#infos-principales; Charles Monnet, *Journée du premier prairial de l'an III (20 mai 1795), Insurrection, la tête du député Féraud amenée au président de l'assemblée de la Convention le 1er Prairial An III (20 mai 1795). 12ème pl. des « Principales journées de la Révolution, »* 1790–1800, 36.2 cm. x 47.3 cm., Musée Carnavalet, Histoire de Paris, http://parismuseescollections.paris.fr/fr/musee-carnavalet/oeuvres/journee-du -premier-prairial-de-l-an-iii-20-mai-1795-insurrection-la-tete-du#infos-principales.

23. Mayo, "Joshua Barney and the French Revolution," 359, 357.

24. *PJM,* 3:30–31, "To the French Convention," Aug. 15, 1794; *ASP-FR,* 1:674, Edmund Randolph to the Committee of Public Safety of the French Republic, June 10, 1794.

25. *PJM,* 3:32, from Douai, Aug. 15, 1794; Morgan, *The Life of James Monroe,* 184.

26. *PJM,* 3:49, to Madison, Sept. 2, 1794; 3:172–73, from Edmund Randolph, Dec. 2, 1794.

27. *PJM,* 3:10, from Edmund Randolph, June 10, 1794; 3:49, to Madison, Sept. 2, 1794; 3:188–89, to Edmund Randolph, Dec. 18, 1794.

28. *PJM,* 3:188–89, to Edmund Randolph, Dec. 18, 1794.

29. Conway, *The Life of Thomas Paine,* 2:168; Ammon, *James Monroe,* 133–37.

30. Paine, *The Writings of Thomas Paine,* 3:246–47, 250.

31. Ibid., 220 and n1.

32. Washington, *Writings,* 35:359, to David Stuart, Jan. 8, 1797.

33. *PJM,* 3:45–46 and n1, from Adrienne Lafayette, Aug. 27, 1794.

34. Ammon, *James Monroe,* 163; Monroe, *Autobiography,* 70–71; Maurois, *Adrienne,* 296–308.

35. *PJM,* 3:198 and n1, "From the Committee of Public Safety," Jan. 7, 1795.

36. *PJM,* 3:188–89, to Edmund Randolph, Dec. 18, 1794.

37. *PJM,* 3:222, from Jay, Feb. 5, 1795.

38. Ibid.

39. Combs, *Jay Treaty,* 160; "The Jay Treaty: Hunter Miller's Notes," Avalon Project, http://avalon.law.yale.edu/18th_century/jaynotes.asp.

40. *PMC,* 15:473, to Jefferson, Feb. 15, 1795; 16:15, from Pierce Butler, June 12, 1795.

41. *PMC,* 16:94, to Henry Tazewell, Sept. 25, 1795; "The Jay Treaty; November 19, 1794," Avalon Project, http://avalon.law.yale.edu/18th_century/jay.asp.

42. *PMC,* 16:168, to Monroe, Dec. 20, 1795; McMaster, *A History of the People of the United States,* 2:213–19.

43. Henry Adams, *Life of Albert Gallatin,* 158; *PAH,* 18:398–401, from Washington, July 3, 1795; 18:404–54 and n1, "Remarks on the Treaty of Amity, Commerce and Navigation Lately Made Between the United States and Great Britain," July 9–11, 1795.

44. Tachau, "George Washington and the Reputation of Edmund Randolph," 21–23, 25, 28.

45. *PMC,* 12:420, from Washington, ca. Sept. 23, 1789.

46. Jefferson, *Complete Anas,* 165; Pickering and Upham, *Life of Timothy Pickering,* 3:224; *PMC,* 15:57, from Jefferson, Aug. 11, 1793.

47. Brant, "Edmund Randolph, Not Guilty!," 182–83, 192–95.

48. Edmund Randolph, *Vindication,* 37.

49. Combs, *Jay Treaty,* 169–70; *PMC,* 16:169, to Monroe, Dec. 20, 1795.

50. Edmund Randolph, *Vindication,* 36–37; Pickering and Upham, *Life of Timothy Pickering,* 3:226–27.

51. *PMC,* 16:204, to Monroe, Jan. 26, 1796; Brant, "Edmund Randolph, Not Guilty!," 180–81.

52. *PMC,* 16:286, to Jefferson, April 4, 1796.

53. *PWP,* 19:640, to Alexander Hamilton, March 31, 1796; *PAH,* 20:81–82, to Washington, March 24, 1796.

54. Washington, *Writings,* 35:2–5, to the House of Representatives, March 30, 1796.

55. Marshall, *The Life of George Washington,* 354; *PMC,* 16:286, to Jefferson, April 4, 1796; 16:329, from Jefferson and enclosure, April 17, 1796.

56. Fisher Ames, *Works,* 1:191, to George Minot, April 2, 1796.

57. *Annals,* 4th Cong., 1st sess., 987, April 15, 1796.

58. Charles, *The Origins of the American Party System,* 118–19; Bemis, *Jay's Treaty,* 372–73.

59. *Annals,* 4th Cong., 1st sess., 1259, 1263, April 28, 1796; *PMC,* 16:352, to Jefferson, May 9, 1796.

60. *PMC,* 16:343, to Jefferson, May 1, 1796; *Adams Family Papers: An Electronic Archive,* John Adams to Abigail Adams, April 28, 1796.

61. Washington, *Writings,* 35:49, to Hamilton, May 15, 1796; Gilbert, *To the Farewell Address,* 125–26; *PMC,* 15:29, to Jefferson, June 13, 1793.

62. Washington, *Writings,* 35:225, "Farewell Address," Sept. 19, 1796.

63. Ibid., 234–35; *PMC,* 16:403, to Monroe, Sept. 29, 1796.

64. Washington, *Writings,* 35:30, to Carroll, May 1, 1796; Leibiger, *Founding Friendship,* 220.

65. *PTJ,* 29:51, to Madison, March 27, 1796.

66. *PTJ,* 29:127–28, to Washington, June 19, 1796.

67. *PTJ,* 29:142, from Washington, July 6, 1796.

68. Ibid., 142–43.

69. Malone, *Jefferson,* 3:269, 308; Elkins and McKitrick, *Age of Federalism,* 528.

70. *PJM,* 4:236 and n3, to Jefferson, Jan. 8, 1798; 3:375–76, to George Logan, June 24, 1795.

71. *PJM*, 4:36, from Pickering, June 13, 1796.

72. *PMC*, 16:443, from Monroe, Jan. 1, 1797.

73. *PJM*, 4:179, from Aaron Burr, Aug. 9, 1797; 4:179, from Hamilton, Aug. 9, 1797.

74. *PAH*, 21:243, "Printed Version of the 'Reynolds Pamphlet,'" 1797.

SIX
INTERREGNUM

1. Jefferson, *Complete Anas*, 184–85; *PWD*, 6:236, March 6, 1797. Jefferson would have ceded the place of honor (the wall side of the walk) to Adams, who would have expected it.

2. After the Twelfth Amendment was ratified, it became possible for parties to field presidential/vice-presidential teams.

3. *PTJ*, 29:235, to John Adams, Dec. 28, 1796; 29:248, "I. To James Madison," Jan. 1, 1797; 29:264, from Madison, Jan. 15, 1797.

4. *PTJ*, 29:280–81, to Madison, Jan. 30, 1797.

5. Jefferson, *Complete Anas*, 184–85; John Adams, *Works*, 9:285; Buchan, *Domestic Medicine*, 434.

6. Jefferson, *Complete Anas*, 185; John Adams, *Works*, 9:285–86.

7. Jefferson, *Complete Anas*, 185.

8. *PTJ*, 2:955, 976 n89, "Memorandum Books, 1797," March 10, 1797; Malone, *Jefferson*, 3:341–46.

9. Jefferson, *Memorandum Books*, 2:956; Malone, *Jefferson*, 3:346–56; *PTJ*, 29:322, to Thomas Mann Randolph, March 23, 1797; 29:332–33, from William Short, March 30, 1797; 29:323, from Peregrine Fitzhugh, March 25, 1797; 29:335–36, to James Wood, March 31, 1797; 29:408, to John Gibson, May 31, 1797; McLaughlin, *Jefferson and Monticello*, 261–62.

10. "James Madison's Autobiography," 203; Kennedy, *Memoirs of the Life of William Wirt*, 1:246; De Coppet Collection, Madison to Delaplaine, memo, Sept. 1816. For an extended treatment of Madison's epilepsy, see Cheney, *James Madison: A Life Reconsidered*.

11. *PTJ*, 29:124, to James Monroe, June 12, 1796.

12. *PTJ*, 29:371–72, to Madison, May 18, 1797.

13. *PTJ*, 29:347, to Fitzhugh, April 9, 1797; Jefferson, *Memorandum Books*, 2:960; John Adams, *Works*, 9:111–18, "Speech to Both Houses of Congress, 16 May, 1797."

14. "Early French Policy Toward the United States," 59; *PTJ*, 29:416, to Fitzhugh, June 4, 1797; John Adams, *Works*, 8:546–47 and n1, to Uriah Forrest, June 20, 1797; Elkins and McKitrick, *Age of Federalism*, 565–66; American Historical Association, *Annual Report of the American Historical Association for the Year 1903*, 2:1030.

15. American Historical Association, *Annual Report of the American Historical Association for the Year 1903*, 2:1030.

16. *PTJ,* 29:437–39, to Aaron Burr, June 17, 1797.

17. Malone, *Jefferson,* 3:322–24. According to Malone, the letter to Burr "marked Jefferson's assumption of the leadership of the Republican Party."

18. *PTJ,* 29:447, from Aaron Burr, June 21, 1797; Henry Adams, *Life of Albert Gallatin,* 186–87; Ammon, *James Monroe,* 157; "Theodosia Prevost and Aaron Burr," Hermitage Museum, http://www.thehermitage.org/history/history_people _prevost_theodosia.html; *PJM,* 2:12, to Theodosia Prevost, Nov. 8, 1778.

19. *PWRT,* 1:327, to Timothy Pickering, Aug. 29, 1797.

20. *PTJ,* 29:61, to Volney, April 10, 1796; 29:273, to Thomas Mann Randolph, Jan. 22, 1797; 29:576, from Monroe, Nov. 1797; McLaughlin, *Jefferson and Monticello,* 257, 261–62, 268–72.

21. *PTJ,* 29:490, to Madison, Aug. 3, 1797.

22. *PMC,* 17:44 and n3, to Jefferson, Aug. 24, 1797; *PTJ,* 29:562–63, from Monroe, Oct. 22, 1797; 29:564, to Monroe, Oct. 25, 1797.

23. *PTJ,* 29:593–94, to Monroe, Dec. 27, 1797; 30:11, to Madison, Jan. 3, 1798; 30:40, from Madison, Jan. 21, 1798; 30:96, from Madison, Feb. 12, 1798.

24. *PWRT,* 1:333, to Pickering, Aug. 31, 1797; 2:20, to Pickering, Jan. 12, 1798; 2:39, to Oliver Wolcott Jr., Jan. 22, 1798; 2:61, from Wolcott, Jan. 30, 1798; 2:76, to Pickering, Feb. 6, 1798; 2:169–70, 199, 206, 184, 183, "Comments on Monroe's *A View of the Conduct of the Executive of the United States,*" ca. March 1798.

25. *PWRT,* 2:192, "Comments on Monroe's *A View of the Conduct of the Executive of the United States,*" ca. March 1798.

26. Charles, *The Origins of the American Party System,* 44.

27. *PJM,* 4:259–60, to Jefferson, March 26, 1798.

28. John Adams, *Works,* 9:190, "To the Inhabitants of the County of Lancaster, Pennsylvania," May 8, 1798; *PJM,* 4:270, from Jefferson, May 21, 1798; 4:275–77, to Jefferson, June 10, 1798.

29. *PJM,* 4:270, from Jefferson, May 21, 1798; 4:272, to Madison, June 8, 1798; 4:276, to Jefferson, June 10, 1798; 4:283, "Response to Speech by John Adams," June 1798; Joanne Freeman, *Affairs of Honor,* xxii–xxiii; *PJM,* 4:302, "Essay: To George Washington," 1798.

30. *PMC,* 17:113, 115 and n2, to Jefferson, April 15, 1798.

31. Everett, "Some Aspects of Pro-French Sentiment," 39; Abigail Adams, *New Letters,* 169, to Mary Cranch, May 7, 1798; James Morton Smith, *Freedom's Fetters,* 192.

32. Farrand, ed., *Records,* 1:465, Madison's notes, June 29, 1787.

33. Schutz and Adair, eds., *The Spur of Fame,* 41, Adams to Benjamin Rush, Sept. 30, 1805.

34. Jefferson, *Works,* 12:446, "Thoughts on Lotteries," Feb. 1826; Logan, *Memoir of Dr. George Logan,* 75.

35. Fehlings, "Storm on the Constitution," 105–10.

36. *Statutes,* 5th Cong., 2nd sess., 596, "An Act in addition to the act, entitled 'An act for the punishment of certain crimes against the United States,'" July 14, 1798.

37. *PTJ*, 31:526, to Martha Jefferson Carr, April 21, 1800; Smelser, "George Washington and the Alien and Sedition Acts," 328; *PWRT*, 3:317–19, to Patrick Henry, Jan. 15, 1799.

38. Jean Edward Smith, *John Marshall*, 240–44.

39. Addison, *Liberty of Speech*, 21–23; *PWRT*, 3:297, to Marshall, Dec. 30, 1798; 3:309, from Marshall, Jan. 8, 1799.

40. James Morton Smith, "The 'Aurora' and the Alien and Sedition Laws," *PMHB*, Jan. 1953, 18–20; James Morton Smith, *Freedom's Fetters*, 175, 188–203.

41. James Morton Smith, *Freedom's Fetters*, 278–305; *PWRT*, 4:221–23 and n1, to Pickering, Aug. 4, 1799.

42. James Morton Smith, *Freedom's Fetters*, 226; "The Alien and Sedition Acts," *Digital History*, www.digitalhistory.uh.edu/disp_textbook.cfm?smtID=3&psid=245.

43. *PTJ*, 30:389, to John Taylor, June 4, 1798.

44. *PTJ*, 30:547, "II. Jefferson's Fair Copy," before Oct. 4, 1798; 30:554, "III. Resolutions Adopted by the Kentucky General Assembly," Nov. 10, 1798.

45. Koch and Ammon, "Virginia and Kentucky Resolutions," 159–61; *The Virginia Report*, 148–50; *PMC*, 17:191, to Jefferson, Dec. 29, 1798; 17:223–24, from Jefferson, Jan. 30, 1799.

46. Frank Maloy Anderson, "Contemporary Opinion," 52; Elliot, *Debates*, 4:532–39.

47. *PTJ*, 31:173-74, to Madison, Aug. 23, 1799.

48. The weekend that Madison was at Monticello (August 31–September 1, 1799), afternoon temperatures were in the eighties. See Jefferson's "Weather Record," 2, image 24, at https://www.loc.gov/resource/mtj7.059_0055_0102/?sp=24; *PMC*, 17:257, from Jefferson, Aug. 23, 1799; *PTJ*, 31:178, from Madison, Aug. 28, 1799; 31:178–79, to Wilson Cary Nicholas, Sept. 5, 1799.

49. *PMC*, 17:278, from Monroe, Nov. 22, 1799.

50. "Kentucky Resolution—Alien and Sedition Acts," Avalon Project, http://avalon.law.yale.edu/18th_century/kenres.asp.

51. *PWRT*, 2:402, to Adams, July 13, 1798; 3:255, 261, to James McHenry, Dec. 13, 1798.

52. *PWRT*, 1:28–29, from Elizabeth Willing Powel, March 11–13, 1797; 1:51–52, to Elizabeth Willing Powel, March 26, 1797.

53. Fields, ed., *"Worthy Partner."* Letters on 263, 296, 297, 301, and 302 provide examples. In some instances, Washington's draft as well Martha's letter has been preserved: See "A Guide to the Martha Washington Letters, 1797," Library of Virginia, https://ead.lib.virginia.edu/vivaxtf/view?docId=lva/vi00505.xml.

54. *PWRT*, 3:242, from Powel, Dec. 3, 1798; 3:246 and n1, from Powel, Dec. 7, 1798.

55. *PWRT*, 3:246, from Powel, Dec. 7, 1798.

56. *PWRT*, 3:247, to Powel, Dec. 7, 1798.

57. *PWRT*, 3:247–48, to Powel, Dec. 9, 1798; 3:243, to Powel, Dec. 4, 1798.

58. *PWRT*, 2:403, to Adams, July 13, 1798; King, *Life and Correspondence*, 2:518, from Sedgwick, Jan. 20, 1799; *PAH*, 22:453, to Sedgwick, Feb. 2, 1799; Chernow, *Hamilton*, 566.

59. *PMC*, 17:227–28, from Walter Jones and Others, Feb. 7, 1799; 17:245–46 and n2, from Taylor, March 4, 1799; Ragosta, *Patrick Henry*, 200; Kukla, *Patrick Henry*, 1.

60. *PMS*, 8:536, to Dolley Madison, Dec. 2, 1799.

61. *PMC*, 17:297, to Jefferson, Dec. 29, 1799; 17:343–44, 310, "The Report of 1800," Jan. 7, 1800; 17:303–6, "The Report of 1800: Editorial Note."

62. *PMC*, 17:357, to Jefferson, Jan. 18, 1800.

63. Augustine Davis, *Virginia Gazette*, Dec. 10, 1799.

64. Lear, *Letters and Recollections of George Washington*, 130.

65. Ibid., 130–35.

66. *PJM*, 4:344, to St. George Tucker, Dec. 26, 1799; *PAH*, 24:155, to Tobias Lear, Jan. 2, 1800.

67. *PMC*, 17:295, "Death of George Washington," Dec. 18, 1799.

68. Malone, *Jefferson*, 3:442–44; John Cotton Smith, *Correspondence and Miscellanies of the Hon. John Cotton Smith*, 224–25.

69. *PTJR*, 7:101, to Jones, Jan. 2, 1814.

70. Cunningham Jr., *The Jeffersonian Republicans*, 197–98; Callender, *The Prospect Before Us*, 1:143.

71. Gibbs, ed., *Memoirs of the Administrations of Washington and John Adams*, 2:399, Tracy to John Adams, Aug. 7, 1800; *PTJ*, 31:10, to Madison, Feb. 5, 1799.

72. *PTJ*, 31:300–301, to Monroe, Jan. 12, 1800.

73. Cunningham Jr., *The Jeffersonian Republicans*, 178–84; Isenberg, *Fallen Founder*, 196–200; *PTJ*, 31:408–9, to Madison, March 4, 1800.

74. Henry Adams, *Life of Albert Gallatin*, 241–42.

75. Egerton, *Gabriel's Rebellion*, 50–68; Schwarz, ed., *Gabriel's Conspiracy: A Documentary History*, 94, "Ben Woodfork [Woolfolk] Affidavit," Sept. 17, 1800.

76. Egerton, *Gabriel's Rebellion*, 68–71; *PJM*, 4:397–98, from Mosby Sheppard, Aug. 30, 1800.

77. *PJM*, 4:410, to Jefferson, Sept. 15, 1800; 4:413, from Jefferson, Sept. 20, 1800; 4:420, to the Virginia Council of State, Sept. 28, 1800; 4:423, to Thomas Newton, Oct. 5, 1800.

78. *PJM*, 4:425, to Madison, Oct. 8, 1800; Schwarz, ed., *Gabriel's Conspiracy: A Documentary History*, 143–44, "Virginia Council Meeting," Oct. 3, 1800. In January 1801 the legislature passed a bill allowing the governor to "sell convicted slaves and have them transported out of the state." *PJM*, 4:450 and n3, to Larkin Smith and Richard Kennon, Dec. 5, 1800.

79. American Historical Association, *Annual Report of the American Historical Association for the Year 1912*, 663; Sutcliff, *Travels in Some Parts of North America*, 50.

80. Burleigh, "No. XII, To the People of the United States," *Connecticut Courant*, Sept. 15, 1800; Margaret Bayard Smith, *First Forty Years*, 6.

81. Maier, *American Scripture*, 169–70.

82. *PAH*, 25:192–234, "Letter from Alexander Hamilton, Concerning the Public Conduct and Character of John Adams, Esq. President of the United States," Oct. 24, 1800; *PTJ*, 32:239, from Bishop James Madison, Nov. 1, 1800.

83. *PMC*, 17:431, from Monroe, Nov. 6, 1800; 17:435, to Monroe, ca. Nov. 10, 1800; 17:438, from Gelston, Nov. 21, 1800; Malone, *Jefferson*, 3:497.

84. Henry Adams, *The Education of Henry Adams*, 44.

85. Abigail Adams, *New Letters*, 257, to Mary Cranch, Nov. 21, 1800.

86. Allen, *History of the United States Capitol*, 44–45.

87. Margaret Bayard Smith, *First Forty Years*, 23–24; *PMC*, 17:444, from Jefferson, Dec. 19, 1800; "President Pro Tempore," United States Senate, https://www.senate.gov /artandhistory/history/common/briefing/President_Pro_Tempore.htm. As of the writing of this book, the vice president is first in line to succeed the president; the Speaker of the House, second; the president pro tempore, third. Presidents pro tempore stay in office until another president pro tempore is elected.

88. *PTJ*, 32:594, to Monroe, Feb. 15, 1801; 33:230, to Thomas McKean, March 9, 1801; 33:391, from Thomas McKean, March 21, 1801; 32:435, from Thomas McKean, Jan. 10, 1801; Henry Adams, *Life of Albert Gallatin*, 249.

89. Jefferson, *Complete Anas*, 240.

90. Matthew L. Davis, *Memoirs of Aaron Burr*, 2:130, "Deposition of the Honorable James A. Bayard."

91. Matthew L. Davis, *Memoirs of Aaron Burr*, 2:130–36, "Deposition of the Honourable James A. Bayard," "Deposition of the Honourable Samuel Smith."

92. *PTJ*, 33:3–4 and n, "Announcement of Election Results," Feb. 17, 1801; 33:414, to William Branch Giles, March 23, 1801; Cook, "Allan McLane, Unknown Hero of the Revolution."

93. Jefferson, *Complete Anas*, 240–41.

94. Matthew L. Davis, *Memoirs of Aaron Burr*, 2:106–8, General Samuel Smith to Richard H. Bayard and James A. Bayard, April 3, 1830.

95. Gallatin, *Writings*, 2:664–65, to Henry A. Muhlenberg, May 8, 1848.

96. Wilentz, "The Electoral College Was Not a Pro-Slavery Ploy," *The New York Times*, April 4, 2019.

SEVEN

THE SPIRIT OF '76

1. *Alexandria Times*, March 6, 1801; *National Intelligencer*, March 6, 1801.

2. "United States Capitol," SAH Archipedia, http://sah-archipedia.org /buildings/DC-01-CH01.

3. *PTJ*, 40:127–28, "Report on the Ground Plan of the Capitol's New Wing," April 4, 1803; *Documentary History of the Construction and Development of the*

United States Capitol Building, 88–89; Margaret Bayard Smith, *First Forty Years,* 26.

4. Allen, *History of the United States Capitol,* 44.

5. *PTJ,* 33:148–49, "III. First Inaugural Address."

6. Margaret Bayard Smith, *First Forty Years,* 25.

7. *PTJ,* 33:149, "III. First Inaugural Address."

8. *PTJ,* 33:16, to Madison, Feb. 18, 1801.

9. *PTJ,* 32:227, to Samuel Smith, Oct. 17, 1800; Malone, *Jefferson,* 4:xvii.

10. *PTJ,* 33:149, "III. First Inaugural Address."

11. *PTJ,* 33:51–52, to Lewis, Feb. 23, 1801; 33:238–39, from Lewis, March 10, 1801; 33:530, from Lewis, April 3, 1801; Abigail Adams, *Letters,* 2:241, to Abigail Smith, Nov. 21, 1800; Gerry Jr., *The Diary of Elbridge Gerry, Jr.,* 181; *PMP,* 1:48, from Benjamin Henry Latrobe, March 14, 1809; *PTJ,* 34:200, to Martha Jefferson Randolph, May 28, 1801; Malone, *Jefferson,* 4:xxv.

12. Donald Jackson, *Thomas Jefferson and the Stony Mountains,* 89, 94–96; Dayton Duncan, interview by Ken Burns et al., *Lewis and Clark: The Journey of the Corps of Discovery,* PBS, Nov. 4–5, 1997, http://www.pbs.org/lewisandclark /living/idx_1.html.

13. *PTJ,* 33:148, "III. First Inaugural Address."

14. *PTJ,* 33:658, to Madison, April 30, 1801; Margaret Bayard Smith, *First Forty Years,* 10–11; Mary Clemmer Ames, *Ten Years in Washington,* 176; "A Beautiful Spot Capable of Every Improvement," White House Historical Association, https://www.whitehousehistory.org/a-beautiful-spot-capable-of-every -improvement.

15. Peterson, *Thomas Jefferson and the New Nation,* 454; *PTJ,* 34:381–84, "Remonstrance of the New Haven Merchants," June 18, 1801; 34:554–56, "To the New Haven Merchants," July 12, 1801.

16. Peterson, *Thomas Jefferson, and the New Nation,* 695.

17. Forte, "Marbury's Travail," 349–400.

18. Jefferson, *Works,* 12:135–37, to Spencer Roane, Sept. 6, 1819.

19. Callender, *The Prospect Before Us,* 143; *PMS,* 1:244–45, to James Monroe, June 1, 1801.

20. *PTJ,* 34:205, to Monroe, May 29, 1801; 34:229–30, from Monroe, June 1, 1801.

21. *PMS,* 1:244–45, to Monroe, June 1, 1801.

22. *PTJ,* 34:205, to Monroe, May 29, 1801.

23. The Monticello website states that "Thomas Jefferson was at Monticello at the likely conception times of Sally Hemings's six known children. There are no records suggesting that she was elsewhere at these times, or records of any births at times that would exclude Jefferson paternity." See "Thomas Jefferson and Sally Hemings: A Brief Account," Monticello, https://www.monticello.org/thomas

-jefferson/jefferson-slavery/thomas-jefferson-and-sally-hemings-a-brief
-account/.

24. *PTJ*, 33:150, "III. First Inaugural Address"; 7:511–12, to Monroe, Nov. 11, 1784.

25. Glenn Tucker, *Dawn Like Thunder,* 19–23.

26. Malone, *Jefferson,* 4:102–3; *PTJ*, 34:384, to Thomas Mann Randolph, June 18, 1801.

27. *PTJ*, 34:159, to Yusuf Qaramanli, May 21, 1801; *PMS,* 1:209, "Circular Letter to American Consuls, Mediterranean," May 21, 1801; Farrand, ed., *Records,* 2:318, Madison's notes, Aug. 17, 1787.

28. *PTJ*, 35:188-89, from Jacob Wagner, Aug. 31, 1801; Glenn Tucker, *Dawn Like Thunder,* 38, 228.

29. Toll, *Six Frigates,* 190–91, 205–11.

30. In 1942, the fourth line became, "We fight our country's battles / In the air, on land, and sea."

31. "The Barbary Treaties 1786–1816—Treaty of Peace and Amity, Signed at Tripoli June 4, 1805," Avalon Project, http://avalon.law.yale.edu/19th_century /bar1805t.asp.

32. Girard, *The Slaves Who Defeated Napoléon,* 1–10, 60–66.

33. Beard, *Toussaint L'Ouverture,* 157–58.

34. Girard, *The Slaves Who Defeated Napoléon,* 276.

35. Bemis, ed., *The American Secretaries of State,* 1–2:116–20, 187; microfilm edition of Adams Papers, Abigail Adams to John Quincy Adams, May 27, 1798.

36. Bemis, ed., *The American Secretaries of State,* 1–2:187; *PMS,* 3:174–76, to Livingston, May 1, 1802.

37. *PTJ*, 37:264–65, to Livingston, April 18, 1802.

38. Foreign Affairs, Political Correspondence, Paris–United States, Louis Pichon to Talleyrand, July 7, 1802.

39. *PMS,* 4:146–47, to Charles Pinckney, Nov. 27, 1802.

40. *ASP-FR,* 2:520–23, extract—Mr. Livingston to the Secretary of State, Aug. 10, 1802.

41. Girard, *The Slaves Who Defeated Napoléon,* 161, 167–68, 267–71, 179, 279.

42. Roederer, *Oeuvres du Comte P. L. Roederer,* 3:461; Kukla, *Wilderness So Immense,* 249; Barbé Marbois, *The History of Louisiana,* 274; *PMS,* 4:500–501, from Livingston, April 11, 1803.

43. Iung, *Lucien Bonaparte et ses mémoires,* 2:148–55.

44. *PMS,* 4:500, from Livingston, April 11, 1803.

45. *PMS,* 4:511, from Livingston, April 13, 1803; *PTJ*, 39:329, to Monroe, Jan. 13, 1803; 39:444, to Livingston, Feb. 3, 1803.

46. LC-JMo, "Undated Memorandum," Account Book and Journal, June 13, 1794–Dec. 10, 1802.

47. *PTJ*, 39:328–29, to Monroe, Jan. 13, 1803; Hunt-Jones, *Dolley and the "Great Little Madison,"* 22–25; *PMS,* 4:396–97 and n1, from Monroe, March 7, 1803; LC-JMo, Thomas Jefferson to Napoleon Bonaparte, April 19, 1803.

48. Monroe, *Writings,* 4:9–12 and n1, to Madison, April 15, 1803; 4:33, to Virginia senators, May 25, 1803.

49. The treaty, dated April 30, 1803, was not actually signed until early May, when an English translation was provided. Ayers, *The Architecture of Paris,* 57–58. Special thanks to my assistant Nicole Penn for finding the location where the treaty was signed and for compiling a history of the Hôtel Tubeuf.

50. Barbé Marbois, *The History of Louisiana,* 310.

51. *PMS,* 4:612–13, from Monroe, May 14, 1803.

52. Malone, *Jefferson,* 4:298–99; Brecher, *Negotiating the Louisiana Purchase,* 93, 97–98.

53. *PMS,* 4:610, from Monroe, May 14, 1803.

54. Henry Adams, *Jefferson,* 316.

55. *PTJ,* 4:237–38, to George Rogers Clark, Dec. 25, 1780.

56. Ambrose, *Undaunted Courage,* 76–91.

57. *PTJ,* 40:181, "IV. Instructions for Meriwether Lewis"; 40:169, "Drafting Instructions for Meriwether Lewis: Editorial Note"; Donald Jackson, *Thomas Jefferson and the Stony Mountains,* 139.

58. *National Intelligencer,* July 4 and July 8, 1803; Margaret Bayard Smith, *First Forty Years,* 38–39.

59. LC-TJ, to Lewis, Oct. 20, 1806; *PTJR,* 8:238, "George Ticknor's Account of a Visit to Monticello," Feb. 4–7, 1815.

60. *PTJ,* 40:672, from Gates, July 7, 1803; Ramsay, *An Oration on the Cession of Louisiana,* 4.

61. Kukla, *Wilderness So Immense,* 292–94; Plumer, *Memorandum,* 13; Fisher Ames, *Works,* 2:353, "The Dangers of American Liberty," Feb. 1805; *PTJ,* 42:54–55, from John Bradford, Nov. 29, 1803; *PTJR,* 5:682, to Benjamin Waterhouse, March 9, 1813.

62. *PTJ,* 39:324–26, from Gallatin, Jan. 13, 1803; *PMS,* 5:323, from Jefferson, Aug. 18, 1803.

63. "*American Insurance Company v. Canter:* 26 U.S. 511 (1828)," Justia US Supreme Court Center, https://supreme.justia.com/cases/federal/us/26/511/; *PTJ,* 41:186, to John Breckinridge, Aug. 12, 1803; 30:543–44, "II. Jefferson's Fairy Copy," before Oct. 4, 1798.

64. *Richmond Recorder,* Sept. 1, 1802.

65. Ellis, *American Sphinx,* 367.

66. "Will and Codicil of Thomas Jefferson," Albert and Shirley Small Special Collections Library, https://small.library.virginia.edu/collections/featured /the-thomas-jefferson-papers/bibliography-of-sources-on-jefferson-and -the-hemings-family/will-and-codicil-jefferson/.

67. *PTJ,* 42:332, to William Short, Jan. 23, 1804; Margaret Bayard Smith, *First Forty Years,* 46.

68. Henry Adams, *Jefferson*, 552–54; *PMS*, 6:363, to Monroe, Jan. 19, 1804.

69. *PTJ*, 42:331–32, to Short, Jan. 23, 1804; Henry Adams, *Jefferson*, 552–54; *PMS*, 6:187 and n1, to Rufus King, Dec. 18, 1803; Allgor, *Perfect Union*, 89.

70. *PTJ*, 42:155, "Canons of Official Etiquette: Editorial Note"; Lester, *Anthony Merry Redivivus*, 39.

71. McCaleb, *The Aaron Burr Conspiracy*, 64; *PTJ*, 42:249–50, to Monroe, Jan. 8, 1804.

72. *PTJ*, 42:249–50, to Monroe, Jan. 8, 1804.

73. *Gazette of the United States*, Jan. 13, 1804.

74. *PTJ*, 42:442, from Mary Jefferson Eppes, Feb. 10, 1804; Boles, *Jefferson*, 379–80; *PTJ*, 42:368, to Joseph Priestley, Jan. 29, 1804.

75. *PTJ*, 42:547, to Mary Jefferson Eppes, Feb. 26, 1804; *PMS*, 7:25, from Jefferson, April 9, 1804; *PTJ*, 42:611, from John Wayles Eppes, March 9, 1804.

76. Sarah N. Randolph, *The Domestic Life of Thomas Jefferson*, 300; Jefferson, *Writings* (Lipscomb), 11:31, to Page, June 25, 1804; 1 Thess. 4:13–14.

77. Jefferson, *Works*, 10:77, to Madison, April 23, 1804; Madison, *Writings*, 7:125, to Livingston, March 31, 1804; Brant, *Madison*, 4:205.

78. *PTJ*, 42:319, from Clinton, Jan. 20, 1804.

79. Chernow, *Hamilton*, 682–87, 700–709.

80. Jefferson, *Writings* (Lipscomb), 18:250, to Thomas Mann Randolph, Nov. 3, 1806; "Constitution for the United States," We the People, http://constitutionus.com/.

81. LC-BC, to Jefferson from Wilkinson, Oct. 21, 1806. Jefferson received this letter on Nov. 25, 1806. See *Annals*, 9th Cong., 2nd sess., 40, Jan. 22, 1807. LC-TJ, "Proclamation on Spanish Dominion Expeditions," Nov. 27, 1806. Wilkinson, it would later be discovered, accepted money from the Spanish. See Cox, "General Wilkinson and His Later Intrigues with the Spaniards," 795–800.

82. *Annals*, 9th Cong., 2nd sess., Appendix, 1012–16; LC-TJ, "Message on Aaron Burr," Jan. 22, 1807; Henry Adams, *Jefferson*, 3:449; Burr, *Political Correspondence and Public Papers of Aaron Burr*, 2:986. The latest scholarly opinion, a result of research by Mary-Jo Kline and her staff, editors of The Aaron Burr Papers at the New-York Historical Society, is that former senator Jonathan Dayton, Burr's deputy and a lifelong friend, wrote the letter. David Robertson, *Reports of the Trials of Colonel Aaron Burr*, 1:128.

83. Hobson, *The Aaron Burr Treason Trial*, 32–33.

84. Newmyer, *Treason Trial of Aaron Burr*, 40–41, 69.

85. LC-TJ, to George Hay, June 12, 1807; Malone, *Jefferson*, 5:320, 333–34; David Robertson, *Reports of the Trials of Colonel Aaron Burr*, 1:209–10.

86. Jefferson, *Writings* (Lipscomb), 11:363–64, to Hay, Sept. 7, 1807; Malone, *Jefferson*, 5:343; Carpenter, *The Trial of Col. Aaron Burr*, 3:14, 45–46.

87. *Ex parte Bollman and Swartwout*, as quoted in Hobson, *The Aaron Burr Treason Trial*, 1, 3–4, 18, 47. Indictment as quoted in ibid., 47.

88. David Robertson, *Reports of the Trials of Colonel Aaron Burr*, 1:396–97, 535–93; 2:446.

89. *Ex Parte Bollman and Ex Parte Swartwout*: 8 U.S. 75 (1807), Justia US Supreme Court Center, https://supreme.justia.com/cases/federal/us/8/75/; Jefferson, *Writings* (Lipscomb), 18:250, to Thomas Mann Randolph, Nov. 3, 1806.

90. Jefferson, *Writings* (Lipscomb), 15:389, to William T. Barry, July 2, 1822.

91. Monroe, *Writings*, 5:5–7, to Jefferson, mistakenly dated June 1, 1807. Context makes it clear that the letter is from at least a year earlier.

92. *PJM*, 5:608–21, from Madison, May 20, 1807; Henry Adams, *Jefferson*, 898–99; *PDM*, to Anna Cutts, March 27, 1807.

93. *Columbian Centinel*, March 18, 1807.

94. *Salem Gazette*, June 16, 1807.

95. MIS, to Jefferson from Norvell, May 9, 1807; LC-TJ, to Norvell, June 11, 1807.

96. *PTJ*, 11:49, to Edward Carrington, Jan. 16, 1787.

97. Toll, *Six Frigates*, 107, 296–300; Tucker and Reuter, *Injured Honor*, 9–17; Perkins, *Prologue to War*, 142.

98. Jefferson, *Writings* (Ford), 9:105, to Bowdoin, July 10, 1807; Brant, *Madison*, 4:381–82. Madison's draft and Jefferson's proclamation of July 2, 1807, can be compared in Jefferson, *Writings* (Ford), 9:89–100 and n1, "Chesapeake Proclamation," July 2, 1807.

99. Malone, *Jefferson*, 5:481; Jefferson, *Writings* (Lipscomb), 11:402, to General John Mason, Dec. 1807.

100. *National Intelligencer*, Dec. 23, 25, and 28, 1807.

101. LC-TJ, from James Lewis, Feb. 16, 1808; Jefferson, *Correspondence*, 166–67, from John Lane Jones, Aug. 8, 1808; *PTJR*, 9:437, to Joseph C. Cabell, Feb. 2, 1816; Coolidge Collection of Jefferson Manuscripts, to Ellen Wayles Randolph Coolidge, March 29, 1808; LC-TJ, to Cornelia Jefferson Randolph, April 3 and 5, 1808.

102. McDonald, *The Presidency of Thomas Jefferson*, 149–51.

103. Toll, *Six Frigates*, 310; Jefferson, *Writings* (Ford), 9:219, "Eighth Annual Message," Nov. 8, 1808.

104. *PTJR*, 3:99, to John B. Colvin, Sept. 20, 1810.

EIGHT

SECURING INDEPENDENCE

1. Allen, *History of the United States Capitol*, 76–79; LC-TJ, from Benjamin Henry Latrobe, Aug. 31, 1805; LC-TJ, from Latrobe, Sept. 17, 1807.

2. "Caucus History," 244.

3. Ammon, *James Monroe,* 271; *PJM,* 5:474–75, from Joseph Nicholson, May 5, 1806; 5:463 and n2, from James Garnett, March 19, 1806; Beckley Papers, to Monroe, July 13, 1806; Ammon, "James Monroe and the Election of 1808," 34, 42–43.

4. LC-JMo, from John Randolph, March 20, 1806; Biddle, "Unforgiving Cousin: John Randolph of Roanoke"; Monroe, *Writings,* 4:414–17, to John Randolph, Feb. 20, 1806; 4:460, to John Randolph, June 16, 1806; 4:480–81, to John Randolph, July 28, 1806.

5. *PJM,* 5:670–71, from Jefferson, Feb. 18, 1808; Monroe, *Writings,* 5:51, to Jefferson, April 18, 1808.

6. Jefferson, *Autobiography,* 55; *PMS,* 4:396–97 and n1, from Monroe, March 7, 1803; 11:413, from Nicholas Voss, March 20, 1806; Ammon, *James Monroe,* 274.

7. Ammon, "James Monroe and the Election of 1808 in Virginia," 47, 50, and n45; *PJM,* 5:706–10, to Taylor, July 13, 1808; 5:710–13, to Taylor, July 19, 1808.

8. Kennedy, *Memoirs of the Life of William Wirt,* 1:241–46.

9. Allgor, *Perfect Union,* 74–75.

10. Hunt, *Life of James Madison,* 273; Mitchill, "Dr. Mitchill's Letters from Washington," 752, to Mrs. Mitchill, Nov. 23, 1807.

11. *Annals,* 10th Cong., 2nd sess., 1422, Feb. 8, 1808; LC-JMa, from Thomas Lehre, Dec. 7, 1808; LC-JMa, from Hubbard Taylor, Dec. 10, 1808; LC-JMa, from Morgan Lewis, Dec. 29, 1808; Cunningham Jr., *The Presidency of James Monroe,* 10.

12. *PJM,* 5:737, to Jefferson, Jan. 18, 1809.

13. Ibid.; Ammon, "James Monroe and the Election of 1808," 54–55; *PJM,* 5:738, from Jefferson, Jan. 28, 1809; 5:739–41, to Jefferson, Feb. 2, 1809; 5:747, to Baring, Oct. 15, 1809.

14. Allen, *History of the United States Capitol,* 63, 71.

15. Margaret Bayard Smith, *First Forty Years,* 59; Taylor and Nicholas, "Of Principles and Men," *VMHB,* July 1988, 359; *PMP,* 1:15–18, "First Inaugural Address," March 4, 1809.

16. Margaret Bayard Smith, *First Forty Years,* 62–63.

17. Gallatin, *Writings,* 1:428, to Jefferson, Nov. 15, 1808; Jefferson, *Writings* (Lipscomb), 12:220, to Logan, Dec. 27, 1808.

18. Stuart, "James Madison and the Militants," 149–55; LC-JMa, ser. 2, from Nicholas, Feb. 6, 1809; LC-JMa, ser. 2, from Nicholas, Feb. 14, 1809; LC-Wilson Cary Nicholas Papers, from Madison, ca. Feb. 15, 1809.

19. Perkins, *Prologue to War,* 218, 234.

20. Few, "The Diary of Frances Few," 355; Perkins, *Prologue to War,* 211–21.

21. *PMP,* 1:317, to Jefferson, Aug. 3, 1809; 1:318, to Dolley Madison, Aug. 7, 1809; LC-JMo, from John Randolph, Jan. 1, 1809; Ketcham, *Madison,* 481–85; *PMP,* 1:327, to Jefferson, Aug. 16, 1809.

22. *PMP,* 2:321, to Jefferson, April 23, 1810; 2:150–51 and n1–3, from Isaac A. Coles, Dec. 29, 1809; Brown, "Satisfaction at Bladensburg," 23–43.

23. George Jackson, *Bath Archives,* 1:116–17, from Francis Jackson, May 1–16, 1810.

24. *PMP,* 2:xxx, "Preface"; 2:347, to William Pinkney, May 23, 1810; 2:460, 463 and n1, from John Armstrong, Aug. 5, 1810; Ketcham, *Madison,* 502, 506; *PMP,* 2:585, to Jefferson, Oct. 19, 1810; Henry Adams, *Madison,* 239.

25. Ketcham, *Madison,* 500–501; Rutland, *The Presidency of James Madison,* 60–61; Stagg, *Borderlines in Borderlands,* 47–69.

26. *PMP,* 2:585, to Jefferson, Oct. 19, 1810.

27. *PMP,* 2:595–96, "Presidential Proclamation," Oct. 27, 1810.

28. Sofaer, *War, Foreign Affairs and Constitutional Power,* 295–99; *PMP,* 2:585, to Jefferson, Oct. 19, 1810.

29. *PMP,* 2:49, to Jefferson, Oct. 30, 1809. Some have argued that Meriwether Lewis did not commit suicide but was the victim of foul play. See Abigail Tucker, "Meriwether Lewis' Mysterious Death."

30. *PMP,* 2:86, to Jefferson, Nov. 27, 1809; 2:95–96, from Jefferson, Nov. 30, 1809; *PTJR,* 4:210, "Notes on Household Consumption," June 3, 1809–Oct. 23, 1811.

31. Ammon, *James Monroe,* 282–83; *PJM,* 5:786, from John Randolph, Jan. 14, 1811; 5:787, from John Randolph, Jan. 15, 1811.

32. *PMP,* 3:255–63, "Memorandum on Robert Smith," ca. April 11, 1811.

33. *PJM,* 5:801–2, from Madison, March 20, 1811; 5:802, to Madison, March 23, 1811; 5:803, from Madison, March 26, 1811; 5:804, to Madison, March 29, 1811; 5:805, from Madison, April 2, 1811.

34. *PJM,* 5:804, from Madison, March 31, 1811; 6:104–5 and n2, to Paul Bentalou, Jan. 1, 1812; Morris, "An Old Washington Mansion," 114–28.

35. Richard Cheney and Lynne V. Cheney, *Kings of the Hill,* 1–10.

36. Clay, *Papers,* 1:498, to Monroe, Nov. 13, 1810; Rutland, *The Presidency of James Madison,* 85–86; *PMP,* 4:8, from Clay, Nov. 6, 1811; Remini, *Henry Clay: Statesman for the Union,* 53–54; Allgor, *Perfect Union,* 274.

37. *PMP,* 4:1–3, "Annual Message to Congress," Nov. 5, 1811.

38. Ibid.; Peterson, *The Great Triumvirate,* 3–4; Sugden, *Tecumseh,* 4–10.

39. Sugden, *Tecumseh,* 231–35; Richard Cheney and Lynne V. Cheney, *Kings of the Hill,* 10–11.

40. *Annals,* 12th Cong., 1st sess., 425, Dec. 9, 1811.

41. Perkins, *Prologue to War,* 355–56.

42. Stagg, *War of 1812,* 41; Elkins and McKitrick, *Age of Federalism,* 295; *PMP,* 4:168, to Jefferson, Feb. 7, 1812; 4:195, from Jefferson, Feb. 19, 1812.

43. Taggart, "Letters of Samuel Taggart," 384–85; *PMP,* 4:228, to Jefferson, March 6, 1812.

44. *PJM,* 6:116–17 and n, to Edward de Crillon, Feb. 2, 1812; 6:119 and n, from John Henry, Feb. 20, 1812; *Annals,* 12th Cong., 1st sess., 1164–65, March 9, 1812; *PJM,* 6:120–21, to Joel Barlow, Feb. 22, 1812.

45. *Annals,* 12th Cong., 1st sess., 1178–81, March 9, 1812; Cruikshank, *The Political Adventures of John Henry,* 68–70.

46. Perkins, *Prologue to War,* 35–36; Henry Adams, *Madison,* 427; Morison, "The Henry-Crillon Affair of 1812," 222 and n35.

47. Rabkin, *Law Without Nations?,* 78–81; *PMS,* 11:53, "An Examination of the British Doctrine, Which Subjects to Capture a Neutral Trade, Not Open in Time of Peace," Jan. 8, 1808; *Annals,* 12th Cong., 1st sess., 1162–63, March 9, 1812; Vattel, *The Law of Nations,* 142, 154, 156.

48. Cruikshank, *The Political Adventures of John Henry,* 155, 159–62, 167, 175.

49. Ibid., 162–66, 176–78.

50. Ibid., 179.

51. Henry Adams, *Madison,* 489–91.

52. *PMP,* 4:436–37, to Congress, June 1, 1812.

53. Henry Adams, *Madison,* 437; Toll, *Six Frigates,* 331–32.

54. *Annals,* 12th Cong., 1st sess., 1387–88, 1407, May 6, 1812; Henry Adams, *Life of Albert Gallatin,* 460.

55. *PJM,* 6:198, to Taylor, June 13, 1812.

56. Powell, *Richard Rush,* 42.

57. *PTJR,* 5:191, to Madison, June 29, 1812; 5:293, to Duane, Aug. 4, 1812.

58. Sugden, *Tecumseh,* 298–303.

59. Henry Adams, *Madison,* 558.

60. U.S. Navy Academy Museum, "Ensigns of HMS Macedonian, Confiance, and Frolic about to be removed for preservation after a century in Mahon Hall," Facebook, Feb. 27, 2018, https://www.facebook.com/usnamuseum /photos/a.766528580031105/2004261622924455; Thomas Buttersworth Jr., *United States and HMS Macedonian,* ca. 1813, oil on canvas, Penobscot Marine Museum, Maine; Washburn, *Illustrated Case Inscriptions from the Official Catalogue of the Trophy Flags of the United States Navy,* 32–33; "United Kingdom: Flags from the War of 1812," Flags of the World website, https://www.crwflags .com/fotw/flags/gb%5Ew1812.html; Taggart, "Letters of Samuel Taggart," 416; Allgor, *Perfect Union,* 292–93.

61. *PMP,* 5:253, from Monroe, Sept. 2, 1812; 5:477, from Eustis, Dec. 3, 1812; *PJM,* 6:316, "Appointment as Acting Secretary of War," Dec. 15, 1812.

62. *Annals,* 12th Cong., 2nd sess., 561–64, 569, 600 and n, Jan. 5 and 6, 1813.

63. *PMR,* 3:281–82, "Review of a Statement Attributed to General John Armstrong, with an Appendix of Illustrative Documents," ca. April 30, 1824.

64. Henry Adams, *Madison,* 591–93.

65. *PJM,* 5:499, 501 and n, to Jefferson, June 15, 1806; 6:375–77 and n, to Madison, Feb. 25, 1813; *PMP,* 6:67–69, from Monroe, Feb. 25, 1813.

66. *PTJR,* 6:171–76, from Monroe, June 7, 1813; Ammon, *James Monroe,* 318–19; *PTJR,* 6:209, to Monroe, June 19, 1813.

67. *PMP,* 6:340–41, to Congress, May 25, 1813; Toll, *Six Frigates,* 404; *PTJR,* 8:214–16, from John Strachan, Jan. 30, 1815.

68. *PDM,* to Hannah Gallatin, May 22, 1814.

69. *PTJR,* 6:241, from Monroe, June 28, 1813; Cheney, *James Madison,* 389–92; Webster, *Letters,* 44, to Chas. March, June 24, 1813.

70. *PJM,* 6:463 and n, from Armstrong, July 15, 1813; 6:463–64, to Armstrong, July 16, 1813; 6:464, to Armstrong, July 17, 1813; 6:465, to Madison, July 18, 1813; *PMP,* 6:447, to Armstrong, July 19, 1813; 6:448, to Monroe, July 19, 1813.

71. *PMP,* 6:493, to Albert Gallatin, August 2, 1813; *PDM,* to Hannah Gallatin, Aug. 30, 1813; Ketcham, *Madison,* 565; Coles, *The War of 1812,* 126–30.

72. Powell, "Some Unpublished Correspondence of John Adams and Richard Rush," *PMHB,* Oct. 1936, 454.

73. *PTJR,* 6:524, to Monroe, Sept. 23, 1813; *PJM,* 6:514, to George Hay, Oct. 17, 1813; *PMC,* 17:277, from Jefferson, Nov. 22, 1799.

74. Coles, *The War of 1812,* 132–35.

75. John Quincy Adams, *Memoirs,* 6:5, June 2, 1822.

76. Ibid.

77. *PMP,* 7:139–40, from Monroe, Dec. 27, 1813; Henry Adams, *Madison,* 902–3; Armstrong, "Answer to the Queries of D. F.," 127.

78. Skeen, *John Armstrong Jr.,* 128–42.

79. *PMP,* 7:461, to Monroe, May 7, 1814; 7:468–69, to Jefferson, May 10, 1814.

80. *PMP,* 7:515 and n1, from Monroe, May 24, 1814; 7:545, "Memorandum on Cabinet Meeting," June 7, 1814; Coles, *The War of 1812,* 164.

81. LC-JMo, from Bayard and Gallatin, May 6, 1814; *PMP,* 7:584, "Memorandum on Cabinet Meeting," June 23–24, 1814; 7:591, "Memorandum on Cabinet Meeting," June 27, 1814.

82. *ASP-MA,* 1:541, "Narrative by Richard Rush," Oct. 15, 1814; 1:540, William Jones's letter, Oct. 31, 1814.

83. Brant, *Madison,* 6:270–71; Cheney, *James Madison,* 399.

84. *PMP,* 8:98–101, to Armstrong, Aug. 13, 1814; 7:513, to Armstrong, May 24, 1814.

85. *ASP-MA,* 1:536, "Letter of Colonel Monroe," Nov. 13, 1814; Ammon, *James Monroe,* 330–31; *PMP,* 8:130–31, from Monroe, Aug. 21, 1814.

86. *PMP,* 8:133, to Dolley Madison, Aug. 23, 1814; *PDM,* to Lucy Todd, Aug. 23, 1814.

87. Barker, *Incidents in the Life of Jacob Barker,* 121.

88. *ASP-MA,* 1:536–37, "Letter of Colonel Monroe," Nov. 13, 1814; Lord, *The Dawn's Early Light,* 111.

89. *ASP-MA,* 1:596–97, William Simmons's letter, Nov. 28, 1814; 1:536–37, "Letter of Colonel Monroe," Nov. 13, 1814.

90. Caffrey, *The Twilight's Last Gleaming,* 236–37; *PMP,* 8:136, "Memorandum of Conversations with John Armstrong," Aug. 24, 1814.

91. *PDM,* to Todd, Aug. 23, 1814; Mattern, "Dolley Madison Has the Last Word," 38–43; Allgor, *Perfect Union,* 2–4.

92. *PMP,* 8:137–41, "The Madisons' Travels in Virginia During the British Occupation of Washington 24–26 August 1814: Editorial Note."

93. Foreign Affairs, Political Correspondence, Paris–United States, Louis Sérurier to Talleyrand, Aug. 27, 1814.

94. Williams, *History of the Invasion and Capture of Washington,* 274–75.

95. *PMP,* 8:149–52, "James Monroe's Draft Memoranda on the Events of 24–28 August 1814 at Washington," post–Aug. 28, 1814; Gilman, *James Monroe,* 219.

96. Margaret Bayard Smith, *First Forty Years,* 109.

97. Thornton, "Diary," 176–77; Monroe, "Letters of James Monroe: Part 4, 1812–1817," 218.

98. *PMP,* 8:153–55, "Memorandum of a Conversation with John Armstrong," Aug. 29, 1814.

99. Ibid., 8:254, from Monroe, Sept. 25, 1814.

100. "The Lyrics," National Museum of American History, https://amhistory.si.edu /starspangledbanner/the-lyrics.aspx.

101. *PMP,* 8:226, "Annual Message to Congress," Sept. 20, 1814; Henry Adams, *Madison,* 978–88; Toll, *Six Frigates,* 438; Roosevelt, *The Naval War of 1812,* 394–99.

102. *PMP,* 8:227, "Annual Message to Congress," Sept. 20, 1814; Henry Adams, *Madison,* 1076–91, 1092–93, 1104–6.

103. *PMP,* 5:165, to Jefferson, Aug. 17, 1812; Kennedy, *Memoirs of the Life of William Wirt,* 1:381, to Mrs. Wirt, Oct. 14, 1814.

104. Henry Adams, *Madison,* 1064–68; "Elbridge Gerry, 5th Vice President (1813–1814)," United States Senate, https://www.cop.senate.gov/artandhistory/history /common/generic/VP_Elbridge_Gerry.htm; Gerry Jr., "Letters of Elbridge Gerry, 1797–1814," 519–20; *PMP,* 8:373, 375 and n11, from Nicholas, Nov. 11, 1814; 5:601, 603, from Carey, Jan. 21, 1813; 8:340, from Carey, Oct. 30, 1814.

105. Ingersoll, *Historical Sketch,* 2:234–35; Clarke, "Thomas Sydney Jesup," 396–97.

106. Monroe received the letter between October 10, when he did not know about Jackson's feud with the Spanish governor, and October 21, when he wrote another letter indicating he did; LC-AJ, to Armstrong, Sept. 9, 1814; *PAJ,* 3:129–31, to Mateo González Manrique, Sept. 9, 1814; 3:170–71 and n3, from Monroe, Oct. 21, 1814; 3:173–74, to Monroe, Oct. 26, 1814; 3:128, from Monroe, Sept. 7, 1814; 3:149–50, from Monroe, Sept. 27, 1814.

107. Stagg, *War of 1812,* 152; "War of 1812," Tennessee Encyclopedia, https:// tennesseeencyclopedia.net/entries/war-of-1812/; Coles, *The War of 1812,* 246; Lossing, *Pictorial Field-Book,* 1046.

108. *PAJ,* 3:239–40, to Monroe, Jan. 9, 1815; Donald R. Hickey in *The War of 1812* puts British losses at over two thousand men. See Hickey, *War of 1812,* 222.

109. *PMP,* 8:554 and n2, from Monroe, Feb. 3, 1815; *Daily National Intelligencer,* Feb. 6, 1815.

110. Pieczynski, "Rediscovering the Treaty of Ghent," 2, 9, 13; "Glorious News!," 385.

111. *Annals,* 14th Cong., 1st sess., 783, Jan. 29, 1816.

112. Powell, "Some Unpublished Correspondence of John Adams and Richard Rush," *PMHB,* Oct. 1936, 454.

113. Barry, "Letters of William T. Barry," 237; *PDM,* to Hannah Gallatin, March 5, 1815.

114. *PDM,* to Hannah Gallatin, March 5, 1815; Cheney, *James Madison,* 114; De Coppet Collection, Madison to Delaplaine, memo, Sept. 1816.

115. *PTJR,* 8:472, "Enclosure: Joseph Milligan's Invoice for Books," May 6, 1815; 12:417–27, "I. Thomas Jefferson's Explanations of the Three Volumes Bound in Marbled Paper (the so-called 'Anas')"; 12:416, "Editorial Note"; 12:431, "III. Joseph C. Cabell's Memorandum on the Introduction to the 'Anas,'" April 9, 1818.

116. LC-JMa, ser. 2, from Monroe, May 4, 1815; LC-JMa, ser. 2, from Monroe, May 16, 1815.

117. Dallas, *Life and Writings,* 436, from Madison, Aug. 8, 1815.

118. Madison, *Writings,* 8:335, "Seventh Annual Message," Dec. 5, 1815.

119. Randolph Papers, John Randolph—J. M. Garnett Letterbook, Randolph to Garnett, Feb. 2, 1816.

120. James Monroe Museum and Memorial Library, "1816 Presidential Election Campaign Essay," Feb. 1816; Cunningham Jr., *The Presidency of James Monroe,* 16.

121. *PDM,* to Anna Cutts, July 5, 1816.

122. Ketcham, *Madison,* 601.

123. Brant, *Madison,* 6:419.

124. Ketcham, ed., "Unpublished Sketch of James Madison by James K. Paulding," *VMHB,* Oct. 1959, 435.

NINE
DYNASTY'S END

1. *National Intelligencer,* March 5, 1817; *Register of Debates,* 24th Cong., 2nd sess., 992, Feb. 28, 1837.

2. Monroe, *Writings,* 6:6–14, "Inaugural Address," March 4, 1817; *National Intelligencer,* March 5, 1817; Morison, *Life and Letters of Harrison Gray Otis,* 2:205; "The Inaugural Speech," 162; Otho Holland Williams Papers, Edward Greene Williams to William Elie Williams, March 17, 1817; Ammon, *James Monroe,* 370–71.

3. *PTJR,* 11:276, from Monroe, April 23, 1817; Monroe, "Letters of James Monroe: Part 4, 1812–1817," 227; *Columbian Centinel,* July 12, 1817.

4. Monroe, "Letters of James Monroe: Part 4, 1812–1817," 227–30.

5. Wirt, *Letters of the British Spy*, 174.

6. Gilman, *James Monroe*, 102–3; Henry Adams, *Madison*, 644.

7. *Diaries of John Quincy Adams: A Digital Collection*, June 4, 1819; Bemis, *John Quincy Adams*, 276.

8. *Diaries of John Quincy Adams: A Digital Collection*, Sept. 20, 1817.

9. *PAJ*, 4:97, to Monroe, March 4, 1817; LC-AJ, from Monroe, Aug. 4, 1817.

10. *PAJ*, 4:145–47, from Monroe, Oct. 5, 1817; *PMR*, 1:142–43 and n1, from Monroe, Oct. 18, 1817.

11. *PMR*, 1:179, from Monroe, Dec. 22, 1817.

12. *PMR*, 1:190, to Monroe, Dec. 27, 1817; Cunningham Jr., *The Presidency of James Monroe*, 166–67.

13. *PTJR*, 13:586, to Monroe, Jan. 18, 1819.

14. *Diaries of John Quincy Adams: A Digital Collection*, July 15–18, July 20, 1818; *PAJ*, 4:224–27, from Monroe, July 19, 1818.

15. *PAJ*, 4:235–39, to Monroe, Aug. 19, 1818; Cunningham Jr., *The Presidency of James Monroe*, 67. Instructions from Secretary of War John C. Calhoun had the "to" that is indicated in brackets: *PAJ*, 4:163, from John Caldwell Calhoun, Dec. 26, 1817; Ammon, *James Monroe*, 417.

16. *Diaries of John Quincy Adams: A Digital Collection*, June 26, July 18, 1818; *PMR*, 1:410 and n2, from Monroe, Feb. 7, 1819.

17. Ammon, *James Monroe*, 423; *Diaries of John Quincy Adams: A Digital Collection*, Feb. 22, 1819, Nov. 6, 1818, Aug. 16, 1819, April 15, 1820, Nov. 12, 1820; Bemis, *John Quincy Adams*, 340.

18. Cunningham Jr., *The Presidency of James Monroe*, 83–85; Jefferson, *Writings* (Ford), 10:147, to John Adams, Nov. 7, 1819.

19. *Annals*, 15th Cong., 2nd sess., 1204, Feb. 16, 1819.

20. *Diaries of John Quincy Adams: A Digital Collection*, Jan. 8, 1820, March 3, 1821; Ammon, *James Monroe*, 452–53; Mason, *Slavery and Politics*, 179.

21. *Annals*, 16th Cong., 1st sess., 266–70, 279, Jan. 26 and 27, 1820.

22. *PMR*, 2:3, from Monroe, Feb. 5, 1820; 2:6, to Monroe, Feb. 10, 1820; LC-TJ, to Monroe, March 3, 1820.

23. Thorpe, *The Federal and State Constitutions*, 4:2149–54; "A Proclamation," 389.

24. *Diaries of John Quincy Adams: A Digital Collection*, Jan. 10, 1820, March 3, 1820; LC-TJ, to William Short, April 13, 1820; LC-TJ, to John Holmes, April 22, 1820.

25. Ammon, *James Monroe*, 164; Cunningham Jr., *The Presidency of James Monroe*, 35, 135–36; NYPL-James Monroe Papers, to Skipwith, March 11, 1823.

26. *PTJ*, 29:576, from Monroe, Nov. 1797; *Will Book G*, Loudoun County, Virginia, 437. Jones Sr. died in 1805 and Jones Jr., unmarried and childless, around 1808, thus making Monroe the senior Jones's heir.

27. Coolidge Collection of Jefferson Manuscripts, from Monroe, Jan. 29, 1823; LC-TJ, to Monroe, Feb. 21, 1823.

28. Ammon, *James Monroe*, 404.

29. Gilman, *James Monroe*, 214–16; *PJM*, 6:479–80, to Skipwith, Aug. 12, 1813; Samuel Latham Mitchill Papers, to Catherine Akerly Cock Mitchill, Feb. 11, 1803.

30. NYPL-James Monroe Papers, to George Hay, Jan. 10, 1820.

31. William Spence Robertson, "The Recognition of the Hispanic American Nations by the United States," 241–58.

32. Monroe, *Writings*, 6:405–7, "The Genesis of the Message of 1823."

33. LC-TJ, from Monroe, Oct. 17, 1823; *PMR*, 3:142–43, from Monroe, Oct. 17, 1823; LC-TJ, to Monroe, Oct. 24, 1823; *PMR*, 3:150, to Monroe, Oct. 30, 1823.

34. *Diaries of John Quincy Adams: A Digital Collection*, Nov. 7, 1823.

35. Ibid., Nov. 21, 1823.

36. Ibid., Nov. 21 1823, Nov. 22, 1823; Bemis, *John Quincy Adams*, 388.

37. *Diaries of John Quincy Adams: A Digital Collection*, Nov. 7, 1823, Nov. 25, 1823; NYPL-James Monroe Papers, "Minutes," Nov. 13, 1823; *Annals*, 18th Cong., 1st sess., 14, Dec. 2, 1823.

38. *Annals*, 18th Cong., 1st sess., 16–22, Dec. 2, 1823.

39. Bemis, *John Quincy Adams*, 394–408.

40. Ammon, *James Monroe*, 533–35.

41. Ibid., 505–7; *Diaries of John Quincy Adams: A Digital Collection*, April 30, 1822.

42. LC-TJ, to Monroe, Feb. 20, 1824.

43. Ibid., to Monroe, Aug. 25, 1824; Coolidge Collection of Jefferson Manuscripts, to Peyton, Aug. 25, 1824; LC-TJ, from Monroe, Aug. 26, 1824.

44. Coolidge Collection of Jefferson Manuscripts, to Peyton, Sept. 3, 1824.

45. LC-TJ, from Monroe, Oct. 18, 1824; Levasseur, *Lafayette in America*, 1:218–20; Monroe, *Writings*, 7:42–43, to Jefferson, Oct. 31, 1824; *Diaries of John Quincy Adams: A Digital Collection*, Nov. 17–Dec. 7, 1824.

46. Levasseur, *Lafayette in America*, 1:220; Malone, *Jefferson*, 6:408.

47. LC-TJ, from Monroe, June 15, 1826.

48. *Diaries of John Quincy Adams: A Digital Collection*, Dec. 14, 1825.

49. "Inaugural Address of John Quincy Adams," Avalon Project, https://avalon.law.yale.edu/19th_century/qadams.asp.

EPILOGUE

1. *PWRT*, 1:391, to Lafayette, Oct. 8, 1797.

2. *PWRT*, 2:272, to Fairfax, May 16, 1798.

3. *PWRT,* 4:479-80, "George Washington's Last Will and Testament," July 9, 1799; "An Act to Authorize the Manumission of Slaves (1782)," Encyclopedia Virginia, https://www.encyclopediavirginia.org/An_act_to_authorize_the_manumission _of_slaves_1782.

4. *PWRT,* 4:311, to Lewis, Sept. 20, 1799; 4:423, to Alexander Addison, Nov. 24, 1799.

5. Haulman, *Virginia and the Panic of 1819,* 28–29, 62; *PMR,* 3:521, from Biddle, April 26, 1825.

6. *PTJR,* 1:281, to John Barnes, June 15, 1809; Margaret Bayard Smith, *First Forty Years,* 76–78.

7. Sarah Randolph, *The Domestic Life of Thomas Jefferson,* 416.

8. Coolidge Collection of Jefferson Manuscripts, to Patrick Gibson, Aug. 11, 1819.

9. Cappon, ed., *Adams-Jefferson Letters,* 611, Adams to Jefferson, Dec. 1, 1825; 612, Jefferson to Adams, Dec. 18, 1825.

10. *PMR,* 3:689, from Jefferson, Feb. 17, 1826; Gordon-Reed, *The Hemingses of Monticello,* 647–48, 655; "The 1827 Slave Auction at Monticello," Monticello, https://www.monticello.org/slaveauction/.

11. Cambreling, "Eulogy," in *A Selection of Eulogies,* 70.

12. *PMR,* 3:687–89, from Jefferson, Feb. 17, 1826; 3:691, to Jefferson, Feb. 24, 1826.

13. Jefferson, *Works,* 12:424–26, to William Branch Giles, Dec. 26, 1825; Cheney, *James Madison,* 276–77; LC-JMa, to Nicholas Trist, May 15, 1832.

14. Martineau, *Retrospect of Western Travel,* 2:2–8.

15. Gawalt, "James Monroe, Presidential Planter," *VMHB,* April 1993, 261; Monroe, *Writings,* 7:68, to Jefferson, Feb. 13, 1826; Wilmerding, *James Monroe: Public Claimant,* 77, 82.

16. *The Virginia Advocate,* Nov. 1, 1828, Nov. 8, 1828, Sept. 13, 1828.

17. Gilman, *James Monroe,* 226.

18. An Act to Provide the Final Settlement and Adjustment of the Various Claims Preferred by James Monroe Against the United States, *Register of Debates,* 21st Cong., 2nd sess., H.R. 330, Feb. 8, 1831.

19. LC-JMo, to Madison, April 11, 1831; LC-JMa, to Monroe, April 21, 1831.

20. *PWP,* 4:552, to Catharine Sawbridge Macaulay Graham, Jan. 9, 1790.

BIBLIOGRAPHY

BOOKS

Adams, Abigail. *Letters of Mrs. Adams, the Wife of John Adams.* With an introductory memoir by Charles Francis Adams. 2 vols. Boston: Charles C. Little and James Brown, 1840.

———. *New Letters of Abigail Adams, 1788–1801.* Edited by Stewart Mitchill. Boston: Houghton Mifflin, 1947.

Adams, Henry. *The Education of Henry Adams: An Autobiography.* Boston: Houghton Mifflin, 1918.

———. *History of the United States of America During the Administrations of James Madison.* New York: Literary Classics of the United States, 1986.

———. *History of the United States of America During the Administrations of Thomas Jefferson.* New York: Literary Classics of the United States, 1986.

———. *The Life of Albert Gallatin.* Philadelphia: J. B. Lippincott, 1880.

Adams, John. *The Adams Papers.* Edited by L. H. Butterfield, Wendell D. Garrett, and Marjorie E. Sprague. 11 vols. Series II: Adams Family Correspondence. Cambridge, Mass.: Belknap Press of Harvard University Press, 1963.

———. *The Adams Papers Digital Edition.* Edited by Sara Martin. Charlottesville: University of Virginia Press, Rotunda, 2008. http://rotunda.upress.virginia.edu/founders/ADMS.html.

———. *Letters of John Adams, Addressed to His Wife.* Edited by Charles Francis Adams. 2 vols. Boston: Charles C. Little and James Brown, 1841.

BIBLIOGRAPHY

——. *Warren-Adams Letters, Being Chiefly a Correspondence Among John Adams, Samuel Adams, and James Warren.* 2 vols. Boston: Massachusetts Historical Society, 1917.

——. *The Works of John Adams, Second President of the United States: With a Life of the Author, Notes, and Illustrations by His Grandson Charles Francis Adams.* 10 vols. Boston: Little, Brown, 1850–1856.

Adams, John Quincy. *The Jubilee of the Constitution: A Discourse Delivered at the Bequest of the New York Historical Society, in the City of New York, on Tuesday, the 30th of April, 1839; Being the Fiftieth Anniversary of the Inauguration of George Washington as President of the United States, on Thursday, the 30th of April, 1789.* New York: Samuel Colman, 1839.

——. *Memoirs of John Quincy Adams, Comprising Portions of His Diary from 1795 to 1848.* Edited by Charles Francis Adams. 12 vols. Philadelphia: J. B. Lippincott, 1874–1877.

Addison, Alexander. *Liberty of Speech, and of the Press. A Charge to the Grand Juries of the County Courts of the Fifth Circuit of the State of Pennsylvania.* Washington, D.C.: John Colerick, 1798.

Alden, John Richard. *General Charles Lee: Traitor or Patriot?* Baton Rouge: Louisiana State University Press, 1951.

Allen, William C. *History of the United States Capitol: A Chronicle of Design, Construction, and Politics.* Washington, D.C.: U.S. Government Printing Office, 2001.

Allgor, Catherine. *A Perfect Union: Dolley Madison and the Creation of the American Nation.* New York: Henry Holt, 2006.

Ambrose, Stephen E. *Undaunted Courage: Meriwether Lewis, Thomas Jefferson, and the Opening of the American West.* New York: Simon & Schuster, 1996.

American Historical Association. *Annual Report of the American Historical Association for the Year 1903.* 2 vols. Correspondence of the French Ministers to the United States, 1791–1797. Washington, D.C.: Government Printing Office, 1904.

——. *Annual Report of the American Historical Association for the Year 1912.* Washington, D.C.: Government Printing Office, 1914.

——. *Annual Report of the American Historical Association for the Year 1913.* 2 vols. Papers of James A. Bayard, 1796–1815. Washington, D.C.: Government Printing Office, 1915.

American State Papers: Documents, Legislative and Executive, of the Congress of the United States. 38 vols. Washington, D.C.: Gales and Seaton, 1832–1861.

Ames, Fisher. *Works of Fisher Ames.* Edited by Seth Ames. 2 vols. Boston: Little, Brown, 1854.

Ames, Mary Clemmer. *Ten Years in Washington: Life and Scenes in the National Capital, as a Woman Sees Them.* Hartford, Conn.: A. D. Worthington, 1875.

BIBLIOGRAPHY

Ammon, Harry. *James Monroe: The Quest for National Identity*. New York: McGraw-Hill, 1971.

Anderson, Troyer Steele. *The Command of the Howe Brothers During the American Revolution*. New York: Oxford University Press, 1936.

Annals of Congress. 42 vols. (1st Cong.–18th Cong., 1st sess.). Washington, D.C.: Gales and Seaton, 1834–1856.

The Annual Register, or a View of the History, Politics, and Literature for the Year 1781. Third Edition. London: J. Dodsley, 1800.

Ayers, Andrew. *The Architecture of Paris: An Architectural Guide*. Stuttgart, Germany: Axel Menges, 2004.

Bacon, Francis. *The Essays or Counsels Civil and Moral of Francis Bacon*. With an introduction by Henry Morley. 6th ed. London: George Routledge and Sons, 1889. First published in 1597.

Bailyn, Bernard. *To Begin the World Anew: The Genius and Ambiguities of the American Founders*. New York: Alfred A. Knopf, 2003.

Barbé Marbois, François. *The History of Louisiana, Particularly of the Cession of That Colony to the United States of America, with an Introductory Essay on the Constitution and Government of the United States*. Translated from the French by an American citizen. Philadelphia: Carey and Lea, 1830.

Barker, Jacob. *Incidents in the Life of Jacob Barker, of New Orleans, Louisiana; with Historical Facts, His Financial Transactions with the Government, and His Course on Important Political Questions, from 1800 to 1855*. Washington, D.C.: n.p., 1855.

Barratt, Carrie Rebora, and Ellen G. Miles. *Gilbert Stuart*. New York: Metropolitan Museum of Art, 2004.

Beard, J. R. *Toussaint L'Ouverture: A Biography and Autobiography*. Boston: James Redpath, 1863.

Bemis, Samuel Flagg, ed. *The American Secretaries of State and Their Diplomacy*. 17 vols. New York: Cooper Square Publishers, 1963.

——. *Jay's Treaty: A Study in Commerce and Diplomacy*. New York: Macmillan, 1923.

——. *John Quincy Adams and the Foundations of American Foreign Policy*. New York: Alfred A. Knopf, 1949.

Bodle, Wayne K., and Jacqueline Thibaut. *Valley Forge Historical Research Report*. 3 vols. Valley Forge, Pa.: United States Department of the Interior, National Parks Service, 1982.

Boles, John B. *Jefferson: Architect of American Liberty*. New York: Basic Books, 2017.

Boucher, François, and Frances Wilson Huard. *American Footprints in Paris*. New York: George H. Doran, 1921.

BIBLIOGRAPHY

Boudinot, Elias. *Journal or Historical Recollections of American Events During the Revolutionary War.* Philadelphia: Frederick Bourquin, 1894.

Brant, Irving. *James Madison.* 6 vols. Indianapolis: Bobbs-Merrill, 1941–1961.

Brecher, Frank W. *Negotiating the Louisiana Purchase: Robert Livingston's Mission to France, 1801–1804.* Jefferson, N.C.: McFarland, 2006.

Buchan, William. *Domestic Medicine; or, A Treatise on the Prevention and Cure of Diseases by Regimen and Simple Medicines.* London: Printed for A. Strahan, 1785.

Burr, Aaron. *Political Correspondence and Public Papers of Aaron Burr.* Edited by Mary-Jo Kline, Joanne Wood Ryan, C. Susan Feuerwerger, Karen L. Judd, and Linda S. Raven. 2 vols. Princeton, N.J.: Princeton University Press, 1983.

Caffrey, Kate. *The Twilight's Last Gleaming: Britain vs. America, 1812–1815.* New York: Stein and Day, 1977.

Callender, James. *The Prospect Before Us.* 2 vols. Richmond, Va., 1800.

Cappon, Lester J., ed. *The Adams-Jefferson Letters: The Complete Correspondence Between Thomas Jefferson and Abigail and John Adams.* Chapel Hill: University of North Carolina Press, 1988.

Carpenter, T. *The Trial of Col. Aaron Burr, on an Indictment for Treason, Before the Circuit Court of the United States, Held in Richmond (Virginia), May Term, 1807: Including the Arguments and Decisions on All the Motions Made During the Examination and Trial, and on the Motion for an Attachment Against Gen. Wilkinson.* 3 vols. Washington City: Westcott & Co., 1808.

Carroll, Frances Laverne, and Mary Meacham. *The Library at Mount Vernon.* Pittsburgh, Pa.: Beta Phi Mu, 1977.

Charles, Joseph. *The Origins of the American Party System: Three Essays.* New York: Harper Torchbooks, 1956.

Cheney, Lynne. *James Madison: A Life Reconsidered.* New York: Penguin Books, 2014.

Cheney, Richard, and Lynne Cheney. *Kings of the Hill: Power and Personality in the House of Representatives.* New York: Touchstone, 1996.

Chernow, Ron. *Alexander Hamilton.* New York: Penguin Press, 2004.

———. *Washington: A Life.* New York: Penguin Press, 2010.

Clark, Kenneth. *Moments of Vision.* London: John Murray, 1981.

Clay, Henry. *The Papers of Henry Clay.* Edited by James F. Hopkins. 11 vols. Lexington: University of Kentucky Press, 1959–1992.

Clinton, Henry. *The American Rebellion: Sir Henry Clinton's Narrative of His Campaigns, 1775–1782, with an Appendix of Original Documents.* Edited by William B. Willcox. Hamden, Conn.: Archon Books, 1971.

Coles, Harry L. *The War of 1812.* Chicago: University of Chicago Press, 1965.

BIBLIOGRAPHY

Combs, Jerald A. *The Jay Treaty: Political Battleground of the Founding Fathers.* Berkeley: University of California Press, 1970.

Conway, Moncure Daniel. *The Life of Thomas Paine.* 2 vols. New York: G. P. Putnam's Sons, 1892.

Cresson, W. P. *James Monroe.* Norwalk, Conn.: Easton Press, 1986.

Cruikshank, E. A. *The Political Adventures of John Henry: The Record of an International Imbroglio.* Toronto: Macmillan, 1936.

Cunningham, Noble E., Jr. *The Jeffersonian Republicans: The Formation of Party Organization, 1789–1801.* Chapel Hill: University of North Carolina Press, 1957.

———. *The Presidency of James Monroe.* Lawrence: University Press of Kansas, 1996.

Custis, George Washington Parke. *Recollections and Private Memoirs of Washington, by His Adopted Son, George Washington Parke Custis, with a Memoir of the Author, by His Daughter.* Edited by Benson J. Lossing. New York: Derby & Jackson, 1860.

Dallas, Alexander. *Life and Writings of Alexander James Dallas.* Edited by George Mifflin Dallas. Philadelphia: J. B. Lippincott, 1871.

Davis, Matthew L. *Memoirs of Aaron Burr. With Miscellaneous Selections from His Correspondence.* 2 vols. New York: Harper & Brothers, 1837.

De Chastellux, Marquis. *Travels in North-America, in the Years 1780, 1781, and 1782.* 2 vols. 2nd ed. London: Printed for G. G. J. and J. Robinson, 1787.

De Lafayette, Marquis. *Lafayette in the Age of the American Revolution. Selected Letters and Papers, 1776–1790.* Edited by Stanley J. Idzerda, Roger E. Smith, Linda J. Pike, and Mary Ann Quinn. 5 vols. Ithaca, N.Y.: Cornell University Press, 1977.

———. *Memoirs, Correspondence and Manuscripts of General Lafayette.* Edited by Jeffry H. Morrison. 3 vols. New York: Saunders and Otley, 1837.

De Luzancy, H. *A Panegyrick to the Memory of His Grace Frederick, Late Duke of Schonberg.* London: R. Bentley, 1690.

de Vattel, Emmerich. *The Law of Nations; or, Principles of the Law of Nature, Applied to the Conduct and Affairs of Nations and Sovereigns. From the French of Monsieur de Vattel.* Edited by Joseph Chitty. Sixth American Edition. Philadelphia: T. & J. W. Johnson, 1844.

Documentary History of the Construction and Development of the United States Capitol Building and Grounds. Washington, D.C.: Government Printing Office, 1904.

The Documentary History of the Ratification of the Constitution. Edited by Merrill Jensen, John P. Kaminski, Gaspare J. Saladino, Richard Leffler, Charles H. Schoenleber, Margaret A. Hogan, et al. 26 vols. Madison: Wisconsin Historical Society, 1981–2013.

Doniol, Henri. *Histoire de la participation de la France à l'éstablissement des États-Unis d'Amérique: Correspondance diplomatique et documents.* 5 vols. Paris: Imprimerie Nationale, 1892.

Drinker, Elizabeth. *Extracts from the Journal of Elizabeth Drinker.* Edited by Henry D. Biddle. Philadelphia: J. B. Lippincott, 1889.

Egerton, Douglas R. *Gabriel's Rebellion: The Virginia Slave Conspiracies of 1800 and 1802.* Chapel Hill: University of North Carolina Press, 1993.

Elkins, Stanley, and Eric McKitrick. *The Age of Federalism.* New York: Oxford University Press, 1993.

Elliot, Jonathan. *The Debates in the Several State Conventions, on the Adoption of the Federal Constitution, as Recommended by the General Convention at Philadelphia in 1787.* Collected and revised by Jonathan Elliot. 5 vols. Washington, D.C.: Printed for the editor, 1836.

Ellis, Joseph J. *American Sphinx: The Character of Thomas Jefferson.* 1996. New York: Vintage Books, 1998.

——. *His Excellency George Washington.* New York: Vintage Books, 2005.

Farrand, Max, ed. *The Records of the Federal Convention of 1783.* 3 vols. New Haven, Conn.: Yale University Press, 1911.

Field, Thomas W. *The Battle of Long Island.* Brooklyn: Long Island Historical Society, 1869.

Fields, Joseph E., ed. *"Worthy Partner": The Papers of Martha Washington.* Westport, Conn.: Greenwood, 1994.

Fithian, Philip Vickers. *Journal, 1775–1776: Written on the Virginia-Pennsylvania Frontier and in the Army Around New York.* Edited by Robert Greenhalgh Albion and Leonidas Dodson. Princeton, N.J.: Princeton University Press, 1934.

Fischer, David Hackett. *Albion's Seed: Four British Folkways in America.* Oxford: Oxford University Press, 1989.

——. *Washington's Crossing.* Oxford: Oxford University Press, 2004.

Flexner, James Thomas. *George Washington in the American Revolution, 1775–1783.* Boston: Little, Brown, 1968.

Fliegelman, Jay. *Declaring Independence: Jefferson, Natural Language & the Culture of Performance.* Stanford, Calif.: Stanford University Press, 1993.

Foner, Philip S., ed. *The Democratic-Republican Societies, 1790–1800: A Documentary Sourcebook of Constitutions, Declarations, Addresses, Resolutions, and Toasts.* Westport, Conn.: Greenwood Press, 1976.

Force, Peter. *American Archives.* 9 vols. Washington, D.C., 1837–1853. https://digital.lib.niu.edu/amarch.

Ford, Paul Leicester, ed. *Pamphlets on the Constitution of the United States, Published During Its Discussion by the People, 1787–1788.* Brooklyn, N.Y.: n.p., 1888.

Fraser, Flora. *The Washingtons: George and Martha, "Join'd by Friendship, Crown'd by Love."* New York: Alfred A. Knopf, 2015.

Freeman, Douglas Southall. *George Washington.* 7 vols. New York: Charles Scribner's Sons, 1951.

Freeman, Joanne B. *Affairs of Honor: National Politics in the New Republic.* New Haven, Conn.: Yale University Press, 2001.

Gallatin, Albert. *The Writings of Albert Gallatin.* Edited by Henry Adams. 3 vols. Philadelphia: J. B. Lippincott, 1879.

Gerry, Elbridge, Jr. *The Diary of Elbridge Gerry, Jr.* With a preface and footnotes by Claude G. Bowers and a foreword by Annette Townsend. New York: Brentano's, 1927.

Gibbes, R. W. *Documentary History of the American Revolution.* 3 vols. New York: D. Appleton, 1857.

Gibbs, George, ed. *Memoirs of the Administrations of Washington and John Adams, Edited from the Papers of Oliver Wolcott, Secretary of the Treasury.* 2 vols. New York: Printed for subscribers, 1846.

Gilbert, Felix. *To the Farewell Address: Ideas of Early American Foreign Policy.* Princeton, N.J.: Princeton University Press, 1961.

Gilman, Daniel C. *James Monroe.* Boston and New York: Houghton, Mifflin and Company, 1883.

Girard, Philippe R. *The Slaves Who Defeated Napoléon: Toussaint Louverture and the Haitian War of Independence, 1801–1804.* Tuscaloosa: University of Alabama Press, 2011.

Goldwin, Robert A. *Why Blacks, Women, and Jews Are Not Mentioned in the Constitution, and Other Unorthodox Views.* Washington, D.C.: AEI Press, 1990.

Golway, Terry. *Washington's General: Nathanael Greene and the Triumph of the American Revolution.* New York: Henry Holt, 2005.

Gordon, William. *The History of the Rise, Progress, and Establishment of the Independence of the United States of America: Including an Account of the Late War; and of the Thirteen Colonies, from Their Origin to That Period.* 2nd ed. Vol. 2. New York: Samuel Campbell, 1794.

Gordon-Reed, Annette. *The Hemingses of Monticello: An American Family.* New York and London: W. W. Norton, 2008.

Grainger, John D. *The Battle of Yorktown, 1781: A Reassessment.* Woodbridge, U.K.: Boydell, 2005.

Graydon, Alexander. *Memoirs of a Life, Chiefly Passed in Pennsylvania, Within the Last Sixty Years.* Edinburgh: William Blackwood and T. Cadell, 1822.

Greene, George Washington. *The Life of Nathanael Greene, Major-General in the Army of the Revolution.* 3 vols. New York: G. P. Putnam and Son, 1867.

Hamilton, Alexander. *The Papers of Alexander Hamilton.* Edited by Harold C. Syrett and Jacob E. Cooke. 27 vols. New York: Columbia University Press, 1961–1987.

BIBLIOGRAPHY

——. *The Papers of Alexander Hamilton Digital Edition*. Edited by Harold C. Syrett. Charlottesville: University of Virginia Press, Rotunda, 2011. http://rotunda.upress.virginia.edu/founders/ARHN.html.

Hamilton, Allan McLane. *The Intimate Life of Alexander Hamilton*. New York: Charles Scribner's Sons, 1911.

Hanser, Richard. *The Glorious Hour of Lt. Monroe*. New York: Atheneum, 1976.

Harris, Matthew L., and Thomas S. Kidd. *The Founding Fathers and the Debate over Religion in Revolutionary America: A History in Documents*. Oxford: Oxford University Press, 2011.

Haulman, Clyde A. *Virginia and the Panic of 1819: The First Great Depression and the Commonwealth*. London: Pickering and Chatto, 2008.

Heath, William. *Heath's Memoirs of the American War*. Reprinted with an introduction and notes by Rufus Rockwell Wilson. New York: A. Wessels, 1904. First published in 1798.

Hening, William Waller. *The Statutes at Large: Being a Collection of All the Laws of Virginia from the First Session of the Legislature, in the Year 1619*. 13 vols. Richmond, Va.: Printed for the editor, 1823.

Hickey, Donald R. *The War of 1812: A Forgotten Conflict*. Urbana: University of Illinois Press, 2012.

Hobson, Charles F. *The Aaron Burr Treason Trial*. Washington, D.C.: Federal Judicial History Office, 2006.

Hollitz, John. *Contending Voices: Biographical Explorations of the American Past*. 3rd ed. 3 vols. Boston: Wadsworth, 2010.

Humphrey, Carol Sue. *The Press of the Young Republic, 1783–1833*. The History of American Journalism. 6 vols. Edited by James D. Startt and Wm. David Sloan. Westport, Conn.: Greenwood Press, 2011.

——. ed. *Voices of Revolutionary America: Contemporary Accounts of Daily Life*. Santa Barbara, Calif.: Greenwood Press, 2011.

Hunt, Gaillard. *The Life of James Madison*. 1902. New York: Russell & Russell, 1968.

Hunt-Jones, Conover. *Dolley and the "Great Little Madison."* Washington, D.C.: American Institute of Architects Foundation, 1977.

Ingersoll, Charles J. *Historical Sketch of the Second War Between the United States of America and Great Britain*. 2 vols. Philadelphia: Lea and Blanchard, 1845–1849.

Irving, Washington. *Life of George Washington*. 5 vols. New York: G. P. Putnam's Sons, 1857.

Isenberg, Nancy. *Fallen Founder: The Life of Aaron Burr*. New York: Viking, 2007.

Iung, Theodore. *Lucien Bonaparte et ses mémoires, 1775–1840*. 3 vols. Paris: G. Charpentier, 1882.

BIBLIOGRAPHY

Jackson, Andrew. *The Papers of Andrew Jackson Digital Edition.* Edited by Daniel Feller. Charlottesville: University of Virginia Press, Rotunda, 2015. https://rotunda.upress.virginia.edu/founders/JKSN.html.

Jackson, Donald. *Thomas Jefferson and the Stony Mountains: Exploring the West from Monticello.* Urbana: University of Illinois Press, 1981.

Jackson, George. *The Bath Archives: A Further Selection from the Diaries and Letters of Sir George Jackson, K.C.H., from 1809 to 1816.* Edited by Lady Jackson. 2 vols. London: Richard Bentley and Son, 1873.

Jay, John. *The Correspondence and Public Papers of John Jay, First Chief-Justice of the United States, Member and President of the Continental Congress, Minister to Spain, Member of Commission to Negotiate Treaty of Independence, Envoy to Great Britain, Governor of New York, Etc.* Edited by Henry P. Johnston. 4 vols. New York: G. P. Putnam's Sons: 1890–1893.

Jefferson, Thomas. *Autobiography of Thomas Jefferson.* Introduction by Dumas Malone. New York: Capricorn Books, 1959.

——. *The Complete Anas of Thomas Jefferson.* Edited by Franklin B. Sawvel. New York: Round Table Press, 1903.

——. *Jefferson's Memorandum Books: Accounts, with Legal Records and Miscellany, 1767–1826.* Edited by James A. Bear Jr. and Lucia C. Stanton. 2 vols. Princeton, N.J.: Princeton University Press, 1997.

——. *Notes on the State of Virginia.* Richmond: J. W. Randolph, 1853.

——. *The Papers of Thomas Jefferson.* Edited by Julian P. Boyd, Charles T. Cullen, John Catanzariti, and Barbara B. Oberg. 39 vols. Princeton, N.J.: Princeton University Press, 1950–2012.

——. *The Papers of Thomas Jefferson Digital Edition.* Edited by James P. McClure and J. Jefferson Looney. Charlottesville: University of Virginia Press, Rotunda, 2008. http://rotunda.upress.virginia.edu/founders/TSJN.html.

——. *The Papers of Thomas Jefferson: Retirement Series.* Edited by J. Jefferson Looney. 10 vols. Princeton, N.J.: Princeton University Press, 2005–2014.

——. *Thomas Jefferson Correspondence: Printed from the Originals in the Collections of William K. Bixby.* With notes by Worthington Chauncey Ford. Boston: Plimpton Press, 1916.

——. *The Works of Thomas Jefferson.* Edited by Paul Leicester Ford. 12 vols. New York: G. P. Putnam's Sons, 1904–1905.

——. *The Writings of Thomas Jefferson.* Edited by Paul Leicester Ford. 10 vols. New York: G. P. Putnam's Sons, 1892–1899.

——. *The Writings of Thomas Jefferson.* Edited by Andrew A. Lipscomb and Albert Ellery Bergh. 20 vols. Washington, D.C.: Thomas Jefferson Memorial Association, 1903–1904.

BIBLIOGRAPHY

Jones, Colin. *The Smile Revolution in Eighteenth-Century Paris*. Oxford: Oxford University Press, 2014.

Jones, Joseph. *Letters of Joseph Jones of Virginia, 1777–1787*. Washington, D.C.: Department of State, 1889.

Journals of the Continental Congress, 1774–1789. Edited by Worthington C. Ford et al. 34 vols. Washington, D.C.: Government Printing Office, 1904–1937.

Kaminski, John P., ed. *Jefferson in Love: The Love Letters Between Thomas Jefferson & Maria Cosway*. Madison, Wisc.: Madison House, 1999.

Kennedy, John P. *Memoirs of the Life of William Wirt, Attorney General of the United States*. 2 vols. Philadelphia: Lea and Blanchard, 1849.

Ketcham, Ralph. *James Madison: A Biography*. 1971. Charlottesville: University of Virginia Press, 1990.

King, George Harrison Sanford, comp. *The Register of Overwharton Parish, Stafford County, Virginia, 1723–1758 and Sundry Historical and Genealogical Notes*. Fredericksburg, Va.: George Harrison Sanford King, 1961.

King, Rufus. *The Life and Correspondence of Rufus King*. Edited by Charles R. King. 6 vols. New York: G. P. Putnam's Sons, 1894–1900.

Kranish, Michael. *Flight from Monticello: Thomas Jefferson at War*. Oxford: Oxford University Press, 2010.

Kukla, Jon. *Patrick Henry: Champion of Liberty*. New York: Simon & Schuster, 2017.

———. *A Wilderness So Immense: The Louisiana Purchase and the Destiny of America*. New York: Alfred A. Knopf, 2003.

Laurens, John. *The Army Correspondence of Colonel John Laurens in the Years 1777–8*. With a memoir by Wm. Gilmore Simms. New York: Bedford Club, 1867.

Lear, Tobias. *Letters and Recollections of George Washington: Being Letters to Tobias Lear and Others Between 1790 and 1799, Showing the First American in the Management of His Estate and Domestic Affairs; with a Diary of Washington's Last Days, Kept by Tobias Lear*. New York: Doubleday, Page, 1906.

Lee, Charles. *The Lee Papers*. 4 vols. New York: New-York Historical Society, 1872.

Leibiger, Stuart. *Founding Friendship: George Washington, James Madison, and the Creation of the American Republic*. Charlottesville: University Press of Virginia, 1999.

Lengel, Edward G. *General George Washington: A Military Life*. New York: Random House, 2005.

Lester, Malcolm. *Anthony Merry Redivivus: A Reappraisal of the British Minister to the United States, 1803–6*. Charlottesville: University Press of Virginia, 1978.

Letters of Delegates to Congress, 1774–1789. 25 vols. Edited by Paul H. Smith et al. Washington, D.C.: Library of Congress, 1976–2000.

BIBLIOGRAPHY

Levasseur, A. *Lafayette in America in 1824 and 1825; or, Journal of a Voyage to the United States.* Vol. 1. Philadelphia: Carey and Lea, 1829.

Lincoln, Abraham. *Collected Works of Abraham Lincoln.* 8 vols. Edited by Roy P. Basler. New Brunswick, N.J.: Rutgers University Press, 1953.

Link, Eugene Perry. *Democratic-Republican Societies, 1790–1800.* Morningside Heights, N.Y.: Columbia University Press, 1942.

Locke, John. *The Works of John Locke in Nine Volumes.* 9 vols. London: Printed for C. and J. Rivington, 1824.

Logan, George. *Memoir of Dr. George Logan of Stenton by His Widow Deborah Norris Logan with Selections from His Correspondence.* Edited by Frances A. Logan, with an introduction by Charles J. Stille. Philadelphia: Historical Society of Pennsylvania, 1899.

Longmore, Paul K. *The Invention of George Washington.* Berkeley: University of California Press, 1988.

Lord, Walter. *The Dawn's Early Light.* New York: W. W. Norton, 1972.

Lossing, Benson J. *Mary and Martha: The Mother and the Wife of George Washington.* New York: Harper & Brothers, 1886.

——. *The Pictorial Field-Book of the War of 1812.* New York: Harper & Brothers, 1868.

Ludlum, David M. *The Weather Factor.* Boston: Houghton Mifflin, 1984.

McBurney, Christian M. *Kidnapping the Enemy: The Special Operations to Capture Generals Charles Lee & Richard Prescott.* Yardley, Pa.: Westholme, 2014.

McCaleb, Walter Flavius. *The Aaron Burr Conspiracy.* New York: Wilson-Erickson, 1936.

McCullough, David. *1776.* New York: Simon & Schuster, 2005.

McDonald, Forrest. *The Presidency of Thomas Jefferson.* Lawrence: University Press of Kansas, 1976.

McGrath, Tim. *James Monroe: A Life.* New York: Dutton, 2020.

Mackenzie, Frederick. *Diary of Frederick Mackenzie: Giving a Daily Narrative of His Military Service as an Officer of the Regiment of Royal Welch Fusiliers During the Years 1775–1781 in Massachusetts, Rhode Island and New York.* 2 vols. Cambridge, Mass.: Harvard University Press, 1930.

McLaughlin, Jack. *Jefferson and Monticello: The Biography of a Builder.* New York: Henry Holt, 1988.

Maclay, William. *Journal of William Maclay: United States Senator from Pennsylvania, 1789–1791.* Edited by Edgar S. Maclay. New York: D. Appleton, 1890.

McMaster, John Bach. *A History of the People of the United States from the Revolution to the Civil War.* 7 vols. New York: D. Appleton, 1907.

BIBLIOGRAPHY

Madison, Dolley. *The Papers of Dolley Madison Digital Edition.* Edited by Holly C. Shulman. Charlottesville: University of Virginia Press, Rotunda, 2008. https://rotunda.upress.virginia.edu/dmde/.

Madison, James. *The Papers of James Madison, Congressional Series.* Edited by J. C. A. Stagg, David B. Mattern, William T. Hutchinson, William M. Rachal, Robert A. Rutland, et al. 17 vols. Chicago: University of Chicago Press; Charlottesville: University Press of Virginia, 1962–1991.

——. *The Papers of James Madison Digital Edition.* Edited by J. C. A. Stagg. Charlottesville: University of Virginia Press, Rotunda, 2010. http://rotunda.upress.virginia.edu/founders/JSMN.html.

——. *The Papers of James Madison, Presidential Series.* Edited by Robert A. Rutland, J. C. A. Stagg, Angela Kreider, et al. 7 vols. Charlottesville: University of Virginia Press, 1984–2012.

——. *The Papers of James Madison, Retirement Series.* Edited by David B. Mattern and J. C. A. Stagg. 2 vols. Charlottesville: University of Virginia Press, 2009–2013.

——. *The Papers of James Madison, Secretary of State Series.* Edited by Robert R. Brugger, Robert A. Rutland, David B. Mattern, J. C. A. Stagg, Mary A. Hackett, et al. 9 vols. Charlottesville: University Press of Virginia, 1986–2011.

——. *The Writings of James Madison.* Edited by Gaillard Hunt. 9 vols. New York: G. P. Putnam's Sons, 1900–1910.

Maier, Pauline. *American Scripture: Making the Declaration of Independence.* New York: Alfred A. Knopf, 1997.

Malone, Dumas. *Jefferson and His Time.* 6 vols. 1948–1981. Charlottesville: University of Virginia Press, 2005.

The Manuscripts of J. B. Fortescue, Esq., Preserved at Dropmore. 6 vols. London: Her Majesty's Stationery Office, 1892–1908.

Marshall, John. *The Life of George Washington, Written for the Use of Schools.* Philadelphia: James Crissy, 1838.

Martin, Joseph Plumb. *A Narrative of a Revolutionary Soldier: Some of the Adventures, Dangers, and Sufferings of Joseph Plumb Martin.* With an introduction by Thomas Fleming. New York: Signet Classics, 2001.

Martineau, Harriet. *Retrospect of Western Travel.* 3 vols. London: Saunders and Otley, 1838.

Mason, Matthew. *Slavery and Politics in the Early American Republic.* Chapel Hill: University of North Carolina Press, 2006.

Maurois, André. *Adrienne, ou la vie de Mme de La Fayette.* Paris: Hachette, 1961.

Maxey, David W. *A Portrait of Elizabeth Willing Powel (1743–1830).* Philadelphia: American Philosophical Society, 2006.

BIBLIOGRAPHY

Monroe, James. *The Autobiography of James Monroe.* Edited and with an introduction by Stuart Gerry Brown. Syracuse, N.Y.: Syracuse University Press, 1959.

———. *The Papers of James Monroe.* Edited by Daniel Preston and Marlena C. Delong. 6 vols. Westport, Conn.: Greenwood Press, 2003–2017.

———. *The Writings of James Monroe.* Edited by Stanislaus Murray Hamilton. 7 vols. New York: G. P. Putnam's Sons, 1898–1903.

Moore, Charles, ed. *George Washington's Rules of Civility and Decent Behaviour in Company and Conversation.* Cambridge, Mass.: Riverside Press, 1931.

Morgan, George. *The Life of James Monroe.* Boston: Small, Maynard, 1921.

Morison, Samuel Eliot. *The Life and Letters of Harrison Gray Otis, Federalist 1764–1848.* 2 vols. Boston and New York: Houghton Mifflin Company, 1913.

Morrison, Jeffry H. *John Witherspoon and the Founding of the American Republic.* Notre Dame, Ind.: University of Notre Dame Press, 2005.

Mowry, William A. *The Territorial Growth of the United States.* New York: Silver, Burdett, 1902.

Nash, Solomon. *Journal of Solomon Nash: A Soldier of the Revolution, 1776–1777.* With an introduction and notes by Charles I. Bushnell. New York: Privately printed, 1861.

Nelson, Paul David. *William Alexander, Lord Stirling.* University, Ala.: University of Alabama Press, 1987.

Newmyer, R. Kent. *The Treason Trial of Aaron Burr: Law, Politics, and the Character Wars of the New Nation.* Cambridge: Cambridge University Press, 2012.

Paine, Thomas. *An Eulogy on the Life of General George Washington Who Died at Mount Vernon, December 14th, 1799, in the 68th Year of His Age.* Newburyport, Mass.: Edmund M. Blunt, 1800.

———. *Life and Writings of Thomas Paine.* Edited and annotated by Daniel Edwin Wheeler. 10 vols. New York: Vincent Parke, 1908.

———. *The Writings of Thomas Paine.* Edited by Moncure Daniel Conway. 4 vols. New York: G. P. Putnam's Sons, 1894–1896.

Papas, Phillip. *Renegade Revolutionary: The Life of General Charles Lee.* New York: New York University Press, 2014.

Peale, Charles Willson. *The Selected Papers of Charles Willson Peale and His Family.* Edited by Lillian B. Miller, Sidney Hart, David C. Ward, Lauren E. Brown, Sara C. Hale, and Leslie K. Reinhardt. 6 vols. New Haven, Conn.: Yale University Press, 2000.

Perkins, Bradford. *Prologue to War: England and the United States, 1805–1812.* Berkeley: University of California Press, 1961.

Peterson, Merrill D. *The Great Triumvirate: Webster, Clay, and Calhoun.* New York: Oxford University Press, 1987.

BIBLIOGRAPHY

——. *The Jefferson Image in the American Mind*. Charlottesville, Va.: Thomas Jefferson Memorial Foundation, 1998.

——. *Thomas Jefferson and the New Nation*. New York: Oxford University Press, 1970.

Pickering, Octavius, and Charles W. Upham. *The Life of Timothy Pickering*. 4 vols. Boston: Little, Brown, 1867–1873.

Pierson, Hamilton W. *Jefferson at Monticello: The Private Life of Thomas Jefferson from Entirely New Materials*. New York: Charles Scribner's Sons, 1862.

Plumer, William. *William Plumer's Memorandum of Proceedings in the United States Senate, 1803–1807*. New York: Macmillan, 1923.

Plutarch. *Plutarch's Lives, Translated from the Original Greek; with Notes, Critical and Historical; and a Life of Plutarch*. Edited by John Langhorne and William Langhorne. 2 vols. London: Richards and Co., 1823.

Poulet, Anne L., Guilhem Scherf, Ulrike D. Mathies, Christoph Frank, Claude Vandalle, Dean Walker, and Monique Barbier. *Jean-Antoine Houdon: Sculptor of the Enlightenment*. Chicago: National Gallery of Art, 2003.

Powell, J. H. *Richard Rush: Republican Diplomat, 1780–1859*. Philadelphia: University of Pennsylvania Press, 1942.

"President Pro Tempore." United States Senate. https://www.senate.gov/artand history/history/common/briefing/President_Pro_Tempore.htm.

Puls, Mark. *Henry Knox: Visionary General of the American Revolution*. New York: St. Martin's Griffin, 2008.

Rabkin, Jeremy A. *Law Without Nations? Why Constitutional Government Requires Sovereign States*. Princeton, N.J.: Princeton University Press, 2005.

Ragosta, John A. *Patrick Henry: Proclaiming a Revolution*. New York: Routledge, 2017.

Ramsay, David. *An Oration on the Cession of Louisiana, to the United States, Delivered on the 12th May, 1804, in St. Michael's Church, Charleston, South-Carolina, at the Request of a Number of the Inhabitants, and Published by Their Desire*. Charleston, S.C.: W. P. Young, 1804.

Randall, Henry S. *The Life of Thomas Jefferson*. 3 vols. New York: Derby & Jackson, 1858.

Randolph, Edmund. *A Vindication of Edmund Randolph*. Richmond, Va.: Charles H. Wynne, Printer, 1855.

Randolph, Sarah N. *The Domestic Life of Thomas Jefferson*. With an introduction by Dumas Malone. New York: Frederick Ungar, 1958.

Reardon, John J. *Edmund Randolph: A Biography*. New York: Macmillan, 1975.

Reed, William. *Life and Correspondence of Joseph Reed*. 2 vols. Philadelphia: Lindsay and Blakiston, 1847.

BIBLIOGRAPHY

Register of Debates in Congress. 14 vols. (18th Cong., 2nd sess.–25th Cong., 1st sess.) Washington, D.C.: Gales and Seaton, 1825–1837.

Remini, Robert V. *Henry Clay: Statesman for the Union.* New York: W. W. Norton, 1991.

The Republic of Letters: The Correspondence Between Thomas Jefferson and James Madison, 1776–1826. Edited by James Morton Smith. 3 vols. New York: W. W. Norton, 1995.

The Revolutionary Diplomatic Correspondence of the United States. Edited by Francis Wharton. 6 vols. Washington, D.C.: Government Printing Office, 1889.

Robertson, Archibald. *His Diaries and Sketches in America: 1762–1780.* Edited and with an introduction by Harry Miller Lydenberg. New York: New York Public Library, 1930.

Robertson, David. *Reports of the Trials of Colonel Aaron Burr (Late Vice President of the United States), for Treason, and for a Misdemeanor.* 2 vols. Philadelphia: Hopkins and Earle, 1808.

Rodney, Caesar. *Letters to and from Caesar Rodney, 1756–1784.* Edited by George Herbert Ryden. Philadelphia: Historical Society of Delaware, 1933.

Rodney, Thomas. *Diary of Captain Thomas Rodney, 1776–1777.* With an introduction by Caesar A. Rodney. Wilmington: Historical Society of Delaware, 1888.

Roederer, A. M. *Oeuvres du Comte P. L. Roederer, Pair de France, Membre de L'Institut.* 8 vols. Paris: Firmin Didot Frères, 1854.

Roosevelt, Theodore. *The Naval War of 1812, or the History of the United States Navy During the Last War with Great Britain, to Which Is Appended an Account of the Battle of New Orleans.* New York: G. P. Putnam's Sons, 1882.

Royster, Charles. *A Revolutionary People at War: The Continental Army and American Character, 1775–1783.* Chapel Hill: University of North Carolina Press, Institute of Early American History and Culture, 1979.

Rutland, Robert Allen. *The Presidency of James Madison.* Lawrence: University Press of Kansas, 1990.

Schauffler, Robert Haven, ed. *Washington's Birthday: Its History, Observance, Spirit, and Significance as Related in Prose and Verse, with a Selection from Washington's Speeches and Writings.* Our American Holidays. New York: Moffat, Yard, 1910.

Scheer, George F., and Hugh F. Rankin. *Rebels and Redcoats.* Cleveland: World Publishing, 1957.

Schutz, John A., and Douglass Adair, eds. *The Spur of Fame: Dialogues of John Adams and Benjamin Rush, 1805–1813.* San Marino, Calif.: Huntington Library, 1966.

Schwarz, Philip J., ed. *Gabriel's Conspiracy: A Documentary History.* Charlottesville: University of Virginia Press, 2012.

BIBLIOGRAPHY

A Selection of Eulogies, Pronounced in the Several States, in Honor of the Illustrious Patriots and Statesmen, John Adams and Thomas Jefferson. Hartford, Conn.: D. F. Robinson & Co. and Norton and Russel, 1826.

Sellers, John R. "The Common Soldier in the American Revolution." In *Military History of the American Revolution: The Proceedings of the Sixth Military History Symposium USAF Academy,* edited by Stanley J. Underdal, 151–66. Honolulu: University Press of the Pacific, 2002.

Shackelford, George Green. *Jefferson's Adoptive Son: The Life of William Short, 1759–1848.* Lexington: University Press of Kentucky, 1993.

Shaw, Samuel. *The Journals of Major Samuel Shaw: The First American Consul at Canton.* With a life of the author by Josiah Quincy. Boston: Wm. Crosby and H. P. Nichols, 1847.

Skeen, C. Edward. *John Armstrong Jr., 1758–1843: A Biography.* Syracuse, N.Y.: Syracuse University Press, 1981.

Slaughter, Thomas P. *The Whiskey Rebellion: Frontier Epilogue to the American Revolution.* New York: Oxford University Press, 1986.

Smith, James Morton. *Freedom's Fetters: The Alien and Sedition Laws and American Civil Liberties.* Ithaca, N.Y.: Cornell University Press, 1956.

Smith, Jean Edward. *John Marshall: Definer of a Nation.* New York: Henry Holt, 1996.

Smith, John Cotton. *The Correspondence and Miscellanies of the Hon. John Cotton Smith, LL.D., Formerly Governor of Connecticut.* New York: Harper & Brothers, 1847.

Smith, Margaret Bayard. *The First Forty Years of Washington Society.* Edited by Gaillard Hunt. New York: Charles Scribner's Sons, 1906.

Sofaer, Abraham D. *War, Foreign Affairs and Constitutional Power: The Origins.* Cambridge, Mass.: Ballinger, 1976.

Sparks, Jared. *The Life of Gouverneur Morris, with Selections from His Correspondence and Miscellaneous Papers. Detailing Events in the American Revolution, the French Revolution, and in the Political History of the United States.* 3 vols. Boston: Gray & Bowen, 1832.

Stagg, J. C. A. *Borderlines in Borderlands: James Madison and the Spanish-American Frontier, 1776–1821.* New Haven, Conn.: Yale University Press, 2009.

——. *The War of 1812: Conflict for a Continent.* Cambridge: Cambridge University Press, 2012.

Statutes at Large of the United States of America. 18 vols. (1st Cong.–18th Cong.). Boston: Charles C. Little and James Brown, 1845–1878.

Stilgoe, John R. *Common Landscape of America, 1580 to 1845.* New Haven, Conn.: Yale University Press, 1982.

BIBLIOGRAPHY

Stryker, William S. *The Battles of Trenton and Princeton.* Cambridge, Mass.: Riverside Press, 1898.

Sugden, John. *Tecumseh: A Life.* New York: John Macrae/Owl Books, 1997.

Sutcliff, Robert. *Travels in Some Parts of North America, in the Years 1804, 1805, and 1806.* York, U.K.: C. Peacock, 1811.

Symonds, Craig L. *A Battlefield Atlas of the American Revolution.* Cartography by William J. Clipson. Baltimore, Md.: Nautical & Aviation Publishing Company of America, 1986.

Thacher, James. *Military Journal During the American Revolutionary War, from 1775 to 1783.* Boston: Richardson & Lord, 1823.

Thayer, Theodore. *Nathanael Greene: Strategist of the American Revolution.* New York: Twayne, 1960.

Thorpe, Francis Newton. *The Federal and State Constitutions Colonial Charters, and Other Organic Laws of the States, Territories, and Colonies Now or Heretofore Forming the United States of America.* 7 vols. Washington, D.C.: Government Printing Office, 1909.

Toll, Ian W. *Six Frigates: The Epic History of the Founding of the U.S. Navy.* New York: W. W. Norton, 2006.

Tucker, Glenn. *Dawn Like Thunder: The Barbary Wars and the Birth of the U.S. Navy.* Indianapolis: Bobbs-Merrill, 1963.

Tucker, Spencer C., and Frank T. Reuter. *Injured Honor: The Chesapeake-Leopard Affair, June 22, 1807.* Annapolis, Md.: Naval Institute Press, 1996.

Tudor, William. *An Oration Delivered March 5, 1779.* Boston: Edes & Gill, 1779.

Van Doren, Carl. *Secret History of the American Revolution: An Account of the Conspiracies of Benedict Arnold and Numerous Others Drawn from the Secret Service Papers of the British Headquarters in North America Now for the First Time Examined and Made Public.* New York: Viking Press, 1941.

Van Tyne, Claude H. *The Founding of the American Republic.* 2 vols. Boston: Houghton Mifflin, 1929.

The Virginia Report of 1799–1800, Touching the Alien and Sedition Laws; Together with the Virginia Resolutions of December 21, 1798, the Debate and Proceedings Thereon in the House of Delegates of Virginia, and Several Other Documents Illustrative of the Report and Resolutions. Richmond, Va.: J. W. Randolph, 1850.

Warren, Mercy. *History of the Rise, Progress, and Termination of the American Revolution.* 3 vols. Boston: Manning and Loring, 1805.

Washburn, H. C. *Illustrated Case Inscriptions from the Official Catalogue of the Trophy Flags of the United States Navy.* Baltimore: Lord Baltimore Press, 1913.

BIBLIOGRAPHY

Washington, George. *The Papers of George Washington, Colonial Series.* Edited by W. W. Abbot. 10 vols. Charlottesville: University Press of Virginia, 1992–1997.

——. *The Papers of George Washington, Confederation Series.* Edited by W. W. Abbot. 6 vols. Charlottesville: University Press of Virginia, 1992–1997.

——. *The Papers of George Washington, Diaries.* Edited by Donald Jackson and Dorothy Twohig. 6 vols. Charlottesville: University Press of Virginia, 1992–1997.

——. *The Papers of George Washington Digital Edition.* Edited by Theodore Crackel. Charlottesville: University of Virginia Press, Rotunda, 2008. http://rotunda .upress.virginia.edu/founders/GEWN.html.

——. *The Papers of George Washington, Presidential Series.* Edited by Dorothy Twohig, Mark A. Mastromarino, Jack D. Warren, Robert F. Haggard, Christine S. Patrick, John C. Pinheiro, David R. Hoth, and Carol S. Ebel. 16 vols. Charlottesville: University Press of Virginia, 1985–2011.

——. *The Papers of George Washington, Retirement Series.* Edited by W. W. Abbot and Edward G. Lengel. 4 vols. Charlottesville: University Press of Virginia, 1998–1999.

——. *The Papers of George Washington, Revolutionary War Series.* Edited by Philander D. Chase, Frank E. Grizzard Jr., Edward G. Lengel, David R. Hoth, and William M. Ferraro. 21 vols. Charlottesville: University Press of Virginia, 1985–2012.

——. *The Writings of George Washington from the Original Manuscript Sources, 1745–1799.* Edited by John C. Fitzpatrick. 39 vols. Washington, D.C.: Government Printing Office, 1937.

Watson, Elkanah. *Men and Times of the Revolution; or, Memoirs of Elkanah Watson, Including Journals of Travels in Europe and America, from 1777 to 1842.* Edited by Winslow C. Watson. New York: Dana and Company, 1856.

Webster, Daniel. *The Letters of Daniel Webster, from Documents Owned Principally by the New Hampshire Historical Society.* Edited by C. H. Van Tyne. New York: McClure, Phillips, 1902.

Wilentz, Sean. *No Property in Man: Slavery and Antislavery at the Nation's Founding.* Cambridge, Mass.: Harvard University Press, 2018.

Wilkinson, James. *Memoirs of My Own Times.* 3 vols. Philadelphia: Abraham Small, 1816.

Williams, John S. *History of the Invasion and Capture of Washington, and of the Events Which Preceded and Followed.* New York: Harper & Brothers, 1857.

Wilmerding, Lucius. *James Monroe, Public Claimant.* New Brunswick, N.J.: Rutgers University Press, 1960.

Wirt, William. *The Letters of the British Spy.* 10th ed. New York: J. & J. Harper, 1832.

Witherspoon, John. *The Selected Writings of John Witherspoon.* Edited by Thomas P. Miller. Carbondale: Southern Illinois University Press, 2015.

Wood, Gordon. *Empire of Liberty: A History of the Early Republic, 1789–1815.* Oxford: Oxford University Press, 2009.

——. *Revolutionary Characters: What Made the Founders Different.* New York: Penguin Press, 2006.

Wright, Robert K., Jr. *The Continental Army.* Washington, D.C.: Center of Military History, 1986.

Wulf, Andrea. *Founding Gardeners: The Revolutionary Generation, Nature, and the Shaping of the American Nation.* New York: Alfred A. Knopf, 2011.

SELECTED ARTICLES

Adair, Douglass. "'That Politics May Be Reduced to a Science': David Hume, James Madison, and the Tenth Federalist." *Huntington Library Quarterly* 20, no. 4 (Aug. 1957): 343–60.

Ammon, Harry. "James Monroe and the Election of 1808 in Virginia." *William and Mary Quarterly* 20, no. 1 (Jan. 1963): 33–56.

Anderson, Frank Maloy. "Contemporary Opinion of the Virginia and Kentucky Resolutions I." *American Historical Review* 5, no. 1 (Oct. 1899): 45–63.

Armstrong, John. "Answer to the Queries of D. F., in Our Third Number, Addressed to the Reviewer of Wilkinson's Memoirs." *Literary and Scientific Repository and Critical Review* 3, no. 5 (July 1821): 106–37.

Barry, William T. "Letters of William T. Barry." *William and Mary Quarterly* 13, no. 4 (April 1905): 236–44.

Becker, Ann. "Smallpox in Washington's Army." *Journal of Military History* 68, no. 2 (April 2004): 381–430.

Biddle, Francis. "Unforgiving Cousin: John Randolph of Roanoke." *American Heritage* 12, no. 5 (Aug. 1961).

Bizardel, Yvon, and Howard C. Rice Jr. "'Poor in Love Mr. Short.'" *William and Mary Quarterly* 21, no. 4 (Oct. 1964): 516–33.

Brant, Irving. "Edmund Randolph, Not Guilty!" *William and Mary Quarterly,* 3rd ser., 7, no. 2 (April 1950): 179–98.

Brown, Stephen W. "Satisfaction at Bladensburg: The Pearson-Jackson Duel of 1809." *North Carolina Historical Review* 58, no. 1 (Jan. 1981): 23–43.

"Caucus History." *Niles' Weekly Register,* Dec. 20, 1823, 244–45.

Clarke, Jack Alden. "Thomas Sydney Jesup: Military Observer at the Hartford Convention." *New England Quarterly* 29, no. 3 (Sept. 1956): 393–99.

BIBLIOGRAPHY

Cook, Fred J. "Allan McLane, Unknown Hero of the Revolution." *American Heritage* 7, no. 6 (Oct. 1956).

Cox, Isaac J. "General Wilkinson and His Later Intrigues with the Spaniards." *American Historical Review* 19, no. 4 (July 1914): 794–812.

Dabney, Virginius. "Jouett Outrides Tarleton and Saves Jefferson from Capture." *Scribner's Magazine* 83 (June 1928): 690–98.

Davis, W. W. H. "Washington on the West Bank of the Delaware, 1776." *Pennsylvania Magazine of History and Biography* 4, no. 2 (1880): 133–63.

Du Ponceau, Peter S. "Autobiographical Letters of Peter S. Duponceau." *Pennsylvania Magazine of History and Biography* 40, no. 2 (1916): 172–86.

Du Ponceau, Peter S., and James L. Whitehead. "Notes and Documents: The Autobiography of Peter Stephen Du Ponceau." *Pennsylvania Magazine of History and Biography* 63, no. 2 (April 1939): 189–227.

"Early French Policy Toward the United States." *Chicago Historical Society Bulletin* 3, no. 7 (Jan. 1926): 56–60.

Everett, Edward G. "Some Aspects of Pro-French Sentiment in Pennsylvania, 1790–1800." *Western Pennsylvania Historical Magazine* 43, no. 1 (March 1960): 23–41.

Fehlings, Gregory. "Storm on the Constitution: The First Deportation Law." *Tulsa Journal of Comparative and International Law* 10, no. 1 (Fall 2002): 63–114.

Few, Frances. "The Diary of Frances Few, 1808–1809." Edited by Noble E. Cunningham Jr. *Journal of Southern History* 29, no. 3 (Aug. 1963): 345–61.

Forte, David F. "Marbury's Travail: Federalist Politics and William Marbury's Appointment as Justice of the Peace." *Catholic University Law Review* 45, no. 2 (Winter 1996): 349–402.

Garnett, James Mercer. "John Francis Mercer, Governor of Maryland, 1801 to 1803." *Maryland Historical Magazine* 2, no. 3 (Sept. 1907): 191–213.

Garrison, Winfred E. "Characteristics of American Organized Religion." *Annals of the American Academy of Political and Social Science* 256 (March 1948): 14–24.

Gawalt, Gerard W. "James Monroe, Presidential Planter." *Virginia Magazine of History and Biography* 101, no. 2 (April 1993): 251–72.

Gerry, Elbridge, Jr. "Letters of Elbridge Gerry, 1797–1814." *Proceedings of the Massachusetts Historical Society*, 3rd ser., 47 (Oct. 1913–June 1914): 480–523.

"Glorious News! Orleans Saved and Peace Concluded." *Niles' Weekly Register*, Feb. 18, 1815, 385.

"The Inaugural Speech." *National Register*, March 15, 1817, 161–62.

"The Ineligibility Clause's Lost History: Presidential Patronage and Congress, 1787–1850." *Harvard Law Review* 123, no. 7 (May 2010): 1727–48.

"James Madison's Autobiography." Edited by Douglass Adair. *William and Mary Quarterly*, 3rd ser., 2, no. 2 (April 1945): 191–209.

Ketcham, Ralph L., ed. "An Unpublished Sketch of James Madison by James K. Paulding." *Virginia Magazine of History and Biography* 67, no. 4 (Oct. 1959): 432–37.

Koch, Adrienne, and Harry Ammon. "The Virginia and Kentucky Resolutions: An Episode in Jefferson's and Madison's Defense of Civil Liberties." *William and Mary Quarterly*, 3rd ser., 5, no. 2 (April 1948): 145–76.

Malone, Dumas. "The Great Generation." *Virginia Quarterly Review* 23, no. 1 (Winter 1947): 108–22.

Mattern, David B. "Dolley Madison Has the Last Word: The Famous Letter." *White House History* 4 (Fall 1998): 38–43.

Mayo, Bernard. "Joshua Barney and the French Revolution." *Maryland Historical Magazine* 36, no. 4 (December 1941): 357–62.

Mitchill, Samuel Latham. "Dr. Mitchill's Letters from Washington: 1801–1813." *Harper's New Monthly Magazine*, April 1879, 740–55.

Monroe, James. "Letters of James Monroe: Part 4, 1812–1817." *Bulletin of the New York Public Library* 6 (Jan.–Dec. 1902): 210–30.

Morison, Samuel Eliot. "The Henry-Crillon Affair of 1812." *Proceedings of the Massachusetts Historical Society*, 3rd ser., 69 (Oct. 1947–May 1950): 207–31.

Morris, Maud Burr. "An Old Washington Mansion (2017 I Street Northwest)." *Records of the Columbia Historical Society, Washington, D.C.* 21 (1918): 114–28.

"Notes and Queries." *Pennsylvania Magazine of History and Biography* 8, no. 2 (June 1884): 223–32.

Powell, J. H. "Some Unpublished Correspondence of John Adams and Richard Rush, 1811–1816." *Pennsylvania Magazine of History and Biography* 60, no. 4 (Oct. 1936): 419–54.

"A Proclamation." *Niles' Weekly Register*, August 18, 1821.

Riley, Edward M. "Philadelphia, the Nation's Capital, 1790–1800." *Pennsylvania History: A Journal of Mid-Atlantic Studies* 20, no. 4 (Oct. 1953): 357–79.

Ring, Malvin E. "John Greenwood, Dentist to President Washington." *Journal of the California Dental Association* 38, no. 12 (Dec. 2010): 846–51.

Robertson, H. "Washington at Monmouth—The Testimony of an Eye-Witness." *American Monthly Magazine* 16, no. 1 (1900): 1189–92.

Robertson, William Spence. "The Recognition of the Hispanic American Nations by the United States." *Hispanic American Historical Review* 1, no. 3 (Aug. 1918): 239–69.

Rush, Benjamin. "Excerpts from the Papers of Dr. Benjamin Rush." *Pennsylvania Magazine of History and Biography* 29, no. 1 (1905): 15–30.

BIBLIOGRAPHY

Smelser, Marshall. "George Washington and the Alien and Sedition Acts." *American Historical Review* 59, no. 2 (Jan. 1954): 322–34.

Smith, James Morton. "The 'Aurora' and the Alien and Sedition Laws: Part 1: The Editorship of Benjamin Franklin Bache." *Pennsylvania Magazine of History and Biography* 77, no. 1 (Jan. 1953): 3–23.

Smith, Sydney. Review of *Statistical Annals of the United States of America,* by Adam Seybert. *Edinburgh Review or Critical Journal* 33, no. 65 (Jan. 1820): 69–80.

Stuart, Reginald C. "James Madison and the Militants: Republican Disunity and Replacing the Embargo." *Diplomatic History* 6, no. 2 (Spring 1982): 145–67.

Tachau, Mary K. Bonsteel. "George Washington and the Reputation of Edmund Randolph." *Journal of American History* 73, no. 1 (June 1986): 15–34.

Taggart, Samuel. "Letters of Samuel Taggart, Representative in Congress, 1803–1814: Part II, 1808–1814." *Proceedings of the American Antiquarian Society* 33, no. 2 (Oct. 1923): 297–438.

Taylor, John, and Wilson Cary Nicholas. "Of Principles and Men: The Correspondence of John Taylor of Caroline with Wilson Cary Nicholas, 1806–1808." Edited by David N. Mayer. *Virginia Magazine of History and Biography* 96, no. 3 (July 1988): 345–88.

Thornton, Anna. "Diary of Mrs. William Thornton: Capture of Washington by the British." Edited by Wilhemus B. Bryan. *Records of the Columbia Historical Society, Washington, D.C.* 19 (1916): 172–82.

Trumbull, Jonathan, Jr. "Minutes of Occurrences Respecting the Siege and Capture of York in Virginia, Extracted from the Journal of Colonel Jonathan Trumbull, Secretary to the General, 1781." *Proceedings of the Massachusetts Historical Society* 14 (1875–1876): 331–38.

Tucker, Abigail. "Meriwether Lewis's Mysterious Death." Smithsonian.com, Oct. 8, 2009. https://www.smithsonianmag.com/history/meriwether-lewis-mysterious -death-144006713/.

Van Rensselaer, May King. "Our Social Ladder: Its Sound and Rotten Rungs—I: When Blood and Breeding Were the Supreme Essentials." *Ladies' Home Journal*, Feb. 1923, 14–15.

Waldo, Albigence. "Valley Forge, 1777–1778. Diary of Surgeon Albigence Waldo, of the Connecticut Line." *Pennsylvania Magazine of History and Biography* 21, no. 3 (1897): 299–323.

Wilson, Douglas L. "The Evolution of Jefferson's *Notes on the State of Virginia.*" *Virginia Magazine of History and Biography* 112, no. 2 (2004): 98–133.

Yoo, John C. "The First Claim: The Burr Trial, *United States v. Nixon,* and Presidential Power." *Minnesota Law Review* 83, no. 5 (May 1999): 1435–79.

BIBLIOGRAPHY

UNPUBLISHED MANUSCRIPTS

Pieczynski, Christopher. "Rediscovering the Treaty of Ghent." Paper presented to the Norfolk Historical Society, Feb. 2015.

Thompson, Mary V. "Statements Regarding the Physical Appearance, Traits and Personal Characteristics of George Washington (1732–1799)." Unpublished manuscript. Prepared for the Mount Vernon Ladies' Association, Jan. 31, 2005–Feb. 5, 2015.

SPECIAL COLLECTIONS

Adams Family Papers: An Electronic Archive. Massachusetts Historical Society, Boston. https://www.masshist.org/digitaladams/archive/.

Adams Papers, 1639–1899. Microfilms. Massachusetts Historical Society, Boston.

The Diaries of John Quincy Adams: A Digital Collection. Massachusetts Historical Society, Boston. http://www.masshist.org/jqadiaries/php/.

John James Beckley Papers, 1773–1807. Transcription. Virginia Historical Society, Richmond.

Coolidge Collection of Thomas Jefferson Manuscripts. Massachusetts Historical Society, Boston.

Andre De Coppet Collection. Manuscripts Division, Department of Rare Books and Special Collections, Princeton University Library.

Frederick Douglass Papers: Digital Edition. Indiana University–Purdue University Indianapolis. https://frederickdouglass.infoset.io/.

Foreign Affairs, Political Correspondence, Paris–United States. Manuscript Division, Library of Congress.

Historic Records & Deed Research, Clerk of the Circuit Court, Loudoun County, Virginia.

Andrew Jackson Papers. Manuscript Division, Library of Congress. https://www.loc.gov/collections/andrew-jackson-papers/.

Thomas Jefferson Collection. Missouri Historical Society, St. Louis. https://mohistory.org/collections/item/resource:103470.

Thomas Jefferson Papers. Manuscript Division, Library of Congress. https://www.loc.gov/collections/thomas-jefferson-papers/.

Jefferson Papers: An Electronic Archive. Massachusetts Historical Society, Boston. http://www.masshist.org/thomasjeffersonpapers.

James Madison Papers. Manuscript Division, Library of Congress. https://www.loc.gov/collections/james-madison-papers/.

BIBLIOGRAPHY

Samuel Latham Mitchill Papers, 1801–1929. Clements Library, University of Michigan.

James Monroe Museum and Memorial Library, Fredericksburg, Va.

James Monroe Papers. Manuscript Division, Library of Congress. https://www
.loc.gov/collections/james-monroe-papers/.

James Monroe Papers. Manuscripts and Archives Division, New York Public Library.

John Randolph Papers, 1806–1832. Manuscript Division, Library of Congress.

Matthew Ridley Papers. Massachusetts Historical Society, Boston.

Colonel Francis Taylor Diary, 1786–1792, 1794–1799. Homer Babbidge Library, University of Connecticut, Storrs.

George Washington Papers. Manuscript Division, Library of Congress. https://www
.loc.gov/collections/george-washington-papers/.

George Weedon Papers, 1776–1789. Personal Papers Collection, Library of Virginia, Richmond.

Otho Holland Williams Papers. Maryland Historical Society, Baltimore.

INDEX

INDEX

INDEX

INDEX